D1368242

Teacher's Edition

by
Bonnie L. Walker

AGS®
American Guidance Service, Inc.
Circle Pines, Minnesota 55014-1796
800-328-2560

About the Author

Bonnie L. Walker taught for sixteen years in secondary schools and college. She holds a Ph.D. in curriculum theory and instructional design from the University of Maryland, an M.Ed. in secondary education, and a B.A. in English. She studied psycholinguistics at the University of Illinois Graduate School, and was a curriculum developer at the Model Secondary School for the Deaf at Gallaudet University. She is the author of *Basic English Grammar, Life Skills English,* and numerous workbooks, learning packages, and sound filmstrips in written expression, grammar, and usage. She was a member of Project EduTech, which investigated promising technologies to improve the delivery of special education services. Dr. Walker has written several papers on the applications of personal computers, video technology, and cable television in education. She has been the director for research and development projects funded by the U.S. Department of Education, the U.S. Department of Agriculture, and the Administration on Youth, Children, and Families. Since 1986, Dr. Walker has been president of a research and development company specializing in development of training and educational materials for special populations.

The publisher wishes to thank the following educators for their helpful comments during the review process for *Basic English Composition*. Their assistance has been invaluable.

Patsy P. Land
Special Education Teacher
Oak Ridge High School
Oak Ridge, TN

Dr. William B. Whitaker
Director of Adult High School and GED
 Programs
Rowan Cabarrus Community College
Salisbury, NC

Marie Ramey
Department Chairperson
West Side High School
Newark, NJ

Sherryl Duff-Conrad
Learning Support Teacher
Penn Hills Senior High School
Pittsburgh, PA

Karen L. Piscopo
Acting Assistant Principal
Frankford High School
Philadelphia, PA

Beverly D. Morrison
Special Education Teacher, Department
 Head
Meade County High School
Brandenburg, KY

Susan Harrington
Special Education Teacher—Option III
Salamanca Middle School
Salamanca, NY

ISBN 0-7854-2301-X (Previously ISBN 0-7854-0540-2)   Product Number 91342

A 0 9 8 7 6 5 4 3 2 1

Table of Contents

Basic English Composition

Teacher's Edition

Student Text

Student Workbook

Teacher's Resource Library

Self-Study Guide

BASIC ENGLISH COMPOSITION is designed to help secondary students and adult learners to develop practical writing skills. Throughout the text, comprehension is enhanced through the use of simple sentence structure and low-level vocabulary. To add motivational interest, the instruction and activities revolve around a group of high school students experiencing a typical school year.

Prior to the development of this text, the author conducted a series of interviews with teachers, curriculum supervisors, and students across the country. As a result, *Basic English Composition* reflects these needs by emphasizing writing sentences, then paragraphs, followed by reports and other projects. All are identified as important skills to be taught.

A major focus of *Basic English Composition* is on writing sentences. Many older students who are in need of basic writing instruction need to develop a sense of good sentence structure. Most writing

textbooks focus on writing complete compositions, which intensifies the frustration of many students who are struggling to master the basics. By focusing on sentence development, students using *Basic English Composition* experience success earlier and are motivated to continue.

An example of a helpful student activity is *sentence lists*. Students are asked to write sentences in list form about a topic. These lists could become paragraphs. By breaking instruction on writing paragraphs into short, step-by-step lessons, students experience success and are thus motivated to proceed to the next step of writing structured paragraphs about a given topic.

The ability to write in clear, correct language is an important skill for most jobs and everyday situations. *Basic English Composition* provides instruction in the basic writing skills needed for success in school and in the workplace.

AGS Worktexts

CHECK OUT AGS WORKTEXTS! AGS offers additional language arts materials to help you tailor instruction to meet the diverse needs of your students. Each worktext contains 96 pages of up-to-date information and motivating skill lessons with lots of opportunities for practice and reinforcement. These may be used to accompany a basal program or as the core instructional tool.

AGS Grammar and Composition Skills

AGS Practical English Skills

For more information on AGS Worktexts, call 1-800-328-2560.

AGS English Textbooks

Basic English Grammar

Basic English Grammar is designed to meet the needs of secondary students and adults who read well below grade level. Prior to the book being written, a series of interviews was conducted with teachers, supervisors, and students across the United States. A need was identified for a textbook that would present grammatical rules and concepts one at a time and provide sufficient opportunities for appropriate practice.

All aspects of the text are carefully controlled, including instructions, examples, directions, and exercises. The sentence structure and vocabulary are clear and straightforward, which helps reluctant readers access the material more easily than they could with traditional grammar textbooks. In addition, the high interest content of the activities appeals to older students.

Reading Level: 3.2 Spache
Interest Level: Grades 6-12, ABE, ESL

Life Skills English

The major goal of *Life Skills English* is to develop language skills that young people and adults need in their everyday lives. The development of this textbook is based on a series of interviews with teachers, supervisors, and students across the country. Topics included in the text are based on these findings.

The primary focus of *Life Skills English* is seeking and evaluating information. The text first emphasizes the skills needed to find information. Students learn how information is organized and how to use reference tools to locate information. The text teaches students how to use and develop skills that they will apply in other subjects and everyday life.

To motivate students, both the sentence structure and the vocabulary are controlled throughout the text, including the directions, examples, and exercises. This allows students to concentrate on content mastery. Chapter openers, examples, and exercises focus on relevant and practical applications. For example, students are taught how to read a food label, read the yellow pages, follow recipe directions, and read the want ads.

Reading Level: 3.7 Spache
Interest Level: Grades 6-12, ABE, ESL

For more information on AGS Textbooks, call 1-800-328-2560.

English for the World of Work

English for the World of Work develops communication skills that are essential for deciding upon a career, obtaining a job, keeping a job, and being prepared for promotions. Students prepare a career portfolio that can be used later during their job searches. This textbook is intended for secondary students and adults who are planning to enter the world of work soon after the course.

This text is designed to be practical and relevant. Activities and exercises are patterned after situations in the working world and are designed to develop better reading, writing, speaking, and listening skills. Effort has been made to keep the reading level below the fourth grade. Some concepts are dealt with at a slightly higher level than others. Suggestions are provided in the Teacher's Edition for directing the students' reading to help them achieve full comprehension.

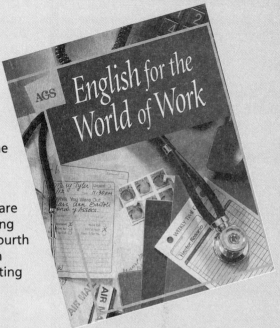

Reading Level: 3.6 Spache
Interest Level: Grades 6-12, ABE, ESL

English to Use

English to Use is designed to meet the communication needs of secondary students and adults who are reading below grade level or learning English as a second language. Grammar and usage are integrated into each lesson to facilitate an understanding of rules and their practical application to the patterns of written and spoken English. Students practice and apply each language skill in a variety of settings, from identification and classification to evaluative thinking and application.

The instructions, examples, directions, and exercises are presented in a systematic, discrete manner. Particular attention is given to organizing the instruction so that only a single rule or a single concept is presented at one time. Numerous exercises allow the teacher frequent review of students' understanding. Lessons build upon each other throughout the book.

Sign language is featured throughout *English to Use*. By including these illustrations, we hope to connect the spoken word and signing. It is not the intention of this text to provide a total program in signing—only an awareness.

Reading Level: 3.3 Spache
Interest Level: Grades 6-12, ABE, ESL

Student Text Highlights

The student texts are designed to motivate even the most reluctant learner. Concise, targeted lessons allow students to focus on a single concept and experience success. Students will demonstrate increased comprehension with the text written at 3.1 reading level.

- ■ Each chapter opens with an engaging photo that relates the chapter content to real-life application.

- ■ Background information is provided to set the stage for learning and to make the material relevant for students.

- ■ *Goals for Learning* are identified at the beginning of each chapter to help students understand the main ideas they will be learning.

Chapter 11

Messages and Memorandums

Imagine this situation. You are waiting at the entrance to a store. You had told your friend to meet you there at three o'clock. It is now three-thirty. Where is your friend? You are worried. Why hasn't your friend arrived? You are also annoyed. "How much longer should I wait?" you ask yourself.

When these mixups occur, the cause is often a missed communication. Maybe your friend left a message for you, but you never got it. Maybe you forgot to tell your friend exactly where to meet you. Missed or confused communications can cause all sorts of problems.

In Chapter 11, you will learn one way to avoid missed communications. You will learn how to write clear, complete messages.

Goals for Learning
- ▶ To write clear messages
- ▶ To include all necessary information in messages and memorandums

231

Lesson 1   **Writing Messages**

Message
Communication, either written or spoken.

A **message** is any kind of communication. Friends and family members often leave messages to inform one another of plans. Taking messages is an important job in many offices.

Messages may be spoken or written. A written message is more often handwritten than typed. Be careful to make your handwriting readable. Also be sure to include all necessary information.

This list shows the main elements to include in any message:

- The time and date that you wrote the message
- The name of the person who told you the information
- The information needed by the person who gets the message
- Your name, to show who wrote the message

Read the message below. It is written completely and correctly. The person receiving the message has been given all the information she needs to know.

> 3:00 PM Monday
> Laura,
> Amanda called at 3:00 PM Call her at home if you get home before 4:30. She'll be at her dancing class until 5:30. Then she'll be home.
> Love,
> Mom

Activity A   Use the message above to answer the following questions. Write your answers on your paper.

1) What time did Amanda call?
2) Who took this message?
3) Who is to get this message?
4) What is Laura supposed to do?
5) It is now 5:00 P.M. Is Amanda home?

Activity B   Read each message below. Decide what important information has been left out. Write the missing information on your paper.

> Mom, I'm going out. I'll be home later.
> Amanda

> Laura, Derek called. Call him back.
> Mom

> MIKE, YOU ARE SUPPOSED TO PLAY TENNIS. Tim

> Dad, someone called about the car.

> Ms. Martin, I stopped by during second period to ask about my homework. I'll be back.
> Amanda

> MS. LAWSON, I NEED AN APPOINTMENT TO TALK TO YOU. I'LL BE BACK AT THREE O'CLOCK.

Activity C   Imagine that you have answered the phone at home. You need to write a message for a family member. List at least five kinds of information that you would want to include in such a message.

- ■ Each lesson is clearly labeled to help students focus on main ideas.

- ■ Graphs and charts present concepts visually to reinforce and clarify instruction.

- ■ Glossary words are boldfaced the first time they appear in the text. In addition to being defined in context, they are also defined in a special vocabulary box in the side column. This provides a quick review for students.

Lesson 1 Adding Adjectives and Adverbs

Modifier
A word that describes another word in a sentence.

The words in a sentence all have jobs. The main job of some words is to describe, or tell about, other words. Describing words give more information about the other words. Because the describing words change, or modify, meaning, they are also called **modifiers**.

You have learned that an adjective describes a noun or pronoun. An adjective tells how many, what kind, or which ones. Look at the bold adjectives in each list below. Think about the question each one answers.

EXAMPLES
How many?
one dog, **few** animals, **nineteen** students

What kind?
furry dogs, **extinct** dinosaurs, **curious** students

Which ones?
those dogs, **the** animals, **other** friends

Adjectives add details to sentences. Adjectives often appear before the words they modify. Read the sentences below. The adjectives are bold. In the first example sentence, adjectives come before the nouns *man, glass, lemonade,* and *gulps.* In the second example sentence, adjectives come before the nouns *kitten* and *yarn.*

EXAMPLES
The thirsty man drank a **tall** glass of **pink** lemonade in **four** gulps.

A **fuzzy black** kitten had wrapped itself in **thick yellow** yarn.

Activity A Think of an adjective that could describe each noun below. Write the adjective on your paper.

1) _____ tree
2) _____ teachers
3) _____ haircut
4) _____ motorcycle
5) _____ elephants

You may write sentences in which an adjective does not come before the noun. The adjective still modifies the noun, but it comes after the verb. An adjective often follows a form of the verb *to be.* An adjective may follow other state-of-being verbs.

Some Forms of *Be*	Some Other State-of-Being Verbs
am	looks
is	feels
was	seems
has been	appears
should have been	becomes

Notice the bold adjectives after the verbs in these example sentences.

EXAMPLES The winner was **surprised**. She looked **shocked**.
"I am **amazed** and **speechless**," she said.

Activity B Complete each sentence with an adjective. Write the adjective on your paper.

1) The trees were _____.
2) My English teacher seems _____.
3) Movies about romance are _____.
4) I would like to drive a car that is _____.
5) Tests can be _____.

Activity C Add adjectives to each sentence. Write new sentences.

1) The _____ girl did a _____ somersault.
2) Did you order _____ jam on _____ toast?
3) After running _____ miles, Derek said, "I feel _____ and _____!"
4) The _____ dessert made everyone feel _____.
5) The United States is a _____ and _____ country.
6) School subjects that are _____ can also be _____.

■ *Chapter Reviews* appear in the student text and allow students and teachers to check skill mastery.

■ The *Chapter Reviews* directly reflect the chapter *Goals for Learning.*

Chapter 11 Review

Part A Read the following conversation between Derek and his mother. Write the message that is to be given to Shirley. Use complete sentences.

Derek: It is nearly three o'clock. I have to go to work. Tell Shirley that I'll be home by six. I'll meet her at school.

Ms. Corelli: You'll have to eat dinner before you go out.

Derek: OK. Tell her I'll meet her at seven.

Ms. Corelli: I'll give her your message.

Part B Imagine that you are baby-sitting for little Tanya at the Jefferson home this evening. You answer the telephone and explain that Ms. Jefferson has gone out for the evening. This is the information the caller gives you:

• "My name is Denise Stith."
• "I am Tanya Jefferson's aunt."
• "I cannot meet Ms. Jefferson tomorrow evening."
• "I will try to call Ms. Jefferson tomorrow."
• "Tell Ms. Jefferson I'm sorry about the change in plans."

Use the information to write a message for Ms. Jefferson, Tanya's mother. Include all necessary information.

Part C Copy the parts of the memo below onto your paper. Write a message to your teacher, a friend, or a family member. Choose any subject you wish. Include all necessary information. Use today's date.

MEMO
Date:
To:
From:
Subject:

Part D Rewrite the message below. Put it into memo form. Use today's date.

> 11:00 A.M., Tuesday
>
> Luis,
>
> The chess club is meeting in room 111 tomorrow. Mr. Harris says he has an important announcement. Try to come early, before three o'clock.
>
> Mia

Part E Find five errors in the following memo. List them on your paper.

MEMO
Date: April 3, 20–
To: Mr. Henry Tso
Subject: Vacation days

I have received your request to take five days of vacation from Monday, June 12, through Friday, June 16, the request has been approved. I hope you have a great time in arizona!

Best wishes,
Fred Lamont

Test Taking Tip When you read test directions, try to restate them in your own words. Tell yourself what you are expected to do. That way, you can make sure your answer will be complete and correct.

Test Taking Tip When you read test directions, try to restate them in your own words. Tell yourself what you are expected to do. That way, you can make sure your answer will be complete and correct.

Teacher's Edition Highlights

The comprehensive, wraparound teacher's edition provides instructional strategies at point of use. Everything from preparation guidelines to teaching tips and strategies are included in an easy-to-use format. Activities are featured at point of use for teacher convenience.

- Quick overview of the lesson saves time.

- Lesson objectives are listed for easy reference.

- Page references are provided for convenience.

- Instructional resources are clearly identified.

- Reading vocabulary classified above fourth grade level is listed on each page. Grade levels are shown in parentheses. Nongraded words show no number.

- An introductory discussion or activity opens each lesson by activating prior knowledge and setting the stage for learning.

- Suggestions are given for introducing and teaching the learning activities.

- Teachers are given suggestions for reviewing skills needed for success in the lesson.

Lesson at a Glance

Chapter 11   Lesson 1

Overview This lesson focuses on written messages that include all necessary information.

Objective

- To write a clear, complete message.

Student Pages 232–234

Teacher's Resource Library

Activities 41–42

Workbook Activity 47

Reading Vocabulary

element (6)	member (5)
handwritten	**message (3)**
handwriting	readable

Teaching Suggestions

- **Introducing the Lesson**
  Have students imagine that they have answered the phone in the school office and are taking down a message for a teacher. Ask them what information they should include in order for the message to be complete.

- **Reviewing Skills** Select five or six words from the "Spelling Demons" list on page 109 of the student book. Have volunteers come to the board to write each word correctly in a sentence.

- **Presenting Activity A**
  Have a volunteer read aloud the sample message shown on this page. Students should refer to it as they answer questions 1–5. Direct students to write their answers in complete sentences.

Activity A Answers

1) Amanda called at three o'clock in the afternoon. 2) Laura's mother took the message.
3) Laura will get this message.
4) Laura should call Amanda before 4:30 or after 5:30.
5) Amanda is not yet home.

Lesson 1

Writing Messages

Message
Communication, either written or spoken.

A **message** is any kind of communication. Friends and family members often leave messages to inform one another of plans. Taking messages is an important job in many offices.

Messages may be spoken or written. A written message is more often handwritten than typed. Be careful to make your handwriting readable. Also be sure to include all necessary information.

This list shows the main elements to include in any message:

- The time and date that you wrote the message
- The name of the person who told you the information
- The information needed by the person who gets the message
- Your name, to show who wrote the message

Read the message below. It is written completely and correctly. The person receiving the message has been given all the information she needs to know.

> 3:00 p.m. Monday
> Laura,
> Amanda called at 3:00 p.m. Call her at home if you get home before 4:30. She'll be at her dancing class until 5:30. Then she'll be home.
> Love,
> Mom

Activity A   Use the message above to answer the following questions. Write your answers on your paper.

1) What time did Amanda call?
2) Who took this message?
3) Who is to get this message?
4) What is Laura supposed to do?
5) It is now 5:00 P.M. Is Amanda home?

Activity B Read each message below. Decide what important information has been left out. Write the missing information on your paper.

Mom, I'm going out. I'll be home later.
Amanda

Laura, Derek called. Call him back.
Mom

MIKE, YOU ARE SUPPOSED
TO PLAY TENNIS. Tim

Dad, someone called about the car.

Mr. Martin, I stopped by during second period to ask about my homework. I'll be back.
Amanda

Ms. Lawson, I NEED AN APPOINTMENT TO TALK TO YOU. I'LL BE BACK AT THREE O'CLOCK.

Activity C Imagine that you have answered the phone at home. You need to write a message for a family member. List at least five kinds of information that you would want to include in such a message.

Messages and Memorandums   Chapter 11   **233**

Activity 41

Reading Vocabulary
appointment (6)   tennis (5)
homework

■ **Presenting Activity B** Tell students to use their imagination in order to complete the information in each message. Refer them to the list on page 232 of their book.

Activity B Answers
The missing information is given below.
1) Add the date and the time. Be more specific about the time "later."   2) Add the date and the time.   3) Add the date, the time, the name of the person who called, and more specific information about where and when the tennis game is being held.   4) Add the date, the time, the name of the caller, and the caller's phone number.
5) Add the date and a detail about when Amanda will be back.   6) Add the date and the message writer's name.

■ **Presenting Activity C**
Review the directions with students. Make sure they understand they are to write categories of information rather than details of any particular call.

Activity C Answers
Answers may vary. A sample answer is given.
1) Name of person receiving message   2) Date and time
3) Name and phone number of caller   4) Most important details of message   5) Name of person taking message

APPLICATION
At Home
Ask students whether any of them have sure-fire methods at home for taking messages completely and accurately. Students may offer ideas for making sure all the people who share a household receive the information they need.

Messages and Memorandums   Chapter 11   **233**

■ Answers are provided in the teacher's edition for all exercises in the student text.

■ The *Global Connection* features will help students connect the lesson to the world community at large. Multicultural issues are emphasized as students view the world as a community.

■ Special helps will assist ESL students with lesson content.

■ *Application:* There are three kinds of applications—At Home, Career Connection, and In the Community. Relating lessons to the world outside of the classroom helps motivate students and makes learning relevant.

■ Community participation and environmental awareness are encouraged with activities in the teacher's edition as extensions of various lessons.

■ Activity and Workbook Activity pages are shown at point of use. The Teacher's Resource Library contains all reproducible activities. Emphasis is placed on including learning activities for reaching a diverse range of learning styles. A variety of teaching and student activities are included at the point of use.

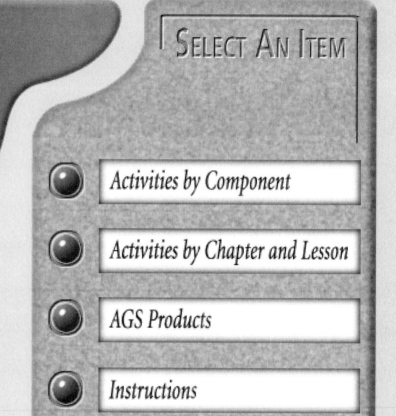

Basic English Composition

Teacher's Resource Library

AGS®

© 1997

American Guidance Service, Inc.
Circle Pines, MN 55014-1796
1-800-328-2560

Permission is granted to print and reproduce
the contents of this disk for classroom use only.

SELECT AN ITEM

- Activities by Component
- Activities by Chapter and Lesson
- AGS Products
- Instructions

 All of the activities you'll need to reinforce and extend the text are conveniently located on the AGS Teacher's Resource Library (TRL) CD-ROM. The reproducible activities featured in the Teacher's Edition are ready to review, select, and print. Additionally, you can preview other materials by directly linking to the AGS web site.

Activities

Lesson activities reinforce the concepts taught in the lesson. Activities are designed to help students see the relevance of the skills being taught. A variety of activities provide additional motivation.

Workbook Activities

Workbook activities may be reproduced as added reinforcement and practice for lessons. These activities are also available in a workbook format.

Community Connections

Relevant activities help students apply their new knowledge in the community and reinforce concepts covered in class.

Writing Tips

Writing Tips are included to extend the text by offering writing suggestions to help students become better writers. The sheets can be used later for reference.

Self-Study Guide

Assignment guides with student/teacher contracts are provided for the entire text. These are suggested lesson plans from the text and workbook.This provides teachers with the flexibility of individualized instruction or independent study.

Mastery Tests

Chapter, midterm, and final mastery tests are conveniently referenced as assessment options.

CHAPTER 2: Punctuating Sentences

Goal 2.1 To end each sentence with the correct punctuation mark

Date	Assignment	Score
_____	1: Read pages 11-12. Complete Activities A-B on page 13.	_____
_____	2: Complete Workbook Activity 4.	_____
_____	3: Read page 14. Complete Activities C-D on page 14.	_____
_____	4: Read page 15. Complete Activity E on page 15.	_____
_____	5: Complete the Lesson 1 Review, Parts A-B on page 16.	_____
_____	6: Complete Workbook Activity 5.	_____

Comments:

Goal 2.2 To punctuate dialogue correctly

...signment	Score
Read page 17. Complete Activity A on page 17.	_____
Read page 18. Complete Activity B on page 18.	_____
Complete Workbook Activity 6.	_____
Read page 19. Complete Activity C on page 19.	_____
Complete Workbook Activity 7.	_____
Read page 20. Complete Activity D on page 20.	_____
Read page 21. Complete Activity E on page 21.	_____

Name	Date	Period	Chapter 3
			Activity
			10

Recognizing Antecedents

Directions: Find the antecedent for each bold pronoun. Then write each pronoun and its antecedent on the lines provided.

EXAMPLE   Amanda is enjoying **her** ice cream.
her — Amanda

1) Derek is playing **his** radio very loud.

2) Our car has a bumper sticker on **it**.

3) Laura went to **her** house after school.

4) Derek and **his** friend went shopping.

5) The teacher told the students **his** story.

6) Laura and Amanda enjoyed **their** summer vacation.

7) Mr. Smith gave **his** students a homework assignment.

8) Amanda said, "**I** would like to go home."

9) The boys ride **their** bikes every day after school.

10) My house has a sidewalk in front of **it**.

Name	Date	Period	Chapter 9
			Mastery Test A
			page 2

Chapter 9 Mastery Test A, continued

Part C Rewrite this paragraph. Improve it by adding five transitional words or phrases. Use *meanwhile, surprisingly, at last, finally, later, at first, for a moment, however,* or *then.*

Ruth once visited the Statue of Liberty in New York. She was fifteen. She climbed and climbed. She reached the top. She was able to see the view of the city and the harbor. It was spectacular! She always remembered that trip.

Name	Date	Period	Chapter 6
			Workbook Activity
			27

Sentences to Improve

A. Directions: • Add at least one prepositional phrase to each sentence below. Write the new sentence.

EXAMPLE   My friend went out.
*My friend **from Knoxville** went out **for a walk.***

1) Everyone was out.

2) The kitten looks sad.

3) The team got three new players.

4) The winters are cold here.

5) Marlene is hungry.

B. Directions: • Combine each pair of sentences below.
• Add a conjunction. Write the new sentence.

EXAMPLE   There was finally enough snow. We went skiing.
There was finally enough snow, so we went skiing.

1) We like the beach. We go there every summer.

2) Jackie's Uncle has a farm. She goes horseback riding.

3) Sometimes there is nothing to do. I just go for a walk.

4) The city streets are noisy. They are also exciting.

5) Dena got tickets for the concert. Karl got tickets for the concert.

...of the comparisons below.

Skills Chart

Basic English Composition

Grammar and Usage Skills	1	2	3	4	5	6	7	8	9	10	11	12	13
Parts of Speech			3			6							
Singular			3	4									
Plural			3	4									
Sentences	1	2	3		5	6	7		9				
Questions		2						8		10			
Subject-Verb Agreement			3										
Antecedents			3										
Case			3										
Phrases			3			6	7						
Clauses						6							
Comparisons						6			9				

Punctuation and Mechanics Skills	1	2	3	4	5	6	7	8	9	10	11	12	13
Period	1	2											
Question Mark	1	2											
Exclamation Mark	1	2											
Comma	1	2			5	6							
Apostrophe				4									
Quotation Marks		2											13
Capitalization	1	2	3									12	
Spelling				4									
Addressing Envelopes												12	
Parts of a Letter												12	

Research and Study Skills	1	2	3	4	5	6	7	8	9	10	11	12	13
Taking Notes													13
Finding Materials in a Library													13
Using the Library Catalog													13
Using a Newspaper													13
Encyclopedias													13
Almanacs													13
Atlases													13
Biographical Dictionaries													13
Finding Relevant Information													13
Bibliography													13

Chapter

Writing Skills	1	2	3	4	5	6	7	8	9	10	11	12	13
Sentences	1	2	3	4	5	6	7	8	9	10	11	12	13
Paragraphs							7	8	9	10	11	12	13
Topic Sentences							7		9	10			13
Conclusions							7			10			
Choosing and Narrowing a Topic													13
Planning to Write						6	7	8		10	11	12	13
Revising and Rewriting								8	9	10	11	12	13
Proofreading								8	9	10	11	12	13
Transitions									9				
Comparisons									9				
Point of View									9				

Types of Writing	1	2	3	4	5	6	7	8	9	10	11	12	13
Answering Questions					5			8		10			
Summaries							7			10			13
Reports													13
Outlines													13
Essay Answers										10			
Short Answers										10			
Stories		2						8					
Dialogue		2						8					
Messages											11		
Memos											11		
Personal Letters												12	
Business Letters												12	
Explanations								8					
Requests								8					

Adapting Activities for Diverse Learning Styles

The learning style activities in the *Basic English Composition* Teacher's Edition provide activities to help students with special needs understand the lesson. These activities focus on the following learning styles: Visual/Spatial, Auditory/Verbal, Body/Kinesthetic, Logical/ Mathematical, Interpersonal/Group Learning, LEP/ESL. These styles reflect Howard Gardner's theory of multiple intelligences. The writing activities suggested in this student text are appropriate for students who fit Gardner's description of Verbal/Linguistic Intelligence.

The activities are designed to help teachers capitalize on students' individual strengths and dominant learning styles. The activities reinforce the lesson by teaching or expanding upon the content in a different way.

Following are examples of activities featured in the *Basic English Composition* Teacher's Edition:

Interpersonal/Group learners benefit from working with at least one other person on activities that involve a process and an end product.

LEARNING STYLES

Interpersonal/Group Learning
Divide the class into groups of nine students each. Point out the nine sentences in Activity E on page 26. Have each group draw nine pictures to illustrate the story in the activity. Afterward, ask each group to decide how it will present its story. Suggest that the groups might stand before the class. Each group member could then show a picture and read the appropriate sentence. Or one member of the group could hold up a picture while the other members mime the action. Encourage group creativity with the pictures and story.

Auditory/Verbal students benefit from having someone read the text aloud or listening to the text on audiocassette. Musical activities appropriate for the lesson may help auditory learners.

LEARNING STYLES

Auditory/Verbal
Divide the class into pairs. Ask each set of partners to write a conversation story as in Activities A–D on pages 17–20. Emphasize that the "tag" line—for example, the words *asked Laura*—tells the reader who says the dialogue. Afterward, invite the partners to record their dialogue on tape. Have the class listen to the tapes and, following the rules on pages 17–20, write the dialogue and tag lines.

Logical/Mathematical students learn by using logical/mathematical thinking in relation to the lesson content.

LEARNING STYLES

Logical/Mathematical
Form a patterned chain of two-word sentences— subject/verb. Begin by saying a sentence such as "Cats meow." Then have a volunteer start the next sentence with a word that begins with the letter *w*—the letter that ended the last word of your sentence. (So, for example, the student might say, "Weather changes." Then the next student would begin a sentence with the *s* from *changes*.) Continue doing this until the students have established a sentence rhythm that they can clap out with a pause for the periods.

Body/Kinesthetic learners benefit from activities that include physical movement or tactile experiences.

LEARNING STYLES

Body/Kinesthetic
Invite the students, one by one, to stand and show singular and plural pronouns by miming them. As they do this, have volunteers guess the pronouns using the chart on page 44. For instance, a student might point to himself to show *I*. The student could using a sweeping motion that encompasses the whole class to show *they* or *us*. The student might pick up a book to show *my* book. The student might point to another student's book to show *her* book. As students do this, print the pronouns on the chalkboard.

Visual/Spatial students benefit from seeing illustrations or demonstrations beyond what is in the text.

LEARNING STYLES

Visual/Spatial
Make three posters by pasting a colorful magazine picture on each one. Above each picture, draw an ending point of punctuation—period, exclamation point, question mark. (Create a poster for each point of punctuation.) Invite the students to write an original sentence on their favorite poster. Explain that the sentence must reflect what they see in the picture and must end with the point of punctuation on the poster. Afterward, invite students to read the sentences aloud with expression.

LEP/ESL students benefit from activities that promote English language acquisition and interaction with English-speaking peers.

LEARNING STYLES

LEP/ESL
Direct the students' attention to the conversation in Activity B on page 13 to which they have added end punctuation. Encourage students for whom English is a second language to read the conversation in their first language. Ask them to use their voices and hands to create the end points of punctuation. If two students have the same primary language, ask them to be partners. Encourage them to use their primary language to speak the two parts of the conversations.

AGS

Basic English Composition

by
Bonnie L. Walker

AGS®
American Guidance Service, Inc.
Circle Pines, Minnesota 55014-1796
800-328-2560

About the Author

Bonnie L. Walker taught for sixteen years in secondary schools and college. She holds a Ph.D. in curriculum theory and instructional design from the University of Maryland, an M.Ed. in secondary education, and a B.A. in English. She studied psycholinguistics at the University of Illinois Graduate School, and was a curriculum developer at the Model Secondary School for the Deaf at Gallaudet University. She is the author of *Basic English Grammar, Life Skills English,* and numerous workbooks, learning packages, and sound filmstrips in written expression, grammar, and usage. She was a member of Project EduTech, which investigated promising technologies to improve the delivery of special education services. Dr. Walker has written several papers on the applications of personal computers, video technology, and cable television in education. She has been the director for research and development projects funded by the U.S. Department of Education, the U.S. Department of Agriculture, and the Administration on Youth, Children, and Families. Since 1986, Dr. Walker has been president of a research and development company specializing in development of training and educational materials for special populations.

Photo Credits: pp. vi, 72, 130, 240—Superstock; pp. 10, 30, 114, 162, 178, 200, 218—Jim and Mary Whitmer; p. 230—Rob Cage/FPG International; p. 258—Jon Riley/Tony Stone Images

Printed in the United States of America

ISBN 0-7854-2300-1 (Previously ISBN 0-7854-0538-0)

Product Number 91340

A 0 9 8 7 6 5 4 3 2 1

Contents

Basic English Composition   *Contents*   **iii**

Planning Guide

Sentences

	Student Pages	Vocabulary	Practice Exercises	Lesson Review
		Student Text Lesson		
Lesson 1 Beginning and Ending a Sentence	2-4	✔	✔	4
Lesson 2 Choosing the Correct End Punctuation	5-7		✔	7

Chapter Activities

Teacher's Resource Library
Writing Tip 1: Basic Rules of Punctuation

Community Connection 1: Sentences in the Newspaper

Assessment Options

Student Text
Chapter 1 Review

Teacher's Resource Library
Chapter 1 Mastery Tests A and B

	Teaching Strategies							Language Skills			Learning Styles						Teacher's Resource Library		
	Reviewing Skills	Teacher Alert	Follow-up Activity	Career Application	Home Application	Global Connection	Community Application	Identification Skills	Writing Skills	Punctuation Skills	Visual/Spatial	Auditory/Verbal	Body/Kinesthetic	Logical/Mathematical	Group Learning	LEP/ESL	Activities	Workbook Activities	Self-Study Guide
	2	3	4					✔	✔	✔			4				1-2	1-3	✔
	5		7		6	5		✔	✔	✔	7						3-4		✔

Chapter at a Glance

Name _____ Period _____ Chapter 1 / Writing Tip / 1

Basic Rules of Punctuation

Capitalization
- Capitalize the first word in a sentence.
- Capitalize proper nouns.
- Do not capitalize common nouns unless they begin a sentence.
- Capitalize the first word of a quotation in conversation.
- Capitalize parts of the country but not compass directions.
- Capitalize the names of languages.
- Capitalize the first word and all important words in a title.
- Capitalize the pronoun *I*.
- Capitalize all proper adjectives in sentences.

End Punctuation
- Use a period (.) at the end of a statement.
- Use a period (.) at the end of a command.
- Use a question mark (?) at the end of a question.
- Use an exclamation mark (!) at the end of a sentence that expresses strong feeling.
- Do not use a comma (,) to end a sentence.

Comma (,)
- Use a comma to set off the name of the person you are addressing.
- Use a comma to separate two or more separate sentences that are joined with *and, but, or, nor,* or *for.*
- Do not separate two complete sentences with only a comma.
- Use a comma to separate a series of three or more words or phrases.

- Put a comma before the conjunction in a series of three or more words or phrases.
- Use a comma after a dependent clause that starts a sentence.
- Do not use a comma in a sentence that ends in a dependent clause.
- Use a comma after these conjunctions to indicate a pause:

  besides   however   furthermore
  accordingly   also   therefore
  moreover   otherwise   consequently
  nevertheless   instead   then

- Use a comma to indicate a pause after a transitional phrase.
- Do not use a comma if there is no pause after a transitional phrase.
- Use a comma after the salutation in a personal letter.
- Use a comma after the closing in a letter.

Apostrophe (')
- Use an apostrophe and add the letter *s* to make a singular noun possessive.
- Add only an apostrophe to make a plural noun possessive.
- Add both an apostrophe and the letter *s* if a plural noun does not end in an *s.*
- Use an apostrophe to replace the missing letters in a contraction.
- Do not use an apostrophe to form the possessive of *it.*

©AGS® American Guidance Service, Inc. Permission is granted to reproduce for classroom use only.   **Basic English Composition**

Name _____ Period _____ Chapter 1 / Writing Tip / 1

Basic Rules of Punctuation (continued)

Semicolon (;)
- Use a semicolon to connect sentences with these conjunctions:

  besides   however   furthermore
  accordingly   also   therefore
  moreover   otherwise   consequently
  nevertheless   instead   then

Colon (:)
- Use a colon after the salutation in a business letter.

Quotation Marks (" ")
- Put quotation marks around a speaker's exact words (direct quotation).
- Do not use quotation marks around the idea that someone said if you do not use the speaker's exact words (indirect quotation).
- If a speaker is named at the start of a quotation, use a comma between the speaker's name and the quotation.

- If a speaker is named at the end of a quotation, use a comma between the quotation and the speaker's name.
- If a speaker asks a question, use a question mark at the end of the quotation.
- If a speaker expresses strong feeling, use an exclamation point at the end of the quotation.
- Put the punctuation mark at the end of a quotation inside the closing quotation marks.
- Start a new paragraph each time a new person speaks.
- If a speaker says more than one sentence, use quotations marks only at the beginning and at the end of the entire speech.
- When words interrupt a quoted sentence, begin the second part with a small letter.
- Use quotation marks around the exact words of an author you use in a report.

©AGS® American Guidance Service, Inc. Permission is granted to reproduce for classroom use only.   **Basic English Composition**

Writing Tip 1

Name _____ Date _____ Period _____ Chapter 1 / Community Connection / 1

Sentences in the Newspaper

A complete sentence begins with a **capital letter.** Each sentence ends with an **end punctuation mark.** An end punctuation mark tells the reader where the complete idea ends.

EXAMPLE   He went to his English class today.

Notice that *He,* the first word of the sentence, begins with a capital letter. The period after *today* ends the statement. It is important to use the correct end punctuation mark. Using a different punctuation mark can change the meaning of a sentence.

The word order of a sentence can vary. Sometimes you can change a sentence by using a different word first.

EXAMPLE   We like to go shopping usually.
          Usually we like to go shopping.

A newspaper is a good place to find sentences you can practice changing. Follow the steps below.

Step 1. Find a newspaper at home or at the library.

Step 2. Choose five complete sentences from the newspaper. Write each sentence on the first line after each number below.

Step 3. Think of a different word order for each sentence. Then rewrite each sentence in that order on the line below it. Be sure to use the correct end punctuation mark.

Step 4. Have your teacher check your work.

1) _____

2) _____

3) _____

4) _____

5) _____

©AGS® American Guidance Service, Inc. Permission is granted to reproduce for classroom use only.   **Basic English Composition**

Community Connection 1

Chapter 1

Sentences

W hat kinds of writing will you do today? Maybe you will write a message to a friend. Maybe you will start your report. Maybe you will send a thank-you note to a relative for a gift. No matter what kind of writing you do, you will try to communicate your ideas clearly. After all, your aim is to be understood! Clear communication depends on clear sentences.

In Chapter 1, you will learn how to build clear, correct sentences.

Goals for Learning

▶ To identify the beginning and end of a thought

▶ To capitalize the first word of a sentence

▶ To end a sentence with the correct punctuation mark

Reading Vocabulary
capitalize (9) identify (6)
communicate (6) relative (5)

Introducing the Chapter

Have students examine the introductory photograph accompanying the first page of Chapter 1. Write the words *clear communication* on the board. Ask students why clear communication is particularly important to the three people in this scene. Write students' answers on the board as complete sentences.

SELF-STUDY GUIDE

Name _____

CHAPTER 1: Sentences

Goal 1.1 *To capitalize the first word of a sentence*

Date	Assignment	Score
_____	1: Read pages 1-2.	_____

Comments:

Goal 1.2 *To identify the beginning and end of a thought*

Date	Assignment	Score
_____	2: Read page 2. Complete Activities A-B on page 2.	_____
_____	3: Read page 3. Complete Activities C-D on page 3.	_____
_____	4: Complete Workbook Activity 1.	_____
_____	5: Complete Workbook Activity 2.	_____
_____	6: Complete Workbook Activity 3.	_____
_____	7: Complete the Lesson 1 Review, Parts A-B on page 4.	_____

Comments:

©AGS® American Guidance Service, Inc. Permission is granted to reproduce for classroom use only. **Basic English Composition**

SELF-STUDY GUIDE

Name _____

CHAPTER 1 Sentences, continued

Goal 1.3 *To end a sentence with the correct punctuation mark*

Date	Assignment	Score
_____	8: Read page 5. Complete Activity A on page 5.	_____
_____	9: Read page 6. Complete Activities B-C on page 6.	_____
_____	10: Complete the Lesson 2 Review, Parts A-B on page 7.	_____
_____	11: Complete the Chapter 1 Review, Parts A-D on pages 8-9.	_____

Comments:

Student's Signature _____ Date _____

Instructor's Signature _____ Date _____

©AGS® American Guidance Service, Inc. Permission is granted to reproduce for classroom use only. **Basic English Composition**

Chapter 1 Self-Study Guide

Chapter 1 Lesson 1

Overview This lesson introduces the sentence as a unit of meaning that must begin with a capital letter and end with a punctuation mark.

Objectives

- To identify a sentence.
- To begin a sentence with a capital letter and end it with an end punctuation mark.
- To vary word order in a sentence.

Student Pages 2–4

Teacher's Resource Library

Activities 1–2

Workbook Activities 1–3

Reading Vocabulary

capital letter
comma
communicate (6)
end punctuation mark
exclamation (8)
sentence (4)

Teaching Suggestions

- **Introducing the Lesson**
  Ask students if they have ever been told to "use complete sentences" in their writing. Have them give their ideas about what that request means.

- **Reviewing Skills** Have students show examples of sentences from written materials they have on hand. Have them identify the capital letter that begins a sentence and the mark of punctuation that ends it.

- **Presenting Activity A**
  Read the directions together, and have students read the items. Ask them to tell why each sentence is only partly correct.

  Activity A Answers
  1) In the fall we like to camp in the mountains. 2) We take plenty of food and water.

Lesson 1 Beginning and Ending a Sentence

Sentence
A group of words containing a subject and a verb and expressing a complete idea.

As a writer and a speaker, you have ideas to communicate. You express each idea in a unit of meaning called a **sentence**.

When you write, you want your readers to understand your ideas. Here are two basic rules for writing sentences.

1. Use a **capital letter** to begin the first word of the sentence. A capital letter tells the reader that a new thought is beginning.

2. End each sentence with an **end punctuation mark**. The mark tells the reader that the thought has ended. Use only a period, a question mark, or an exclamation point to end a sentence. The period is the most common end mark. Never end a sentence with a comma.

Capital letter
The uppercase form of a letter: A, B, C, and so on.

End punctuation mark
A mark that comes at the end of a sentence and tells the reader where the complete idea ends. Here are the three end punctuation marks:
- period .
- question mark ?
- exclamation point !

| EXAMPLE | Not clear: | do you know my friend Derek Corelli he lives a few blocks away |
| | Clear: | Do you know my friend Derek Corelli? He lives a few blocks away. |

Get in the habit of reading your sentences aloud. You can hear where the thoughts begin and where they end.

Activity A List the four sentences below on your paper. Add capital letters and end punctuation marks to make them correct.

> in the fall we like to camp in the mountains. we take plenty of food and water We hike on the trails most of the day we are asleep by eight o'clock at night!

Activity B Read the following words. Decide how to turn them into five sentences. List the five sentences on your paper. Make sure to use capital letters and end punctuation marks.

> my neighbor has a garden on the roof she grows tomatoes there she shares them with everyone in the building how do they taste they are delicious

---

(Activity A Answers, continued)
3) We hike on the trails most of the day. 4) We are asleep by eight o'clock at night!

- **Presenting Activity B** After reading the directions together, have students read the three lines of text aloud. Have them give their ideas about the five separate ideas contained in the three lines.

Activity B Answers

1) My neighbor has a garden on the roof. 2) She grows tomatoes there. 3) She shares them with everyone in the building. 4) How do they taste? 5) They are delicious!

| Name | Date | Period | Chapter 1 Activity 1 |

Looking for Sentences

Directions: Read each group of words below. Find three sentences and write them in order. Capitalize the first word in each sentence. Put the correct punctuation mark at the end of each sentence.

EXAMPLE	School will end soon Laura is ready for summer her last day is June 12
	1) School will end soon.
	2) Laura is ready for summer.
	3) Her last day is June 12.

1) in the spring we have cheerleading tryouts they last two weeks twelve girls are chosen to be on the squad

2) Amanda received her yearbook today she had her friends autograph it the book was full of color pictures

3) the seniors will graduate at the Capital Center this is an exciting event Derek will miss his friends

4) during the summer Derek will work at a full-time job he needs to make money for college he hopes to work many hours

5) college is expensive it is important to plan Derek will need to choose his classes

Basic English Composition

Activity 1

Word Order in Sentences

When you write, think about word order in each sentence. Sometimes you can move the words around without changing the meaning of the sentence.

Read the three example sentences. Notice how they all begin differently. Notice how they all give the same meaning.

 EXAMPLES   The day usually warms up by noon.

Usually the day warms up by noon.

By noon the day usually warms up.

Activity C   Rewrite each sentence below. Change the word order. Find a different word in the sentence to put at the beginning. Capitalize the first word in your new sentence.

1) We go to the lake every Sunday.

2) It is too cold for camping now.

3) We decided to hike instead.

4) We walked steadily for three hours.

5) We saw a deer on the way.

6) Quickly it hid from us.

7) We rested twice.

8) We finally reached the end of the trail.

9) It was time to turn back then.

10) We got a lot of exercise that day.

Activity D   Study the example sentences at the top of this page. Then rewrite each of the following sentences in two different ways. First find a different word in the sentence to put at the beginning. Then make a second sentence by moving this word to a new place. Capitalize the first word of each new sentence.

1) They later saw a deer.

2) It stared quietly at them.

3) It then ran back into the woods.

■ **Presenting Activity C** Ask students to read aloud the example sentences on page 3. Then have them discuss which placement of *usually* in the sentence *The day warms up by noon* sounds more natural to them. Does their choice change when they emphasize different words in the sentence? After reading the directions for Activity C together, direct students to look for single words and for groups of words that can be shifted to the first position in the sentence.

Activity C Answers
Students may be able to justify other responses.

1) Every Sunday we go to the lake.   2) Now it is too cold for camping.   3) Instead we decided to hike.   4) For three hours we walked steadily.   5) On the way we saw a deer.   6) It quickly hid from us.   7) Twice we rested.   8) Finally we reached the end of the trail.   9) Then it was time to turn back.   10) That day we got a lot of exercise.

■ **Presenting Activity D** After reading the directions together, make sure students understand they are to write two sentences for each one given.

Activity D Answers
1) Later they saw a deer. They saw a deer later.   2) Quietly it stared at them. It stared at them quietly.   3) Then it ran back into the woods. It ran back into the woods then.

TEACHER ALERT

Make the point that writers can add variety to their sentences by changing the word order. Emphasize that a changed word order may also change the meaning of the sentence. Students should read their sentences aloud to make sure that the word order gives exactly the meaning they want.

Workbook Activity 1

Name _____ Date _____ Period _____ | Chapter 1 / Workbook Activity / 1

Finding Sentences

Directions: • Read each group of words below.
• Find the sentences and list them in order.
• Capitalize the first word in each sentence.
• Put a punctuation mark at the end.

EXAMPLE everyone in my family likes ice cream our favorite flavor is chocolate we often have ice cream for dessert

1) Everyone in my family likes ice cream.
2) Our favorite flavor is chocolate.
3) We often have ice cream for dessert.

1) in the spring we planted a garden we planted cabbages and peas first later we planted tomatoes

2) my aunt sent me a book for my birthday I wrote a letter to thank her she was pleased

3) my friends and I started a band we practiced three times a week soon we sounded very good

4) last night it snowed again the streets were slippery this morning we looked in the garage for our sleds

5) there was an ad in the newspaper for a file clerk the person had to put papers in alphabetic order I decided to apply for the job

6) yesterday my sister went to the library she wanted to find a book about guitars her music teacher told the class to write a report about a musical instrument

7) today there was an announcement on the public address system at school the coach is having tryouts for the basketball team my friend and I decided to go

8) every year the senior class produces a play usually it is a musical we have a lot of talent at our school

9) what two things must a writer always do a writer must capitalize the first work of a sentence he or she also must put a punctuation mark at the end

©AGS® American Guidance Service, Inc. Permission is granted to reproduce for classroom use only.   **Basic English Composition**

Activity 2

Name _____ Date _____ Period _____ | Chapter 1 / Activity / 2

Expressing Ideas in Different Order

Directions: Rewrite each sentence below in two different ways. Change the words around. Start each sentence in a different way. Always capitalize the first word in a sentence. Add the correct end punctuation mark.

EXAMPLE I enjoy going shopping sometimes.   1) *I sometimes enjoy going shopping.*
2) *Sometimes I enjoy going shopping.*

1) We immediately got into traffic.

2) Everyone usually goes on vacation in the summer.

3) Suddenly I saw a huge black rain cloud.

4) The weather has been hot and humid lately.

5) Often they have a picnic to celebrate.

6) We finally finished our last exam.

7) They carefully ran down the hill.

8) The sun is always shining on a gorgeous day.

©AGS® American Guidance Service, Inc. Permission is granted to reproduce for classroom use only.   **Basic English Composition**

Reading Vocabulary
civil (5)　　　　movement (6)

Part A Answers
Sometimes one person can make a big difference. Have you ever heard of Rosa Parks? She changed American history. She refused to give up her seat on a bus. The civil rights movement began with her brave action.

Part B Answers
1) Every evening Mike listens to music.　2) Lately he enjoys rock.　3) Sometimes he plays the music loudly.　4) Usually his mother complains.　5) Then he turns the music down.

Follow-up Activity

Have each student copy a sentence from a book or newspaper. The sentence should have fewer than twelve words. Each student then writes each word of the sentence on a separate slip of paper, beginning all words with lowercase letters. After shuffling the slips of paper, each student challenges classmates to reorder the words into a meaningful sentence. Classmates try to write the sentence correctly. More than one sentence may be made with each group of words.

Lesson 1　Review

- Before writing a sentence, think about the words that you are going to use.
- Decide which word would be best to put at the beginning. Make sure it begins with a capital letter.
- Remember to put an end punctuation mark at the end of each sentence.

Part A　Read the words below. Find five sentences. Rewrite them correctly on your paper. Capitalize the first word in each sentence. End each sentence with the correct end punctuation mark.

> sometimes one person can make a big difference have you ever heard of Rosa Parks she changed American history she refused to give up her seat on a bus the civil rights movement began with her brave action

Part B　Change the order of the words in each sentence below. Find a different word to put first. Rewrite the sentences on your paper. Remember to capitalize the new first word. Remember to include an end punctuation mark.

1) Mike listens to music every evening.
2) He enjoys rock lately.
3) He sometimes plays the music loudly.
4) His mother usually complains.
5) He turns the music down then.

Name _____ **Date** _____ **Period** _____　| Chapter 1 / Workbook Activity 2 |

Expressing Ideas

The same idea can be expressed with the same words in different ways. The words of a sentence can be placed in a different order.

EXAMPLE　Every year the family usually goes camping.
The family usually goes camping every year.
Usually the family goes camping every year.

Directions: Rewrite each sentence below. Change the words around. Find a different word in the sentence to put at the beginning. Capitalize the first word. Remember end punctuation.

1) We seldom watch television in the summer.
2) We are usually too busy with outdoor activities.
3) Always the weather is sunny and warm where we live.
4) Lately we have not had much rain in our town.
5) Suddenly I heard thunder rumbling in the background.
6) Everyone immediately was sure that we would have rain.
7) In a few minutes the thunder stopped.
8) Slowly we opened the door and looked outside.
9) At that moment the sky was clear as far as we could see.
10) Someday soon, I'm sure, we finally will get some rain.

©AGS® American Guidance Service, Inc. Permission is granted to reproduce for classroom use only.　**Basic English Composition**

Workbook Activity 2

Name _____ **Date** _____ **Period** _____　| Chapter 1 / Workbook Activity 3 |

Writing in Sentences

Directions: Answer each question by writing a complete sentence. Capitalize the first word in each sentence. Put a punctuation mark at the end.

EXAMPLE　What is you favorite holiday?
My favorite holiday is Christmas.

1) What is today's date?
2) What is your name?
3) How old are you?
4) In which state do you live?
5) What is the capital city of your state?
6) Who is president of the United States?
7) What is your favorite color?
8) Do you have cable television in your community?
9) What is the name of your teacher?
10) Which is your favorite sport or hobby?
11) Who is your favorite singer?
12) What is the name of the last movie you saw?
13) Did you enjoy the movie?

©AGS® American Guidance Service, Inc. Permission is granted to reproduce for classroom use only.　**Basic English Composition**

Workbook Activity 3

Always put a punctuation mark at the end of a sentence. It tells the reader where the idea ends. It also helps the reader understand what kind of idea you have written. Here are four rules to learn.

1. Use a period (.) to end a statement.
2. Use a question mark (?) to end a question.
3. Use an exclamation mark (!) to end a sentence that expresses strong feeling.
4. Do not use a comma to end a sentence.

Activity A   Copy each of these sentences on your paper. Capitalize the first word. Add the correct punctuation mark at the end of each sentence.

1) sports are important to Derek
2) he likes to play basketball and soccer
3) he enjoys watching football
4) baseball bores him
5) do you agree with Derek
6) baseball is exciting
7) picture the bases loaded and a power hitter coming to bat
8) what happens next
9) the hitter strikes out
10) there are plenty of surprises in baseball

Lesson at a Glance

Chapter 1   Lesson 2

Overview This lesson focuses on the connection between sentence meaning and the correct end punctuation mark.

Objective
- To choose a period, a question mark, or an exclamation mark to end a sentence.

Student Pages 5–7

Teacher's Resource Library
Activities 3–4

Reading Vocabulary
bore (5)   soccer (6)

Teaching Suggestions

- **Introducing the Lesson**
Ask students what their reaction would be if they were reading a page in which no end punctuation marks were used. They may express their understanding that end punctuation breaks up the text into meaningful units. They may also see that the particular mark used helps the reader understand the writer's meaning.

- **Reviewing Skills** Draw a period, an exclamation point, a question mark, and a comma on the board. Have students name each symbol and tell which three are end punctuation marks.

- **Presenting Activity A**
After reading the directions together, have students read the ten items to themselves. Ask them to point out one sentence that should end with a period, another that should end with an exclamation point, and a third that should end with a question mark.

Activity A Answers
1) Sports are important to Derek.
2) He likes to play basketball and soccer.   3) He enjoys watching football.   4) Baseball bores him.

GLOBAL CONNECTION

Students who are familiar with written Spanish may know that upside-down question marks and exclamation points precede sentences. A volunteer may offer an example in Spanish of each kind of sentence and mark. Ask students why the Spanish method of punctuating is a useful signal to readers.

(Activity A Answers, continued)
5) Do you agree with Derek?
6) Baseball is exciting! (or) Baseball is exciting.   7) Picture the bases loaded and a power hitter coming to bat.   8) What happens next?   9) The hitter strikes out! (or) The hitter strikes out.   10) There are plenty of surprises in baseball. (or) There are plenty of surprises in baseball!

Reading Vocabulary

detail (5)   junior (5)

fitness   physical (5)

■ Presenting Activity B

Read the directions together. Have students read the paragraph aloud quietly to themselves. Explain that reading aloud can help writers hear the beginning and end of a sentence.

Activity B Answers

1) When Derek was a junior in high school, he met Amanda and Laura. **2)** They liked him very much. **3)** He liked them also. **4)** Derek was in good physical shape. **5)** The girls shared Derek's interest in physical fitness. **6)** They wanted to improve their fitness. **7)** The girls and Derek decided to work on their fitness together. **8)** In six months Derek, Amanda, and Laura all looked and felt much better.

■ Presenting Activity C

Have volunteers take turns reading aloud the directions and the three paragraphs of boxed text. Briefly discuss the meaning of the idiom "hit it off," and have students tell why friends sometimes hit it off from the start. Then read aloud the second set of directions with students.

Activity C Answers

Answers will vary. Sample answers are given.

1) Before he met Amanda and Laura, Derek was shy. **2)** Most of the time, Derek ran, worked out, or studied alone before he met Amanda and Laura.

3) After he met the girls, Derek spent less time alone, had lots of friends, and became popular.

4) Derek changed because of his new friends.

Activity B   The paragraph below has eight sentences. List them on your paper. Capitalize the first word of each sentence. Add the correct end punctuation.

> When Derek was a junior in high school, he met Amanda and Laura they liked him very much he liked them also Derek was in good physical shape the girls shared Derek's interest in physical fitness they wanted to improve their fitness the girls and Derek decided to work on their fitness together in six months Derek, Amanda, and Laura all looked and felt much better

Activity C   Read more about Derek, Amanda, and Laura. Notice the details that describe the kind of person Derek is.

> Before he met Amanda and Laura, Derek was shy. He spent most of his time alone running and working out or studying.
>
> Amanda and Laura were very friendly. They decided to become friends with Derek. The girls and Derek hit it off from the start.
>
> Soon Derek, Amanda, and Laura became good friends. They were always together. After a few months, Derek spent less time alone. He had lots of friends, too. He became very popular.

Read each question about Derek. Answer each question on your paper. Use complete sentences. Begin each sentence with a capital letter. Add the correct mark of end punctuation.

1) What was Derek like before he met Amanda and Laura?

2) What did Derek do with most of his time before he met Amanda and Laura?

3) How was Derek different after he met the girls?

4) Why did Derek change?

APPLICATION

At Home

Students may examine mailings delivered to their homes. Have them look for end punctuation marks in sentences. Ask them to copy sentences containing the three marks of end punctuation.

Activity 3

- Use an end punctuation mark to show your readers where your idea ends.
- Use *only* a period, a question mark, or an exclamation point to end a sentence.
- Do not end a sentence with a comma.

Part A   Read the words below. Find five sentences. Rewrite them in a list on your paper. Capitalize the first word of each sentence. End each sentence with the correct punctuation mark.

> Derek has a job at a gas station he likes to work with his hands is he thinking about becoming a mechanic he has not decided on a career his main interest is sports right now

Part B   Follow these directions.

1) Select a topic from the list below.
   - Driving a car
   - Riding a bicycle
   - Listening to music
   - Playing basketball
   - Wearing the right clothes

2) Write five questions about the topic you chose. End each question with a question mark.

3) Then write the answers to your five questions. End each answer with a period.

4) Check your work to make sure that each sentence is a complete thought. Make sure that every sentence begins with a capital letter.

Sentences   *Chapter 1*   **7**

Reading Vocabulary

career (6)   topic (5)
mechanic (6)

Part A Answers

1) Derek has a job at a gas station. **2)** He likes to work with his hands. **3)** Is he thinking about becoming a mechanic?   **4)** He has not decided on a career.   **5)** His main interest is sports right now.

Part B Answers

Answers will vary. Allow time for students to read aloud their questions and answers. Listeners may identify the end mark of punctuation in each sentence heard.

Follow-up Activity

Have several students each copy a paragraph of text from any published work. Ask them to leave out the end marks. Classmates then read the copied paragraphs and try to tell what punctuation mark belongs at the end of each sentence.

LEARNING STYLES

Visual/Spatial
Make three posters by pasting a colorful magazine picture on each one. Above each picture, draw an ending point of punctuation—period, exclamation point, question mark. (Create a poster for each point of punctuation.) Invite the students to write an original sentence on their favorite poster. Explain that the sentence must reflect what they see in the picture and must end with the point of punctuation on the poster. Afterward, invite students to read the sentences aloud with expression.

Name _____ Date _____ Period _____ | Chapter 1 |
                                              | Activity |
Find the Sentences | 4 |

Directions: Read the paragraph below. Find 9 sentences and write them in order. Capitalize the first word of each sentence. Add the correct punctuation mark at the end of each sentence.

George Washington
The first president of the United States was George Washington he was the son of Augustine Washington and Mary Ball his early childhood was spent on the Ferry farm near Fredericksburg, Virginia at the age of 16, he went to live with his half brother Lawrence, who built and named Mount Vernon Lawrence died in 1752, and George acquired his property by inheritance in 1759, he married Martha Dandridge Custis and managed his family estate at Mount Vernon he was unanimously elected president by the electoral college and inaugurated on April 30, 1789, on the balcony of New York's Federal Hall he was reelected in 1792 but refused to consider a third term and retired to Mount Vernon he had acute laryngitis after a ride in the snow and rain around his estate and died on December 14, 1799

1) _____
2) _____
3) _____
4) _____
5) _____
6) _____
7) _____
8) _____
9) _____

©AGS® American Guidance Service, Inc. Permission is granted to reproduce for classroom use only.   **Basic English Composition**

Activity 4

Chapter 1 Review

The Teacher's Resource Library includes two parallel forms of the Chapter 1 Mastery Test. The difficulty level of the two forms is equivalent. You may wish to use one form as a pretest and the other form as a posttest.

Part A Answers

Answers will vary. Sample answers are given.

1) A sentence is a group of words that expresses a complete thought.
2) The three end punctuation marks are the period, the question mark, and the exclamation point.
3) The most common end punctuation mark is the period.
4) A sentence must begin with a capital letter to show the reader that a new thought is beginning.
5) Writers can make their sentences better by changing the word order.

Part B Answers

Answers will vary. Remind students that reading their sentences aloud will help them hear any problems that need to be fixed.

APPLICATION

In the Community
Show students headlines from a newspaper. Point out that headline writers rarely have the space for complete sentences. Have students choose headlines that they turn into complete sentences.

Part A Answer each question by writing a complete sentence. Capitalize the first word. Put a punctuation mark at the end.

1) What is a sentence?

2) What are the names of the three end punctuation marks?

3) What is the most common end punctuation mark?

4) Why must a sentence begin with a capital letter?

5) How can writers make their sentences better?

Part B Before you write a sentence, you must have an idea. Only you know the beginning and ending of each idea. Follow these directions.

1) Write five sentences.

2) Tell about something you know. You may write about your neighborhood or your friends. You may write about a game, a sport, or a hobby.

3) Put your sentences in a list. Number them from 1 to 5.

4) Check to make sure each sentence begins with a capital letter.

5) Make sure the sentence ends with the correct punctuation mark.

Name	Date	Period	Chapter 1 Mastery Test A page 1

Chapter 1 Mastery Test A

Part A Rewrite each of these sentences on the blank line. Capitalize the first word in each sentence. Add the correct end punctuation mark.

1) in the fall Derek likes to go to the school basketball games

2) he decided to call Amanda and see if she wanted to go

3) what time does the basketball game start

4) amanda finished her work and got ready for the game

5) she could not wait for the game to begin

6) derek met Amanda in front of her house

7) they walked several blocks to the school

8) unfortunately, it started to rain

9) luckily, they were almost at the school

10) which players will be starting the game today

©AGS® American Guidance Service, Inc. Permission is granted to reproduce for classroom use only. **Basic English Composition**

Name	Date	Period	Chapter 1 Mastery Test A page 2

Chapter 1 Mastery Test A, continued

Part B Rewrite the sentences in each paragraph. Add capital letters and end punctuation marks to make them correct.

1) in area, Canada is the second largest country in the world it stretches 3,223 miles from east to west the United States is on its southern border

2) many stories are told about who designed the United States flag no one knows for sure who really did some people think that Betsy Ross made the first flag however, there is no historical proof that she did

3) have you ever heard of the Pulitzer Prizes they have been given since 1917 they are given to writers for outstanding work receiving a Pulitzer Prize is a great honor

4) do you know anyone who lives in Mobile, Alabama more than 200,000 people live in this city it is the second largest city in Alabama the largest city is Birmingham

5) almanacs are books of facts do you want to know how many calories are in a banana do you need to know what the capital of Lesotho is you can find the answers to these questions in an almanac

©AGS® American Guidance Service, Inc. Permission is granted to reproduce for classroom use only. **Basic English Composition**

Chapter 1 Mastery Test A

Part C Find two sentences in each group of words below. Write the two sentences with correct capitalization and end punctuation.

1) my grandfather spent a week at the lake he learned to swim

2) the moon was full last week what makes it seem smaller tonight

3) our class is going to the art museum will you join us

4) this biography tells about Eleanor Roosevelt she led an amazing life

5) what is the most important invention of the twentieth century I believe it is the computer

Part D Change the order of the words in each sentence below. Find a different word to put first. Rewrite the sentences on your paper. Remember to capitalize the new first word. Remember to include an end punctuation mark.

1) William listens to the radio every night.

2) He discovered a jazz station last year.

3) Jazz was new to him then.

4) He is fascinated by jazz now.

5) He bought a ticket this week for a Jazz Greats concert.

Test Taking Tip After you have completed a test, reread each question and answer. Ask yourself: Have I answered the question that was asked? Have I answered it completely?

Chapter 1 Mastery Test B

Name _____ Date _____ Period _____

Chapter 1 Mastery Test B
page 1

Chapter 1 Mastery Test B

Part A Rewrite each of these sentences on the blank line. Capitalize the first word in each sentence. Add the correct end punctuation mark.

1) derek and Amanda saw Mike in the stands at the basketball game

2) amanda always asks Derek questions during the game

3) which team will get this tip-off

4) which player is the best free thrower

5) sometimes the school pep group sells snacks at halftime

6) oh boy, they have hot dogs today

7) do they have any mustard

8) yes, and they have ketchup, too

9) derek wants two hot dogs and a cold drink

10) amanda just wants a cold drink

©AGS® American Guidance Service, Inc. Permission is granted to reproduce for classroom use only.   **Basic English Composition**

Name _____ Date _____ Period _____

Chapter 1 Mastery Test B
page 2

Chapter 1 Mastery Test B, continued

Part B Rewrite the sentences in each paragraph. Add capital letters and end punctuation marks to make them correct.

1) the average person watches television almost 30 hours each week do you think that men or women watch the most TV the answer is women they watch about five hours more each week than men do

2) do you know what snowflakes are made of snowflakes are clumps of ice crystals they form around bits of dust when the temperature is very cold ice crystals bump into each other and form snowflakes

3) the skeleton is the body's framework it is made up of large and small bones do you know how many bones are in the human body there are 206 bones that provide the framework for your body

4) did you ever watch Lassie did you wish you had a collie of your own the collie is a very smart dog it is capable of showing a great deal of affection you could not find a better friend and protector

5) erosion wears down hills and forms valleys and canyons did you ever see water running down a hill after it rains running water, ice, wind, ocean waves, and gravity are all part of the erosion process

©AGS® American Guidance Service, Inc. Permission is granted to reproduce for classroom use only.   **Basic English Composition**

Planning Guide

Punctuating Sentences

	Student Pages	Vocabulary	Practice Exercises	Lesson Review
Lesson 1 The Purpose of a Sentence	12-16	✔	✔	16
Lesson 2 Writing Dialogue	17-24	✔	✔	24
Lesson 3 Writing Sentences	25-27		✔	27

Chapter Activities

Teacher's Resource Library
Writing Tip 2: The Purpose of a Sentence

Community Connection 2: The Rules for Writing Dialogue

Assessment Options

Student Text
Chapter 2 Review

Teacher's Resource Library
Chapter 2 Mastery Tests A and B

	Teaching Strategies							Language Skills			Learning Styles						Teacher's Resource Library		
Reviewing Skills	Teacher Alert	Follow-up Activity	Career Application	Home Application	Global Connection	Community Application	Identification Skills	Writing Skills	Punctuation Skills	Visual/Spatial	Auditory/Verbal	Body/Kinesthetic	Logical/Mathematical	Group Learning	LEP/ESL	Activities	Workbook Activities	Self-Study Guide
12	12	16	15			14	✔	✔	✔						13	5-6	4-5	✔
17	21	24		19			✔	✔	✔		20					7-8	6-8	✔
25		27				26	✔	✔	✔					26				✔

Chapter 2: Punctuating Sentences pages 10–29

Writing Tip 2

The Purpose of a Sentence

A **sentence** is a group of words containing a subject and a verb. It expresses a complete idea. You write a sentence for several purposes. They are:

1) To Make a Statement
A **statement** is a sentence that states a fact or gives information to another person.
A statement is also called a **declarative sentence**.
A statement ends with a period (.).

EXAMPLES   Denzel Washington is an actor.
Mexico is south of the United States.

2) To Ask a Question
A **question** is a sentence that asks for information.
A question is also called a **declarative sentence**.
A question ends with a question mark (?).

EXAMPLES   Who is Denzel Washington?
Where is Mexico?

3) To Give a Command or Make a Request
A **command** tells or orders someone to do something.
A **request** politely asks someone to do something.
A request often includes the word *please*.
A command or request is also called an **imperative sentence**.
A command or request ends with a period.

EXAMPLES   Please open the window.
Play that CD for me, Tam.

4) To Express Strong Feeling
An **exclamation** is a sentence that expresses strong feeling.
An exclamation is also called an **exclamatory sentence**.
An exclamation ends with an exclamation point (!).

EXAMPLES   Stop here!
What a hard question!

5) To Tell a Story
A story may include dialogue, or conversation. Study the rules in Chapter 2 Lesson 2 for punctuating dialogue.

©AGS® American Guidance Service, Inc. Permission is granted to reproduce for classroom use only.   **Basic English Composition**

Community Connection 2

The Rules for Writing Dialogue

Dialogue is words said between people or story characters. In Chapter 2, you learned eleven rules for writing dialogue. These rules will help you to write dialogue correctly. The rules can also help you to understand dialogue better when you read it.

You probably have seen dialogue in things you have read. Dialogue is used in short stories and novels when characters talk. Use stories you have read to practice identifying the eleven rules of dialogue. Follow these steps.

Step 1. Go to the library or your bookshelf at home. Find a novel or short story that interests you.

Step 2. Look at the dialogue in the story. Copy five complete sentences of dialogue from the story. Each sentence must be an example of a different rule. Then write in your own words the rule that each sentence represents.

EXAMPLE   The policeman asked, "Do you know how fast you were driving?"
Rule: Punctuation at the end of a quotation goes inside the closing quotation mark.

1) _____

2) _____

3) _____

4) _____

5) _____

Step 3. Share your sentences with your class.

©AGS® American Guidance Service, Inc. Permission is granted to reproduce for classroom use only.   **Basic English Composition**

Writing Tip 2   **Community Connection 2**

Punctuating Sentences

How can you tell that someone is asking you a question? The speaker's voice usually ends with a rising tone. How can you tell that someone is giving an order? The speaker's voice has a firm tone. In speech, changes in tone are clues to meaning.

When you write, you want your words to "speak" from the page. How can you help readers to hear how the words sound? Use punctuation marks in your sentences.

In Chapter 2, you will learn how to punctuate your sentences so that readers will hear exactly what you mean.

Goals for Learning

▶ To recognize the purpose of a sentence

▶ To end each sentence with the correct punctuation mark

▶ To punctuate dialogue correctly

▶ To distinguish direct and indirect quotations

11

Reading Vocabulary

clue (5)   punctuation (7)
distinguish (6)   tone (6)
punctuate (7)

Introducing the Chapter

Have students examine the introductory photograph accompanying the first page of Chapter 2. Tell them that the person in the photograph is reading aloud from a book. Have them give their ideas about the mood or idea the reader could be conveying with her facial expression and voice—what does she seem to be saying? Ask students why someone who is reading aloud must pay attention to where sentences begin and end. Then ask for their ideas about what makes an oral reader interesting to listen to and easy to understand.

SELF-STUDY GUIDE

Name _____

CHAPTER 2: Punctuating Sentences

Goal 2.1 To end each sentence with the correct punctuation mark

Date	Assignment	Score
_____	1: Read pages 11–12. Complete Activities A–B on page 13.	_____
_____	2: Complete Workbook Activity 4.	_____
_____	3: Read page 14. Complete Activities C–D on page 14.	_____
_____	4: Read page 15. Complete Activity E on page 15.	_____
_____	5: Complete the Lesson 1 Review, Parts A–B on page 16.	_____
_____	6: Complete Workbook Activity 5.	_____

Comments:

Goal 2.2 To punctuate dialogue correctly

Date	Assignment	Score
_____	7: Read page 17. Complete Activity A on page 17.	_____
_____	8: Read page 18. Complete Activity B on page 18.	_____
_____	9: Complete Workbook Activity 6.	_____
_____	10: Read page 19. Complete Activity C on page 19.	_____
_____	11: Complete Workbook Activity 7.	_____
_____	12: Read page 20. Complete Activity D on page 20.	_____
_____	13: Read page 21. Complete Activity E on page 21.	_____

Comments:

SELF-STUDY GUIDE

Name _____

CHAPTER 2 Punctuating Sentences, continued

Goal 2.3 To distinguish direct and indirect quotations

Date	Assignment	Score
_____	14: Read page 22. Complete Activity F on page 22.	_____
_____	15: Complete Activities G–H on page 23.	_____
_____	16: Complete Workbook Activity 8.	_____
_____	17: Complete the Lesson 2 Review on page 24.	_____

Comments:

Goal 2.4 To recognize the purpose of a sentence

Date	Assignment	Score
_____	18: Read page 25. Complete Activities A–C on page 25.	_____
_____	19: Complete Activities D–E on page 26.	_____
_____	20: Complete the Lesson 3 Review, Parts A–B on page 27.	_____
_____	21: Complete the Chapter 2 Review, Parts A–C on pages 28-29.	_____

Comments:

Student's Signature _____ Date _____

Instructor's Signature _____ Date _____

Chapter 2 Self-Study Guide

Lesson at a Glance

Chapter 2 Lesson 1

Overview This lesson discusses the four main purposes of a sentence: to make a statement, to ask a question, to give a command or make a request, and to make an exclamation. The lesson also shows the connection between sentence purpose and end punctuation.

Objectives

- To distinguish four types of sentences.
- To use appropriate end punctuation with each type of sentence.

Student Pages 12–16

Teacher's Resource Library

Activities 5–6

Workbook Activities 4–5

Reading Vocabulary

command (4)	imperative (10)
declarative	interrogative
democracy (6)	**question (2)**
determine (5)	register (6)
exclamation (8)	**request (6)**
exclamatory	**statement (4)**
expression (5)	

Teaching Suggestions

■ Introducing the Lesson

Write the three words *You are here* on the board. End the sentence in turn with a period, a question mark, and an exclamation point. Discuss how meaning and tone change as the end punctuation changes.

■ Reviewing Skills
Ask students to think about the answer to this question: How does a writer show readers that a new idea is beginning? Have students use the words *capital letter* and *end punctuation* in a written sentence that answers the question.

Command
A sentence that tells or orders someone to do something.

Exclamation
An expression of strong feeling.

Question
A sentence that asks for information.

Request
A mild command. It politely tells someone to do something. It often includes the word please.

Statement
A sentence that expresses a fact or gives information.

A sentence has one of four main purposes. The purpose of the sentence determines the end punctuation.

1. **Purpose: to make a statement**
   A statement expresses a fact or gives information. A statement is also called a declarative sentence. A statement ends with a period.

EXAMPLES	I am hungry.
	The United States is a democracy.

2. **Purpose: to ask a question**
   A question is a sentence that asks for information. A question is also called an interrogative sentence. A question ends with a question mark.

EXAMPLES	Are you hungry?
	What is a democracy?

3. **Purpose: to give a command or make a request**
   A command tells or orders someone to do something. A request politely asks someone to do something. It often includes the word *please*. A command or request is also called an imperative sentence. A command or request usually ends with a period.

EXAMPLES	Eat this sandwich if you are hungry.
	Please register to vote.

4. **Purpose: to make an exclamation**
   An exclamatory sentence expresses strong feeling. It may make a statement or give a strong command. It ends with an exclamation point.

EXAMPLES	I'm really hungry!
	Vote today!

---

12   *Chapter 2   Punctuating Sentences*

TEACHER ALERT

As you discuss purpose 4 on this page, "to make an exclamation," point out to students that the examples show complete exclamatory sentences. The term *exclamation* also applies to expressions of strong feelings that are not complete sentences. Write a few exclamations on the chalkboard, and have students note how the exclamation point signals strong feeling. Spend a little time discussing why these are not considered complete sentences:

Wow!

What a day!

How amazing!

Activity A Read the following conversation between Derek and Amanda. Write the purpose of each sentence on your paper. Choose from these four purposes:

- to make a statement
- to ask a question
- to give a command or make a request
- to express strong feeling

1) Amanda: What do you think of Mr. Lamar's music class?

2) Derek: I like the old recordings.

3) Amanda: Tell me more.

4) Derek: I wish I could have heard Robert Johnson.

5) Amanda: Wasn't he a blues musician?

6) Derek: He was the greatest!

7) Amanda: That music sounds old-fashioned to me.

8) Derek: Give it another chance.

Activity B Read the following conversation between Amanda and Laura. The end punctuation is missing. Copy each sentence on your paper. Add the end punctuation that matches the purpose of the sentence.

1) Laura: Are you as hungry as I am

2) Amanda: I'm starving

3) Laura: Is it lunchtime yet

4) Amanda: Look at your watch

5) Laura: It's only ten o'clock

6) Amanda: I need a snack

7) Laura: I have an apple

8) Amanda: Please cut it in half

Reading Vocabulary
blues
conversation (5)
old-fashioned (5)

■ Presenting Activity A
Make sure students focus on the sentence that follows the character identification. Remind them that a period may end a statement, but it also may end a request or command.

Activity A Answers
1) to ask a question 2) to make a statement 3) to give a command or make a request 4) to make a statement 5) to ask a question 6) to express strong feeling 7) to make a statement 8) to give a command or make a request

■ Presenting Activity B
Students may read the conversation aloud to hear the speakers' tones and make judgments about sentence purpose.

Activity B Answers
1) Are you as hungry as I am? 2) I'm starving! 3) Is it lunchtime yet? 4) Look at your watch. 5) It's only ten o'clock. (or) It's only ten o'clock! 6) I need a snack. (or) I need a snack! 7) I have an apple. 8) Please cut it in half.

LEARNING STYLES

LEP/ESL
Direct the students' attention to the conversation in Activity B on page 13 to which they have added end punctuation. Encourage students for whom English is a second language to read the conversation in their first language. Ask them to use their voices and hands to create the end points of punctuation. If two students have the same primary language, ask them to be partners. Encourage them to use their primary language to speak the two parts of the conversations.

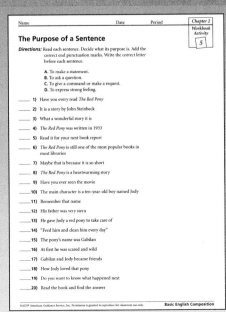

Workbook Activity 5

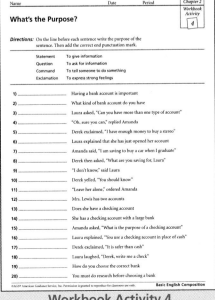

Workbook Activity 4

Reading Vocabulary

capital (5)   mousse
chill (5)   rewrite

■ Presenting Activity C

Help students to see that the sentences represent a conversation between two people. Have them look at both the beginning and ending of each sentence to determine what, if any, corrections are needed. Tell them to choose either a question mark or a period for the end mark. Provide the tricky pronunciation of *mousse,* if necessary.

Activity C Answers

1) What is your favorite dessert?
2) I like chocolate ice cream.
3) Have you ever eaten chocolate mousse?   **4)** No, I haven't.
5) What is chocolate mousse?
6) Chocolate mousse is a chilled dessert.   **7)** It is very sweet, very filling, and very delicious.
8) I do not think that I should try mousse.   **9)** Why not?   **10)** I am determined to stay away from sweets.

■ Presenting Activity D

Have students look back at the examples on this page for ideas about how to ask and answer questions.

Activity D Answers

Answers will vary.

Punctuation: Questions and Answers

Always put a question mark after a question. An answer is a statement. Use a period at the end of an answer. Study the punctuation in the examples below.

> **EXAMPLES**
>
> Question: When did John F. Kennedy become president of the United States?
>
> Answer: John F. Kennedy became president in 1961.
>
> Question: Who invented the telephone?
>
> Answer: Alexander Graham Bell invented the telephone.

Activity C   Rewrite the following questions and answers. Some of these sentences begin with a capital letter and end with the correct mark of end punctuation. Other sentences have errors. Find and correct any mistakes.

1) What is your favorite dessert.

2) i like chocolate ice cream.

3) Have you ever eaten chocolate mousse?

4) No, I haven't?

5) What is chocolate mousse.

6) Chocolate mousse is a chilled dessert.

7) it is very sweet, very filling, and very delicious.

8) I do not think that I should try mousse?

9) Why not.

10) I am determined to stay away from sweets,

Activity D   Write five questions about famous people. Write the answer to each question. Check to be sure each sentence starts with a capital letter and ends with the correct punctuation mark.

Punctuation: Exclamations

Say the following sentences aloud. Listen for the difference in tone. The words are the same, but the sentence with the exclamation point has the stronger feeling. Remember that most sentences end with a period. Use an exclamation point only when you want extra power.

EXAMPLES		
	Statement:	It is late.
	Exclamation:	It is late!
	Statement:	Arnold looks good.
	Exclamation:	Arnold looks good!
	Command:	Write to me.
	Exclamation:	Write to me!

Activity E Copy the following sentences on your paper. End the sentence with an exclamation point if it shows strong feeling. If it does not show strong feeling, end the sentence with a period.

1) Amanda is learning to drive

2) Her mother used to race cars

3) Amanda's mother is a great driver

4) Amanda took a lesson from her mother

5) One lesson was enough

6) Watch out

7) Pay attention

8) You're going too fast

9) Amanda signed up at Patience Driving School

10) The instructor is very calm

Reading Vocabulary
instructor (7)   patience (5)

■ Presenting Activity E

Remind students that a command may end with a period or an exclamation point. Tell them that the exclamation point appears only if the command is a strong one.

Activity E Answers

1) Amanda is learning to drive. 2) Her mother used to race cars. 3) Amanda's mother is a great driver. (or) Amanda's mother is a great driver! 4) Amanda took a lesson from her mother. 5) One lesson was enough. (or) One lesson was enough! 6) Watch out! 7) Pay attention! 8) You're going too fast! 9) Amanda signed up at Patience Driving School. 10) The instructor is very calm.

APPLICATION

 Career Connection
Tell students that in business writing, exclamation points should be used sparingly. Write the following two sentences on the board, and have students tell why the first one is more appropriate for a business communication:

Please send me the information.

Send me the information!

Ask students to brainstorm other examples that may be different in business.

Reading Vocabulary

assign (6)   tennis (5)
biography (7)

Part A Answers

1) To ask a question (?)   2) To make a statement (.)   3) To ask a question (?)   4) To make a statement (.)   5) To make a statement (.)
6) To ask a question (?)   7) To show strong feeling (!)   8) To make a statement (.) (or) To show strong feeling (!)   9) To ask a question (?)
10) To make a statement (.)

Part B Answers

Answers will vary.

Follow-up Activity

Have students brainstorm a list of topics to write about—sports, music, computers, and so on. Together, choose one topic, and have everyone write four sentences on that topic. Each sentence should serve one of the four main purposes students have learned.

Lesson 1 Review

Here are four main purposes for saying or writing a sentence:

- To make a statement
- To ask a question
- To request or command
- To show strong feeling

Part A   Read each sentence below. The end punctuation mark is missing. Decide on the main purpose of the sentence. Number your paper from 1 to 10. Write the purpose of each sentence. Then write the punctuation mark that belongs at the end.

1) Did Ms. Ruiz assign books to read
2) Derek chose a biography
3) What is a biography
4) It tells the story of someone's life
5) Derek's book is about Arthur Ashe
6) Wasn't he a tennis player
7) That's not all
8) Ashe was a true hero
9) What book will you choose
10) I think I'll read a biography

Part B   Write ten sentences on your paper. Include three statements, three questions, two commands or requests, and two exclamations. Be sure to use the correct punctuation mark at the end of each sentence.

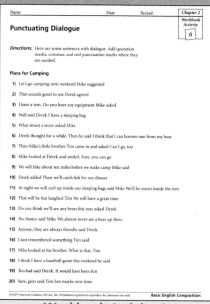

Workbook Activity 6

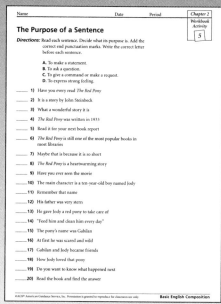

Workbook Activity 5

Lesson 2 Writing Dialogue

Dialogue
The words that people or story characters say to each other.

Quotation
A passage containing someone's exact spoken or written words. The words are enclosed in quotation marks (" ").

Dialogue is conversation. The speaker's exact words are called a **quotation**. This lesson has eleven rules for writing dialogue.

1. Put quotation marks around a speaker's exact words.

> **EXAMPLE** "Where are you going?" asked Amanda.

2. Capitalize the first word of a quotation.

> **EXAMPLE** Laura answered, "Now I'm going to lunch."

3. You may name the speaker before the quotation. Then use a comma before the quotation.

> **EXAMPLE** Amanda said, "I will see you later."

4. You may name the speaker after the quotation. If the quotation is a statement, use a comma (not a period) to separate the speaker's name from the quotation. Set the comma inside the closing quotation marks.

> **EXAMPLE** "I'll see you at the bus stop," said Laura.

5. If the quotation is a question, use a question mark at the end of the quotation. If the speaker's sentence expresses strong feeling, use an exclamation point.

> **EXAMPLES** "Will you be on time?" asked Amanda.
> "Of course, I will!" said Laura.

Activity A Rewrite these sentences. Punctuate them correctly.

1) I am going to Centerville said Laura.
2) Why are you going there asked Amanda.
3) I want to see a rodeo answered Laura.
4) Take me with you said Amanda.
5) Sure, come along replied Laura.

Punctuating Sentences *Chapter 2* **17**

■ **Presenting Activity A**
Remind students to study the five rules on this page to determine all the punctuation that belongs in each sentence.

Activity A Answers
1) "I am going to Centerville," said Laura. **2)** "Why are you going there?" asked Amanda. **3)** "I want to see a rodeo," answered Laura. **4)** "Take me with you," said Amanda. **5)** "Sure, come along," replied Laura.

Lesson at a Glance

Chapter 2 Lesson 2

Overview This lesson presents how to write dialogue with correct punctuation and capitalization.

Objectives

■ To use quotation marks around a speaker's exact words.
■ To use capital letters correctly in dialogue.
■ To use commas and end punctuation correctly in dialogue.
■ To break dialogue into paragraphs correctly.
■ To use words of direct address correctly.
■ To distinguish direct and indirect quotations and to use them correctly.

Student Pages 17–24

Teacher's Resource Library
Activities 7–8
Workbook Activities 6–8

Reading Vocabulary

capitalize (9)   enclose (5)
comma   exact (6)
conversation (5) passage (5)
dialogue (7)   **quotation (6)**

Teaching Suggestions

■ **Introducing the Lesson**
Ask students what writers do to show conversations among story characters. Have students give their ideas about why writers choose to show the exact words of characters. Students may express their understanding that writers want to make story characters come alive for readers.

■ **Reviewing Skills** Leave out the end punctuation as you write a declarative, an imperative, an exclamatory, and an interrogative sentence on the chalkboard. Have students add correct end punctuation to each sentence.

Punctuating Sentences *Chapter 2* **17**

Reading Vocabulary

broncs   wrestling (5)
comment (5)

■ **Presenting Activity B**

Tell students that as they read each sentence, they should look for the character's name and the accompanying word, such as *said, asked, added,* or *answered.* Then they can determine which words should be enclosed in quotation marks.

Activity B Answers

1) "How far are we from Centerville?" asked Amanda.
2) "About two hundred miles," said Laura.   3) Amanda asked, "When does the rodeo begin?"
4) "The rodeo begins at noon," Laura answered.   5) "I am getting excited!" Amanda said with a laugh.   6) "The first event is the steer wrestling," Laura said.   7) Then Amanda said, "I can hardly believe that we will soon be there!"
8) "I have never seen a rodeo," added Laura.   9) "Neither have I," commented Amanda.
10) "Do you think that you will like the rodeo?" asked Laura.
11) "I know I will," said Amanda.

6. The whole sentence must end with the correct end punctuation mark. Study the end punctuation marks used in the examples. The first example is a statement; it ends with a period. The second example is a question; it ends with a question mark.

EXAMPLES "We are leaving for Centerville tomorrow."
Amanda asked, "How long will we be there?"

7. The punctuation mark at the end of the quotation goes inside the closing quotation marks.

EXAMPLES "I want to see the steer wrestling!"
"I want to see the broncs," said Laura.
"I am looking forward to seeing my first rodeo."

Activity B   Check your knowledge of writing dialogue. Rewrite the following sentences. Punctuate them correctly. Follow the rules and examples given on pages 17–18.

1) How far are we from Centerville asked Amanda.

2) About two hundred miles said Laura.

3) Amanda asked when does the rodeo begin

4) The rodeo begins at noon Laura answered

5) I am getting excited Amanda said with a laugh

6) The first event is the steer wrestling Laura said

7) Then Amanda said I can hardly believe that we will soon be there.

8) I have never seen a rodeo added Laura.

9) Neither have I commented Amanda.

10) Do you think that you will like the rodeo asked Laura.

11) I know I will said Amanda.

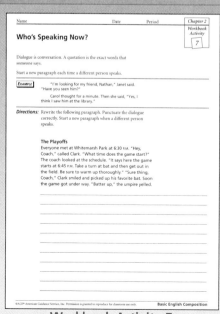

Workbook Activity 7

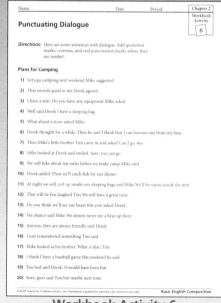

Workbook Activity 6

8. Start a new paragraph with each new speaker. Study the examples.

EXAMPLES   "Here we are at last!" said Laura.

"I am pleased to be in Centerville to see a rodeo," said Amanda.

"Me, too!" added Laura.

9. You may want the speaker to say several sentences. Use quotation marks only at the beginning and at the end of the entire speech. Study the example.

EXAMPLE   "Just think, only yesterday we were back home in Springfield. Now we are in Centerville. Soon we will be seeing a rodeo," Amanda said to Laura.

Activity C   Review the rules for writing dialogue given on pages 17–19. Then read the following sentences carefully. Each of these quotations is incorrect. Find the errors. Then rewrite each sentence on your paper. Make the necessary corrections.

1) "let's buy a postcard for Derek," suggested Amanda.

2) "Which card do you like best," asked Laura.

3) I like them all, "said Amanda."

4) Laura added. "Let's buy one of each."

5) That's a good idea, Amanda agreed.

6) "We can put some in our scrapbooks," Laura suggested

7) "Now let's go to the rodeo," " The show is about to begin," Amanda said.

8) "I hope we have good seats," Laura said. "I would like to be in the front row," Amanda added.

■ Presenting Activity C
Remind students to review the preceding nine rules for dialogue as they hunt for errors in these sentences. Discuss the problems in each item before students work on their corrected versions.

Activity C Answers
1) "Let's buy a postcard for Derek," suggested Amanda.
2) "Which card do you like best?" asked Laura.   **3)** "I like them all," said Amanda.
4) Laura added, "Let's buy one of each."   **5)** "That's a good idea," Amanda agreed.   **6)** "We can put some in our scrapbooks," Laura suggested.   **7)** "Now let's go to the rodeo. The show is about to begin," Amanda said.
8) "I hope we have good seats," Laura said. "I would like to be in the front row," Amanda added.

APPLICATION

At Home
Tell students that they can develop an "ear" for dialogue by listening to their friends and family members talk during dinner. They may write a few paragraphs of the dialogue to capture a bit of real-life conversation.

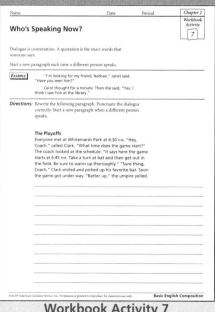

Workbook Activity 7

Reading Vocabulary

capitalization   item (6)
identify (6)   lowercase

■ **Presenting Activity D**

Remind students to review all eleven rules. Have them try to hear the character's exact words in order to determine where to put the opening and closing quotation marks and what kind of end punctuation to use.

Activity D Answers

End punctuation within a quotation may vary.

1) "There are ten riders in this contest," Amanda said. "Which one will win?"   **2)** "The first rider will be Rudy Mendez," said the announcer.   **3)** Laura called out, "Come on, Rudy!"
4) "That was a great ride!" Amanda said.   **5)** "Give Rudy a big cheer," said the announcer.
6) "How long did Rudy stay on?" asked Laura. "Did you hear the count?"   **7)** Amanda said, "He must have been on close to eight seconds."

10. You may want to interrupt a one-sentence quotation with words that identify the speaker. In an interrupted quotation, the second part begins with a lowercase letter.

> **EXAMPLES**   "Maybe we'll see the bronc riding first," said Amanda, "or the calf roping."
>
> "We want to see every event," she added, "if we can stay long enough."

11. Do not capitalize the first word of the words identifying the speaker unless it is a person's name. Compare the following examples. *Amanda* is capitalized, but *she* is not.

> **EXAMPLES**   "Here comes a bull rider," Amanda shouted.
> "There are the rodeo clowns," she added.

Activity D   Review all the rules for writing dialogue on pages 17–20. Then read the following dialogue carefully. Notice that it has no punctuation and no capitalization. Rewrite the entire dialogue on your paper. Add the correct punctuation and capitalization.

Hint: There may be more than one sentence in each numbered item.

1) there are ten riders in this contest Amanda said which one will win

2) the first rider will be Rudy Mendez said the announcer

3) Laura called out come on, Rudy

4) that was a great ride Amanda said

5) give Rudy a big cheer said the announcer

6) how long did Rudy stay on asked Laura did you hear the count

7) Amanda said he must have been on close to eight seconds

Words of Direct Address

When you are writing a letter or a message, you may want to name the person you are addressing. Use commas to set off the name or words from the rest of the sentence. Study these examples.

> **EXAMPLES**   Joel, thank you for the gift.
> (The sentence begins with the name of the person being addressed. Use one comma.)
>
> Thank you for the gift, my friend.
> (The sentence ends with words that name the person being addressed. Use one comma.)
>
> Thank you, Joel, for being such a good friend.
> (The name is in the middle of the sentence. Use two commas.)

When you write dialogue, you will use words of direct address more often. Use commas to set off the name of or words identifying the person being spoken to. Study these examples.

> **EXAMPLES**   "Look over there, Laura, at that clown," said Amanda.
> (The speaker is Amanda. She is addressing Laura.)
>
> "Amanda, I don't see the clown."
> (Amanda is being addressed. The speaker must be Laura.)
>
> Amanda said, "Laura, he's letting the bull chase him."
> (The speaker is Amanda. She is addressing Laura.)

Activity E   Copy these sentences on your paper. Add quotation marks and punctuation. Make sure to use commas to set off words of direct address.

1) What is the next event Amanda
2) Amanda said I'm not sure Laura so let's ask someone
3) Excuse me sir what is the next event Laura asked
4) Laura said That man told me the bronc riding is next Amanda

■ **Presenting Activity E** Go over the first item together, helping students to see that Amanda is being addressed—by Laura, most likely. Point out that two names appear in each of the other items. Tell students to read each item aloud softly, to distinguish the speaker from the person being addressed.

Activity E Answers
1) "What is the next event, Amanda?"   2) Amanda said, "I'm not sure, Laura, so let's ask someone."   3) "Excuse me, sir, what is the next event?" Laura asked.   4) Laura said, "That man told me the bronc riding is next, Amanda."

TEACHER ALERT

As students practice developing dialogue in their own stories, remind them that correct punctuation will help their readers figure out who is speaking and what is being said. Students should also think about the main purposes of dialogue: to bring characters to life and to move the story along. Have students find samples of dialogue in stories they are reading. Set aside time to read aloud selected portions, so that students can see how authors use dialogue.

■ **Presenting Activity F** Ask students how they plan to determine whether a sentence contains an indirect or a direct quotation. They should refer to the instruction and examples to make the distinction.

Activity F Answers
1) Direct 2) Direct 3) Indirect
4) Direct 5) Indirect 6) Direct
7) Direct 8) Indirect 9) Direct

Direct quotation

Sentences reporting the exact words that someone said. Quotation marks enclose these exact words.

Indirect quotation

Sentences that report what someone said without using the speaker's exact words.

Direct and Indirect Quotations

In this lesson, you have been writing **direct quotations**. You have used quotation marks to enclose a speaker's exact words. You may also tell about conversations with **indirect quotations**. When you write indirect quotations, you do not need quotation marks. The word *that* often appears in indirect quotations.

Look at these examples to compare direct and indirect quotations.

| **EXAMPLES** | Direct quotation: | "I had a good time," said Amanda. |
| | Indirect quotation: | Amanda said that she had a good time. |

Activity F   Read the following sentences carefully. Identify each sentence as either a direct quotation or an indirect quotation. Write *Direct* or *Indirect* on your paper.

1) "Do you come to the rodeo often?" Laura asked the woman sitting next to them.

2) "Yes, I enjoy rodeos," answered the woman.

3) The woman added that she lived nearby.

4) "Do you live in Centerville?" she asked Amanda and Laura.

5) Laura explained that she and Amanda lived in Springfield.

6) Amanda told the woman, "This is my first rodeo."

7) "Mine, too!" added Laura.

8) Amanda said that she couldn't wait to tell their friends all about the rodeo.

9) "It was so exciting!" she said.

Activity G Study the examples of direct and indirect quotations on page 22. Then change each of these indirect quotations to a direct quotation. Write the direct quotations on your paper. Punctuate and capitalize each sentence correctly. Remember to use quotation marks. If necessary, review the rules for writing dialogue on pages 17–20.

1) Laura said that she enjoyed the rodeo.

2) Their new friend said that she hoped the girls would come again.

3) Amanda told her that they would definitely come back.

4) Laura said that she liked the bull riding best.

5) The woman said that she liked the bull riding, too.

6) Amanda decided that she still liked calf roping better.

7) The woman wondered how they had heard about the rodeo in Centerville.

8) Laura explained that she had read about it in the newspaper.

Activity H Rewrite these direct quotations as indirect quotations. Review the examples on page 22. Remember that indirect quotations do not use quotation marks.

1) "Next time let's bring Derek," Amanda said.

2) Laura agreed, "He would enjoy the rodeo."

3) "Who is Derek?" the woman asked.

4) "He is a friend of ours from school," Amanda told her.

5) The woman said, "Be sure to bring him when you come again."

6) "When is the next rodeo?" asked Laura.

7) The woman said, "We have a rodeo every Saturday for the next three weeks."

8) "We'll try to come again someday," Amanda said.

9) "Maybe Derek can come with us the next time," added Laura.

Name _____ Date _____ Period _____ | Chapter 2 Activity **8**

Direct and Indirect Quotations

A. Directions: Change each of these indirect quotations to a direct quotation. Rewrite your sentences on the lines provided. Punctuate and capitalize each sentence correctly.

Indirect Quotation: They said that they would be home soon.
Direct Quotation: They said, "We will be home soon."

1) Amanda said that she enjoyed the movie.

2) They said they would go to the movies together again.

3) Laura said that she would choose the movie next time.

4) She asked if she could call for next week's shows.

5) Derek laughed and said that he was not paying.

B. Directions: Now change each of these direct quotations to an indirect quotation. Rewrite your sentences on the lines provided. Do not use quotation marks. Be sure to punctuate each sentence correctly.

1) The lady answered, "I'm not sure what movies are playing next week."

2) "When will you know?" asked Laura.

3) "We change our movies every Friday," answered the lady.

4) Laura said, "I'll call back on Friday."

5) "I should have my allowance by Friday," said Amanda.

©AGP® American Guidance Service, Inc. Permission is granted to reproduce for classroom use only.   **Basic English Composition**

Activity 8

■ **Presenting Activity G**
Discuss what is required in order to change an indirect quotation into a direct one. Point out to students that they should try to hear the speaker's exact words. Then they will know whether to change a word such as *she* or *they* into a word such as *I* or *you.*

Activity G Answers
Answers will vary. Sample answers are given.

1) Laura said, "I enjoyed the rodeo." 2) Their new friend said, "I hope you girls will come again." 3) Amanda told her, "We will definitely come back." 4) Laura said, "I liked the bull riding best." 5) The woman said, "I liked the bull riding, too." 6) Amanda said, "I still liked the calf roping better." 7) The woman asked, "How did you hear about the rodeo in Centerville?" 8) Laura answered, "I read about it in the newspaper."

■ **Presenting Activity H** Tell students to read each item and imagine that they have overheard that bit of spoken conversation. Then they should ask themselves how they might report what they heard. Their answer may be the indirect quotation they are looking for as they do this activity. Remind them that many indirect quotations contain the word *that.*

Activity H Answers
Answers will vary. Sample answers are given.

1) Amanda said that they should bring Derek next time. 2) Laura agreed that he would enjoy the rodeo. 3) The woman wanted to know who Derek was. 4) Amanda told her that Derek was a friend from school. 5) The woman said that the girls should bring Derek when they come again. 6) Laura asked when the next rodeo was.

(Activity H Answers, continued)
7) The woman said that there would be a rodeo every Saturday for the next three weeks.
8) Amanda said that they would try to come again someday.
9) Laura added that maybe Derek would come with them next time.

Reading Vocabulary

describe (5)
due (5)
identification (8)

Lesson Review Answers

1) "Wasn't the rodeo exciting?" Laura asked.
"Yes, I'm glad we came," answered Amanda.
2) "I have a paper in English due on Monday," Laura said.   3) "The teacher said that we could write about anything we wanted," Laura added.   4) "You could describe the woman we met," suggested Amanda.   5) Laura said, "That's a good idea!"

Follow-up Activity

Have a pair of volunteers come to the front of the room to have a very short conversation of two sentences each. They may be themselves or pretend to be characters. They should include words of direct address in their conversation. The rest of the group listens to the conversation. Everyone tries to transcribe the dialogue accurately. Allow time for students to read aloud the dialogue they wrote.

Lesson 2 Review

Use dialogue to show what your characters say.

- Put quotation marks around a speaker's exact words.
- Capitalize the first word of a quotation.
- If you name the speaker first, use a comma before the quotation.
- If you name the speaker after the quotation, use a comma after the quotation. Set the comma inside the closing quotation marks.
- If the quotation is a question, use a question mark at the end of the quotation. If the speaker's sentence expresses strong feeling, use an exclamation point.
- Use the correct end punctuation mark at the end of the whole sentence.
- Place the punctuation mark at the end of the quotation inside the closing quotation marks.
- Start a new paragraph with each new speaker.
- Use quotation marks only at the beginning and at the end of a character's entire speech.
- If you interrupt a one-sentence quotation, begin the second part with a lowercase letter.
- Do not capitalize the first word of the speaker identification unless it is a person's name.
- Use commas to set off words of direct address.

Lesson Review   When you write dialogue, use quotation marks around the exact words that someone says. Find the mistake in each of the items below. Then write the sentences correctly on your paper.

1) "Wasn't the rodeo exciting?" Laura asked. "Yes, I'm glad we came," answered Amanda.
2) "I have a paper in English due on Monday, Laura said."
3) The teacher said, "that we could write about anything we wanted," Laura added.
4) "You could describe the woman we met", suggested Amanda.
5) Laura said. "That's a good idea!"

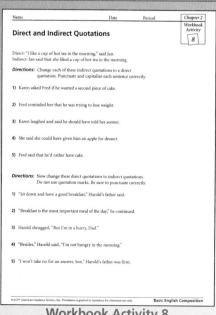

Workbook Activity 8

You write sentences for many reasons. You may want to give information or directions. You may want to express your feelings. You may want to ask for information. You may use sentences to tell a story.

Activity A Some sentences give information. Read these statements that Derek wrote about himself. Notice that no two sentences begin with the same word. Every sentence begins with a capital letter. Every sentence ends with a period.

a) Right now I am a high school student.
b) My hobby is collecting sports cards.
c) I live with my family in an apartment.
d) People say that my brown eyes sparkle.
e) Someday I want to be a diesel mechanic.
f) In the winter I like to ski and ice skate.

Study Derek's sentences. Then write at least six sentences about yourself on your paper. Start each sentence with a different word. Begin each sentence with a capital letter. Punctuate each sentence correctly.

Activity B Some sentences express feelings. Read the topics below. Choose one topic. Write five sentences about this topic. List your sentences on your paper. Begin each sentence with a capital letter. End each sentence with the correct punctuation mark.

• How I feel on a rainy day
• How I feel about the future
• The best day of my life
• The kindest person I have ever known

Activity C Some sentences give directions. These sentences are written as commands. Choose one of the topics below. Tell someone how to get from the first place to the second. Use an atlas or a map if necessary.

• Directions from your house to the nearest food store
• Directions from school to your house
• Directions from your classroom to the school library
• Directions from your town or city to the state capital

Lesson at a Glance

Chapter 2   Lesson 3

Overview This lesson offers practice in writing sentences for a variety of reasons.

Objectives

■ To write sentences to give information or directions.

■ To write sentences to express feelings.

■ To write sentences to ask for information.

■ To write sentences to tell a story.

Student Pages 25–27

Reading Vocabulary

atlas (7)   mechanic (6)
diesel (5)   topic (5)

Teaching Suggestions

■ **Introducing the Lesson**
Ask students to name as many forms of writing as they can—from stories to news articles to bulletin board announcements. List their suggestions on the board. Explain that in almost all forms of writing, the writer's message is conveyed in sentences. Make the point that the reasons for writing sentences are varied.

■ **Reviewing Skills** Write the terms *statement, request, exclamation,* and *question* on the board. Ask students to give an oral example of each kind of sentence.

■ **Presenting Activity A** Go over the first set of directions with students. Have them refer to sentences a–f to name the different word that begins each sentence and to name the capital letter that begins each sentence. Remind them that they can model their own sentences on the ones given.

Activity A Answers
Sentences will vary.

■ **Presenting Activity B**
After students read the directions to themselves, brainstorm a list of words that describe feelings: *sad, worried, enthusiastic, loving,* and so on. Suggest that students use such words in their sentences. Offer your own examples of sentences that express feelings to get them started.

Activity B Answers
Sentences will vary.

■ **Presenting Activity C**
Remind students that sentences that give commands often begin with a word that shows what action the reader should take: *Start, Turn, Walk, Look,* and so on.

Activity C Answers
Sentences will vary.

Reading Vocabulary

occupation (6)   soggy
quiz (6)

■ Presenting Activity D

Help students formulate questions by providing a list of words used to start questions: *Who, How, What, Where, When, Why, Which.*

Activity D Answers

Questions and answers will vary.

■ Presenting Activity E

Have students take turns reading aloud the brief narrative in sentences a–i. Make sure they understand their own story can be a simple recounting of an event.

Activity E Answers

Sentences will vary. Students are to punctuate dialogue correctly.

GLOBAL CONNECTION

 Tell students that the kinds of questions people ask one another vary from culture to culture. In some cultures, for example, it is impolite to ask anyone a personal question. Ask students for their own ideas about polite and impolite questioning.

LEARNING STYLES

 Interpersonal/Group Learning
Divide the class into groups of nine students each. Point out the nine sentences in Activity E on page 26. Have each group draw nine pictures to illustrate the story in the activity. Afterward, ask each group to decide how it will present its story. Suggest that the groups might stand before the class. Each group member could then show a picture and read the appropriate sentence. Or one member of the group could hold up a picture while the other members mime the action. Encourage group creativity with the pictures and story.

Activity D   Some sentences ask for information. These sentences are written as questions. Such sentences end with a question mark. Choose a topic that you know something about. Here are some possible topics:

- Your favorite book, movie, or television show
- Your favorite sport or team
- A famous person you would like to meet
- Your town or your school
- An occupation

1) Make up a quiz about your topic. Write five questions that ask for information. Punctuate each question correctly.

2) On another piece of paper, write the answers to your five questions. Punctuate each sentence correctly.

Activity E   Some sentences tell a story. A story often includes dialogue. Read the story given in the sentences below.

a) One day Amanda's dog ran away.

b) Amanda and Laura walked all over the neighborhood.

c) Night came, and it began to rain.

d) The girls came home.

e) "We'll probably never see Benjy again," Amanda said.

f) Suddenly they heard a scratching at the door.

g) "It must be Benjy!" they cried.

h) A wet, tired dog was at the door.

i) Amanda bent down and hugged the soggy dog.

Write your own brief story. List as many sentences as necessary to tell your story. Capitalize all names and the first word of each sentence. Punctuate all sentences correctly.

Be sure to include some dialogue! Remember to include quotation marks around any direct quotations.

You may write sentences for different purposes. Some sentences give information. Other sentences give directions, express feelings, or tell a story. Questions, or interrogative sentences, ask for information.

Part A   Match each sentence purpose in Column A with a sentence in Column B. Write the correct letter on your paper.

Column A

1) To express feelings
2) To give directions
3) To ask for information
4) To give information

Column B

a) How do I get to Derek's house?
b) Take the Number 6 bus to get to Derek's house.
c) Amanda's dog is named Benjy.
d) A lost dog brings tears to my eyes.

Part B   Follow each direction below.

1) Write two sentences that give information about a place.
2) Write two sentences that could be part of a scary story.
3) Write two sentences that give directions for playing a game.
4) Write two sentences that tell how you feel after a long day.
5) Write two questions to ask about something you have always wanted to know.

Reading Vocabulary
scary

Part A Answers
1) d 2) b 3) a 4) c

Part B Answers
Sentences will vary.

Follow-up Activity

Write the name of a broad topic on the board: *Animals* or *Sports,* for example. Then call out one sentence-writing purpose discussed in this lesson: to express feelings, to tell a story, to give information, to give directions, to ask a question. Have students quickly write a topic-related sentence with that purpose. Continue until you have called out all the purposes at least once. Volunteers may then read aloud and compare their sentences.

The Teacher's Resource Library includes two parallel forms of the Chapter 2 Mastery Test. The difficulty level of the two forms is equivalent. You may wish to use one form as a pretest and the other form as a posttest.

Reading Vocabulary

application (8)   terrific (5)
Bravo

Part A Answers

1) a 2) a 3) b 4) a 5) b
6) b 7) a 8) a 9) b 10) b

Part A   Read each of the following pairs of sentences. Find the sentence that has correct punctuation and capitalization. Write the letter of that sentence on your paper.

1) a) Write to tell me how to get to your house.
   b) Write to tell me how to get to your house?

2) a) What a terrific party you gave!
   b) What a terrific party you gave?

3) a) This book tells the life story of a great man!
   b) This book tells the life story of a great man.

4) a) Please send me an application.
   b) Please send me an application?

5) a) Ms. Ruiz clapped wildly. "Bravo!" "Bravo!", she shouted.
   b) Ms. Ruiz clapped wildly. "Bravo! Bravo!" she shouted.

6) a) Blanca sighed, "this has been a hard day."
   b) Blanca sighed, "This has been a hard day."

7) a) "My first job is over," sighed Blanca, "but my next one is about to begin."
   b) "My first job is over," sighed Blanca, "But my next one is about to begin."

8) a) Chantal told Robbie that he looked fine.
   b) Chantal told Robbie that "he looked fine."

9) a) "What is your answer?" Derek, asked Ms. Ruiz.
   b) "What is your answer, Derek?" asked Ms. Ruiz.

10) a) "Hamlet, can't decide what to do," replied Derek.
    b) "Hamlet can't decide what to do," replied Derek.

Chapter 2 Mastery Test A

Part B   Change these indirect quotations to direct quotations. Write the direct quotations on your paper. Capitalize and punctuate each sentence correctly.

1) Laura told Derek that she had gone to Centerville to see a rodeo.
2) Derek asked who had gone with her.
3) Laura told him that she had gone with Amanda.
4) Derek asked if they were going again.
5) He said that he had never seen a rodeo.
6) Amanda told him that she planned to go to the rodeo again.
7) Laura asked Derek if he wanted to go with them.
8) Derek said that the rodeo sounded like fun.
9) He said that he wanted to see the bull riding.
10) Amanda said that Derek would enjoy the rodeo.

Part C   Follow each direction.

1) Write a sentence that expresses a fact or gives information.
2) Write a sentence that asks a question.
3) Write a sentence that expresses strong feeling.
4) Write a sentence to request information.
5) Write a sentence that tells someone what to do.
6) Write a sentence that gives a command.
7) Write a direct quotation spoken by a character named Alphonse.
8) Write an indirect quotation that tells what a character named Claude said.
9) Write a direct quotation in which Alphonse speaks to Claude.
10) Write at least two sentences of dialogue between two characters.

Test Taking Tip   Always read directions more than once. Underline words that tell *how many* examples or items you must provide.

Part B Answers

Answers will vary. Sample answers are given.

1) Laura told Derek, "I went to Centerville to see a rodeo."
2) "Who went with you?" Derek asked.   3) "I went with Amanda," Laura said.   4) "Are you going again?" Derek asked.   5) He added, "I've never seen a rodeo."
6) "I plan to go to the rodeo again," Amanda told Derek.
7) Laura asked, "Derek, do you want to go with us?"   8) "It sounds like fun," Derek said.   9) "I would like to see the bull riding," Derek said.   10) Amanda said, "You would enjoy the rodeo, Derek."

Part C Answers

Answers will vary.

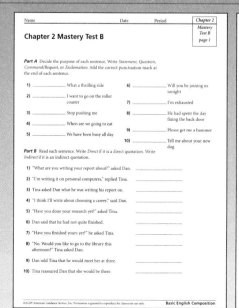

Chapter 2 Mastery Test B

Planning Guide

Writing Correct Sentences

	Student Pages	Vocabulary	Practice Exercises	Lesson Review
Lesson 1 Agreement of Subject and Verb	32-39	✔	✔	39
Lesson 2 Using Pronouns Correctly	40-46	✔	✔	46
Lesson 3 Capitalizing Words	47-49	✔	✔	49
Lesson 4 Using Verbs Correctly	50-54	✔	✔	54
Lesson 5 Regular and Irregular Verbs	55-64	✔	✔	64
Lesson 6 Possessives and Plurals	65-69	✔	✔	69

Column header spanning group: Student Text Lesson

Chapter Activities

Teacher's Resource Library
Writing Tip 3: Correcting Common Writing Mistakes

Community Connection 2: Correct Sentences

Assessment Options

Student Text
Chapter 3 Review

Teacher's Resource Library
Chapter 3 Mastery Tests A and B

	Teaching Strategies							Language Skills			Learning Styles						Teacher's Resource Library		
Reviewing Skills	Teacher Alert	Follow-up Activity	Career Application	Home Application	Global Connection	Community Application	Identification Skills	Writing Skills	Punctuation Skills	Visual/Spatial	Auditory/Verbal	Body/Kinesthetic	Logical/Mathematical	Group Learning	LEP/ESL	Activities	Workbook Activities	Self-Study Guide
32	34, 37	39		32		38	✔	✔	✔				39			9	9	✔
40	40, 44	46			42		✔	✔	✔			44				10	10	✔
47	47	49					✔	✔	✔							11	11	✔
50		54				52	✔	✔	✔	51						12		✔
55	55, 63	64					✔	✔	✔						64			✔
65		69	66				✔	✔	✔		68						12-13	✔

Name _____ Period _____ | Chapters 3,5 Writing Tip 3

Correcting Common Writing Mistakes

You can avoid eight common writing mistakes if you remember these rules:

1) Make subjects and verbs agree
- A singular subject must have a singular verb.
- A plural subject must have a plural verb.
- A compound subject must have a plural verb.

2) Make pronouns agree with their antecedents
- A pronoun must agree with its antecedent in gender.
  –Replace the name of a male person with a masculine pronoun.
  –Replace the name of a female person with a feminine pronoun.
  –Replace the name of singular nouns with *it* or *its.*
  –Replace the name of plural nouns with *they, them,* or *their.*
- A pronoun must agree with its antecedent in number.
  –Make the pronoun singular if its antecedent is singular.
  –Make the pronoun plural if its antecedent is plural.

3) Capitalize proper nouns and proper adjectives
- Capitalize proper nouns.
- Capitalize a common noun only when it is the first word of a sentence.
- Capitalize the first word of any sentence.
- Capitalize parts of the country but not compass points.
- Capitalize the names of languages.
- Capitalize the first word and all important words in a title.
- Capitalize the pronoun *I.*
- Capitalize all proper adjectives in sentences.

4) Use correct verb tenses
- Use an action verb to tell what someone did.
- Use a state-of-being verb to express the condition of the subject.
- Use a helping verb to help the main verb express tense, or time.
  –Use only one main verb in a verb phrase.
  –Use one or more helping verbs in a verb phrase.
  –Make the main verb last in a verb phrase.
- Make sure the verb tenses are logical.
- You may use more than one main verb in a sentence.
  –Use the same verb tenses if the actions occurred at the same time.
  –Use different verb tenses if the actions occurred at different times.

©AGS® American Guidance Service, Inc. Permission is granted to reproduce for classroom use only   **Basic English Composition**

Name _____ Period _____ | Chapters 3,5 Writing Tip 3

Correcting Common Writing Mistakes (continued)

5) Use and spell regular and irregular verb forms correctly
- Form the past tense of a regular verb by adding *-ed* or *-d.*
- Use the past participle to form the past perfect tenses.
- Study Chapter 3 Lesson 5 for how to form the past tense of irregular verbs.

6) Use and spell possessives and plurals correctly
- Use a possessive noun to show ownership or a relationship between two things.
- Make a singular noun possessive by adding an apostrophe (') and the letter *s.*
- Make a plural noun possessive by adding only an apostrophe.
- Add both an apostrophe and the letter *s* if the plural noun does not end in an *s.*

7) Avoid run-on sentences
- Begin each sentence with a capital letter.
- End each sentence with a period, question mark, or exclamation point.
- Do not end a sentence with a comma.
- Do not separate two sentences with a comma.
- Use a comma plus a conjunction to connect two complete ideas.

8) Avoid sentence fragments
- Make sure each sentence has a subject and a verb that express a complete idea.
- Complete sentences have a subject and a predicate.
- Do not capitalize the first word of a phrase that does not begin a new idea.

©AGS® American Guidance Service, Inc. Permission is granted to reproduce for classroom use only   **Basic English Composition**

Name _____ Date _____ Period _____ | Chapter 3 Community Connection 3

Correct Sentences

There is a lot to remember when trying to write a correct sentence. For example, in a correct sentence, the **subject** and the **verb** must have **agreement**. A subject is a person, place, or thing that the sentence is talking about. If these two parts fit together logically within a sentence, there is **agreement**.

EXAMPLE   The child sings.

The noun *child* is singular. Therefore, the verb *sings* is singular.

You also must capitalize **proper nouns** and **proper adjectives** for a sentence to be correct. Look at these examples.

EXAMPLE

Proper Nouns	Proper Adjectives
California	Japanese
New York Yankees	Democratic
George Washington	British

Practice using what you know about subject and verb agreement and capitalizing proper nouns and proper adjectives. Follow these steps.

Step 1. Record at least five minutes of a radio or television news program.

Step 2. Play back the recording. Find a sentence that has correct subject and verb agreement. Find a sentence that has a proper noun or proper adjective. Write the sentences on the lines below.

1) _____

2) _____

Step 3. Look at your sentence that shows subject and verb agreement. Circle the subject and underline the verb.

Step 4. Look at the other sentence. Circle the proper noun or proper adjective.

Step 5. Have your teacher check your work.

©AGS® American Guidance Service, Inc. Permission is granted to reproduce for classroom use only   **Basic English Composition**

Writing Tip 3   Community Connection 3

Chapter 3

Writing Correct Sentences

W hen you write correct sentences, your readers get your message clearly. They are not spending time trying to figure out exactly what you mean. Correctly written sentences also make a good impression. Suppose that two people are writing letters to apply for a job. Person A has written correct sentences. Person B has written sentences with errors. It's easy to see that Person A has the better chance of being called.

Can you recognize common writing mistakes? Do you know how to fix them? In Chapter 3, you will learn how to recognize and to correct six common writing mistakes.

Goals for Learning

▶ To find and correct errors in subject-verb agreement

▶ To find and correct errors in pronoun usage

▶ To recognize proper nouns and proper adjectives

▶ To follow rules of capitalization

▶ To use verb tenses correctly

▶ To use and spell regular and irregular verb forms correctly

▶ To use and spell possessives and plurals correctly

31

Introducing the Chapter

Have students examine the introductory photograph accompanying the first page of Chapter 3. Ask for their ideas about where the scene is taking place. When they suggest a business office, point out that the man in the photograph appears to be reviewing job applications. Have students suppose that he is looking at two applications from two people he has never met. Ask students why one application might make a more favorable impression than the other.

SELF-STUDY GUIDE

Name _____

CHAPTER 3: Writing Correct Sentences

Goal 3.1 To find and correct errors in subject-verb agreement

Date	Assignment	Score
_____	1: Read pages 31-32. Complete Activities A-C on page 33.	_____
_____	2: Read page 34. Complete Activity D on page 34. Read page 35. Complete Activity E on page 35.	_____
_____	3: Read page 36. Complete Activity F on page 36. Read page 37. Complete Activity G on page 37.	_____
_____	4: Read page 38. Complete Activity H on page 38.	_____
_____	5: Complete Workbook Activity 9.	_____
_____	6: Complete the Lesson 1 Review, Parts A-B on page 39.	_____

Comments:

Goal 3.2 To find and correct errors in pronoun usage

Date	Assignment	Score
_____	7: Read page 40. Complete Activities A-B on page 41.	_____
_____	8: Read page 42. Complete Activity C on page 42. Read page 43. Complete Activity D on page 43.	_____
_____	9: Complete Workbook Activity 10.	_____
_____	10: Read page 44. Complete Activity E on page 44. Read page 45. Complete Activity F on page 45.	_____
_____	11: Complete the Lesson 2 Review, Parts A-B on page 46.	_____

Comments:

Goal 3.3 To recognize proper nouns and proper adjectives and to follow rules of capitalization

Date	Assignment	Score
_____	12: Read page 47. Complete Activities A-B on page 48.	_____
_____	13: Complete Workbook Activity 11.	_____
_____	14: Complete the Lesson 3 Review, Parts A-B on page 49.	_____

Comments:

©AGS® American Guidance Service, Inc. Permission is granted to reproduce for classroom use only. **Basic English Composition**

SELF-STUDY GUIDE

Name _____

CHAPTER 3 Writing Correct Sentences, continued

Goal 3.4 To use verb tenses correctly

Date	Assignment	Score
_____	15: Read page 50. Complete Activity A on page 50. Read page 51. Complete Activity B on page 51.	_____
_____	16: Read page 52. Complete Activity C on page 52. Read page 53. Complete Activity D on page 53.	_____
_____	17: Complete the Lesson 4 Review, Parts A-B on page 54.	_____

Comments:

Goal 3.5 To use and spell regular and irregular verb forms correctly

Date	Assignment	Score
_____	18: Read page 55. Complete Activity A on page 55. Read page 56. Complete Activity B on page 56. Complete Activity C on page 57.	_____
_____	19: Complete Activity D on page 57. Read page 58. Complete Activities E-F on page 58.	_____
_____	20: Read page 59. Complete Activity G on page 59. Read page 60. Complete Activity H on page 60. Read page 61. Complete Activity I on page 61.	_____
_____	21: Complete Activity J on page 61. Read page 62. Complete Activity K on page 62. Read page 63. Complete Activity L on page 63.	_____
_____	22: Complete the Lesson 5 Review, Parts A-B on page 64.	_____

Comments:

Goal 3.6 To use and spell possessives and plurals correctly

Date	Assignment	Score
_____	23: Read page 65. Complete Activity A on page 65. Read page 66. Complete Activity B on page 66.	_____
_____	24: Complete Activity C on page 67 and Activity D on page 68.	_____
_____	25: Complete Workbook Activity 12.	_____
_____	26: Complete the Lesson 6 Review, Parts A-B on page 69.	_____
_____	27: Complete Workbook Activity 13.	_____
_____	28: Complete the Chapter 3 Review, Parts A-D on pages 70-71.	_____

Comments:

Student's Signature _____ Date _____

Instructor's Signature _____ Date _____

©AGS® American Guidance Service, Inc. Permission is granted to reproduce for classroom use only. **Basic English Composition**

Chapter 3 Self-Study Guide

Lesson at a Glance

Chapter 3 Lesson 1

Overview This lesson presents nouns and pronouns as subjects of sentences. It also explains how to make the verb agree with the subject in number.

Objectives

- To recognize that present-tense verbs may require an -s ending.
- To identify singular and plural nouns.
- To identify singular and plural pronouns.
- To use the correct form of the verbs *to be* and *to have*.
- To use correct subject-verb agreement when words separate the subject and verb.
- To use correct subject-verb agreement with compound subjects.

Student Pages 32–39

Teacher's Resource Library

Activity 9

Workbook Activity 9

Reading Vocabulary

agreement (6)   noun
boom (6)   **plural (6)**
element (6)   **singular (8)**
heroism   **subject (5)**
logical (8)   **verb**

Teaching Suggestions

- ### Introducing the Lesson
  Write this sentence on the board, and have students identify the error: *Every day, the man ride the bus.* Explain that this lesson will help students recognize when to add -s to words such as *ride*.

- ### Reviewing Skills Write a
  question and an answer on the board, using all lowercase letters and leaving out the end punctuation. (Example: *what is the weather like today it is sunny and cool today*) Have students rewrite the sentences correctly.

Agreement
The logical match between two elements of a sentence.

Noun
The name of a person, place, thing, or idea: teacher, museum, ball, heroism.

Plural
Referring to more than one person, place, or thing: houses, nations, doctors, they.

Singular
Referring to one person, place, or thing: house, nation, doctor, it.

Subject
The person, place, or thing that the sentence tells about. Donald ate a sandwich. *(subject:* Donald*)*

Verb
A word used to express action or state of being. Donald ate a sandwich. *(action verb:* ate*)* Donald was hungry. *(state-of-being verb:* was*)*

Each part of a sentence should fit logically with every other part. That logical fit is called **agreement**. Every sentence has a **subject** and a **verb**. The subject of the sentence is the person, place, or thing that the sentence is talking about. Often a subject is a **noun**. The verb tells what the subject is doing. The subject may be **singular** or **plural**.

Study these rules.

1. Singular nouns usually do not end in -s. Singular verbs that name present actions usually do end in -s.

   EXAMPLES
   Sam runs.
   The wheel squeaks.
   A dog barks.

2. Plural nouns usually do end in -s. Plural verbs that name present actions usually do not end in -s.

   EXAMPLES
   The boys run.
   The wheels squeak.
   Dogs bark.

3. If the subject is singular, the verb must also be singular. If the subject is plural, the verb must also be plural.

   EXAMPLES

Singular subjects and verbs:	The student reads. A drum booms. That baby cries.
Plural subjects and verbs:	Students read. Drums boom. Babies cry.

APPLICATION

 At Home
As you discuss the material on page 32, make the point that different varieties of English are spoken by different groups in North America. In some varieties of English, the added -s on verbs is not pronounced. In written standard English, however, the -s should appear when needed. (Example: *The bus waits.* not *The bus wait.*)

Activity A Read the following list of nouns. Copy them on your paper in two columns. In the left column, write the singular nouns. In the right column, write the plural nouns. Twelve words belong in each column.

dogs	dress	reports
sentences	movie	dangers
garage	puppies	musician
verbs	teams	fruits
visitors	subject	Derek
box	teacher	science
classes	trees	vacation
cars	dance	weather

Activity B Read the sentences below. Label each bold subject as *Singular* or *Plural*. Write your answers on your paper.

1) The **snow** falls gently.
2) **Knowledge** of rules helps writers.
3) The **answers** pop into my head.
4) My **friends** like music.
5) Those **dancers** whirl like tops.

Activity C Look at the bold subject of each sentence below. Read the verbs in parentheses. On your paper write the verb that agrees with the subject.

1) Sometimes **Benjy** (run, runs) away.
2) That **dog** (jump, jumps) the fence.
3) His **owners** (call, calls) him.
4) The **neighbors** (chase, chases) him.
5) Other **dogs** (bark, barks) at Benjy.
6) Finally the **adventurer** (return, returns).

Reading Vocabulary

adventurer	label (6)
column (5)	parentheses
gently (6)	science (5)

■ Presenting Activity A

Have several students use their own words to tell what the difference is between a singular noun and a plural noun.

Activity A Answers

Singular Nouns	Plural Nouns
garage	dogs
dress	visitors
subject	classes
musician	puppies
Derek	trees
vacation	reports
box	sentences
movie	verbs
teacher	cars
dance	teams
science	dangers
weather	fruits

■ Presenting Activity B

Help students to see that there may be more than one noun in each sentence, but that only the noun subject is in bold type. Refer students to page 32 to review the definition of a subject.

Activity B Answers

1) Singular 2) Singular
3) Plural 4) Plural 5) Plural

■ Presenting Activity C

Have students look back to Activity B to find the verb in each sentence. Tell them that they can use those sentences as models as they choose the correct verb in each sentence in Activity C.

Activity C Answers

1) runs 2) jumps 3) call
4) chase 5) bark 6) returns

Reading Vocabulary
pronoun

■ Presenting Activity D

Have students read aloud the subject-verb phrases in the table. Tell them to use those items as models for the fourteen sentences they are to write for this activity.

Activity D Answers

1) You eat. You talk.   **2)** They eat. They talk.   **3)** I eat. I talk.   **4)** He eats. He talks.   **5)** She eats. She talks.   **6)** It eats. It talks.   **7)** We eat. We talk.

TEACHER ALERT

Help students to understand that the *-s* ending is added to singular verbs only in the present tense. The present tense is used to describe actions that are occurring now or actions that occur regularly.

Pronoun
A word used in place of a noun.

Singular and Plural Pronouns

The subject of a sentence is not always a singular or plural noun. The subject may be a singular or plural **pronoun** instead. The verb must agree in number with the subject pronoun.

Notice when *-s* (or *-es*) is added to the verb *go* and the verb *sing* below. Each verb is made to agree with each pronoun listed.

Singular		Plural	
I go.	I sing.	We go.	We sing.
You go.	You sing.	You go.	You sing.
He goes.	He sings.	They go.	They sing.
She goes.	She sings.		
It goes.	It sings.		

Activity D   Copy each of the pronouns listed below. Use it as the first word of a two-word sentence. The second word of the sentence should be the correct form of the verb *eat*.

1) You

2) They

3) I

4) He

5) She

6) It

7) We

Now write another two-word sentence beginning with each pronoun listed after numbers 1-7. Use the correct form of the verb *talk* as the second word of the sentence.

Some kinds of pronouns refer in a general way to people, places, and things. Some of these pronouns are singular, and some are plural. Others may be either singular or plural, depending on what meaning is intended. Read the examples below.

Singular			
anyone	somebody	neither	no one
anybody	each	everybody	nobody
someone	either	everyone	

EXAMPLE	Everybody works. (singular verb: *works*)

Plural			
several	few	many	both

EXAMPLE	Both need help. (plural verb: *need*)

Singular or Plural				
all	any	most	none	some

EXAMPLES	All go quickly. (plural verb: *go*) All goes well. (singular verb: *goes*)

Activity E Choose the correct form of the verb to agree with each bold subject. Write your answers on your paper.

1) **Someone** (knock, knocks) at the door.

2) The friends are talking. **Nobody** (hear, hears) the knocks at first.

3) The knocks grow louder. **Several** (make, makes) the door shake.

4) **Everybody** (look, looks) at everybody else.

5) A voice calls out, "Pizza delivery! Two pies here!" **Both** (smell, smells) wonderful!

Reading Vocabulary
pizza   refer (6)

■ **Presenting Activity E**
Have students find each bold subject in one of the tables on this page before they choose the correct verb.

Activity E Answers
1) knocks 2) hears 3) make
4) looks 5) smell

■ **Presenting Activity F**
Have students read aloud the subject-verb items in the tables. Ask them to explain why the verbs *to be* and *to have* are called irregular verbs.

Activity F Answers
1) has **2)** is **3)** runs
4) enjoy **5)** have **6)** am
7) are **8)** are **9)** am

Verbs With Different Forms

To agree with a singular subject, a verb often ends with *-s*. Here are two examples:

Verb	Singular	Plural
to know	Jon *knows*	the boys *know*
to plan	he *plans*	they *plan*

Some verbs do not change in a regular way. Their singular and plural forms vary. Their forms vary with different subject pronouns, too. Study these examples of two common verbs with different forms: *be* and *have*.

Verb	Singular	Plural
to be	Jon *is* I *am* you *are* he *is;* she *is;* it *is*	the boys *are* we *are* you *are* they *are*
to have	Jon *has* I *have* you *have* he *has;* she *has;* it *has*	the boys *have* we *have* you *have* they *have*

Activity F Make each subject and verb agree. Write the correct verb form for each sentence.

1) Derek (have, has) a glass of juice every morning.

2) He (is, am, are) still keeping in shape.

3) After breakfast he (run, runs) a mile.

4) "I (enjoy, enjoys) running," Derek says.

5) "You (have, has) the right attitude!" says Amanda.

6) "I (is, am, are) lifting weights," adds Laura.

7) "We (is, are) all keeping in shape!" says Amanda.

8) "Tell me what you (is, am, are) doing," says Laura.

9) "I (am, are) taking dance lessons with my mom!"

Finding the Subject

In order to make a verb agree with its subject, you must know what the subject is. Sometimes words come between the subject and the verb in a sentence. Ignore those words. The number of the subject is not changed by any word or words that follow it. Study the examples below.

> **EXAMPLES**
> **One** of the girls **knows** Mike.
> (singular subject: *one*; verb: *knows*)
>
> The **rules** in this book **are** important.
> (plural subject: *rules*; verb: *are*)
>
> One **rule** in these books **is** especially important.
> (singular subject: *rule*; verb: *is*)
>
> That **car** often **makes** noise.
> (singular subject: *car*; verb: *makes*)
>
> Those **cars** often **make** noise.
> (plural subject: *cars*; verb: *make*)

Activity G   Find the subject in each of the sentences below. Write the correct form of the verb that agrees with each subject. Remember to ignore any words that come between the subject and the verb in a sentence.

1) The subject of a sentence (is, am, are) either singular or plural.

2) One of Derek's friends (run, runs) thirty miles a week.

3) The girl with red sneakers (dance, dances) well.

4) The actors in the school play (seem, seems) talented.

5) All of the actors (has, have) worked very hard to learn their parts.

6) Neither of the guys (has, have) entered the marathon yet.

7) Both of them (hope, hopes) to do well in their first race.

8) The soccer players on the field (has, have) one ball.

9) The player in the stands (has, have) another ball.

10) Some of the plants (is, am, are) tall.

Reading Vocabulary

guy (6)   sneakers
ignore (5)   soccer (6)
marathon   talented (5)

■ **Presenting Activity G**
Have students identify the subject in each sentence before they choose the correct verb form.

Activity G Answers
1) is   2) runs   3) dances
4) seem   5) have   6) has
7) hope   8) have   9) has
10) are

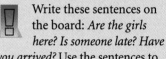

TEACHER ALERT

Write these sentences on the board: *Are the girls here? Is someone late? Have you arrived?* Use the sentences to point out that questions must have subject-verb agreement, even though the subject follows the verb. Have students turn each question into a declarative sentence to see the connection between subject and verb.

Reading Vocabulary

aerobics
**compound
 subject**
daily (10)
firefighter
freestyle
golf (5)
gracefully
provide (5)
tennis (5)
workout

■ Presenting Activity H

Have students identify the sentences that begin with compound subjects before they proceed with the activity.

Activity H Answers

1) like   2) lifts   3) wants
4) run   5) play   6) are
7) provides   8) swim   9) are
10) dive

APPLICATION

In the Community
Have students look for compound subjects in commercial signs ("Photocopying and Faxing," "Smith and Jones," "Moving and Storage," and so on). After they compile a list, work together to come up with sentences that use each as the compound subject.

> **Compound subject**
> Two subjects joined by *and*.

Compound Subjects

Sometimes a sentence has two subjects joined with *and*. A **compound subject** needs a plural verb.

> **EXAMPLES**
> Amanda and Laura exercise daily.
> (compound subject: *Amanda, Laura*
> plural verb: *exercise*)
>
> Science and math are Amanda's favorite subjects.
> (compound subject: *science, math*
> plural verb: *are*)

Activity H   Find the subjects in the sentences below. Some subjects are compound. Choose the correct form of the verb to agree with each subject. Write your answers on your paper.

1) Amanda and her mom (like, likes) aerobics.

2) Laura (lift, lifts) weights.

3) She (want, wants) to be a firefighter.

4) Derek and his friend Mike (run, runs).

5) Both Derek and Mike also (play, plays) tennis on the weekends.

6) Golf and bowling (is, am, are) popular sports.

7) Stair climbing (provides, provide) a good workout.

8) Laura and Amanda (swims, swim) at the town pool.

9) Freestyle and the butterfly stroke (is, am, are) Amanda's strengths.

10) The girls (dives, dive) gracefully.

| Name | Date | Period | Chapter 3 Activity 9 |

Subject and Verb Agreement

Directions: Find the bold subject of each of these sentences. The verbs are in parentheses. Complete each sentence by writing the correct form of the verb on the line provided.

EXAMPLE   Derek *is* excited about getting a motorcycle for a graduation present.
(is, are)

1) **He** _____ to receive many gifts.
(plans, plan)

2) **Both Amanda and Laura** _____ baby kittens.
(loves, love)

3) **Everyone** _____ about the graduation party.
(knows, know)

4) **Each of the girls** _____ excellent cookies.
(makes, make)

5) **Amanda** usually _____ in the front of the class.
(sits, sit)

6) **One of the cheerleaders** _____ the football captain.
(likes, like)

7) **The dog** _____ over the gate all the time.
(jumps, jump)

8) **Some students** _____ all their homework correctly.
(completes, complete)

9) **Several girls** _____ him every night.
(calls, call)

10) **Neither Amanda nor Laura** _____ to go.
(wants, want)

©AGS® American Guidance Service, Inc. Permission is granted to reproduce for classroom use only.   Basic English Composition

Activity 9

| Name | Date | Period | Chapter 3 Workbook Activity 9 |

Making Your Subject and Verb Agree

A singular subject needs a singular verb form.
A plural subject needs a plural verb form.

EXAMPLES   Singular subject — One **girl** walks home.
Plural subject — Many **girls** walk home.

Directions: The subject of each of these sentences is in bold print. The verbs are in parentheses. Complete each sentence by writing the correct form of the verb on the line.

1) **Both of my friends** _____ going to the party. (is, are)

2) **Carolyn** _____ a party every year. (gives, give)

3) **She** _____ the best snacks you ever tasted.
(makes, make)

4) **Carolyn** _____ a recreation room in her basement.
(has, have)

5) **Her mother and father** _____ upstairs. (stays, stay)

6) **Carolyn** _____ Fred for her date.
(invites, invite)

7) **He and Carolyn** _____ parties. (loves, love)

8) **They** both _____ to eat. (likes, like)

9) **Fred** always _____ there early. (gets, get)

10) **Everyone** _____ that they'd better come on time or there may be nothing left! (knows, know)

11) **Carolyn's father** always _____ the same thing. (does, do)

12) **There** _____ a large **clock** on the wall. (is, are)

13) **Her dad** always _____ downstairs about midnight. (comes, come)

14) **He** checks to be sure the **clock** still _____ (works, work)

©AGS® American Guidance Service, Inc. Permission is granted to reproduce for classroom use only.   Basic English Composition

Workbook Activity 9

Lesson 1 · Review

To write correct sentences, make your subjects and verbs agree. Check your understanding of this rule by completing the activities below.

Part A Write the correct form of the verb for each sentence below.

1) The capital of Puerto Rico (is, am, are) San Juan.

2) Laura (likes, like) her Spanish class.

3) Both Laura and Amanda (takes, take) Spanish.

4) "All of us (likes, like) Spanish," they said to Derek.

5) "I (want, wants) Spanish next semester," he said.

6) "Spanish (helps, help) you to learn English."

7) "I (agrees, agree) with that," Derek said.

8) "Everyone (tells, tell) me that learning another language helps me to understand my own," said Amanda.

9) "I (hear, hears) that, too," said Derek.

10) "I (sign, signs) up today!" he said.

Part B Each of these sentences has a mistake. Find each mistake. Rewrite the sentences correctly.

1) Mr. Chang's class and Ms. Ricci's class is preparing a play.

2) One of my friends have a leading part in the play.

3) She play the role of Lady Macbeth.

4) Toward the end, Lady Macbeth lose her mind.

5) "I am made for this role!" my friend say proudly.

Writing Correct Sentences Chapter 3 **39**

Follow-up Activity

Ask these questions about subject-verb agreement; have students answer the questions orally:

- How is a compound subject like a plural subject?

- When you add the ending -s to a singular noun, what do you get?

- What is different about subject-verb agreement with a singular noun and with the singular pronoun *I*?

- What is unusual about the verb *to be*?

LEARNING STYLES

Logical/Mathematical
Form a patterned chain of two-word sentences—subject/verb. Begin by saying a sentence such as "Cats meow." Then have a volunteer start the next sentence with a word that begins with the letter *w*—the letter that ended the last word of your sentence. (So, for example, the student might say, "Weather changes." Then the next student would begin a sentence with the *s* from *changes*.) Continue doing this until the students have established a sentence rhythm that they can clap out with a pause for the periods.

Lesson at a Glance

Chapter 3 Lesson 2

Overview This lesson covers pronoun usage. It explains how to make each pronoun refer clearly and correctly to its antecedent and how to use the correct case of a pronoun.

Objectives

- To make sure each pronoun has a clear antecedent.
- To make sure each pronoun agrees in gender and in number with its antecedent.
- To use the nominative, objective, and possessive cases of pronouns correctly.

Student Pages 40–46

Teacher's Resource Library

Activity 10

Workbook Activity 10

Reading Vocabulary

antecedent (11) principal (5) compare (5)

Teaching Suggestions

- **Introducing the Lesson**
Ask students what is wrong with this sentence: *Me am a teacher.* Students should have no difficulty recognizing that the pronoun *me* is used incorrectly and in a babyish way, and that the correct pronoun to use in that sentence is *I.* Explain that adult speakers and writers rarely make that kind of pronoun error, but that other kinds of pronoun errors are much more common. Students must be alert to common kinds of pronoun errors in order to use standard, correct English in their writing.

- **Reviewing Skills** Ask students to use their own words to define a pronoun. Have them list the pronouns they recall from Lesson 1. Then have them look back to Lesson 1 to see which ones they should add to their list.

A pronoun is a word that is used in place of a noun in a sentence. Pronouns are used to avoid repeating nouns. In each first sentence below, the noun is bold. In each second sentence, the pronoun is bold. Compare each pronoun with the noun it refers to.

The **school** is on Maple Avenue. **It** is an old building.

Have the **students** entered? Have **they** begun their classes?

The **principal** is outside. **She** is waiting for the last bus.

It, they, and *she* are pronouns. Here are other common pronouns:

I	me	our	myself
you	us	his	yourself
we	them	her	herself
he	him	theirs	themselves

When you write, your readers must be able to tell what each of your pronouns refers to. Make sure each pronoun has a clear **antecedent**. The word part *ante* means "before," and the antecedent often comes before the pronoun. A pronoun is near the antecedent, but it is not always in the same sentence.

Antecedent
The noun to which a pronoun refers.

EXAMPLES	Amanda and **Amanda's** mother go to dance class.
	Amanda and **her** mother go to dance class.
	(*Amanda* is the antecedent for the pronoun *her.*)
	The **school** is on Maple Avenue.
	It is an old building.
	(*School* is the antecedent for the pronoun *it.*)

TEACHER ALERT

The reflexive (-*self*) pronouns are listed in the table. These pronouns are often misused. Have students try to give oral sentences in which each pronoun is used correctly. (Examples: *I am going by myself. Did you do it yourself? She hurt herself.*) Point out that it is incorrect to use the -*self* pronouns as sentence subjects, as in *My sister, my brother, and myself entered the room.* The subject pronoun *I* should replace *myself.*

Activity A   Find the antecedent for the bold pronoun in each sentence below. List each pronoun and its antecedent on your paper. Follow the example.

Example   Does a dog protect **its** human family?
its—dog

1) Derek is studying **his** Spanish lesson.
2) Amanda and Laura enjoy **their** Spanish class.
3) Derek and the girls are helping each other understand **their** Spanish lesson.
4) Derek thought **his** friend Mike would like to take Spanish.
5) The girls enjoy **their** times studying Spanish with Derek.
6) Amanda and Laura enjoyed **their** trip to Texas.
7) Both girls found **their** Spanish useful on the trip.
8) Amanda said, "**I** understood what the names of Texas towns mean because of my Spanish."
9) Derek said that **he** would like to go to Texas with Mike.
10) Mike said they could use **his** car for the trip.

Activity B   Read the sentences below. These sentences are all about the same topic. Find the pronouns and list them on your paper. Beside each pronoun, write its antecedent. There are twelve pronouns in all.

1) Mike said he read about a national park in Kentucky.
2) It is called Mammoth Cave.
3) "I would like to visit Mammoth Cave," said Mike.
4) Derek said to Mike, "Tell me about Mammoth Cave."
5) "It has 144 miles of underground passages," Mike told him.
6) "A river runs underground," he added, "and it is 360 feet below the surface."
7) Derek said, "I wish we could go tomorrow."
8) Mike held up a road map as he said, "Our route is already marked."

Reading Vocabulary
mammoth (5)   topic (5)
passage (5)   underground

■ **Presenting Activity A**
Refer students to the second example on page 40. Have them use their own words to explain why *school* is the antecedent for the pronoun *it.* Have them come up with their own sentences in which *schools* is the antecedent for the pronoun *they.*

Activity A Answers
1) his—Derek
2) their—Amanda and Laura
3) their—Derek and the girls
4) his—Derek
5) their—the girls
6) their—Amanda and Laura
7) their—both girls
8) I—Amanda
9) he—Derek
10) his—Mike

■ **Presenting Activity B**
Read through the eight sentences together, and have students find the pronouns before they proceed with the activity.

Activity B Answers
1) he—Mike
2) It—national park
3) I—Mike
4) me—Derek
5) It—Mammoth Cave
him—Derek
6) he—Mike
it—river
7) I—Derek
we—Derek and Mike
8) he—Mike
Our—Mike and Derek

Name		Date	Period	Chapter 3
				Activity
Recognizing Antecedents				**10**

Directions: Find the antecedent for each bold pronoun. Then write each pronoun and its antecedent on the lines provided.

EXAMPLE	Amanda is enjoying **her** ice cream.
	her — Amanda

1) Derek is playing **his** radio very loud.

2) Our car has a bumper sticker on **it.**

3) Laura went to **her** house after school.

4) Derek and **his** friend went shopping.

5) The teacher told the students **his** story.

6) Laura and Amanda enjoyed **their** summer vacation.

7) Mr. Smith gave **his** students a homework assignment.

8) Amanda said, "**I** would like to go home."

9) The boys ride **their** bikes every day after school.

10) My house has a sidewalk in front of **it.**

©AGS® American Guidance Service, Inc. Permission is granted to reproduce for classroom use only.   **Basic English Composition**

Activity 10

Reading Vocabulary

assignment (6)
characteristic (6)
female (5)
feminine pronoun
gender (10)
male (5)
masculine pronoun
neuter pronoun
prefer (6)
rewrite

■ Presenting Activity C

Before students proceed with this activity, have them look at each example on this page. Ask them to identify the antecedent for each bold pronoun.

Activity C Answers

1) their 2) his 3) it, he
4) I, her 5) you

GLOBAL CONNECTION

Point out that the English language has far fewer gender distinctions than other languages. Students who are familiar with Spanish, French, or other Latin-based languages may share examples of masculine and feminine nouns and articles.

Gender
The characteristic of nouns and pronouns that tells they are masculine (man, he), feminine (woman, she), or neuter (puppy, it).

Feminine pronoun
A word that replaces a noun naming a female person. The feminine pronouns are she, her, hers, herself.

Masculine pronoun
A word that replaces a noun naming a male person. The masculine pronouns are he, him, his, himself.

Neuter pronoun
A word that replaces the name of any place, thing, or idea in a sentence. Neuter singular pronouns are it, its, itself.

Gender

Make each pronoun refer clearly to its antecedent. The **gender** of the pronoun should agree with the gender of its antecedent. Study the following rules about using gender.

1. Replace the name of a male person with a **masculine pronoun**.

> **EXAMPLE**   Harry drives **his** car to work.

2. Replace the name of a female person with a **feminine pronoun**.

> **EXAMPLE**   The actress played **her** part well.

3. Replace the names of any other singular noun with a **neuter pronoun**.

> **EXAMPLE**   Our house has a fence around **it**.

4. If the singular noun could be either male or female or both, use the words *his or her*. Since those words can sound stiff, you may prefer to change the noun to a plural.

> **EXAMPLE**   Each student signed up for **his or her** classes. (singular)
> The students signed up for **their** classes. (plural)

5. Replace plural nouns with plural pronouns such as *they, their, ours,* and *yourselves*. It does not matter whether the group includes males, females, or both.

> **EXAMPLE**   Ten families came. **They** brought **their** food.

Activity C   Rewrite the following bold nouns as pronouns.

1) Amanda and Laura went to **Amanda and Laura's** Spanish class.
2) Mr. Martin gave **Mr. Martin's** class an assignment.
3) "Did everyone do **the assignment**?" **Mr. Martin** asked.
4) "**Amanda** did," said Amanda. "Laura has **Laura's** work, too."
5) "My, my! Aren't **Amanda and Laura** wonderful!" Mr. Martin said with a grin.

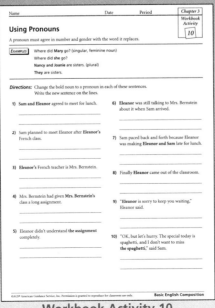

Workbook Activity 10

Case

The form of a noun or pronoun that tells its relation to other words in a sentence.

Nominative case

The form of a pronoun that shows it is being used as a subject: I *sing;* he *dances;* we *perform.*

Number

The characteristic of a noun or pronoun that tells whether it is singular or plural.

Objective case

The form of a pronoun that shows it is being used as an object: Sing with me; *hold* him; *perform for* us.

Possessive case

The form of a pronoun that shows ownership or relationship: The song is mine; *hold* his *hand; watch* our *performance.*

Number

Make your pronouns agree with their antecedents in **number**. If the antecedent is singular, the pronoun must be singular. If the antecedent is plural, the pronoun must be plural. Study the examples below.

> **EXAMPLES** Tran liked **the class**. Tran liked **it**. (singular)
>
> Tran liked **the classes**. Tran liked **them**. (plural)

Activity D Each item below has an error. A pronoun does not agree in number with its antecedent. Find the error. Rewrite the sentences correctly.

1) Springfield shares a recycling center with their neighboring towns.

2) The recycling center is off Main Street. They are located behind the supermarket.

3) Three huge bins are there. It is for glass, newspaper, and plastic.

4) "Trash is a big problem, and landfills are not a way to solve them," said Laura.

5) Amanda agreed, "Each household in town should recycle their trash."

Case

Think about how a pronoun works in a sentence. Then use the correct **case** of the pronoun. A pronoun used as the subject of a sentence should be in the **nominative case**. A pronoun that receives action should be in the **objective case**. A pronoun used to show ownership should be in the **possessive case**.

Examples of each case are shown in the box on the top of the next page.

Reading Vocabulary

bin (5)   plastic (6)
household (6)   recycle
item (6)   supermarket
landfill   trash (6)
number (2)

■ **Presenting Activity D**

Help students to identify the pronouns in the five items before they rewrite the sentences. Point out that a verb may need to change in number, along with the pronoun.

Activity D Answers

1) Springfield shares a recycling center with its neighboring towns. 2) The recycling center is off Main Street. It is located behind the supermarket.
3) Three huge bins are there. They are for glass, newspaper, and plastic. 4) "Trash is a big problem, and landfills are not a way to solve it," said Laura.
5) Amanda agreed, "Each household in town should recycle its trash."

Reading Vocabulary

boss (5)
case (3)
nominative case
objective case
ownership (7)
personal (6)
possessive case

■ **Presenting Activity E**

Have students take turns using the pronouns in the table in oral sentences. Go over the first two sentences with them, discussing their reasons for their choice of pronouns.

Activity E Answers

1) his **2)** It, his **3)** She, him
4) He, him **5)** her **6)** She, her
7) they, their

TEACHER ALERT

Even advanced students make errors in pronoun case. Familiarize students with correct usage. Offer a pair of oral sentences (Examples: *Give the books to John and I, Give the books to John and me*), ask students to choose the one they think is correct. Tell students which pronoun is correct and why (in the example, the pronoun *me* is correct because the pronoun receives action). Have students practice saying sentences that are modeled on the correct example.

EXAMPLES		
Nominative pronoun:	**She** called Denise. Denise and **I** called back.	
Objective pronoun:	Graciela called **her**. Denise called Graciela and **me**.	
Possessive pronoun:	Where are **their** phones? Are the phones **theirs** or **yours**?	

Personal Pronouns			Nominative	Objective	Possessive
Singular	First person		I	me	my, mine
	Second person		you	you	your, yours
	Third person		he, she, it	him, her, it	his, her, hers, its
Plural	First person		we	us	our, ours
	Second person		you	you	your, yours
	Third person		they	them	their, theirs

Activity E Study the table above. Then write the personal pronoun on your paper that correctly completes each sentence.

1) Derek had to go to _____ job at the gas station.

2) _____ was a good job, and Derek liked _____ boss.

3) Mabel Lentz owns the station. _____ also liked _____.

4) _____ hired _____ to work part-time.

5) Mabel Lentz started _____ hobby twenty-five years ago.

6) _____ has hundreds of model cars in _____ collection.

7) Derek collects sports cards; _____ show _____ collections to each other.

LEARNING STYLES

 Body/Kinesthetic
Invite the students, one by one, to stand and show singular and plural pronouns by miming them. As they do this, have volunteers guess the pronouns using the chart on page 44. For instance, a student might point to himself to show *I*. The student could using a sweeping motion that encompasses the whole class to show *they* or *us*. The student might pick up a book to show *my* book. The student might point to another student's book to show *her* book. As students do this, print the pronouns on the chalkboard.

Using Pronouns and Antecedents

Avoid the error of using a pronoun that has no clear antecedent. Correct the error by changing the pronoun to a noun. Compare these examples:

> **EXAMPLES**
>
> Not clear: **They** say the Giants will win.
>
> Clear: **Sportscasters** say the Giants will win.

Watch out for pronouns that could refer to more than one antecedent. To fix the problem, rewrite the sentence. Or change the pronoun to a noun.

> **EXAMPLES**
>
> Not clear: Laura told Amanda that she would be late.
> (Does *she* refer to Laura or to Amanda?)
>
> Clear: "You will be late," Laura told Amanda.
>
> Not clear: When the dog chases the cat, it always knocks something over.
> (Does *it* refer to the dog or the cat?)
>
> Clear: When the dog chases the cat, the dog always knocks something over.

Activity F   Find the unclear pronoun antecedent in each sentence below. Rewrite the sentence to make it correct. (There is more than one way to correct each sentence. Choose just one way.)

1) Amanda gave Laura her book.

2) They say that California always has great weather.

3) Mike told Derek he would be taking his brother to the game.

4) When Mike plays ball with Derek, he always says he has to go home.

5) It says that prices are going up.

Reading Vocabulary
sportscaster   unclear

■ **Presenting Activity F**

Have students use their own words to explain why each first example has an unclear pronoun antecedent. Go over item 1 together to come up with two or more correctly rewritten versions. (*Amanda gave her book to Laura; Amanda gave Laura's book back to her; Amanda gave Laura Amanda's book* and so on.)

Activity F Answers

Answers may vary. Sample answers are given.

1) Amanda gave her book to Laura.   **2)** Californians say that California always has great weather.   **3)** Mike told Derek, "I will be taking your brother to the game."   **4)** When Mike plays ball with Derek, Mike always says he has to go home.   **5)** This newspaper article says that prices are going up.

Reading Vocabulary

binoculars (8)	cardinal
birdwatching	collector
bluejay	lent (5)

Part A Answers

1) Everyone in my family has his or her own hobby. 2) My mother gave her stamp collection to my sister. 3) Only I had no special interest. 4) My father showed me some old baseball cards he had saved. 5) They were interesting to look at. 6) So I decided to collect sports cards. (correct as is) 7) A store on Main Street sells them. 8) Ms. Lentz, my boss, has small model cars in her collection. 9) They are exactly like the full-size cars. 10) We are both collectors.

Part B Answers

Answers will vary. Sample answers are given.

1) Many people say that birdwatching can be fun. 2) At the park, my friend Derek and I met a birdwatcher. 3) This woman made birdwatching sound interesting. 4) She lent Derek and me her binoculars. 5) The two of us saw a cardinal and a bluejay on a tree together. Their colors seemed so bright!

Follow-up Activity

Have students select a piece of their own writing that is at least one paragraph long. Each student should identify the pronouns, decide whether there are any pronoun usage problems, and fix any pronoun errors.

Lesson 2 Review

Check your writing for careful use of pronouns. Make sure you can answer yes to each of these questions:

- Does every pronoun have a clear antecedent?
- Does every pronoun agree in number with its antecedent?
- Does every pronoun agree in gender with its antecedent?
- Is the correct case of the pronoun used?

Part A Rewrite the sentences that Derek wrote about his hobby. Find and correct all the pronoun usage errors.

1) Everyone in my family had their own hobby.
2) My mother gave my sister her stamp collection.
3) Only me had no special interest.
4) My father showed me some old baseball cards him had saved.
5) Them were interesting to look at.
6) So I decided to collect sports cards.
7) A store on Main Street sells it.
8) Ms. Lentz, my boss, has small model cars in their collection.
9) Them are exactly like the full-size cars.
10) Us are both collectors.

Part B The sentences below tell about the same topic. There is at least one pronoun error in each item. Rewrite the sentences to correct the errors. (There is more than one way to correct the errors. Choose just one way.)

1) They say that birdwatching can be fun.
2) At the park, my friend Derek and me met a birdwatcher.
3) This woman made it sound interesting.
4) She lent Derek and I his binoculars.
5) The two of us saw a cardinal and a bluejay on a tree together. Them colors seemed so bright!

Capitalize the first word of a sentence. Always capitalize the pronoun *I*. Here are other capitalization rules.

Adjective
A word that describes a noun or pronoun. It tells how many, what kind, or which one.

Common noun
The general name of a person, place, thing, or idea. It begins with a lowercase letter: child, playground, swing, happiness.

Proper adjective
A describing word formed from a proper noun: French food.

Proper noun
The name of a particular person, place, thing, or idea. It begins with a capital letter: Frances, Osgood Park, U.S. Senate, Stone Age.

1. Most nouns are **common nouns**. Use a lowercase letter to begin a common noun. Capitalize a common noun only if it is the first word of a sentence. Some nouns are **proper nouns**. Capitalize a proper noun.

EXAMPLES

Common Nouns	Proper Nouns
athlete	Carl Lewis
city	Houston
building	Shea Stadium
day	Tuesday

2. An **adjective** usually begins with a lowercase letter. Capitalize an adjective only when it is a **proper adjective**. Proper adjectives are formed from proper nouns.

EXAMPLES

Proper Nouns	Proper Adjectives
Islam	Islamic
Africa	African

3. Capitalize parts of the country but not compass directions.

EXAMPLES Ms. Lentz lives in the South.
She lives south of our house.

4. Capitalize the names of languages. Capitalize the name of a course that has a number. Do not capitalize the names of school subjects except languages.

EXAMPLES Sign up for Music 101.
Who is taking music and history?

5. Capitalize the first, last, and all important words in a title.

EXAMPLE I read *The Heart Is a Lonely Hunter.*

Lesson at a Glance

Chapter 3   Lesson 3

Overview This lesson presents common rules of capitalization.

Objectives

- To capitalize the first word of a sentence and the pronoun *I*.
- To distinguish common and proper nouns and to capitalize proper nouns.
- To identify proper adjectives and capitalize them.
- To capitalize parts of the country but not compass directions.
- To capitalize the names of languages and numbered courses but not the names of school subjects.
- To capitalize the first, last, and all important words in a title.

Student Pages 47–49

Teacher's Resource Library

Activity 11

Workbook Activity 11

Reading Vocabulary

adjective	lowercase
athlete (6)	**proper**
capitalize (9)	**adjective**
common noun	**proper noun**
compass (5)	senate (6)
describe (5)	stadium (7)

Teaching Suggestions

- **Introducing the Lesson**
  Write the words *lake, sunset,* and *Lake Sunset* on the board. Ask students to identify the initial lowercase and capital letters. Have them give their ideas about why neither *lake* nor *sunset* is capitalized when the word stands alone, yet both are capitalized in the name *Lake Sunset.*

- **Reviewing Skills** Ask students to use each singular and plural subject pronoun (*I, you, he, she, it, we, you, they*) with the verbs *to be* and *to dance.*

TEACHER ALERT

Point out that the book title in the example for rule 5 is given in italic type. Explain that if students are using a word processor, they should be able to italicize titles. If they are handwriting or typing, they should underline titles of books and movies. Titles of stories, articles, poems, and songs are usually enclosed in quotation marks. Have students find titles on and within books, magazines, and newspapers; they may practice writing the titles correctly.

Reading Vocabulary

impress (6)   narrative (7)
jay (6)   series (5)

■ **Presenting Activity A**

Direct students to the appropriate rule for each bold item in sentence 1. Students should note that *Derek, Olympics,* and *Springfield High School* are proper nouns; *track team* is a common noun; and *American* is a proper adjective. Students should continue referring to the rules on page 47 as they complete Activity A.

Activity A Answers

1) Derek, American, Olympics, track team, Springfield High School **2)** miles, day, Friday **3)** cross-country course, Macarthur Park, weekend **4)** finish line, minutes, Coach Jones **5)** man, coach, Springfield Springers, winner

■ **Presenting Activity B**

Tell students to look carefully at the three items to find differences before they choose the correct answer.

Activity B Answers

1) c **2)** b **3)** b **4)** c **5)** a

Activity A   Read the following sentences. List the bold words on your paper. Capitalize them only if they are proper nouns or proper adjectives.

1) **Derek** watched the **american** runners at the **olympics**. He decided to join the **track team** at **springfield high school**.

2) To prepare, he ran five **miles** every **day** except **friday**.

3) He tried out at a **cross-country course** at **macarthur park** last **weekend**.

4) He crossed the **finish line** in sixteen **minutes** and impressed **coach jones**.

5) "I think we can use you, young **man**," said the smiling **coach**. "The **springfield springers** may have a future **winner**."

Activity B   Read each set of sentences below. Decide which sentence uses correct capitalization. Write the letter of the correct sentence on your paper.

1) **a)** what is the name of your high school?
  b) What is the name of your High School?
  c) What is the name of your high school?

2) **a)** Order french toast for breakfast.
  b) Order French toast for breakfast.
  c) Order French Toast for breakfast.

3) **a)** When did the Blue Jays win the world series?
  b) When did the Blue Jays win the World Series?
  c) When did the blue jays win the World Series?

4) **a)** The bank is north of Bigelow avenue.
  b) The Bank is North of Bigelow Avenue.
  c) The bank is north of Bigelow Avenue.

5) **a)** The book *Narrative of the Life of Frederick Douglass* was written long ago.
  b) The book *Narrative Of The Life Of Frederick Douglass* was written long ago.
  c) The book *Narrative of the life of Frederick Douglass* was written long ago.

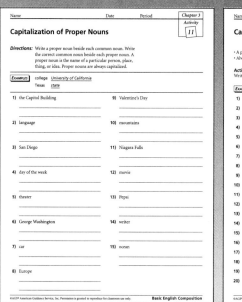

Activity 11

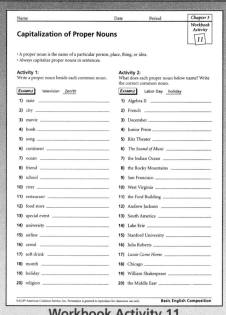

Workbook Activity 11

Lesson 3 Review

Check your writing for careful use of capital and lowercase letters. Review these rules.

- Always capitalize the first word in a sentence.
- Always capitalize the pronoun *I*.
- Capitalize proper nouns and proper adjectives.
- Capitalize parts of the country, languages, exact course names, and important words in a title.
- Do not capitalize common nouns.

Part A   Number your paper from 1 to 10. Read each of the following sentences. If the sentence is correct, write *Correct* after the number. If the sentence has a capitalization error, rewrite the sentence correctly after the number.

1) Thanksgiving is an American Holiday.
2) Mr. Chang teaches english at the High School.
3) My mother was born in North Carolina.
4) Did you receive any Valentines last february 14?
5) The last book Amanda read was *Kiss of Death*.
6) The football team in Springfield is called the Cubs.
7) what is the most popular Television Show this year?
8) Laura said, "i want to learn to play Chess."
9) Coronado was a spanish explorer who reached the southwest.
10) New York was once a Dutch colony.

Part B   Write one sentence about each of the following topics. Follow the rules for correct capitalization and punctuation.

1) A movie you have seen (include the title)
2) A place you have visited
3) Something that happened at your school (include the school name)
4) Someone in your family
5) Something that happens on a particular day of the week

Reading Vocabulary

chess (7)   punctuation (7)
exact (6)   review (5)
popular   southwest

■ **Lesson Review** Have students read aloud the bulleted list of rules at the top of this page. They should refer to the rules and examples in this lesson as they make decisions about the items in these activities.

Part A Answers

1) Thanksgiving is an American holiday. 2) Mr. Chang teaches English at the high school.
3) Correct 4) Did you receive any valentines last February 14?
5) Correct 6) Correct
7) What is the most popular television show this year?
8) Laura said, "I want to learn to play chess." 9) Coronado was a Spanish explorer who reached the Southwest. 10) Correct

Part B Answers
Answers will vary.

Follow-up Activity

Make a list of common nouns with students. Then have students give a corresponding proper noun to list beside it. Examples:

hotel—Harrington Hotel

college—Trinity College

mountain range—Rocky Mountains

river—Mississippi River

Overview This lesson identifies verbs and verb phrases and focuses on correct and consistent use of verb tenses.

Objectives

- To identify an action verb and a state-of-being verb.
- To recognize helping verbs in verb phrases.
- To use six verb tenses correctly and consistently.

Student Pages 50–54

Teacher's Resource Library

Activity 12

Reading Vocabulary

action verb	state-of-being
helping verb	verb
jog (5)	verb phrase
plus (6)	

Teaching Suggestions

■ Introducing the Lesson

Students have been introduced to verbs in Lesson 1 of this chapter. Ask volunteers to come to the board to write complete sentences on any topic. The group then identifies the verb in each sentence.

■ Reviewing Skills Write the

following sentences on the board. Have students rewrite them with correct capitalization:

the pittsburgh steelers are a football team.

i would like to visit oregon and then travel farther north.

■ Presenting Activity A

Make true-false statements based on the information on this page; have students tell whether the statement is true or false and why. Example statements: *All sentences need verbs. Verbs always show action. A verb is always just one word.*

Activity A Answers

1) has **2)** need **3)** must know
4) will be **5)** find

Action verb
A word that expresses action in a sentence. It tells what someone or something does. (Throw the ball. They run *fast. Please think* of *an answer.)*

Helping verb
A verb form that helps main verbs to express time. (We must *go. I have* cooked. *Laura will* see *us. The dog has been* eating).

State-of-being verb
A word that expresses the condition of the subject. It connects the subject with a noun, pronoun, or adjective. (Richard is *my brother. The woman* looks *tired.)*

Verb phrase
A group of words including a main verb and any helping verbs.

Every sentence must have a verb. A verb is a word expressing action or state of being. Study the examples below.

1. A verb can express action in a sentence. **Action verbs** tell what the subject does or did.

> **EXAMPLES** Derek **runs** five miles almost every day.
> Amanda **met** Laura at the corner.

2. A verb can also express a condition of someone or something. A **state-of-being verb** does not suggest action.

> **EXAMPLES** Amanda and Laura **are** friends.
> Derek **seems** friendly, too.

3. A verb can be made of more than one word. A main verb often has a **helping verb**. The helping verb helps complete the meaning of the main verb. The helping verb plus the main verb form a **verb phrase**.

> **EXAMPLES** Derek **will jog** tomorrow.
> Cal and Denise **have been** friends for years.
> Everyone **should leave** at noon.

Activity A Write the verb or verb phrase in each of these sentences on your paper.

1) Every sentence has a verb.

2) You need a verb in every sentence.

3) Everyone must know the rules.

4) Soon you will be an expert!

5) Find the verb in this sentence.

Verb Phrases

A verb phrase includes a helping verb and a main verb. The main verb expresses action or state of being. The helping verb helps to express time. Study the following list of common helping verbs.

have	am	was	been	will	would	must
has	is	were	do	shall	could	may
had	are	be	did	can	should	might

A verb phrase has only one main verb. It may have more than one helping verb. The main verb is always last. Study the bold verb phrases in the sentences below. The helping verbs are underlined.

> **EXAMPLES** By nine in the morning, Derek **had trained** for an hour.
>
> He **has been running** on the track every afternoon.

Activity B Find the verb phrase in each sentence. Copy the verb phrase on your paper. Underline each helping verb.

1) Amanda was writing a letter to her aunt.

2) Cal has been playing in a band for a year.

3) The band is practicing now.

4) Laura must go to the gym this evening.

5) Amanda has known Laura for several years.

6) Mr. Chang has given the class a difficult assignment.

7) He will collect the papers tomorrow.

8) Coach Jones might make an announcement Friday.

9) The students did answer correctly.

10) You should have arrived sooner!

Reading Vocabulary

announcement   include (5)
gym (5)   underline

■ Presenting Activity B

Write the main verbs *run, eat,* and *grow* on the board. Have students give oral sentences using each boxed helping verb, with or without other helping verbs, before each main verb. Then have them proceed with Activity B.

Activity B Answers

1) <u>was</u> writing 2) <u>has been</u> playing 3) <u>is</u> practicing
4) <u>must</u> go 5) <u>has</u> known
6) <u>has</u> given 7) <u>will</u> collect
8) <u>might</u> make 9) <u>did</u> answer
10) <u>should have</u> arrived

LEARNING STYLES

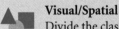 **Visual/Spatial**
Divide the class into pairs and give each pair a colorful and detailed magazine picture. Encourage one member of each pair to create the beginnings of ten sentences by writing down ten nouns that appear in the picture. For example, a student might write the following: *The woman; The curtains; The light;* and so on. Then have the other pair member select five of these sentence beginnings and add a verb to shows what the noun is doing. For example, the second student might write *"The woman speaks"; "The curtains are lace"; "The light shines."* Note: Keep these magazine pictures for use with the Learning Styles activity on page 141.

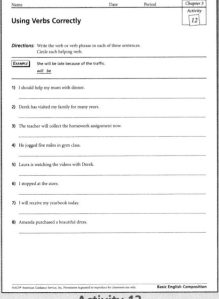

Activity 12

Reading Vocabulary

county (5)   student (5)
local (6)   **tense (6)**

■ **Presenting Activity C** As students decide how to label the bold verbs in this activity, have them look back at the examples for matching helping verbs and verb endings.

Activity C Answers

1) announced—past **2)** talked—past **3)** had started—past perfect **4)** runs—present
5) will have run—future perfect
6) takes—present **7)** will enter—future **8)** has planned—present perfect **9)** wishes—present

---

APPLICATION

In the Community Interested students may look over the sports pages of a local newspaper for information about high school sports. Examine the articles together for information about what has happened, had happened, and will happen.

Tense
The form of a verb that expresses time.

Tense

People talk and write about events that happen at different times. They use verbs to express **tense**. Study the following examples of six verb tenses:

EXAMPLES	Present:	Derek **starts** his training today.
	Past:	Derek **started** his training yesterday.
	Future:	Derek **will start** his training tomorrow.
	Present perfect:	Derek **has started** his training.
	Past perfect:	Derek **had started** his training earlier.
	Future perfect:	Derek **will have started** his training by next Tuesday.

Activity C Read the paragraph below. Find the bold verbs or verb phrases. List each one on your paper. Label it with the verb tense.

HIGH SCHOOL STUDENT TRAINS FOR COUNTY MEET

Today Derek Corelli **announced** his training plan for the County Meet. When he **talked** with reporters, he already **had started** his training. Derek **runs** at least five miles every day. He said he **will have run** thirty miles by the end of this week. He always **takes** Friday off. He **will enter** some local meets soon. Corelli **has planned** for more training. Springfield High School **wishes** you luck, Derek!

Consistency of Tenses

Consistent

Following the same rules; staying the same.

As a writer, you must decide whether the tense of each verb is logical. All the verbs in a sentence should be **consistent**. Some sentences may include more than one main verb. Generally, all verbs should be in the same tense if the actions occur at the same time. However, different tenses can show that actions occur at different times. Study the following examples.

EXAMPLES

Since Derek **wanted** to win, he **practiced** every day.
(Both verbs are past tense.)

Every weekday Amanda **gets** up and **goes** to school.
(Both verbs are present tense.)

Mike **hopes** that Derek **will win** the race.
(The verb *hopes* is present tense. The verb phrase *will win* is future tense. Right now, Mike hopes that Derek will win in the future.)

Activity D   Read each pair of sentences below. Study the bold verbs. Decide which sentence shows correct, consistent use of tenses. Write the letter of the correct sentence on your paper.

1) **a)** When Amanda **smiles**, the room **seems** brighter.
   b) When Amanda **smiled**, the room **seems** brighter.

2) **a)** The starting gun **fired**, and the runners **dashed** off!
   b) The starting gun **fired**, and the runners **dash** off!

3) **a)** As Derek **jogged** around the track, he **waved** to his friends.
   b) As Derek **jogs** around the track, he **waved** to his friends.

4) **a)** **Pay** attention to verbs, and your writing **improves**.
   b) **Pay** attention to verbs, and your writing **will improve**.

5) **a)** Because Derek **trained** hard, he **has raced** well.
   b) Because Derek **trained** hard, he **raced** well.

■ **Presenting Activity D**

Before students begin Activity D, have them look back at the example sentences on this page. Ask them to change the verbs in the first sentence to present tense and the verbs in the second sentence to future tense. Then ask for ideas about verb changes that would make sense in the third sentence.

Activity D Answers

1) a   2) a   3) a   4) b   5) b

Part A Answers

1) looked　2) jumped　3) fixed
4) asked　5) remarked
6) churned　7) wanted
8) celebrated　9) intend
10) will practice

Part B Answers

Students' sentences will vary.

Follow-up Activity

Find a short passage in a literature book to read aloud to students. Have students identify each verb and the verb tense. Discuss whether the author has used verb tenses consistently and logically. Draw students' attention to adverbs of time in the sentences.

Lesson 4 Review

To write clear sentences, pay attention to verbs.

- Make sure that you have used the correct verb tense.
- Make sure that your verb tenses are consistent.

Part A　Find the verbs in the following sentences. Check the tense. Correct any mistakes. Rewrite the verbs correctly.

The Big Race
by Derek Corelli

1) Last Saturday I look forward to my first big race.
2) That morning the alarm sounded, and I jump up.
3) My mother fixes me a good breakfast and I ate it all.
4) I had already ask Ms. Lentz about having the day off.
5) "I believe that you will succeed," my mother remarks to me.
6) My stomach churns and I tensed up, too.
7) I never doubted that I want to win that race.
8) When the race ended, I celebrate.
9) Now I plan for next week's race, which I intended to win, too!
10) I practice every day next week.

Part B　Practice using verbs correctly. Write ten sentences about a topic of your choice. Here are suggested topics:

- A school event
- A book, a movie, or a television show
- A sport
- Use of technology

Number your sentences. Underline the verbs and verb phrases. (You may have more than one verb in a sentence.)

Most of the verbs in the English language are regular. To form the past tense of a regular verb, you add -ed or -d. You may also want to write the present perfect, past perfect, and future perfect tenses of a regular verb. To write the perfect tenses, you add -ed or -d to form the **past participle** of a regular verb. Below are two examples of regular verbs. Notice that the past tense and the past participle are the same.

Past participle

A principal part of a verb, used to form the perfect tenses.

EXAMPLES

Regular verb:	*to paint*
Present tense:	the man *paints*, they *paint*
Past tense:	he *painted*
Past participle used to form perfect tense:	she has *painted*
Regular verb:	*to promise*
Present tense:	I *promise*, she *promises*
Past tense:	they *promised*
Past participle used to form perfect tense:	they have *promised*

Activity A Write six sentences that include the regular verb *stop*. Write one sentence for each of the tenses listed below. (Look at the examples above for models.)

Present

Past

Future

Present perfect

Past perfect

Future perfect

Now write a sentence that includes the regular verb *dance* in each of the tenses listed.

TEACHER ALERT

Spend some time discussing the meaning relationships among the simple and perfect tenses. On the board, write examples such as these: *We talk daily. We talked yesterday. We will talk tomorrow. We have talked for an hour. We had talked for hours before reaching an agreement. We will have talked three times before next week.* Have students use their own words to explain how verb tense signals meaning.

Activity A Answers

Students' sentences will vary. Sample sentences are given.

1) The man stops. The children dance. (present) **2)** The man stopped. The children danced. (past) **3)** The man will stop. The children will dance. (future) **4)** The man has stopped. The children have danced. (present perfect) **5)** The man had stopped. The children had danced. (past perfect) **6)** The man will have stopped. The children will have danced. (future perfect)

Overview This lesson focuses on the variant past and past participle forms of irregular verbs.

Objectives

- To review the formation of the past tense and perfect tenses in regular verbs.

- To learn the past and past participle forms of irregular verbs and use them correctly.

Student Pages 55–64

Reading Vocabulary
past participle

Teaching Suggestions

- **Introducing the Lesson**
Tell students that it is common for a very young English-speaking child to say a sentence such as *I runned fast* or *Grandma bringed me a present.* Discuss with students why young children might make such mistakes in forming verbs. Help students to see that the -ed ending is the regular way to form past tenses. Ask students how they think children learn the correct forms of irregular past tenses such as *ran* and *brought.*

- **Reviewing Skills** Write the verbs *to practice* and *to jog* on the board. Have students give oral sentences using each verb in the present tense, past tense, and future tense.

- **Presenting Activity A**
Before students proceed with this activity, have them identify the past participle of each verb in the example. They should note that it looks the same as the past tense. Remind them that the present perfect tense is formed with the helping verb *has* or *have*; the past perfect tense is formed with the helping verb *had*; and the future perfect tense is formed with the helping verbs *will have.*

Reading Vocabulary

irregular verb

- ## Presenting Activity B

Have students use each of the boxed verbs in an oral sentence before proceeding with this activity.

Activity B Answers

Students' sentences will vary. Sample sentences are given.

1) I <u>was</u> at home this morning.
2) Now I <u>am</u> at school.
3) Today I <u>have had</u> cereal for breakfast. **4)** I <u>have been</u> here for three hours. **5)** My favorite sport <u>is</u> hockey. **6)** The Detroit Red Wings <u>have</u> a good team.

Irregular verb
A verb that does not form its past and past participle by adding -ed to the present tense form. (eat, ate, eaten)

Some verbs are not regular. **Irregular verbs** change their forms in the different tenses. Two common irregular verbs are *be* and *have*. Study their forms.

Verb	Present	Past	Past Participle
be	am, is, are	was, were	been
have	has, have	had	had

Activity B Write a sentence to answer each question below. Use a form of the verb *be* or *have* in each of your answers. Underline the verb in your sentence.

1) Where were you this morning?

2) Where are you now?

3) What have you had to eat today?

4) How long have you been here?

5) What is your favorite sport?

6) Which team has good players?

Study the irregular verbs in the table below.

Present	Past	Past Participle
begin	began	begun
bend	bent	bent
bite	bit	bitten
blow	blew	blown
break	broke	broken
bring	brought	brought
burst	burst	burst
buy	bought	bought

Activity C   Write the correct form of the verb for each of the following sentences. Remember that the past participle is used with *has, have,* or *had.*

1) The bottle in the freezer has (burst).

2) The wind (blow) the old tree over yesterday.

3) We have finally (begin) the lesson.

4) Last week we (buy) new tires.

5) That gate (break) years ago.

6) He (bend) over and touched his toes.

7) He (bite) into a juicy apple.

8) They (bring) a chocolate cake to the party.

9) The teacher (begin) to speak.

10) What has the dog (break)?

Activity D   Write each word below in a correct sentence. Use the word as a verb.

1) burst

2) bought

3) blew

4) bent

5) begun

6) bitten

7) began

8) blown

9) broken

10) bit

Reading Vocabulary
freezer   juicy

■ **Presenting Activity C** Tell students to refer to the three lists in the table on page 56 as they think about the verb tense in each sentence in this activity.

Activity C Answers
1) burst 2) blew 3) begun
4) bought 5) broke 6) bent
7) bit 8) brought 9) began
10) broken

■ **Presenting Activity D** Go over the list with students to help them identify the past participle forms. Remind students to use the helping verb *has, have,* or *had* with past participles.

Activity D Answers
Sentences will vary.

Reading Vocabulary

drunk (5)
homework

■ **Presenting Activity E** Go over the sentences with students, and have them identify the tense of the verb that belongs in the sentence. They then make the correct substitution in their rewritten sentences.

Activity E Answers

1) Last night Laura did her homework.   2) The coach has chosen the starting players.
3) We have already dug our garden.   4) Yesterday I drove my old car to work.   5) She had drunk a glass of water before lunch.   6) You have drawn a clear picture.

■ **Presenting Activity F** Students may read each sentence softly to themselves, listening for the error and thinking about the form of the verb that sounds correct.

Activity F Answers

1) have done   2) cost   3) cut
4) came   5) have done
6) caught

Study the irregular verbs in the table below.

Present	Past	Past Participle
catch	caught	caught
choose	chose	chosen
come	came	come
cost	cost	cost
cut	cut	cut
dig	dug	dug
do	did	done
draw	drew	drawn
drink	drank	drunk
drive	drove	driven

Activity E   Change each bold verb to either the past tense or to the past participle form. Write the correct sentence on your paper.

1) Last night Laura **do** her homework.

2) The coach has **choose** the starting players.

3) We have already **dig** our garden.

4) Yesterday I **drive** my old car to work.

5) She had **drink** a glass of water before lunch.

6) You have **draw** a clear picture.

Activity F   Find the verb that is not correct. Rewrite the verb correctly.

1) "You done a fine job on this report," Mike said.

2) Last year that coat costed only sixty-five dollars.

3) "I cutted my finger!" the worker cried.

4) Almost all of my friends come to our last party.

5) I have finally did all of my work.

6) They caughted eight large fish.

Study the irregular verbs in the table below.

Present	Past	Past Participle
eat	ate	eaten
fall	fell	fallen
feed	fed	fed
feel	felt	felt
fight	fought	fought
find	found	found
fly	flew	flown
forget	forgot	forgotten
forgive	forgave	forgiven
freeze	froze	frozen

Activity G   Change each bold verb to either the past tense or the past participle form. Rewrite the sentences correctly.

1) Last year Mr. Corelli **flied** to Canada on business.

2) "I nearly **freezed** to death up there," he said.

3) He saw a woman who had **fell** on the ice.

4) "I **fighted** to stay on my feet myself," he said.

5) "I have **forgave** my boss for sending me on this trip," he said.

6) Mr. Corelli **finded** a wonderful gift for his wife.

7) He **eaten** in the hotel restaurant every night.

8) "They **feeded** me very well," he told his family.

9) After he **flown** home, he gave his wife the present.

10) "I have not **forget** you," he told his wife.

11) Ms. Corelli opened the box and **felted** the soft wool throw.

12) "You **founded** the perfect gift," she told her husband.

13) Mr. Corelli **feeled** that the trip was interesting.

■ **Presenting Activity G**
Read the directions with students. Go over the first few items with them, helping them to name the correct form of the verb.

Activity G Answers
1) Last year Mr. Corelli flew to Canada on business.   2) "I nearly froze to death up there," he said.   3) He saw a woman who had fallen on the ice.
4) "I fought to stay on my feet myself," he said.   5) "I have forgiven my boss for sending me on this trip," he said.   6) Mr. Corelli found a wonderful gift for his wife.   7) He ate in the hotel restaurant every night.
8) "They fed me very well," he told his family.   9) After he flew home, he gave his wife the present.   10) "I have not forgotten you," he told his wife.
11) Ms. Corelli opened the box and felt the soft wool throw.
12) "You found the perfect gift," she told her husband.
13) Mr. Corelli felt that the trip was interesting.

Presenting Activity H

Have students look for the helping verb *has* or *have* to decide if a past participle is needed.

Activity H Answers

1) "Has Derek gone yet?" asked Mike. **2)** Aunt Marie has given me a birthday gift. **3)** Have you heard the latest news? **4)** A storm hit town last night. **5)** Mr. Corelli, Derek's father, has grown a beard. **6)** Mike kept a flashlight in the car. **7)** "I knew that I would win the race," said Derek. **8)** Derek got down at the starting block and waited. **9)** He waited until he heard the whistle. **10)** Benjy hid his bone in the garden.

Study the irregular verbs in the table below.

Present	Past	Past Participle
get	got	got, gotten
give	gave	given
go	went	gone
grow	grew	grown
hear	heard	heard
hide	hid	hidden
hit	hit	hit
keep	kept	kept
know	knew	known

Activity H   Change each bold verb to either the past tense or the past participle form. Rewrite the sentences correctly.

1) "Has Derek **went** yet?" asked Mike.

2) Aunt Marie has **gave** me a birthday gift.

3) Have you **hear** the latest news?

4) A storm **hitted** town last night.

5) Mr. Corelli, Derek's father, has **grew** a beard.

6) Mike **keeped** a flashlight in the car.

7) "I **knows** that I would win the race," said Derek.

8) Derek **get** down at the starting block and waited.

9) He waited until he **heared** the whistle.

10) Benjy **hided** his bone in the garden.

Study the irregular verbs in the table below.

Present	Past	Past Participle
lead	led	led
leave	left	left
lie	lay	lain
lose	lost	lost
make	made	made
mean	meant	meant
put	put	put
read	read	read
ride	rode	ridden
ring	rang	rung

Activity I   Find the verb error in each sentence below. Write each sentence correctly.

1) That cowboy has never rode in a rodeo before.

2) She putted the groceries on the shelves.

3) The cat lain on the sofa all morning.

4) We all leaved work at five o'clock yesterday.

5) Who has rang the doorbell?

6) I have readed that book before.

Activity J   Some verbs do not change their forms at all. Copy the verbs in these sentences. Decide whether each verb is present or past tense. Write *Present* or *Past* for each verb.

1) I **read** that book yesterday.

2) They **cut** fresh flowers every day.

3) Cooks often **put** on aprons.

4) Last week Jason **hit** a home run for the team.

5) Today apples **cost** less than yesterday.

Reading Vocabulary
sofa (5)

■ **Presenting Activity I** Have students read each sentence softly to themselves to decide which word or words sound incorrect. Point out that there may be more than one way to correct the verb.

Activity I Answers
1) That cowboy has never ridden in a rodeo before. (or) That cowboy never rode in a rodeo before.   **2)** She put the groceries on the shelves.   **3)** The cat lay on the sofa all morning. (or) The cat has lain on the sofa all morning.   **4)** We all left work at five o'clock yesterday.   **5)** Who has rung the doorbell? (or) Who rang the doorbell?   **6)** I have read that book before. (or) I read that book before.

■ **Presenting Activity J** Have students look back at the tables on pages 56 through 61 to find examples of verbs that are unchanged in present, past, and past participle form. Before students identify each verb in Activity J, remind them that the present tense is used for events that happen at the present time and for events that happen regularly.

Activity J Answers
1) Past **2)** Present **3)** Present **4)** Past **5)** Present

Reading Vocabulary

swear (6)   witness (5)
trial (5)

■ Presenting Activity K

Remind students that the past participle form of the verb should be used if the helping verb *has, have,* or *had* appears in the sentence.

Activity K Answers

1) swore   2) stolen   3) sung
4) swung   5) set   6) sat
7) stood   8) swam   9) sent
10) shook   11) spread
12) seen   13) saw

Study the irregular verbs in the table below.

Present	Past	Past Participle
see	saw	seen
send	sent	sent
set	set	set
shake	shook	shaken
sing	sang	sung
sit	sat	sat
spread	spread	spread
stand	stood	stood
steal	stole	stolen
swear	swore	sworn
swim	swam	swum
swing	swung	swung

Activity K   Read the following sentences. Decide whether the past or the past participle form should be used. Write the correct verb forms.

1) The witness (swear) she heard the thief.

2) The man on trial had (steal) a ring.

3) Where have you (sing) before?

4) The batter (swing) but missed.

5) Paul (set) the vase on the table.

6) Someone has (sit) on this chair.

7) I have (stand) in line for hours!

8) Last summer we (swim) at the lake.

9) Have you (send) that package yet?

10) We (shake) the package, and it rattled.

11) We (spread) the tablecloth for the picnic.

12) Have you (see) Mike?

13) Yes, I (see) him in English class.

Study the irregular verbs in the table below.

Present	Past	Past Participle
take	took	taken
teach	taught	taught
tear	tore	torn
think	thought	thought
wake	woke	woken
wear	wore	worn
weep	wept	wept
win	won	won
wring	wrung	wrung
write	wrote	written

Activity L   Find the verb error in each of the following sentences. Rewrite the sentence using the correct verb form on your paper. Use the table above to help you.

1) At least once a year, Amanda has wrote to her aunt Frances.

2) The nurse wringed out the wet towel.

3) Everyone was glad that Derek winned the race.

4) Laura is glad that she has took Spanish 1.

5) Mike thinked, and then he answered the question.

6) Derek weared his good shoes to school.

7) "Thanks for this wonderful award," weeped the actor.

8) Who has teared a hole in this paper?

9) The fire alarm wokened everyone.

10) "Now that you have teached me all of these verbs, I will never make a mistake," said the student.

Reading Vocabulary
award (5)   wring (6)

■ **Presenting Activity L** Go over the sentences with students, and have them identify the tense of the verb that belongs in the sentence. They then make the correct substitution in their rewritten sentences.

Activity L Answers

1) At least once a year, Amanda has written to her aunt Frances. 2) The nurse wrung out the wet towel. 3) Everyone was glad that Derek won the race. 4) Laura is glad that she has taken Spanish 1. 5) Mike thought, and then he answered the question. 6) Derek wore his good shoes to school. 7) "Thanks for this wonderful award," wept the actor. 8) Who has torn a hole in this paper? 9) The fire alarm woke everyone. 10) "Now that you have taught me all of these verbs, I will never make a mistake," said the student.

TEACHER ALERT

One common mistake speakers and writers make with irregular verbs is to use *has, have,* or *had* with the past tense instead of with the past participle form of the verb. (Examples of common errors: *I had fell on the ice; They have sang nicely.*) Model standard use of the past participle form, and draw students' attention to the sound of correct usage.

Reading Vocabulary

incorrect

Part A Answers

Sentences will vary.

Part B Answers

1) froze 2) done 3) swung
4) stolen 5) saw 6) gone
7) grown 8) lost 9) lay
10) flew

Follow-up Activity

Direct students to one of the tables in this lesson. Have them take turns making short sentences that contain the subject I, you, she, or he and each verb listed. (Example: I see it. I saw it. I have seen it.) Continue with another table.

Remember to use and spell regular and irregular verb forms correctly.

Part A Write each verb below in a correct sentence. Write a different sentence for each word.

1) brought
2) fallen
3) taken
4) stood
5) driven
6) set
7) bit
8) came
9) caught
10) forgotten

Part B The bold verb in each sentence below is incorrect. Correct the sentence by changing the verb. You will need to change it either to the past or the past participle form. Write the verb on your paper.

1) Last night the ice **freeze** on the lake.
2) What have you **did**?
3) "I **swang** from that tree as a child," said Mr. Luca.
4) A robber has **stealed** the money.
5) "I **seen** him do it!" said the witness.
6) You have already **goed** to the gym once.
7) The tomato plants have **growed** tall.
8) The team **losed** the game by one point.
9) Amanda felt ill and **lied** in bed all morning.
10) The butterflies **fly** north last spring.

Possessive noun

A noun that names the owner of something or names a relationship between people or things. A possessive noun must have an apostrophe (Mary's coat; the woman's car; the voters' opinions).

Apostrophe

A punctuation mark used to replace missing letters in a contraction (doesn't) or to show possession (Mary's coat).

A **possessive noun** shows ownership or a relationship. You may confuse possessive nouns with plural nouns because the two forms sound alike: *dog's* and *dogs,* for example. Remember to use an **apostrophe** in a possessive noun—and NOT to use one in a plural noun.

Study the examples below. Notice the different spellings of the bold plural and possessive forms.

EXAMPLES	Plurals	Possessives
	The **friends** meet here.	The **friend's** house is nearby.
	The family has two **dogs**.	The spotted **dog's** collar is broken.
	Two **cars** are parked on the street.	Which **car's** tire is flat?

Activity A   Read each sentence. Copy the bold plural nouns on your paper under the heading *Plurals*. The bold possessive nouns are missing apostrophes. Rewrite them correctly under the heading *Possessives*.

1) Both **teams** met at the stadium.

2) Where is the **poodles** leash?

3) Everyone in **Lauras** class liked learning Spanish.

4) Knowing about irregular **verbs** is important.

5) Where is **Benjys** collar?

6) Where are my running **shoes**?

Chapter 3   Lesson 6

Overview This lesson distinguishes between plural nouns and possessive nouns and shows correct use of an apostrophe with the latter.

Objective

■ To use and spell possessive nouns and plural nouns correctly.

Student Pages 65–69

Teacher's Resource Library
Workbook Activities 12–13

Reading Vocabulary

apostrophe	poodle
confuse (5)	**possessive noun**
contraction (9)	relationship (6)
leash (5)	

Teaching Suggestions

■ **Introducing the Lesson**
Have students listen as you say each of the phrases below; have them "translate" each into the succinct form that is more commonly used in English:
• the home of my aunt ("my aunt's home")
• the pencil of my classmate ("my classmate's pencil")
• the sister of Donald ("Donald's sister")
Students may be able to give additional examples orally.

■ **Reviewing Skills** Ask students to define a singular noun and a plural noun. Have students list five singular nouns and five plural nouns.

■ **Presenting Activity A**
Review the directions with students, making sure they understand the difference between plural nouns and possessive nouns.

Activity A Answers

Plurals	Possessives
teams	poodle's
verbs	Laura's
shoes	Benjy's

Reading Vocabulary

■ Presenting Activity B

Read the directions with students. Help them to understand that the term *singular possessive* means "one owner" and has nothing to do with how many things are owned. The term *plural possessive* means "more than one owner," regardless of whether one thing or many things are owned.

Activity B Answers

1) Plural 2) Plural 3) Singular
4) Plural 5) Singular

APPLICATION

Career Connection
Tell students that if they are working at a job that requires word processing, they may use spell-checking software to find misspellings. Explain that they cannot use a spell checker to find mistakes in possessives and plurals, however. The software can only find words that are not real words; it does not find words that have been confused.

Study these rules for forming singular and plural possessive nouns. Remember that the placement of an apostrophe makes your meaning clear.

1. If the noun is singular, add an apostrophe before the letter *s*.

> Cal's house
> one child's room
> Jo Jones's car

2. If the noun is plural, add an apostrophe after the letter *s*.

> states' rights
> two actors' parts
> cities' problems

Irregular plural noun

A noun that forms its plural in an unusual way, not with the usual -s or -es (*mouse*, mice; *foot*, feet; *man*, men).

---

3. Be careful with **irregular plural nouns**. If the plural does NOT end in -s, add an apostrophe before the letter *s*.

> people's opinions
> children's game
> women's clothes

Activity B   Read each sentence. Decide whether the bold word is a singular possessive or a plural possessive. Write *Singular* or *Plural* after each number.

1) The **sisters'** room is painted blue.
2) What time is the **teachers'** meeting?
3) The students answered the **teacher's** questions.
4) **Men's** shirts are on sale.
5) The **dancer's** feet hurt.

Activity C Read the singular and plural forms of each of the words below. Write the singular possessive form and the plural possessive form of each word. Here are examples with the singular word *wolf* and the plural word *wolves*.

Examples Singular possessive: *wolf's* Plural possessive: *wolves'*

	Singular	Plural
1)	child	children
2)	man	men
3)	tree	trees
4)	Wilson	Wilsons
5)	family	families
6)	boss	bosses
7)	friend	friends
8)	class	classes
9)	team	teams
10)	woman	women
11)	baby	babies
12)	shelf	shelves
13)	goose	geese
14)	mouse	mice
15)	city	cities
16)	animal	animals
17)	artist	artists
18)	day	days
19)	uncle	uncles
20)	Ruiz	Ruizes

■ **Presenting Activity C**
Have students use each of the example words, *wolf's* and *wolves'*, in an oral sentence. Make sure they understand the difference in meaning between a singular possessive and a plural possessive.

Activity C Answers
1) child's, children's 2) man's, men's 3) tree's, trees'
4) Wilson's, Wilsons' 5) family's, families' 6) boss's, bosses'
7) friend's, friends' 8) class's, classes') 9) team's, teams')
10) woman's, women's
11) baby's, babies' 12) shelf's, shelves' 13) goose's, geese's
14) mouse's, mice's 15) city's, cities' 16) animal's, animals'
17) artist's, artists' 18) day's, days' 19) uncle's, uncles'
20) Ruiz's, Ruizes'

Name _____ Date _____ Period _____ | Chapter 3 Workbook Activity 12

Plurals and Possessives

A. Directions: Look at each noun in bold print. Decide whether it is singular or plural. Look for the word in the list below the sentences. Beside the word write S for Singular or P for Plural.

1) One **day** Mrs. O'Hara got a **letter** in the **mail**.
2) The **letter** said that she had jury **duty**.
3) A **jury** is a **group** of twelve **people**
4) Its **members** listen to **evidence**.
5) They judge the defendant's **guilt** or **innocence**.
6) All twelve **men** and **women** must agree.

1) day _____   3) jury _____   5) guilt _____
   Mrs. O'Hara _____   group _____   innocence _____
   letter _____   people _____   6) men _____
   mail _____   4) members _____   women _____
2) letter _____   evidence _____
   duty _____

B. Directions: The apostrophes have been left out of the phrases below. Read each phrase. If it has a possessive noun, write the phrase on the line. Put an apostrophe in the correct place.

EXAMPLES: the lady's hat (singular possessive)
the ladies' club; the men's club (plural possessives)

1) the wolfs howl _____   6) your two cents worth _____
2) the calves pen _____   7) a days pay _____
3) all of the teams _____   8) two weeks a year _____
4) the childrens room _____   9) the familys home _____
5) the students book _____   10) the cars tire _____

©AGS® American Guidance Service, Inc. Permission is granted to reproduce for classroom use only.   **Basic English Composition**

Workbook Activity 12

Reading Vocabulary

memories (5)   unbelievable
sincerely (5)

■ **Presenting Activity D**
Have students find the words ending in *-s* and tell whether each should be a plural or a possessive.

Activity D Answers
1) weeks   2) broncs   3) riders'
4) clowns   5) friends
6) memories

Activity D   The letter below contains six errors in the use of possessives and plurals. List the incorrect words. Write the correct form for each.

May 4, 20--

Dear Ms. Quigley,

    Laura and I enjoyed watching the rodeo with you in Centerville a few weeks' ago. We both liked the bucking broncs' very much. The riders skill was unbelievable. The rodeo clown's were also fun to watch. All of our friend's have heard about the rodeo. One of our best memories' is meeting you! We are looking forward to seeing you again.

        Sincerely,
        Amanda O'Hara

Pay attention to plural nouns and possessive nouns. Remember the rules for using them correctly.

- Do NOT add an apostrophe to make a plural noun. Most of the time, just add -s.
- Add apostrophe -s to make a singular possessive noun.
- Add just an apostrophe to make a plural possessive noun.
- If the plural noun is irregular, add apostrophe -s to make it a possessive.

Part A Choose the correct sentence in each pair below. Write the letter of that sentence on your paper.

1) a) The Wilsons' home is on Third Street.
   b) The Wilson's home is on Third Street.

2) a) Both team's were ready for the big event.
   b) Both teams were ready for the big event.

3) a) Childrens' toys were scattered everywhere.
   b) Children's toys were scattered everywhere.

4) a) My neighbors cat climbed up a tree.
   b) My neighbor's cat climbed up a tree.

5) a) The fire department brought some ladders.
   b) The fire department brought some ladder's.

Part B Write the possessive form of each word below. Use the possessive form in a sentence.

1) neighbors
2) baby
3) people
4) teacher
5) mice

■ **Lesson Review** Go over the bulleted review items. Have volunteers come to the board to write an illustration of each rule.

Part A Answers
1) a 2) b 3) b 4) b 5) a

Part B Answers
Sentences will vary. Sample sentences are given.

1) neighbors'
   Our neighbors' cars are parked on the street.
2) baby's
   Is the baby's blanket soft?
3) people's
   Some people's ideas are interesting.
4) teacher's
   I try to listen to my teacher's lessons.
5) mice's
   What happened to those mice's tails?

Follow-up Activity

Write the phrases below on the board, and have students identify (a) the owner or owners and (b) the thing or things possessed. Ask students to use each phrase in an oral sentence.

- worker's wages
- singers' notes
- robin's wing
- students' assignment
- student's grades

Workbook Activity 13

Chapter 3 Review

The Teacher's Resource Library includes two parallel forms of the Chapter 3 Mastery Test. The difficulty level of the two forms is equivalent. You may wish to use one form as a pretest and the other form as a posttest.

Reading Vocabulary
foul (6)   referee (6)
novelist

Part A Answers
1) are   2) Money   3) building
4) me   5) Stadium   6) children's
7) run   8) caught   9) saw
10) families

Part B Answers
Some sentences may be corrected in more than one way.

1) Each of the students is ready to begin.   2) "My favorite class is English," said Denise.   3) The novelist Jack London wrote <u>The Call of the Wild.</u>   4) All of the students remembered their books.   5) Every pronoun must agree with its antecedent.   6) Rain and snow often fall in November.   7) Denise gave her lunch to her friend.   8) Researchers say that children watch too much TV.   9) Derek knew that he wanted to win that race.   10) When the race was over, Derek jogged happily around the track.

Part A Choose the word that correctly completes each sentence. Write the word on your paper.

1) The leaves on the tree (is, are) red.

2) The movie *Take the* (money, Money) *and Run* is silly.

3) What is the tallest (building, Building) in the world?

4) Denise went with Cal and (I, me) to the game.

5) Yankee (stadium, Stadium) is in New York.

6) The library has a (childrens', children's) room.

7) Today Derek has (ran, run) five miles.

8) The campers (catched, caught) fish for dinner.

9) The referee (saw, seen) the foul.

10) How many (families', families) live in this house?

Part B Find the one error in each sentence below. Then write each sentence correctly on your paper.

1) Each of the students are ready to begin.

2) "My favorite class is english," said Denise.

3) The novelist Jack London wrote *The Call Of the Wild.*

4) All of the students remembered them books.

5) Every pronoun must agree with their antecedent.

6) Rain and snow often falls in November.

7) Denise gave her friend her lunch.

8) They say that children watch too much TV.

9) Derek knew that he want to win that race.

10) When the race were over, Derek jogged happily around the track.

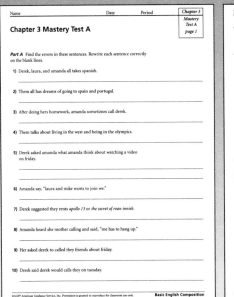
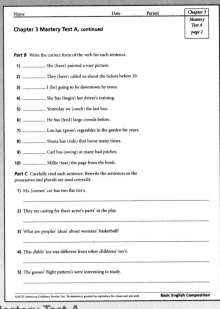

Chapter 3 Mastery Test A

Part C   Read each set of sentences. Decide which one is correct. Write the letter of that sentence on your paper.

1) a) We have driven fifty miles.
   b) We have drived fifty miles.
   c) We have driven fifty mile's.

2) a) The twin's do not look at all alike.
   b) The twins do not look at all alike.
   c) The twins' do not look at all alike.

3) a) The runners has broke a record!
   b) The runners have broke a record!
   c) The runners have broken a record!

4) a) The Hongs live west of Southville.
   b) The Hongs' live west of Southville.
   c) The Hongs live West of Southville.

5) a) Who wrote the book *Nothing But the Truth?*
   b) Who wrote the book *Nothing but the truth?*
   c) Who has wrote the book *Nothing but the Truth?*

Part D Answers
Answers will vary. Sample sentences are given.

1) They ate dinner.   2) Where is my hat?   3) I will go on vacation next week.   4) A person's dreams are important.   5) The three dogs' barks sound different.

Part D   Follow each direction.

1) Write a sentence in which a pronoun is used as the subject.

2) Write a sentence that includes a possessive pronoun.

3) Write a sentence in which at least one of the verbs is in the future tense.

4) Write a sentence containing a singular possessive noun.

5) Write a sentence containing a plural possessive noun.

Test Taking Tip | When taking a short-answer test, first answer the questions you know. Then go back to spend time on the questions you are less sure of.

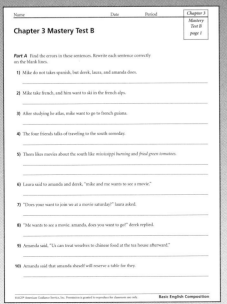

Chapter 3 Mastery Test B

Planning Guide

Spelling Counts!

	Student Pages	Vocabulary	Practice Exercises	Lesson Review
Lesson 1 Words That Sound Alike	74-80	✔	✔	80
Lesson 2 Words That Are Almost Alike	81-85		✔	85
Lesson 3 Contractions and Possessive Pronouns	86-90	✔	✔	90
Lesson 4 Plural Nouns	91-98		✔	98
Lesson 5 Words With *ie* or *ei*	99-101		✔	101
Lesson 6 Doubling the Final Consonant	102-105		✔	105
Lesson 7 Dropping the Final –e	106-108		✔	108
Lesson 8 Spelling Demons	109-111		✔	111

(Column group header: Student Text Lesson)

Chapter Activities

Teacher's Resource Library
Writing Tip 4: Basic Spelling Rules

Community Connection 2: Spell It Right

Assessment Options

Student Text
Chapter 4 Review

Teacher's Resource Library
Chapter 4 Mastery Tests A and B

Teaching Strategies							Language Skills			Learning Styles						Teacher's Resource Library		
Reviewing Skills	Teacher Alert	Follow-up Activity	Career Application	Home Application	Global Connection	Community Application	Identification Skills	Writing Skills	Punctuation Skills	Visual/Spatial	Auditory/Verbal	Body/Kinesthetic	Logical/Mathematical	Group Learning	LEP/ESL	Activities	Workbook Activities	Self-Study Guide
74	75-76	80				77	✔	✔	✔						78	13-14	14-16	✔
81	81	85	83				✔	✔	✔					84		15	17	✔
86		90		87			✔	✔	✔			89					18	✔
91	94	98			92	96	✔	✔	✔			97						✔
99		101					✔	✔	✔									✔
102	105	105					✔	✔	✔									✔
106	107	108					✔	✔	✔	108								✔
109		111					✔	✔	✔							16	19	✔

Chapter 4: Spelling Counts! pages 72–113

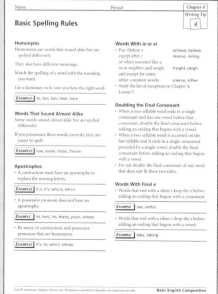

Name ___ Period ___ Chapter 4 / Writing Tip 4

Basic Spelling Rules

Homonyms

Homonyms are words that sound alike but are spelled differently.

They also have different meanings.

Match the spelling of a word with the meaning you want.

Use a dictionary to be sure you have the right word.

EXAMPLES to, too, two; hear, here

Words That Sound Almost Alike

Some words sound *almost* alike but are spelled differently.

If you pronounce these words correctly, they are easier to spell.

EXAMPLES lose, loose; chose, choose

Apostrophes

- A contraction must have an apostrophe to replace the missing letters.

EXAMPLES it is, it's; who is, who's

- A possessive pronoun does not have an apostrophe.

EXAMPLE its, hers, his, theirs, yours, whose

- Be aware of contractions and possessive pronouns that are homonyms.

EXAMPLES it's, its; who's, whose

Words With *ie* or *ei*

- Put *i* before *e*
  except after *c*
  or when sounded like *a*
  as in *neighbor* and *weigh*,
  and except for some
  other common words.

  achieve, believe
  receive, ceiling
  freight, sleigh
  science, either

- Study the list of exceptions in Chapter 4, Lesson 5.

Doubling the Final Consonant

- When a one-syllable word ends in a single consonant and has one vowel before that consonant, double the final consonant before adding an ending that begins with a vowel.
- When a two-syllable word is accented on the last syllable and it ends in a single consonant preceded by a single vowel, double the final consonant before adding an ending that begins with a vowel.
- Do not double the final consonant of any word that does not fit these two rules.

Words With Final *e*

- Words that end with a silent *e* keep the *e* before adding an ending that begins with a consonant.

EXAMPLE use, useful

- Words that end with a silent *e* drop the *e* before adding an ending that begins with a vowel.

EXAMPLE take, taking

©AGS® American Guidance Service, Inc. Permission is granted to reproduce for classroom use only. **Basic English Composition**

Name ___ Period ___ Chapter 4 / Writing Tip 4

Basic Spelling Rules (continued)

Irregular Plural Nouns

- Make most nouns plural by adding the letter *s*.

EXAMPLE town, towns

- If a noun ends in *s*, *x*, *ch*, *sh*, or *z*, make the plural by adding *-es*.

EXAMPLE ax, axes

- If a noun ends in the letter *y* and the letter before the *y* is a consonant, make the plural by changing the *y* to *i* and adding *-es*.

EXAMPLE city, cities

- If a noun ends in the letter *y* and the letter before the *y* is a vowel (*a, e, i, o, u*), make the plural by adding the letter *s*.

EXAMPLE boy, boys

- If a noun ends in the letters *f* or *fe*, make the plural by changing the *f* or *fe* to *v* and adding *-s* or *-es*.

EXAMPLE leaf, leaves

or just adding *-s*.

EXAMPLE roof, roofs

- If a noun ends in the letter *o*, make the plural by adding *-s*

EXAMPLE radio, radios

or adding *-es*.

EXAMPLE potato, potatoes

- If a musical term ends in the letter *o*, make the plural by adding *-s*.

EXAMPLE pianos, altos

- Do not add the letter *s* to some very irregular nouns to make them plural.

EXAMPLES child—children, goose—geese, man—men

- The singular and plural forms of some nouns are alike.

EXAMPLE deer, sheep

- Make a proper noun like a family name plural by adding the letter *s*.

EXAMPLE Smith, Smiths

- If a proper noun ends in the letter *s*, make the plural by adding *-es*.

EXAMPLE Jones, Joneses

- Make the plural of a letter by adding the letter *s* if it would not be confusing.

EXAMPLE Bs

- Make the plural of a letter by adding an apostrophe and the letter *s* if it would be confusing.

EXAMPLE i's

- Make the plural of a number by adding the letter *s*.

EXAMPLE 1990s

©AGS® American Guidance Service, Inc. Permission is granted to reproduce for classroom use only. **Basic English Composition**

Name ___ Period ___ Chapter 4 / Writing Tip 5

Spell It Right

Good writers check their words for spelling. They use a dictionary to check words they are not sure of. They memorize the spelling of words they use most often.

Here is a list of 50 words that people often misspell. Use it to check what you write. Use a dictionary for words that are not on this list.

acquaint	different	interesting	secretary
across	disappear	knowledge	separate
athletic	disappoint	library	similar
beautiful	doctor	minute	since
benefit	experience	necessary	speech
business	false	ninety	surprise
character	February	occasion	thorough
clothes	film	once	together
committee	finally	pleasant	true
decision	forty	privilege	usually
definite	government	realize	Wednesday
describe	grammar	recommend	which
description	immediately		

Here is a place to write words you often misspell. Look them up in a dictionary first to be sure the spelling is right. You can also use your own list to check what you write.

©AGS® American Guidance Service, Inc. Permission is granted to reproduce for classroom use only. **Basic English Composition**

Writing Tip 4   **Writing Tip 5**

Chapter 4

Spelling Counts!

M ost of the writing you will do in your lifetime will be for others to read. Be kind to your readers! Don't confuse them by writing one word when you mean another. Don't let misspelled words slow down your readers. Don't let misspellings make your readers think your message is not important. Your message *is* important. Make sure each word says what you mean.

Memorize the spelling of the words you use often. Keep a dictionary handy to check the spelling of words you use less often.

In Chapter 4, you will learn spelling rules and patterns. You will practice spelling words correctly.

Goals for Learning

▶ To choose the right homonym or the right word from easily confused pairs

▶ To use apostrophes correctly

▶ To spell plural nouns correctly

▶ To spell words with endings correctly

▶ To memorize the spellings of words that are often misspelled

73

Reading Vocabulary

apostrophe   memorize (6)
confuse (5)   misspell
lifetime   plural (6)

Introducing the Chapter

Have students examine the introductory photograph accompanying the first page of Chapter 4. Ask students for their ideas about who the two people in the photograph might be and what they seem to be doing. Tell students that anyone studying a school subject has many new terms to learn and to write about. Students may be able to suggest some terms associated with school subjects, including chemistry, which is being studied by the people in the photograph. Ask students why it is important to learn the spellings of new terms.

Name _____ Date _____ Period _____

Chapter 4
Community Connection
4

Using the Dictionary to Check Spellings

Some words are hard to spell. Sometimes special rules can help you to spell a word correctly. But for other words, you simply have to know which spelling is right. You can use a dictionary to help with spellings of these kinds of words. Follow these steps.

Step 1. Go back to Chapter 4 in the textbook. The chapter discusses words such as piece—peace, affect—effect, tomato—tomatoes, forgetting, and privilege. Write down five words from the chapter that are difficult for you to spell. Use the lines below.

1) _____

2) _____

3) _____

4) _____

5) _____

Step 2. Use a dictionary to look up each word. After each word, write the part of speech for the word.

EXAMPLE piece (noun)

Step 3. After the part of speech, write the definition.

Step 4. Get into a group with two of your classmates. Share with one another the problems you have with spelling the words correctly. Talk about tricks or hints that can help you use the correct spelling.

Step 5. Have your teacher check your work.

©AGS® American Guidance Service, Inc. Permission is granted to reproduce for classroom use only. Basic English Composition

Community Connection 4

SELF-STUDY GUIDE

Name _____

CHAPTER 4: Spelling Counts!

Goal 4.1 To choose the right homonym or the right word from easily confused pairs

Date	Assignment	Score
	1: Read pages 73-74. Complete Activities A-B on page 74.	
	2: Complete Activity C on page 75, Activity D on page 76, and Activity E on page 77.	
	3: Complete Activity F on page 78 and Activity G on page 79.	
	4: Complete the Lesson 1 Review, Parts A-B on page 80.	
	5: Complete Workbook Activity 14.	
	6: Complete Workbook Activity 15.	
	7: Complete Workbook Activity 16.	
	8: Read page 81. Complete Activity A on page 81 and Activity B on page 82.	
	9: Complete Activity C on page 83 and Activity D on page 84.	
	10: Complete the Lesson 2 Review, Parts A-B on page 85.	
	11: Complete Workbook Activity 17.	

Comments:

Goal 4.2 To use apostrophes correctly

Date	Assignment	Score
	12: Read page 86. Complete Activity A on page 86. Read page 87. Complete Activity B on page 87.	
	13: Read page 88. Complete Activity C on page 88 and Activities D-E on page 89.	
	14: Complete Workbook Activity 18.	
	15: Complete the Lesson 3 Review, Parts A-B on page 90.	

Comments:

©AGS® American Guidance Service, Inc. Permission is granted to reproduce for classroom use only. Basic English Composition

---

SELF-STUDY GUIDE

Name _____

CHAPTER 4 Spelling Counts!, continued

Goal 4.3 To spell plural nouns correctly

Date	Assignment	Score
	16: Read page 91. Complete Activity A on page 91. Read page 92. Complete Activity B on page 92. Read page 93. Complete Activity C on page 93.	
	17: Read page 94. Complete Activity D on page 94. Read page 95. Complete Activities E-G on page 95.	
	18: Read page 96. Complete Activity H on pages 96-97. Read page 97. Complete Activities I-J on page 97.	
	19: Complete the Lesson 4 Review, Parts A-B on page 98.	

Comments:

Goal 4.4 To spell words with endings correctly

Date	Assignment	Score
	20: Read page 99. Complete Activity A on page 99. Read page 100. Complete Activity B on page 100.	
	21: Complete the Lesson 5 Review, Parts A-B on page 101.	
	22: Read pages 102-103. Complete Activities A-C on page 103. Read page 104. Complete Activity D on page 104.	
	23: Complete the Lesson 6 Review, Parts A-B on page 105.	
	24: Read page 106. Complete Activity A on page 106. Complete Activities B-C on page 107.	
	25: Complete the Lesson 7 Review, Parts A-B on page 108.	

Comments:

Goal 4.5 To memorize the spellings of words that are often misspelled

Date	Assignment	Score
	26: Read page 109. Complete Activity A on page 109. Complete Activity B on page 110.	
	27: Complete the Lesson 8 Review, Parts A-B on page 111.	
	28: Complete Workbook Activity 19.	
	29: Complete the Chapter 4 Review, Parts A-C on pages 112-113.	

Comments:

Student's Signature _____ Date _____

Instructor's Signature _____ Date _____

©AGS® American Guidance Service, Inc. Permission is granted to reproduce for classroom use only. Basic English Composition

Chapter 4 Self-Study Guide

Lesson at a Glance

Chapter 4 Lesson 1

Overview This lesson distinguishes commonly confused homonyms, words that sound alike but have different meanings and spellings.

Objectives

- To recognize that some words that sound alike have different meanings and spellings.
- To choose the correct spelling of a homonym.

Student Pages 74–80

Teacher's Resource Library

Activities 13–14

Workbook Activities 14–16

Reading Vocabulary

homonyms (13)   verb
relationship (6)

Teaching Suggestions

■ Introducing the Lesson

Pronounce the word *to*, and ask students to spell it. Help them to see that unless the word appears in context, it is difficult to know which spelling to choose. Explain that with some English words, it is important to think about meaning—the choice of spelling depends on meaning.

■ Reviewing Skills Dictate

the following sentence to students: *Three dogs took my dog's toy*. After students write the sentence, review the sound-alike plural and possessive forms, *dogs* and *dog's*.

■ Presenting Activity A

Read and discuss the differences in meaning shown in the box on this page. Have students read aloud each sentence in Activity A before deciding which homonym fits in each position in the sentence.

Activity A Answers

1) two, to, to   2) too, to
3) two, to   4) too, to   5) too, to, two

> **Homonyms**
> *Words that sound alike but have different meanings and spellings.*

Say these words aloud: *to, two, too*. These words are **homonyms**. The English language has many sound-alike words, or homonyms. Make sure that you spell the homonym that fits with your meaning. Study the meanings and examples below.

to	Moving toward or showing a relationship. The bus drove **to** Dallas. Let's walk **to** the store. Stand next **to** me!	**too**	Very; also. I ate **too** much. Did you eat a lot, **too**?
to	A word used before a verb. We like **to** dance, **to** sing, and **to** have a good time.	**two**	A number. It is **two** o'clock. Do you want one or **two** bananas?

Activity A   Read each sentence below. Write the homonyms that correctly complete each sentence.

1) Mike ran (to, too, two) miles (to, too, two) get (to, too, two) school in time.

2) Mike was (to, too, two) out of breath (to, too, two) talk.

3) We have (to, too, two) questions (to, too, two) ask the mayor.

4) "I, (to, too, two), would like (to, too, two) know the answers," said the mayor.

5) If you have (to, too, two) many things (to, too, two) do at the same time, just do one or (to, too, two).

Activity B   Write one sentence on your paper that uses the words *to, too,* and *two*.

■ Presenting Activity B

Have students offer oral sentences using *to, two,* and *too* before proceeding to write of their own.

Activity B Answers

Sentences will vary. A sample sentence is given.

My two sisters want to come with me, too.

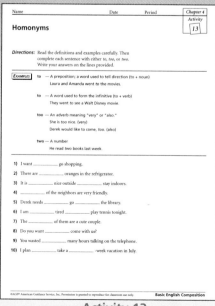

Activity 13

Activity C   Read about each pair of homonyms. Rewrite each sentence using the correct homonym.

all ready	Completely prepared. We are **all ready** for the party.	already	Before; previously. We have **already** finished our work.

1) Derek is (all ready, already) for his next race.

2) Derek has (all ready, already) won his first race.

3) The students have done their homework (all ready, already).

4) Are we (all ready, already) for the show?

hear	To receive a sound through the ears. I **hear** you loud and clear.	here	In this place. We'll meet **here** later.

5) Did you (hear, here) the news?

6) I did not (hear, here) what you said.

7) Laura will be (hear, here) soon.

8) Which people were (hear, here) first?

weak	Not strong. Illness makes people feel **weak**.	week	Seven days. Carlos works two evenings a **week**.

9) Ms. Lentz likes to drink (weak, week) tea.

10) Derek runs thirty miles every (weak, week).

11) This is the third (weak, week) of the month.

12) Have you ever felt (weak, week) in the knees?

Reading Vocabulary

homework   previously
illness   rewrite

■ Presenting Activity C

Before students proceed with the activity, write each pair of homonyms on the board. Read aloud the sentences in the example box, and have students tell which spelling fits with each meaning.

Activity C Answers

1) Derek is all ready for his next race.   **2)** Derek has already won his first race.   **3)** The students have done their homework already.   **4)** Are we all ready for the show?   **5)** Did you hear the news?   **6)** I did not hear what you said.   **7)** Laura will be here soon.   **8)** Which people were here first?   **9)** Ms. Lentz likes to drink weak tea.   **10)** Derek runs thirty miles every week.   **11)** This is the third week of the month.   **12)** Have you ever felt weak in the knees?

TEACHER ALERT

Some students may have learned the term *homophone* for words that sound alike but have different spellings. Point out that *homonym* names a more general category. In addition to words that sound alike but have different spellings, homonyms may be words that look alike but have different meanings. (When I came up to *bat,* a *bat* flew overhead.)

Reading Vocabulary

absence (6)   hip (5)
atmosphere (5) playoff
carelessly   section (5)
forecast (6)

■ **Presenting Activity D**

Have students use their own words to explain the difference in meaning between each pair of homonyms.

Activity D Answers

1) piece 2) piece 3) peace
4) piece 5) weather
6) whether 7) whether
8) weather 9) waist 10) waste
11) waste 12) waist

TEACHER ALERT

Offer students this memory helper to remember that the spelling *piece* refers to a part or section: a **pie**ce of **pie**.

Activity D   Read about each pair of homonyms. Write the homonym that correctly completes each sentence.

piece	A part or section. Take another **piece** of pie.	**peace**	The absence of war; calm. Can we have some **peace** and quiet, please?

1) One (piece, peace) is missing from the puzzle.

2) The town set aside a (piece, peace) of land for a park.

3) The fighting stopped, and (piece, peace) arrived at last.

4) Put a (piece, peace) of cheese on that sandwich.

whether	A word used to introduce two choices. **Whether** the team wins or loses, it will still be in the playoffs.	**weather**	The condition of the atmosphere at a certain time and place. The **weather** changed from hot to cold.

5) The (whether, weather) is clear and sunny today.

6) Derek does not know (whether, weather) to go to his job.

7) Can you tell (whether, weather) it will rain?

8) It is not easy to forecast the (whether, weather) in New England.

waist	Part of the body between hips and ribs. A belt fits around the **waist**.	**waste**	Trash; to use up carelessly. That basket is for **waste**. Do not **waste** paper.

9) Those pants are too big around the (waist, waste).

10) The factory dumped (waist, waste) into the river.

11) Do not (waist, waste) your time.

12) Step into the water up to your (waist, waste).

Activity E Read about each pair of homonyms. Rewrite each sentence using the correct homonym.

brake	Something that stops or slows motion; to stop or slow the motion. The driver used the **brake** to **brake** the car.	break	To separate into pieces; an interruption or pause. Did that cup **break** while you were on a coffee **break**?

1) The TV show had one commercial (brake, break).

2) The child did not mean to (brake, break) the window.

3) When you wish to (brake, break), step on the pedal.

4) Mike needs to fix the (brake, break) on his bicycle.

past	Of a time gone by; times that have gone by. We studied the **past** and learned about **past** events.	passed	Past tense of pass. The student **passed** the test.

5) During the (past, passed) week, Derek ran thirty miles.

6) When he ran, Derek (past, passed) Ms. Lentz's station.

7) Derek was happy when he (past, passed) his test.

8) The storm finally (past, passed).

council	A group that meets to discuss issues or to govern. The town **council** has six members.	counsel	Advice; to give advice. The king ignored his minister's wise **counsel**. The minister tried to **counsel** against war.

9) The teacher offered to (council, counsel) the student.

10) The student listened to the teacher's (council, counsel).

11) The student (council, counsel) meets every week.

12) The (council, counsel) voted against a tax increase.

Reading Vocabulary

advice (5)	interruption
brake (5)	issue (6)
commercial (6)	member (5)
council (4)	minister (5)
counsel (6)	separate (5)
discuss (5)	student (5)
govern (6)	tax (5)
ignore (5)	tense (6)
increase (5)	

■ **Presenting Activity E**
Have students use their own words to explain the difference in meaning between each pair of homonyms.

Activity E Answers

1) The TV show had one commercial break. **2)** The child did not mean to break the window. **3)** When you wish to brake, step on the pedal. **4)** Mike needs to fix the brake on his bicycle. **5)** During the past week, Derek ran thirty miles. **6)** When he ran, Derek passed Ms. Lentz's station. **7)** Derek was happy when he passed his test. **8)** The storm finally passed. **9)** The teacher offered to counsel the student. **10)** The student listened to the teacher's counsel. **11)** The student council meets every week. **12)** The council voted against a tax increase.

APPLICATION

In the Community
Tell students that businesses often use word plays based on homonyms. Write on the board this advertisement from an auto repair shop: *We'll fix it so it brakes.* Discuss the meaning of the ad, and have students offer their own examples of word plays from businesses in the community. (The names of hairstyling shops might be a good place to begin: "Shear Pleasure," "Hair Today," and so on.)

Reading Vocabulary

farmland   woodworking
shorten

■ Presenting Activity F

Before students proceed with the activity, write each pair or set of homonyms on the board. Read aloud the example sentences, and have students tell which spelling fits with each meaning.

Activity F Answers

1) through   2) threw
3) through   4) through
5) plain   6) plane   7) plain
8) plane   9) There   10) their
11) there

Activity F   Read about each pair or set of homonyms. Write the homonym that correctly completes each sentence.

through	Finished; in and out of. We will be **through** with our trip after we pass **through** this tunnel.	threw	Past tense of throw. Who **threw** that tomato?

1) Mike walked (through, threw) the door.
2) Mike (through, threw) the basketball to Derek.
3) We hope that your troubles are (through, threw).
4) The storm passed (through, threw) quickly.

plain	Clear and simple; not fancy. The woman wore a **plain** dress.	plane	A woodworking tool for making a surface smooth and flat; to use a plane to smooth a surface. The carpenter used a **plane** to **plane** the shelf.
plain	A flat area of land. Grass grew on the **plain**.		
plane	A flat surface; an airplane. The math students learned about lines that form a **plane**.		

5) "I like (plain, plane) cooking," said Mr. O'Hara.
6) Have you ever flown on a (plain, plane)?
7) Settlers found good farmland on the (plain, plane).
8) Before you sand the wood, (plain, plane) it.

their	Belonging to them. All the students have **their** homework.	there	A word used to introduce a sentence. **There** are three children in the family.
there	At that place or time. Park the car over **there**.	they're	A shortened form of *they are*. If Luis and Tom are late, **they're** in trouble.

9) (Their, There, They're) is more than one way to solve a problem.
10) Which towns have (their, there, they're) own libraries?
11) We're driving to Savannah. Will it take us long to get (their, there, they're)?

Activity G   Read about each set of homonyms. Rewrite each sentence using the correct homonym.

principal	First in importance; the head of a school. What is the **principal** job of a school **principal**?	**principle**	A basic truth; a rule. The **principle** of freedom must be protected.
principal	The amount of money on which interest is charged or paid. Loan payments include interest and **principal**.		

1) The _____ city of Massachusetts is Boston.
2) We hope our leaders have high _____.
3) This bank charges high interest on the _____ of a loan.
4) An important _____ in America is freedom.
5) The _____ of the middle school is Mr. Chang.

capital	The city in which state or national government is based; relating to the seat of government. Washington, D.C. is the **capital** of the United States. What is the **capital** city of your state?	**capital**	A sum of money. To set up a business, a person needs **capital**.
capital	An uppercase letter. A proper noun begins with a **capital**.	**capitol**	A building in which state lawmakers meet. The state **capitol** has a statue on top of it.
capital	Punishable by death. Treason is a **capital** crime.	**Capitol**	The building in Washington, D.C. in which the Congress of the United States meets. The senator spoke on the steps of the **Capitol**.

6) Mr. Takemura visited Paris, the _____ of France.
7) Always use a _____ letter to begin the name of a month.
8) Mike visited the _____ in Washington, D.C.
9) The two women agreed to combine their _____ to start a business.
10) A golden dome is on the _____ in Des Moines, Iowa.
11) Would it be unjust to make burglary a _____ offense?

Reading Vocabulary

basic (7)	offense (6)
burglary	payment (7)
capital (5)	principal (5)
capitol (5)	principle (5)
combine (6)	punishable
Congress (5)	relate (6)
crime (5)	senator (6)
lawmaker	treason (6)
loan (5)	unjust
noun	uppercase

■ Presenting Activity G

Write the words *principle, principal, capital, capitol,* and *Capitol* on the board. Have students use each in an oral sentence before proceeding with Activity G.

Activity G Answers

1) The principal city of Massachusetts is Boston.   **2)** We hope our leaders have high principles.   **3)** This bank charges high interest on the principal of a loan.   **4)** An important principle in America is freedom.   **5)** The principal of the middle school is Mr. Chang.   **6)** Mr. Takemura visited Paris, the capital of France.   **7)** Always use a capital letter to begin the name of a month.   **8)** Mike visited the Capitol in Washington, D.C.   **9)** The two women agreed to combine their capital to start a business.   **10)** A golden dome is on the capitol in Des Moines, Iowa.   **11)** Would it be unjust to make burglary a capital offense?

Name	Date	Period	Chapter 4
			Activity
			14

Sound-Alike Words

Directions: Read all the meanings for the words listed below. Complete each sentence with *capital* or *capitol*. Write your answers on the lines provided. Capitalize the word *capitol* only if it refers to the building in Washington, D.C.

capital	(noun)	the seat of government of a state or a country
capital	(noun)	a sum of money
capital	(adjective)	punishable by death
capital	(noun or adjective)	an uppercase letter
capitol	(noun)	a building in which lawmakers meet
Capitol	(noun)	the building in Washington, D.C., where the United States senators and representatives meet to make laws

1) A _____ letter is always used at the beginning of a sentence.
2) Many people believe in _____ punishment.
3) I visited the _____ in Washington, D.C.
4) The _____ of Texas is Austin.
5) On a field trip, we visited the state _____ building.
6) The man was convicted of a _____ crime.
7) The United States senators and representatives meet in the _____ building.
8) What is the _____ of your state?
9) The lawmakers meet in the _____ .
10) Proper nouns always begin with a _____ letter.

Activity 14

Reading Vocabulary

adult (6)   original (5)
cloudy   parentheses
decision (5)   repay (5)

Part A Answers

1) council   2) weather   3) capital
4) hear   5) their   6) passed
7) principal   8) capital
9) principal   10) too

Part B Answers

Sentences will vary.

Follow-up Activity

Offer students oral riddles in which the answer is a pair of homonyms; have students who guess the answer come to the board to write the homonyms in the correct order. Examples: *What do you call a 747 that is not fancy?* (a plain plane) *What do you answer when someone asks, "Why aren't they here?"* (They're there.) Students may offer their own riddles using homonyms in addition to those in this lesson.

Homonyms are words that sound alike but have different meanings and spellings. When you are writing, you must think about which meaning you want your readers to understand. Then use the spelling that matches that meaning.

Part A   Choose the word in parentheses that correctly completes the sentence. Write the word on your paper.

1) The members of the queen's (counsel, council) met in a large hall.

2) Is the (whether, weather) expected to turn cloudy?

3) What city is the (capitol, capital, Capitol) of Ecuador?

4) No one could (here, hear) the speaker.

5) Adults may make (there, their, they're) own decisions.

6) After being rescued, the woman said, "My life (past, passed) before my eyes!"

7) "To be honest with others has been my (principle, principal) rule in life," said Mr. Corelli.

8) "Say, Dad," Derek said. "I seem to need a little (capital, capitol, Capitol)."

9) "I'll make you a loan. You can repay the (principal, principle) at five dollars a week."

10) "OK, that's not (to, too, two) much," Derek agreed.

Part B   Write an original sentence with each word below.

1) through   6) week
2) threw   7) plain
3) waste   8) plane
4) waist   9) already
5) weak   10) break

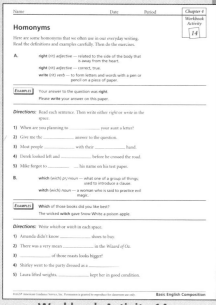

Workbook Activity 14

Workbook Activity 15

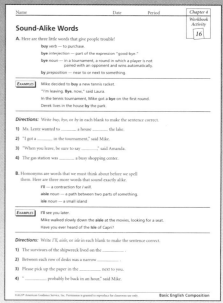

Workbook Activity 16

Some pairs of English words can confuse a speller. The words look and sound *almost* alike. It helps to pronounce each word exactly. Then you can choose the correct spelling.

Be sure to choose the spelling that fits your meaning. Try using the word in your sentence. Look at the dictionary to be sure you have the spelling that fits your meaning.

Compare the spellings of these two words. Pronounce each one carefully. Read about their different meanings and uses.

advice	Suggestions or information. Used as a noun. The counselor gave helpful **advice**.	**advise**	To give suggestions or information. Used as a verb. What did the counselor **advise** you to do?

Activity A Read each sentence below. Write the word on your paper that correctly completes each sentence.

1) The president's cabinet gives him (advice, advise).

2) Cabinet members (advice, advise) the president.

3) Some people like to give (advice, advise) to others.

4) People don't always take others' (advice, advise).

5) "I need someone to (advice, advise) me," said Mike.

6) The counselor gave Mike useful (advice, advise).

Lesson at a Glance

Chapter 4   Lesson 2

Overview This lesson treats common "confusables"—pairs of words that sound similar but have different spellings and meanings.

Objective
- To choose the right word from easily confused pairs.

Student Pages 81–85

Teacher's Resource Library
Activity 15
Workbook Activity 17

Reading Vocabulary

cabinet (5)   exact (6)
compare (5)   speller
counselor   suggestion (5)

Teaching Suggestions

- **Introducing the Lesson**
Tell students to listen especially carefully to this sentence: *It was quite quiet.* Have them pronounce the two different words that end the sentence. Volunteers may come to the board to write the words.

- **Reviewing Skills** Review the distinction between a noun and a verb. Have students give examples of nouns and of verbs. Then have students use the word *break* as a noun and as a verb.

- **Presenting Activity A**
Pronounce the words *advise* and *advice* with slight exaggeration. Have students tell which one is used as a verb and which is used as a noun.

Activity A Answers
1) advice 2) advise 3) advice
4) advice 5) advise 6) advice

TEACHER ALERT

Hearing slight differences in pronunciation may be difficult for nonnative English speakers. Pronunciation may also vary in different regions. Pronounce the words in this lesson with extra emphasis on the phonic distinctions as needed.

Activity 15

Activity B   Read about each pair of words. Write the word on your paper that correctly completes each sentence.

than	A word used in a comparison. Jon's feet are bigger **than** his father's.	**then**	At that time; soon afterward. **Then** what happened?

1) Laura likes swimming more (than, then) tennis.

2) Back (than, then), my family lived in Mexico.

3) I think that Amanda is older (than, then) Laura.

4) First we cried, and (than, then) we laughed.

quite	Completely; truly. I am not **quite** done reading.	**quiet**	Silent; making almost no noise. It's peaceful and **quiet** here.

5) We took a walk through the (quite, quiet) woods.

6) We took (quite, quiet) a long walk!

7) This car has such a (quite, quiet) ride!

8) "Please be (quite, quiet)," said the librarian.

were	Past tense of the verb *be*. The children **were** in bed.	**where**	At or in what place. **Where** did the children sleep?

9) (Were, Where) is Mexico?

10) We (were, where) waiting for you for an hour!

11) Carlos and his brother (were, where) sharing a room.

12) "I do not know (were, where) I put my glasses," said Mr. Corelli.

Activity C Read about each pair of words. Rewrite each sentence using the word that correctly completes it.

affect	To influence someone or something. Used as a verb. How does hot weather **affect** you?	**effect**	The result; the influence that one thing has on something else. Used as a noun. One **effect** of cold weather is dry skin.

1) Sleepiness is one side (affect, effect) of this medicine.

2) The sad song had no (affect, effect) on Valerie.

3) Smoke from factories does (affect, effect) air quality.

personal	Private; having to do with a particular person. A diary is a **personal** form of writing.	**personnel**	The employees of a business. A company vice president was in charge of **personnel**.

4) Send your job application to the (personal, personnel) office.

5) Please lock your (personal, personnel) belongings in the safe.

6) This is a (personal, personnel) matter between my friend and me.

formally	In a formal or socially polite way; according to ceremony or rules. The guests dressed **formally** for the wedding.	**formerly**	Of a former, or earlier, time. Computers now do much of the work **formerly** done by bank tellers.

7) The city held a parade to honor the hero (formally, formerly).

8) Ms. Hall (formally, formerly) lived in Chicago.

9) Do you know how to write (formally, formerly)?

Reading Vocabulary

affect (5)	formerly (7)
application (8)	influence (6)
ceremony (5)	personal (6)
computer (8)	personnel (11)
diary (6)	quality (5)
employee (6)	sleepiness
formally	

■ **Presenting Activity C**

Have students read each pair of words aloud with extra emphasis on the sound distinctions.

Activity C Answers

1) Sleepiness is one side effect of this medicine. 2) The sad song had no effect on Valerie.
3) Smoke from factories does affect air quality. 4) Send your job application to the personnel office. 5) Please lock your personal belongings in the safe.
6) This is a personal matter between my friend and me.
7) The city held a parade to honor the hero formally.
8) Ms. Hall formerly lived in Chicago. 9) Do you know how to write formally?

APPLICATION

 Career Connection
Ask students why it would be extremely important to spell *personnel* correctly when applying for a job to a personnel department. Help students to recognize that using correct spelling may not get them the job, but using incorrect spelling may prevent them from being considered.

Reading Vocabulary

adjective   prefer (6)
apology (7)   select (5)
democracy (6) style (5)
misplace (8)   willingly

■ Presenting Activity D

Go over the pronunciations and meanings of each word with students. Then have them offer their own oral sentences with each word to show each meaning given.

Activity D Answers

1) loose 2) lose 3) lose
4) loose 5) choose 6) chose
7) choose 8) choose
9) except 10) accept
11) accept 12) except

LEARNING STYLES

Interpersonal/Group Learning

Divide the class into groups of four. Ask each group to write a story that uses the "sound-alike" words on pages 81–84. Encourage all the members in each group to participate in creating the characters, situation, and plot of the story. Afterward, invite each group to read its story. As the group reads, ask the other students to raise their hand when they hear one of the sound-alike words and to spell it aloud.

Activity D Read about each pair of words. Write the word on your paper that correctly completes each sentence.

loose	Free; not tight. Used as an adjective. **Loose** clothing is in style.	lose	To misplace; to fail to win. Used as a verb. One team must **lose**.

1) Laura preferred a (loose, lose) belt.

2) Did you (loose, lose) your money?

3) I hope that Derek does not (loose, lose) the race.

4) Don't let Benjy get (loose, lose); he might run away.

choose	To pick out or select. In a democracy, voters **choose** their leaders.	chose	Past tense of *to choose*; picked out or selected. (The word *chose* is never used with a helping verb such as *must, did, have,* or *should.*) Last month the voters **chose** their leaders.

5) "Did you (choose, chose) your dessert yet?" asked Laura.

6) "Yes, I (choose, chose) the orange," said Amanda.

7) "I think I will (choose, chose) the pineapple," said Laura.

8) "Maybe I should (choose, chose) the banana," said Amanda.

accept	To receive willingly. Used as a verb. I **accept** your apology.	except	Other than; if not for the fact that; but. Everyone was there **except** me.

9) Laura always says, "I have everything I need (accept, except) money."

10) Amanda would not (accept, except) the gift.

11) The company did (accept, except) Mike for the job.

12) That cat never comes home (accept, except) to eat.

Lesson 2 | Review

Words that sound nearly alike can confuse spellers. When you write, choose the spelling that fits with your meaning. Pronounce the word especially carefully to remember which spelling fits.

Part A Read the sentence or sentences. Choose the word in parentheses that correctly completes each sentence. Write the words in the correct order on your paper.

1) Amanda always thought she was more interested in art (then, than) math, but (then, than) she discovered geometry.

2) "I can give you (advise, advice)," said Ms. Lawson. "But I also (advise, advice) you to make your own decision."

3) Students (formerly, formally) dressed more (formerly, formally) for school than they do today.

4) At day's end, Mr. Corelli felt (quiet, quite) tired. He hoped for a (quiet, quite) evening at home.

5) How did the storm (affect, effect) the land? The loss of trees was one (affect, effect).

6) Someone in the (personal, personnel) department may be able to help workers who have (personal, personnel) problems.

7) Laura feared she might (lose, loose) the ring because it was so (lose, loose) on her finger.

8) Ms. O'Hara wondered (were, where) the lost keys (were, where).

9) Mike (choose, chose) a course that would help him (choose, chose) a career.

10) "I will (accept, except) every excuse (accept, except) laziness," said Mr. Chang.

Part B Write one original sentence for each word below.

1) personal
2) quiet
3) except
4) formerly
5) chose

Reading Vocabulary

geometry (8)   loss (5)
laziness

Part A Answers

1) than, then 2) advice, advise
3) formerly, formally 4) quite, quiet 5) affect, effect
6) personnel, personal 7) lose, loose 8) where, were 9) chose, choose 10) accept, except

Part B Answers

Sentences will vary.

Follow-up Activity

Have students work with partners to write one sentence that contains pairs of words from this lesson. Encourage partners to work with nearly all the word pairs. They may use the Part A sentences as models, and you may offer other examples: *We were here, but where were you? Watch out for that loose shoelace, or we might lose the race.*

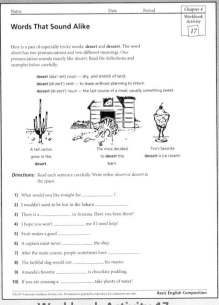

Workbook Activity 17

Chapter 4   Lesson 3

Overview This lesson focuses on the distinction between a contraction, which is made with an apostrophe, and a possessive pronoun, which has no apostrophe.

Objectives

- To use an apostrophe correctly in contractions.
- To spell contractions and possessive pronouns correctly.

Student Pages 86–90

Teacher's Resource Library
Workbook Activity 18

Reading Vocabulary
contraction (9)   informal (7)
dialogue (7)

Teaching Suggestions

■ Introducing the Lesson
Write the word *contract* on the board, and use it in this oral sentence: *The pupil of your eye will contract in bright light.* Discuss the meaning of *contract* that applies in that sentence: "to shrink or get smaller." Then change the word *contract* to *contraction.* Discuss with students why words such as *aren't* and *I'll* are called contractions.

■ Reviewing Skills In Chapter 3, Lesson 6, students worked with apostrophes in possessive nouns. Have students look again at the items from Part A of the Lesson Review on page 69. Discuss the correct answers.

■ Presenting Activity A
Have students use each of the boxed contractions in an oral sentence before proceeding with Activity A.

Activity A Answers
1) hadn't 2) wouldn't
3) Shouldn't 4) Aren't
5) haven't 6) doesn't
7) don't 8) isn't

Contraction

A shortened form of one or two words. An apostrophe stands for the missing letters (they're, he'll, jumpin').

In Chapter 3, you saw how an apostrophe (') is used to show possession in nouns. Notice the apostrophe in these three examples: *Marie's dog, the students' homework, the children's room.*

The apostrophe is also used to stand for missing letters in a **contraction**.

Contractions are most often used in informal writing—notes and friendly letters, for example. You may want to use contractions to show spoken words in dialogue, too.

Here is a list of some commonly used contractions. They are all made of a verb and the word *not.*

aren't = are not	**hasn't** = has not
isn't = is not	**haven't** = have not
can't = cannot	**hadn't** = had not
doesn't = does not	**wouldn't** = would not
don't = do not	**couldn't** = could not
weren't = were not	**shouldn't** = should not
won't = will not	**didn't** = did not

Activity A Find the eight contractions in the following paragraphs. Rewrite each contraction correctly on your paper.

> Derek Corelli hadnt missed a day of practice in weeks. He wouldnt go anywhere but the track.
> "Shouldnt your coach give you a rest?" asked his mother. "Arent you working too hard?"
> "I want to be ready for the next meet," Derek replied. "I havent got much time left."
> "I sent a note to Aunt Lydia," said Ms. Corelli. "She doesnt want to miss your event. We will cheer for you. But please dont worry about winning or losing. Just have fun!"
> "That is what mothers are supposed to say," said Derek. "But losing isnt in my plans!"

Here are more contractions. Study the list.

I'd = I would, I had	**we'll** = we will
I'll = I will	**we're** = we are
I'm = I am	**we've** = we have
I've = I have	**they'd** = they would, they had
you'll = you will	**they're** = they are
you're = you are	**they've** = they have
you've = you have	**that's** = that is, that has
he's = he is, he has	**what's** = what is, what has
she's = she is, she has	**who's** = who is, who has
it's = it is, it has	**there's** = there is
let's = let us	**here's** = here is

Activity B   Rewrite the bold words as contractions on your paper.

1) **I had** never seen a rodeo before.

2) Now **I would** like to see a rodeo again.

3) Amanda says that **she has** never been in a plane.

4) The Leungs say that **they are** sure that **they will** take the trip.

5) **It is** true that **they have** gone.

6) **There is** still time to get to a movie, so **let us** find out **what is** playing.

Reading Vocabulary
definition (6)   possessive
ownership (7)   purr

■ Presenting Activity C
Write *it's* and *its* on the board. Read aloud the example sentences from the first box, and have students tell which word fits with each meaning.

Activity C Answers
1) it's **2)** its **3)** Its, its **4)** its, It's **5)** It's, its **6)** its

---

Some possessive pronouns and contractions are homonyms. They sound alike. Only the contraction is spelled with an apostrophe, however. Be careful NOT to use an apostrophe with a possessive pronoun. Two commonly confused homonyms are *its* and *it's*.

its	A possessive pronoun used to show ownership. Do you see that house? **Its** roof needs fixing.	**it's**	A contraction of *it is.* Whenever **it's** raining, the roof leaks.

Activity C   Read the sentences. Choose the word or words that correctly complete the sentence. Write the words in the correct order on your paper.

1) "That kitten is crying. I think (its, it's) hungry," said Laura.

2) "I wonder where (its, it's) owner is," she added.

3) "(Its, It's) name is on (its, it's) collar," said Amanda.

4) She looked at (its, it's) tag. "(Its, It's) called Fluffy."

5) "(Its, It's) friendly," said Amanda as the kitten purred and licked (its, it's) fur.

6) Then Fluffy trotted off to (its, it's) home.

Study the definitions and example sentences for the following homonyms. Notice that the possessive pronouns do NOT have apostrophes.

your	A possessive pronoun used to show ownership.	**whose**	A possessive pronoun used to show ownership.
you're	A contraction of *you are.* If **you're** late for practice, **your** coach may be angry.	**who's**	A contraction of *who is* or *who has.* **Who's** that tall player? No one knows **whose** team he is on.

Activity D Look for the words *your, you're, whose,* and *who's* in the sentences below. Copy each correct word on your paper. Rewrite each incorrect word.

1) "Where are your shoes, Derek?" asked the coach.

2) "I don't know," Derek said. "Whose seen my lucky shoes?"

3) "Do you all have you're own shoes?" the coach asked the team.

4) "Aren't you're shoes always in your bag?" asked the coach.

5) "Look whose coming! Look whose shoes Benjy has!"

6) "Your a good dog, Benjy," cried Derek.

Study the definitions and example sentences for the following homonyms. Notice that the possessive pronouns do NOT have apostrophes.

their	A possessive pronoun used to show ownership.	**theirs**	A possessive pronoun used to show ownership.
they're	A contraction of *they are.*	**there's**	A contraction of *there is.*
	Springfield fans wait for **their** team to score. **They're** ready to give a big cheer.		**There's** a mixup over sandwiches. Which sandwiches are ours? Which are yours? Which are **theirs**?

Activity E Choose the word that correctly completes the sentence. Write the word on your paper.

1) "(Theirs, There's) my dad!" Derek called out.

2) Derek's parents waved from (their, they're) seats in the stands.

3) When your neighbors are home, please ring (their, they're) bell.

4) If (there's, theirs) no answer, leave a note.

5) We made our plans, and they made (there's, theirs).

6) (There's, Theirs) no chance to change our plans.

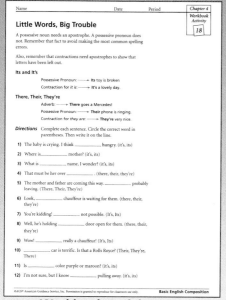

Workbook Activity 18

Reading Vocabulary
mixup

- **Presenting Activity D**
Write *your, you're, whose,* and *who's* on the board. Read aloud each example sentence from the second box on page 88. Have students give the spelling of each word that fits in the sentence.

Activity D Answers
1) your **2)** Who's **3)** your
4) your, your **5)** who's, whose
6) You're

- **Presenting Activity E**
Write the words *their, they're, theirs,* and *there's* on the board. Have students use each in an oral sentence.

Activity E Answers
1) There's **2)** their **3)** their
4) there's **5)** theirs **6)** There's

LEARNING STYLES

 Logical/Mathematical
Ask each student to list in alphabetical order the contractions on pages 86–89. Then challenge them to create a short sentence for each one to illustrate its use. Discuss the sentences and devise a group list of contractions and sentences. Invite interested students to memorize the list. In the following days, call on these students to recite from memory the list of contractions and the sample sentences.

Reading Vocabulary

competition (7)   leash (5)
error (6)   shoelace

Part A Answers

1) I'm 2) you've 3) I've 4) I'd
5) couldn't 6) wasn't 7) wasn't
8) I'll 9) I'm 10) There's

Part B Answers

1) It's about time they changed
their minds! 2) If there's a
problem, let's solve it. 3) Last
month Derek was strong, but now
he's even stronger. 4) We'd like to
join your team. 5) "Your story
isn't easy to believe," said the
coach. 6) "There's a dog named
Benjy that's fond of chewing up
shoelaces," explained Derek.
7) Shouldn't you be resting before
your big game? 8) "If this isn't my
coat, whose is it?" asked Mr. Corelli.
9) The dog needs its walk; here's its
leash. 10) Some of his friends are
also hers.

Follow-up Activity

Write the pairs of words below on the
board. Have students work with partners to write one or two sentences in
which both words are used correctly.

• theirs, there's

• whose, who's

• they're, their

• its, it's

• your, you're

To spell a word that may or may not have an apostrophe,
remember these rules.

• A contraction must have an apostrophe. The apostrophe
  stands for the missing letters.
• A possessive pronoun NEVER has an apostrophe.
• When a possessive pronoun and a contraction are
  homonyms, be especially careful. Remember to use the
  spelling that fits with your meaning.

Part A   Read Derek's paragraphs. Find ten mistakes made
with contractions. Write each word correctly on your paper.

My Second Race

  Im sure youve guessed by now that Ive won my second
race. Id arrived at the track before eight in the morning.
I just couldnt sleep! The competition wasnt so good at
the first race. I must say, the second school wasnt much
better! Ha!
  "Ill win by several seconds," I said to myself.
  And I did! Im planning to set a new record in my third
race! Theres more to come, fans.

Part B   Find the error in each of these sentences. Rewrite the
sentence correctly on your paper.

1) Its about time they changed their minds!
2) If theres a problem, let's solve it.
3) Last month Derek was strong, but now hes' even stronger.
4) We'd like to join you're team.
5) "Your story isnt easy to believe," said the coach.
6) "There's a dog named Benjy thats fond of chewing up
   shoelaces," explained Derek.
7) Shouldn't you be resting before you're big game?
8) "If this isn't my coat, who's is it?" asked Mr. Corelli.
9) The dog needs it's walk; here's its leash.
10) Some of his friends are also her's.

A singular noun names one person, place, thing, or idea. A plural noun names more than one person, place, thing, or idea. Here are two rules for making plural nouns.

1. Add -s to make most nouns plural.

EXAMPLES	Singular	Plural
	noun	nouns
	rule	rules
	subject	subjects
	key	keys

2. If a noun ends in -s, -z, -x, -sh, or -ch, then add -es to make it plural.

EXAMPLES	Singular	Plural
	guess	guesses
	buzz	buzzes
	ax	axes
	leash	leashes
	watch	watches

Activity A   Write the plural form of each of these singular nouns on your paper.

1) speech		11) box	
2) teacher		12) word	
3) house		13) noun	
4) waltz		14) letter	
5) branch		15) church	
6) dish		16) fox	
7) beach		17) desk	
8) shoe		18) paper	
9) school		19) bus	
10) race		20) book	

Lesson at a Glance

Chapter 4   Lesson 4

Overview This lesson presents spelling patterns for forming plurals.

Objective

■ To spell plural nouns correctly.

Student Pages 91–98

Reading Vocabulary

buzz	subject (5)
singular (8)	waltz (6)

Teaching Suggestions

■ **Introducing the Lesson**
Play a rapid naming game with students. Call out a noun, either singular or plural, and have them name the corresponding plural or singular form.

■ **Reviewing Skills** Write each of the following sentence subjects on the board. Have students make an oral sentence using each subject and the verb *are/is* or *has/have*.

• Many people . . .

• One person . . .

• Animals . . .

• This street . . .

• Cities . . .

■ **Presenting Activity A**
Go over the two rules on this page. Have students listen for the slightly different ending sounds in the plural nouns. They should hear the *s* and *z* sounds, as well as an unstressed vowel sound in words with the *-es* ending.

Activity A Answers

1) speeches 2) teachers
3) houses 4) waltzes
5) branches 6) dishes
7) beaches 8) shoes
9) schools 10) races
11) boxes 12) words
13) nouns 14) letters
15) churches 16) foxes
17) desks 18) papers
19) buses 20) books

Reading Vocabulary

bully (5)   guy (6)
column (5)   relay (6)
consonant   salary (5)
delay (5)   vowel (6)

■ Presenting Activity B

Tell students that when they are spelling a plural, they must think about the singular form of the word. For example, if they are writing *cities*, they should picture the word *city* in order to add the ending correctly.

Activity B Answers

1) fly   flies
2) toy   toys
3) valley   valleys
4) activity activities
5) turkey   turkeys
6) delay   delays
7) bully   bullies
8) salary   salaries
9) cry   cries
10) copy   copies
11) army   armies
12) candy   candies

GLOBAL CONNECTION

Point out that all over the world, speakers have developed ways of distinguishing singular and plural forms. List a few singular nouns on the board. Ask students who speak languages other than English to name the corresponding word in another language and pronounce the plural form for classmates.

Nouns Ending With -*y*

Some nouns end with a vowel before the letter *y*. If there is a vowel before *y*, just add -*s* to make a plural noun. (The vowels include *a*, *e*, *i*, *o*, and *u*.)

EXAMPLES	Singular	Plural
	boy	boys
	monkey	monkeys
	guy	guys
	relay	relays

Some nouns end with a consonant before the *y*. Then you must change the *y* to *i* and add -*es* to make a plural noun.

EXAMPLES	Singular	Plural
	city	cities
	story	stories
	penny	pennies

Activity B   Make two columns on your paper. Write the following twelve nouns in column 1. Then write the plural of each noun in column 2.

1) fly
2) toy
3) valley
4) activity
5) turkey
6) delay
7) bully
8) salary
9) cry
10) copy
11) army
12) candy

Nouns Ending With -f or -fe

Some singular nouns end with -f or -fe. Sometimes you just add -s to make a plural noun. At other times, you must change the f to v and add -s or -es. How can you tell what to do? Try pronouncing the plural noun carefully. Listen for the f or v sound.

EXAMPLES	Singular	Plural
	roof	roofs
	belief	beliefs
	leaf	leaves
	wife	wives

Activity C   Read each singular noun below. Then say its plural form aloud. Write the correct plural on your paper.

1) calf

2) thief

3) life

4) knife

5) chief

6) cliff

7) wolf

8) giraffe

9) shelf

10) chef

Reading Vocabulary
chef (7)

- **Presenting Activity C**
Pronounce each of the listed words and its plural form. Then have students repeat the singular and plural forms aloud.

Activity C Answers
1) calves 2) thieves 3) lives
4) knives 5) chiefs 6) cliffs
7) wolves 8) giraffes
9) shelves 10) chefs

Reading Vocabulary

banjo (5)   stereo
bore (5)   tattoo (7)
shampoo (6)   veto (8)
solo (6)   video

■ **Presenting Activity D**

Have students read aloud the words listed in the boxes. Discuss meanings of any unfamiliar words.

Activity D Answers

1) shampoos   2) videos
3) rodeos   4) potatoes
5) echoes   6) banjos

TEACHER ALERT

Although the plural of a musical term ending in consonant -o is generally made by adding -s, there is no hard rule about forming plurals of other words ending in consonant -o. Show students how to use a dictionary to check plural formation. Look up the words *hero*, *mosquito*, and *halo*.

Nouns Ending With -o

A few nouns end with the letter *o*. If there is a vowel before the *o*, just add *-s* to make a plural noun.

EXAMPLES	Singular	Plural
	radio	radios
	stereo	stereos
	tattoo	tattoos

If a singular noun ends with a consonant before the letter *o*, you usually add *-es* to make a plural.

EXAMPLES	Singular	Plural
	potato	potatoes
	echo	echoes
	veto	vetoes
	tomato	tomatoes

With musical terms, just add *-s* to form the plural.

EXAMPLES	Singular	Plural
	piano	pianos
	solo	solos
	banjo	banjos

Activity D   Complete each sentence with the plural form of the bold noun. Write the plural on your paper.

1) Amanda has tried the **shampoo** in the pink bottle. Are some _____ better than others?

2) Which music **video** do you like? Some of the _____ are boring.

3) The girls went to the **rodeo**. How many _____ have you seen?

4) Laura is eating a baked **potato**. Mike ordered mashed _____ .

5) We shouted and listened to our **echo**. The tunnel was great for _____!

6) Mike plays the **banjo**. He has two _____ .

Irregular Plural Nouns

Some plural nouns are irregular. An irregular plural noun does not form its plural with the usual -s or -es. Study the following irregular plural nouns.

Singular	Plural	Singular	Plural
child	children	tooth	teeth
man	men	goose	geese
woman	women	mouse	mice
foot	feet		

Activity E   Choose four of the plural nouns from the list above. Write each one in a separate sentence on your paper.

Sometimes the singular and plural forms of the noun are the same. Here is a list of nouns that do not change their spellings.

Singular	Plural	Singular	Plural
one deer	several deer	one fish	a few fish
one sheep	many sheep	a trout	many trout
one moose	two moose		

Activity F   Number your paper from 1 to 4. Read each sentence below. If the sentence has no errors, write *Correct* after the number. If the sentence has an error, rewrite the sentence.

1) The man and his dog herded the sheeps into the pen.
2) The pet store sells tropical fish.
3) Do mooses live in Maine?
4) The fisherman caught a dozen trout during the afternoon.

Activity G   Review the proper spelling of plurals. Find one mistake in each sentence. Rewrite the word correctly.

1) Springfield has fifteen churchs.
2) Around Springfield are several valleyes.
3) There are also mountaines.
4) In the fall the leafs on the trees all turn to red and gold.
5) People often see deers in the hills.
6) Springfield parents care about their childrens.
7) Farms around Springfield are famous for their potatos.
8) The people's lifes in Springfield are usually pleasant.

Reading Vocabulary
irregular   proper (5)

■ **Presenting Activity E**
Have students use their own words to explain why *women* and *teeth* are called irregular plurals.

Activity E Answers
Sentences will vary. Students should write four sentences.

■ **Presenting Activity F**
After students have read the directions, have them read the four sentences to themselves. Ask them which sentences are correct.

Activity F Answers
1) The man and his dog herded the sheep into the pen.
2) Correct   **3)** Do moose live in Maine?   **4)** Correct

■ **Presenting Activity G**
Have students look back at pages 91–95 to review the spelling patterns covered so far. After students determine the misspelled word in each sentence in Activity G, have them explain which spelling pattern they should apply to fix the error.

Activity G Answers
1) churches   **2)** valleys
3) mountains   **4)** leaves
5) deer   **6)** children
7) potatoes   **8)** lives

Reading Vocabulary
restaurant (5)

- **Presenting Activity H** Go over rules 1–3 with students. Ask them to use their own words to tell what these terms mean: *plural proper noun, singular possessive proper noun, plural possessive proper noun.*

Activity H Answers
1) Adamses   2) Marys
3) Nuccis'

APPLICATION

In the Community Have students look for plural proper names and plural possessive proper names on signs in their neighborhood. Ask them to copy the names exactly as shown. The group can then decide whether the plural or possessive form is spelled according to the rules in this lesson.

Plurals of Proper Nouns

You may want to write the plural of a proper noun such as a family name. Here are rules for writing the plurals of proper nouns.

1. Add *-s* or *-es* to make a name plural.

> **EXAMPLES**   Ms. O'Hara and her family the O'Haras
> Coach Jones and his family the Jones**es**
> Laura Gonzales and her family the Gonzales**es**

2. If a name ends with a consonant before the letter *y*, do NOT change the *y* to *i*.

> **EXAMPLES**   Sophie Stansky invited all the Stansky**s** to a party.
> Kelly Takemura and Kelly Harte are in our class; our class has two Kelly**s**.

3. Do NOT use an apostrophe to make a plural. Use an apostrophe only to make a possessive.

> **EXAMPLES**   **Plural Proper Nouns**
> the Moyers**es**   the O'Haras
> The Ruiz**es**   the Palombos
>
> **Singular Possessive Proper Nouns**
> James**'s** hat   Kelly**'s** book   Mr. Takemura**'s** family
>
> **Plural Possessive Proper Nouns**
> the Jones**es'** car   the Takemuras' house

Activity H Find the error in each sentence below and at the top of the next page. Write the proper noun correctly on your paper.

1) John Adams and other Adams' were famous in American history.

2) The Lowrys have six Mary's in their family.

3) Have you ever eaten at the Nucci's restaurant?

4) The Gonzaleses' have lived in Texas for more than 100 years.

5) Charles Dickens books are still popular.

6) Choon-Cho stayed with the Kim's when she came from Korea.

Activity I   Write the plural of each family name in a sentence on your paper. Then write the plural possessive of each family name in a sentence.

Example   The Carters came to dinner last Sunday.
Have you seen the Carters' new car?

1) Chang

2) Ruiz

3) Williams

4) Corelli

Plurals of Letters and Numbers

An apostrophe is not used to make a plural. If a plural letter would be confusing without an apostrophe, use one to make the letter plural.

> **EXAMPLES**   How many *s*'s are in Mississippi?
> Oona's name has two *o*'s in it.
> Children learn their ABCs.

When making a plural with a number, use no apostrophe.

> **EXAMPLES**   The Vietnam War was fought in the 1960s.
> When were Boeing 727s first made?

Activity J   Write five sentences. Use a plural number or letter in each sentence.

(Activity H Answers, continued)
4) Gonzaleses   5) Dickens's
6) Kims

■ **Presenting Activity I** Go over the example sentences with students. Have them use their own words to tell why *Carters* and *Carters'* are spelled as shown.

Activity I Answers

Sentences will vary. Sample sentences are given.

1) The Changs live on Maple Avenue. The Changs' house is pink.   **2)** The Ruizes have ten grandchildren. The Ruizes' grandchildren visit often.   **3)** Are the Williamses at home? The Williamses' mailbox is full.   **4)** The Corellis had a party. The Corellis' party ended late.

■ **Presenting Activity J** Have students tell why the plurals of letters might be confusing if spelled without an apostrophe.

Activity J Answers

Sentences will vary. A plural number or letter should be used in each sentence.

LEARNING STYLES

   Body/Kinesthetic Have students—one by one—walk around the room, pick up or point to an object, print its name on the chalkboard, and then print its plural. To make this more difficult, ask students to pick up several examples of the same object—for example, several books—and print the plural form on the chalkboard and then work backward to the singular form.

Reading Vocabulary

brace (5)   wealthy (6)

Part A Answers

1) beaches   2) watches
3) students   4) glasses   5) cities
6) shelves   7) wolves   8) plays
9) leaves   10) feet   11) teeth
12) Corellis   13) countries
14) deer   15) families

Part B Answers

Sentences will vary. Sample
sentences are given.

1) One goose landed, but the other
geese flew on.   2) Does a cat have
one life or nine lives?   3) The first
flash of lightning was followed by
three quick flashes.   4) Bill Wilson's
grandfather started the business
run by the Wilsons.   5) One fly is
annoying. Many flies are even more
annoying.

Follow-up Activity

Have students look again at the sentences in Part A on this page. Ask
them to find the correctly spelled plural in each sentence. Have them write
the singular form of that plural and
tell how they know the plural is
spelled correctly.

Lesson 4 Review

Plural nouns name more than one person, place, thing, or idea.
Pay attention to plural nouns in your writing. Make sure that
you have spelled them correctly. Remember these points.

- With most nouns, add -s or -es to make a plural.
- If a singular noun ends with a consonant followed by y,
  change the y to i before adding -es.
- If a singular noun ends with -f or -fe, you may need to form a
  plural that ends with -ves.
- Do not add -s or -es to form the plural of an irregular noun.
- Do not use an apostrophe when writing plurals of proper
  names.
- Use an apostrophe to write the plural of a letter if it would be
  confusing without one.
- Do not use an apostrophe to write a plural number.

Part A   Find the one spelling error in each sentence below.
Write the word correctly on your paper.

1) There are many beautiful beachs in these states.
2) Mike and Derek left their watchs in their lockers.
3) Why are the students' playing their radios in class?
4) These glass are filled with berries.
5) Will taxes rise in the cityes?
6) Put the potatoes on the shelfs.
7) We heard the cries of the wolfs.
8) The class read three playes and two stories.
9) The leafs on these bushes are gold and red.
10) Each of these dancers has two left foot.
11) Elana wears braces to straighten her teeths.
12) The Corellis' give two parties a year.
13) The Ostrowskys lived in three countrys in the 1980s.
14) Three deers wandered through the Nguyens' yard.
15) The Vanderbilts and the Astors were wealthy familys.

Part B   Write one or two sentences with each pair of nouns.

1) goose, geese   3) flash, flashes   5) fly, flies
2) life, lives   4) Wilson's, Wilsons

Words with *ie* or *ei* may confuse spellers. How can you tell which letter to put first? Try memorizing this verse:

> Put *i* before *e*
> Except after *c*
> Or when sounded like *A*
> As in *neighbor* and *weigh*.

EXAMPLES   "i before e"—achieve, believe, thief
"except after c"—receive, ceiling, deceit
"Or when sounded like *A*"—neighbor, weigh, freight

Activity A   Look at each pair of words below. Think about the verse above. Decide which word is spelled correctly. Copy the correct spelling on your paper.

1) chief, cheif
2) reins, riens
3) sliegh, sleigh
4) releif, relief
5) niece, neice
6) peice, piece
7) receipt, reciept
8) thieves, theives
9) freind, friend
10) greif, grief

11) acheive, achieve
12) cieling, ceiling
13) beleive, believe
14) feild, field
15) conceited, concieted
16) freight, frieght
17) reign, riegn
18) relieved, relieved
19) shriek, shreik
20) diesel, deisel

Lesson at a Glance

Chapter 4   Lesson 5

Overview This lesson presents spelling patterns for words with *ie* and *ei*.

Objective
- To spell words with *ie* and *ei* correctly.

Student Pages 99–101

Reading Vocabulary

achieve (5)   niece (5)
conceit (7)   receipt (6)
deceit (8)   reign (7)
diesel (5)   relieve (6)
grief (6)   verse (5)

Teaching Suggestions

- **Introducing the Lesson**
  Read aloud the verse on this page. Discuss with students the value of verses and other memory devices.

- **Reviewing Skills** Write the words *chief* and *thief* on the board. Have students spell the plural form of each (*chiefs, thieves*).

- **Presenting Activity A**
  Read aloud the 20 words listed. Have students tell how each one fits with the verse on this page.

Activity A Answers

1) chief 2) reins 3) sleigh
4) relief 5) niece 6) piece
7) receipt 8) thieves 9) friend
10) grief 11) achieve
12) ceiling 13) believe
14) field 15) conceited
16) freight 17) reign
18) relieved 19) shriek
20) diesel

Reading Vocabulary

athlete (6)	immigrant (6)
biology (10)	leisure (6)
caffeine	protein
conscience (6)	pyramid (7)
exception (7)	unfortunately
foreign (5)	weird (6)
geology (7)	

■ Presenting Activity B

Demonstrate the strategy for memorizing spelling words:

- Look at the word
- Spell it aloud
- Write it
- Compare it to the correct spelling
- Rewrite it if necessary

Activity B Answers

1) caffeine 2) either 3) weird
4) height 5) foreign
6) ancient 7) leisure
8) protein 9) science
10) Neither 11) seize
12) conscience

Unfortunately, some words do not follow the pattern in the verse. You can learn these exceptions. Look at each word, spell it aloud, and write it. The correct spellings will become familiar to you.

Exceptions	
either	science
neither	conscience
height	ancient
seize	
weird	
foreign	
leisure	
protein	
caffeine	

Activity B Look over the 12 words in the list of exceptions. Decide which one fits best in each sentence below. Write the word on your paper.

1) Mr. O'Hara does not like coffee with _____ in it.

2) Choose _____ the black shoes or the white shoes.

3) "That noise sounded _____!" whispered Mike. "I'm scared!"

4) Ruben's _____ is five feet nine inches.

5) Immigrants come to the United States from _____ countries.

6) The Egyptians built pyramids in _____ times.

7) Do the workers have enough time for _____ activities?

8) Athletes must eat foods that have _____.

9) Biology and geology are _____ subjects.

10) _____ Valerie nor her brother has been on a plane.

11) The police tried to _____ the thief.

12) The thief's _____ bothered him, so he returned the money.

When you are trying to decide whether to spell a word with *ie* or *ei*, remember the verse about using those letters. Also make yourself familiar with spellings that are exceptions to the rule.

Part A Read the sentences. Find the words with *ie* or *ei*. Decide whether each one is spelled correctly. Write all the words correctly on your paper.

1) "I beleive that waiting tables is the hardest job in the world," said Loreen. "What a relief to sit down at last!"

2) Footprints were on the cieling. Someone had been up to mischief!

3) Amanda won an award for acheivement. When her name was announced, she shrieked loudly.

4) The child's weight was forty pounds. Her hieght was forty inches.

5) The driver did not yeild to the cars on the highway. The driver received a ticket.

Part B Write one or two sentences on your paper using each pair of words below. You do not have to match the order shown.

1) either, conscience

2) shield, piece

3) foreign, ancient

4) chief, niece

5) fierce, seize

6) freight, weigh

7) believe, thieves

8) weird, science

9) friend, grief

10) briefly, deceived

Reading Vocabulary

achievement (5)	loudly
award (5)	shield (5)
briefly	yield (6)
footprint	

Part A Answers

1) believe, relief 2) ceiling, mischief 3) achievement, shrieked 4) weight, height 5) yield, received

Part B Answers

Sentences will vary. Sample sentences are given.

1) You may either lie or tell the truth. Let your conscience be your guide. 2) The children made a shield from a piece of broken roof. 3) Which foreign rulers had power in ancient times? 4) The niece and her aunt are the chief owners of the business. 5) The fierce tiger will seize the meat. 6) How much does all that freight weigh? 7) I believe that two thieves stole the money. 8) We heard a weird noise and saw smoke. The science experiment was working. 9) Friends comfort each other in times of grief. 10) We were briefly deceived by the magician.

Follow-up Activity

Small groups may work together to examine a page from a reading or literature book. Have all groups study the same page. Students list all the words with *ei* or *ie* they can find. Have the groups then compare their findings.

Lesson at a Glance

Chapter 4   Lesson 6

Overview This lesson presents the rule for doubling the final consonant before endings in one- and two-syllable words.

Objective

■ To double the final consonant correctly in words with endings added.

Student Pages 102–105

Reading Vocabulary

describe (5)	drug (6)
double (5)	druggist (6)

Teaching Suggestions

■ **Introducing the Lesson**
In order to apply the rules in this lesson, students must be able to identify vowels, consonants, and syllables. Use the example words in this lesson to point out and discuss those concepts.

■ **Reviewing Skills** Write the words *quite* and *quiet* on the board, and have students use each in an oral sentence. Then add the word *quit* to the list. Have students tell how the word is different from the others in the way it looks and sounds. Challenge them to use all three words in one or two oral sentences.

Many words have endings added to them. You may need to make a spelling change in the word before you add the ending. For example, you may need to double the final consonant. Suppose that you are describing what a frog did. If you write *hoped* when you mean *hopped*, your readers will be confused.

Look at these words:

hop	big	slam	shut	wet

These words have three things in common.

1. They all have just one syllable.
2. They all end in just one consonant.
3. They all have just one vowel before the final consonant.

Study this rule. It tells you when to double a final consonant.

• Double the final consonant of a word before adding an ending if:
— the word has just one syllable,
— the word has one final consonant, and
— the word has one vowel before the final consonant.

Here are some endings that begin with vowels:

-ing	-ed	-er	-est	-y	-ist

EXAMPLES   **Words in Which the Final Consonant Is Doubled:**

hop + ed = hopped	shut + ing = shutting
big + er = bigger	wet + est = wettest
slam + ed = slammed	pin + ed = pinned
mud + y = muddy	drug + ist = druggist

Words in Which the Final Consonant is NOT Doubled:

sweet + er = sweeter	(*Two* vowels come before the final consonant.)
jump + ed = jumped	(*Two* consonants come at the end.)
sad + ly = sadly	(The ending begins with a *consonant.*)

Activity A Double the final consonant before adding each ending below. Write the new word in a sentence.

1) ship + ed
2) big + est
3) hop + ing
4) hem + ed
5) plan + er

Activity B The final consonant should be doubled in only some of the words below. Add the ending to each word. Write the new word on your paper.

1) sharp + er
2) sweet + er
3) chop + ed
4) sun + y
5) art + ist
6) grab + ed
7) star + y
8) dig + ing
9) mad + ly
10) hurt + ing

Activity C Find the one misspelled word in each sentence below. Write the sentence correctly on your paper.

1) The frog hoped into the water and made a plopping noise.
2) Someone has been digging in the mudy pond.
3) Was Derek a winer at the track meet?
4) The cook stired the soup and added salt.
5) The trail ended, and we steped into the clearing.

Two-Syllable Words

Sometimes you will need to double the final consonant in a two-syllable word. Look at these two-syllable words:

begin	forgot	control

These words have three things in common.

1. They all end in just one consonant.
2. They all have just one vowel before the final consonant.
3. The second syllable is stressed, or spoken with greater force than the first syllable.

Reading Vocabulary
art (5)   plop
hem (6)

■ **Presenting Activity A**
Have students identify the one vowel and one final consonant in each base word in Activity A and name the vowel letter that begins the ending to be added.

Activity A Answers
Sentences will vary. Words with endings are given.

1) shipped 2) biggest
3) hopping 4) hemmed
5) planner

■ **Presenting Activity B**
Read the ten words with students. Have them tell whether they will double the final consonant before adding the ending. Discuss reasons.

Activity B Answers
1) sharper 2) sweeter
3) chopped 4) sunny
5) artist 6) grabbed
7) starry 8) digging
9) madly 10) hurting

■ **Presenting Activity C**
Read the five sentences with students. Have them find the misspelled word and tell how they plan to correct it.

Activity C Answers
1) The frog hopped into the water and made a plopping noise. 2) Someone has been digging in the muddy pond.
3) Was Derek a winner at the track meet? 4) The cook stirred the soup and added salt.
5) The trail ended, and we stepped into the clearing.

Reading Vocabulary

■ Presenting Activity D

Have students identify the base word within each word listed in Activity D before they choose the correctly spelled word.

Activity D Answers

1) offering   2) controller
3) difference   4) referral
5) equipped   6) equipment
7) beginning   8) piloted

Here is the rule to follow for doubling the final consonant in words of more than one syllable.

• If the final syllable is stressed and has just one vowel before one final consonant, double that final consonant before an ending that begins with a vowel.

EXAMPLES	Words in Which the Final Consonant Is Doubled:
	begin + er = beginner
	control + ed = controlled
	forget + ing = forgetting

Words in Which the Final Consonant Is NOT Doubled:

return + ed = returned	(The final syllable, *turn*, ends in *two* consonants.)
travel + er = traveler	(The final syllable, *el*, is not stressed.)
repeat + ed = repeated	(*Two* vowels come before the final consonant.)
forget + ful = forgetful	(The ending begins with a *consonant*.)

Activity D   Look at each pair of words below. Decide which word is spelled correctly. Copy the correct spelling on your paper.

1) offering, offerring

2) controller, controler

3) difference, differrence

4) referral, referal

5) equipped, equiped

6) equippment, equipment

7) beginning, begining

8) piloted, pilotted

Look carefully at words with endings. Make sure that you have doubled final consonants when needed. Make sure that you have not doubled final consonants unless needed. Here are the two rules to follow.

- When a word has just one syllable, one final consonant, and one vowel before that consonant, double the final consonant before an ending that begins with a vowel. *Example* big + er = bigger

- In a two-syllable word, if the final syllable is stressed and has just one vowel before one final consonant, double that final consonant before an ending that begins with a vowel. *Example* begin + er = beginner

Part A Put each word and ending together. Write the new word on your paper.

1) color + ful
2) admit + ed
3) swim + er
4) run + ing
5) hop + ed
6) open + ed
7) fat + est
8) sit + ing
9) wait + er
10) hand + y
11) nut + y
12) great + est
13) limit + ed
14) hot + est
15) begin + ing
16) occur + ence
17) permit + ed
18) bat + er
19) number + ed
20) refer + ing

Part B Look at each pair of words below. Decide which word is spelled correctly. Write a sentence with the correctly spelled word.

1) choper, chopper
2) prefered, preferred
3) patroling, patrolling
4) hiting, hitting
5) sadest, saddest

Reading Vocabulary

limit (5)	patrol (5)
occur (6)	permit (5)

Part A Answers

1) colorful 2) admitted
3) swimmer 4) running
5) hopped 6) opened 7) fattest
8) sitting 9) waiter 10) handy
11) nutty 12) greatest
13) limited 14) hottest
15) beginning 16) occurrence
17) permitted 18) batter
19) numbered 20) referring

Part B Answers

Sentences will vary. Correct spellings are given.

1) chopper 2) preferred
3) patrolling 4) hitting
5) saddest

Follow-up Activity

Provide a list of ten base words from this lesson, along with this list of endings: *-ed, -ing, -er, -est, -y, -ous, -ence.* Have students combine words and endings to make as long a list of words as they can.

TEACHER ALERT

Most mistakes with the doubling rule involve failing to double the final consonant (rather than doubling unnecessarily). Draw students' attention to their own written errors, and emphasize the importance of thinking about the base word when adding an ending.

Chapter 4   Lesson 7

Overview This lesson presents the rule for dropping the final silent -*e* before endings.

Objective

- To drop the final silent -*e* correctly in words with endings added.

Student Pages 106–108

Teaching Suggestions

- ### Introducing the Lesson
  Have students look over a random page from a written work and list all the words with a final -*e*. Write ten of the words on the board, and discuss the endings that could be added to them.

- ### Reviewing Skills
  Write the words *hopping* and *starred* on the board. Have students identify the base word in each. Then write *hoping* and *stared* on the board, and ask students to name the base word in each. Point out that correct spelling of words with endings helps readers know which meaning is intended.

- ### Presenting Activity A
  Have students pronounce each word with its ending before writing the words.

Activity A Answers

1) strangely   2) safety
3) believable   4) arranging
5) choosing   6) hoped
7) wiggling   8) hopeful
9) writing   10) surprising
11) refusal   12) baker

Many words have endings added to them. You may need to make a spelling change in the word before you add the ending. For example, you may need to drop a silent final -*e*. Or you may need to keep a silent final -*e*.

These two rules will help you decide how to add endings to words that have a silent final -*e*.

1. Keep the silent -*e* before an ending that begins with a consonant.

 EXAMPLES   safe + ly = safely
use + ful = useful
excite + ment = excitement

2. Drop the silent -*e* before an ending that begins with a vowel.

 EXAMPLES   take + ing = taking
noise + y = noisy
receive + ed = received

Activity A   Put each word and ending together. Write the new word on your paper.

1) strange + ly
2) safe + ty
3) believe + able
4) arrange + ing
5) choose + ing
6) hope + ed
7) wiggle + ing
8) hope + ful
9) write + ing
10) surprise + ing
11) refuse + al
12) bake + er

Activity B   Find the one misspelled word in each sentence below. Write it correctly on your paper.

1) We are hopeing that Keisha will be pleased with the gift.

2) I am writing to inform you that I am changing my address.

3) The detectives were puzzleing over the confusing clues.

4) The roller coaster is the most exciting ride at any amusement park.

5) After separating the egg whites and yolks, whip each part separatly.

6) Please be carful when arranging those flowers.

7) The diver has a wirey build.

8) "The car makes a noisy, whineing sound," said the owner.

9) The littlest child has an adoreable smile.

10) Smokeing is no longer allowed in many offices.

Activity C   Add the ending *-ing* to each word below. Write the new word in a sentence.

1) come

2) admire

3) care

4) dance

5) divide

6) argue

7) circle

8) apologize

9) compare

10) chase

Reading Vocabulary

adore (6)	inform (6)
amusement (7)	roller (5)
apologize (5)	yolk (6)

■ Presenting Activity B

Direct students to read aloud each sentence and identify the words with endings. Have them tell which word is misspelled before they proceed with writing the word correctly.

Activity B Answers

1) hoping   2) writing
3) puzzling   4) amusement
5) separately   6) careful
7) wiry   8) whining
9) adorable   10) smoking

■ Presenting Activity C   Ask
students to tell what will happen to each base word listed when the ending *-ing* is added.

Activity C Answers

Sentences will vary. Correct spellings are given.

1) coming   2) admiring
3) caring   4) dancing
5) dividing   6) arguing
7) circling   8) apologizing
9) comparing   10) chasing

TEACHER ALERT

You may want to point out that a final silent *-e* is retained in words that end with a soft *c* or *g* sound, as in *peaceable* and *courageous*. The pattern occurs only if the ending does not begin with *i* or *e*.

Reading Vocabulary

advertise (6)   restrung

challenge (5)   rewooded

debate (6)   tickle (5)

passage (5)

Part A Answers

1) tasteful, tasty **2)** advertisement, advertising **3)** exciting, excitement
4) careless, caring **5)** using, useful
6) arrangement, arranger
7) debatable, debating **8)** scary, scaring **9)** troubling, troublesome
10) ticklish, tickler

Part B Answers

1) practicing **2)** chasing
3) arriving **4)** blazing
5) confused

Follow-up Activity

Have students look over their own writing for words with endings. Ask them to list three words in which the base word ends with final -e. Collect students' words and list them on the board. Have students explain how each word with an ending should be spelled, and why.

Many words end in silent -e. Remember to drop the -e before an ending IF that ending begins with a vowel.

Part A   Add each ending to the word shown. Write the new words on your paper.

1) taste + ful
   taste + y

2) advertise + ment
   advertise + ing

3) excite + ing
   excite + ment

4) care + less
   care + ing

5) use + ing
   use + ful

6) arrange + ment
   arrange + er

7) debate + able
   debate + ing

8) scare + y
   scare + ing

9) trouble + ing
   trouble + some

10) tickle + ish
   tickle + er

Part B   Find five spelling errors in the passage below. Write each word correctly on your paper.

The Tennis Match
by Mike Kaplan

My friend, Derek Corelli, and I had been practiceing for several weeks. At first, we were mostly chaseing the ball around. Finally, we decided that we were good enough to make a challenge. There was a lot of excitement in Springfield as the news got around. That day we saw several of our friends arriveing to watch us play.

To make a long story short, we were not exactly blazeing the ball. No one confusd us with Pete Sampras and Andre Agassi.

"It's hard to play well with a tree growing in the middle of the court," Derek complained to me after we lost 6–0, 6–0.

"Oh, yeah!" I said. "Well, most people I know need to have their rackets restrung from time to time. You need to have your racket rewooded!"

Some words are misspelled more often than other words. These spelling demons may be troublesome to you, too. The way to learn spelling demons is to practice writing them correctly again and again.

Read this list of fifty commonly misspelled words.

1) acquaint	18) experience	35) pleasant
2) across	19) false	36) privilege
3) athletic	20) February	37) realize
4) beautiful	21) film	38) recommend
5) benefit	22) finally	39) secretary
6) business	23) forty	40) separate
7) character	24) government	41) similar
8) clothes	25) grammar	42) since
9) committee	26) immediately	43) speech
10) decision	27) interesting	44) surprise
11) definite	28) knowledge	45) thorough
12) describe	29) library	46) together
13) description	30) minute	47) true
14) different	31) necessary	48) usually
15) disappear	32) ninety	49) Wednesday
16) disappoint	33) occasion	50) which
17) doctor	34) once	

Activity A Study the list above.

1) Say each word aloud. Cover the word with your hand. Spell it aloud. Check your spelling.

2) Then have someone else read aloud each word on the list. Write each word on your paper.

3) Check to see which words you misspelled. Cross out each misspelled word and write it correctly three times.

Lesson at a Glance

Chapter 4   Lesson 8

Overview This lesson presents fifty common spelling demons for students to memorize.

Objective

- To spell fifty common spelling demons correctly.

Student Pages 109–111

Teacher's Resource Library

Activity 16

Workbook Activity 19

Reading Vocabulary

acquaint (6)	grammar (5)
athletic (5)	occasion (5)
benefit (5)	privilege (6)
decision (5)	recommend (6)
definite (6)	secretary (5)
demon (6)	similar (6)
description (6)	thorough (6)
film (6)	troublesome

Teaching Suggestions

- **Introducing the Lesson**
  Discuss with students why some words are called spelling demons—why are certain words especially tricky? Students may note that words are not always pronounced as they are spelled, so spellers may leave out letters, reverse them, or add extra ones.

- **Reviewing Skills** List the words *scarred/scared, caning/canning, carful/careful,* and *hopped/hoped* on the board. Have students identify the base word in each.

- **Presenting Activity A**
  Have volunteers demonstrate how to memorize the spelling of a troublesome word, based on the three steps in Activity A.

  Activity A Answers
  Students' responses will vary.

Reading Vocabulary

absolutely (6)   lawyer (5)
effort (5)   witness (5)
federal (6)

■ Presenting Activity B

Read all the sentences aloud with students before they proceed to proofread for the one misspelled word in each sentence.

Activity B Answers

1) library 2) privilege
3) finally 4) athletic 5) false
6) doctor 7) film 8) separate
9) definite 10) knowledge
11) describe 12) acquaint
13) disappoints 14) experience
15) minute

Activity B Find the one misspelled word in each sentence below. Write the word correctly on your paper.

1) You can add to your knowledge by finding interesting books in the libary.

2) "It is my privlege to recommend Keisha for committee secretary," said Loreen.

3) Mr. Corelli finaly turned forty in February.

4) Derek has certainly benefited from his atheletic efforts.

5) "On which occasion did you make a fasle statement?" the lawyer asked the witness.

6) The docter made a thorough examination of the ninety-year-old man.

7) The characters in this flim wore beautiful clothes.

8) The federal government is divided into seperate branches.

9) Is your decision definate, or could you change your mind at the last minute?

10) It is absolutely necessary for a secretary to have knowlege of grammar and spelling rules.

11) How did the writer descibe the different characters?

12) Let me aquaint you with the business owners across the hall.

13) The decision is not a surprise, but it still disapoints us.

14) Can you give a description of the pleasant experence you had Wednesday?

15) The character in the film gave a speech that lasted one minite.

The fifty words in this lesson are difficult for many people to spell. It helps to pronounce each word carefully before writing it. With study and practice, you can learn to spell these words correctly.

Part A   Read both spellings of the ten words listed below. Write the correct spelling of each word on your paper.

1) accrost, across

2) benifit, benefit

3) separate, seperate

4) nessary, necessary

5) togehter, together

6) February, Febuary

7) atheletic, athletic

8) libary, library

9) simler, similar

10) usually, usally

Part B   Look over the list of fifty words. Choose ten that are hard for you to spell. Write each one in a sentence on your paper.

■ Lesson Review Have students try the activities without looking back at the list on page 109. Then have them check their work against that list.

Part A Answers
1) across 2) benefit
3) separate 4) necessary
5) together 6) February
7) athletic 8) library 9) similar
10) usually

Part B Answers
Word choices and sentences will vary.

Follow-up Activity

Mnemonic devices are used to help people remember things. A well-known mnemonic is used for spelling arithmetic—a rat in the house might eat the ice cream. Have students create mnemonics to help them remember spelling demons.

Name _____ Date _____ Period _____ Chapter 4 / Activity 16

Find the Misspelled Words

Directions: Find the spelling errors in the sentences below. Circle each error. Then rewrite these words correctly on the line below each sentence.

EXAMPLE Ocasionally we go to the (libary) on (Wensdays).
Occasionally, library, Wednesdays

1) My freind is a long distance runer.

2) Finaly I beleived my mother's desicion.

3) Stoping was a releif after steping down those steep stairs.

4) The secretery gave me a peice of paper to write on.

5) Everyone was experenced in a diferent way.

6) The suprize birthday party was great.

7) I only have fourty days of school left.

8) We realised the minite hand on the timer was broken.

9) Imedately the nurse recomended something for my headache.

10) You are very privleged to be taking this class.

©AGS® American Guidance Service, Inc. Permission is granted to reproduce for classroom use only. **Basic English Composition**

Activity 16

Name _____ Date _____ Period _____ Chapter 4 / Workbook Activity 19

A Camping Trip

Directions: Find the spelling errors in this story and circle them. Write the words correctly on the lines below each sentence.

1) David and Robert are going on a camping trip Wensday.

2) They are excited becuse the whether is supposed twoo be good.

3) They got all of there supplys together.

4) David bought close and other things at the store.

5) Robert packed too sleeping bags and a tent.

6) The boys' parents will drive them too the camp they were staying.

7) Robert said, "Let's go two bed now. I know you want to get up too hours before dawn."

8) The boys where awake early the next moring.

9) Father asked, "Do you have everything neccessary four you're trip?"

10) Both boys replied, "Were ready to go!"

11) The boys were gone fore one weak.

12) They had a terrific experience.

13) They hiked threw the mountains and swam in a lake.

14) "Did you sea any wild animals?" asked Mother.

15) "Wonc we saw rabbits and squirrels," laughed David.

©AGS® American Guidance Service, Inc. Permission is granted to reproduce for classroom use only. **Basic English Composition**

Workbook Activity 19

Chapter 4 Review

The Teacher's Resource Library includes two parallel forms of the Chapter 4 Mastery Test. The difficulty level of the two forms is equivalent. You may wish to use one form as a pretest and the other form as a posttest.

Reading Vocabulary

guidance (9)   unbelievable
pave (6)   woodworker

Part A Answers

1) their   2) quite   3) loose
4) passed   5) two   6) advice
7) careful   8) its   9) There's
10) your   11) planing
12) pinned   13) hopping
14) staring   15) canned

Part B Answers

1) The business owner finally reached a decision on Wednesday.
2) The guidance counselor spoke to the school principal.   3) "We're already through with a week's work," said the committee members.   4) State governments are usually located in the capital cities.   5) The weather today is affecting the geese strangely.

Part A   Choose the word in parentheses that correctly completes the sentence. Write the word on your paper.

1) The players threw (there, their) hats into the air.

2) The workers are not (quiet, quite) done paving the road.

3) One shoe feels tight, and the other feels (lose, loose).

4) We were busy, so time (past, passed) quickly.

5) Drive (two, to) or three blocks north on Main Street.

6) Will people follow good (advice, advise)?

7) Please be (carful, careful) near a hot stove.

8) The dog has a white spot on (it's, its) back.

9) (Theirs, There's) more than one way to reach our house.

10) "Is that (your, you're) scarf or mine?" Amanda asked Laura.

11) A woodworker smoothes a shelf by (planning, planing) it.

12) The general (pined, pinned) the medal on the war hero.

13) Two rabbits were (hoping, hopping) quickly across the road.

14) "Unbelievable!" the man said, (staring, starring) wide-eyed at the scene.

15) Do (caned, canned) peas taste as good as fresh ones?

Part B   Each sentence below and at the top of the next page contains at least one spelling error. Rewrite each sentence on your paper. Make sure that all words are spelled correctly.

1) The business owner finaly reached a desion on Wenesday.

2) The guidence councilor spoke to the school principal.

3) "Were already through with a week's work," said the commitee members.

4) State governments are usally located in the capitol cityes.

5) The whether today is effecting the gooses strangely.

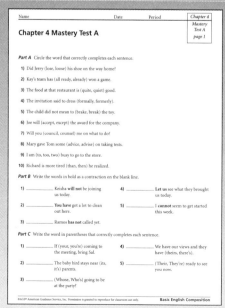

Chapter 4 Mastery Test A

6) Its true that male foxs are careing fathers of there families.

7) The buses stoped runing last Febuary.

8) I read a library book about the lifes of sports heroes.

9) It's likly that the potatos are on the shelfs.

10) "I cant beleive how many spelling errors your makeing!" Mr. Martin repeatted to all his class.

Part C   Write a sentence with each pair of words below. You do not have to match the order shown.

1) since, February

2) necessary, together

3) speeches, exciting

4) preferred, beginner

5) hottest, biggest

6) you're, your

7) they're, their

8) weird, receiving

9) piece, peaceful

10) woman, women

Test Taking Tip   To prepare for a test, study in short sessions rather than one long session. In the week before the test, spend time each evening reviewing your notes.

Spelling Counts!   Chapter 4   **113**

Reading Vocabulary
session (6)

(Part B Answers, continued)
6) It's true that male foxes are caring fathers of their families.
7) The buses stopped running last February.   8) I read a library book about the lives of sports heroes.
9) It's likely that the potatoes are on the shelves.   10) "I can't believe how many spelling errors you're making!" Mr. Martin repeated to all his classes.

Part C Answers
Sentences will vary. Sample sentences are given.

1) It has not snowed since February.
2) Is it necessary for us to arrive together?   3) We heard three exciting speeches at the meeting.
4) I preferred to play a beginner, but I was matched against a good player.   5) I would like the hottest and biggest cup of cocoa.   6) Your father wants to know if you're going home.   7) They're playing quietly in their room.   8) We were receiving weird messages on the computer.   9) We listened to a piece of peaceful music.   10) One woman spoke to the group of women.

Name _____ Date _____ Period _____   Chapter 4 Mastery Test B page 2

Chapter 4 Mastery Test B, continued

Part D Write the plural form of each of these words.

1) _____ fox   6) _____ ruby
2) _____ bay   7) _____ turkey
3) _____ lady   8) _____ giraffe
4) _____ self   9) _____ pinto
5) _____ foot   10) _____ sheep

Part E Circle the word in each pair that is spelled correctly.

1) releif, relief   6) triped, tripped
2) sleigh, sliegh   7) permited, permitted
3) weight, wieght   8) cooled, coolled
4) sceince, science   9) wasteful, wastful
5) pumped, pumpped   10) noseing, nosing

Part F Rewrite each sentence on the blank line. Spell all the words correctly.

1) We our geting knowlege of writting in this class.
   _____

2) It is helping us with hour grammer and ability to discribe things beutifully with words.
   _____

3) After fourty weeks we will relize wich words are spelt write.
   _____

4) We go to the libary and throughly study topiccs that we chose.
   _____

5) We will suprise ourselfs by how much we bennefit from this experience.
   _____

©AGS® American Guidance Service, Inc. Permission is granted to reproduce for classroom use only.   **Basic English Composition**

Chapter 4 Mastery Test B

Chapter 5

Planning Guide

Writing Complete Sentences

	Student Text Lesson			
	Student Pages	Vocabulary	Practice Exercises	Lesson Review
Lesson 1 Run-On Sentences	116-121	✔	✔	121
Lesson 2 Sentence Fragments	122-127	✔	✔	127

Chapter Activities

Teacher's Resource Library

Writing Tip 3: Correcting Common Writing Mistakes

Community Connection 5: Sentence Fragments

Assessment Options

Student Text

Chapter 5 Review

Teacher's Resource Library

Chapter 5 Mastery Tests A and B

	Teaching Strategies							Language Skills			Learning Styles						Teacher's Resource Library		
	Reviewing Skills	Teacher Alert	Follow-up Activity	Career Application	Home Application	Global Connection	Community Application	Identification Skills	Writing Skills	Punctuation Skills	Visual/Spatial	Auditory/Verbal	Body/Kinesthetic	Logical/Mathematical	Group Learning	LEP/ESL	Activities	Workbook Activities	Self-Study Guide
	116	118	121	117	120			✔	✔	✔		121					17-18	20-21	✔
	122		127			126	123	✔	✔	✔					126		19-20	22-23	✔

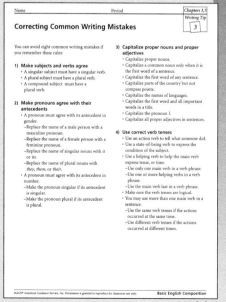

Writing Tip 3

Community Connection 5

Chapter 5

Writing Complete Sentences

Think about the last conversation you had with someone. Can you remember what each of you said? It is likely that neither of you spoke in complete sentences. Speakers can usually understand each other even when their sentences are incomplete or run together.

Writing, however, is not the same as speaking. When you write, you need to pay close attention to your sentences. If your sentences are incomplete, your readers may be puzzled. If your sentences run together, your readers may be lost.

You have learned that a sentence is a group of words containing a subject and a verb and expressing a complete idea. In Chapter 5, you will learn to look for and fix two common sentence errors that can confuse readers.

Goals for Learning

▶ To recognize and fix run-on sentences
▶ To recognize and fix sentence fragments

115

Introducing the Chapter

Have students examine the introductory photograph accompanying the first page of Chapter 5. Ask students how face-to-face communication, such as is shown in this scene, differs from telephone communication. They may recognize that on the telephone speakers can get information from what is said and the tone of voice; face-to-face speakers can also get information by reading each other's expressions. Then ask students how written communication differs even more from conversations. Students should recognize that writers must express ideas more clearly and completely than speakers because writers cannot use their voices or faces to express meaning and cannot get reactions from their readers.

Chapter 5 Self-Study Guide

Lesson at a Glance

Chapter 5   Lesson 1

Overview This lesson teaches how to recognize and repair run-on sentences.

Objectives

- To identify run-on sentences.
- To split a run-on sentence into separate sentences.
- To fix a run-on sentence with correct use of conjunctions and punctuation.

Student Pages 116–121

Teacher's Resource Library

Activities 17–18

Workbook Activities 20–21

Reading Vocabulary

capitalization
capitalize (9)
challenge (5)
comma
exclamation (8)

punctuation (7)
rewrite
run-on sentence
separate (5)
tennis (5)

Teaching Suggestions

- **Introducing the Lesson**
  Read aloud the first paragraph on page 116 as if it were written as a run-on sentence. Have students listen for the separate ideas. Before they read the paragraph for themselves, have them give their ideas about where to put the periods.

- **Reviewing Skills** Write on the board a sentence that begins with a lowercase letter and has no end punctuation mark. Have a volunteer show how to make the sentence correct.

- **Presenting Activity A**
  Read the directions with students. Have students read each group of words to themselves and tell where they think the ideas should be split.

Run-on sentence

Two or more complete ideas that are not connected correctly. (I have read that book many times I'll read it again, it is my favorite and you'll like it too.)

When a sentence seems to run on without coming to a stop, it is called a **run-on sentence**. A run-on sentence has too many ideas in it. The ideas should be clearly separated.

Before you can fix run-on errors, you need to know what they look like. A run-on sentence is often made of two or more sentences with no punctuation between them.

EXAMPLE   Derek and Mike like tennis they play as often as they can.

The easiest way to correct a run-on sentence is to split it into separate sentences. Review the rules for writing a sentence.

1. Capitalize the first word in a sentence.

2. End a sentence with the correct punctuation mark. A period is the most common end punctuation mark. The only other end marks are the question mark and the exclamation point.

3. Do not end a sentence with a comma.

Here is the easiest way to fix the run-on sentence shown in the example above.

EXAMPLE   Derek and Mike like tennis. They play as often as they can.

Activity A   Each group of words below is a run-on sentence. Decide where the first idea ends and the second idea begins. Rewrite the ideas in two correct sentences on your paper. Check for correct capitalization and end punctuation.

1) Do you have an extra tennis racket mine is lost.

2) Meet me at the courts after school we can play for an hour before dark.

3) Derek and Mike practiced for several days then they challenged two players to a tennis match and lost.

116   *Chapter 5   Writing Complete Sentences*

Activity A Answers

1) Do you have an extra tennis racket? Mine is lost.   2) Meet me at the courts after school. We can play for an hour before dark.
3) Derek and Mike practiced for several days. Then they challenged two players to a tennis match and lost.

Activity B Each group of words below is a run-on sentence containing three ideas. Find the beginning and the end of each complete thought. Write the three sentences on your paper. Use capital letters and end punctuation correctly.

Example   Run-on:
Thank you for talking with me on the phone last week my job application is enclosed I look forward to meeting with you

Three sentences:
Thank you for talking with me on the phone last week.
My job application is enclosed.
I look forward to meeting with you.

1) Amanda stayed up too late last night she was reading an interesting book all day she kept yawning

2) Mike has set up another tennis match he thinks that he and Derek will win Derek is not so sure

3) last year Derek wanted to be a diesel mechanic now he likes sports he is thinking about becoming a physical education teacher

4) the tennis match was held at noon on Saturday Mike and Derek lost again Derek decided to stick to track

5) Springfield Senior High has a weight room every day Laura goes there for an hour she feels strong and fit

6) the county track meet will be held next week Derek wants to set a new record everyone hopes that he will win

application (8)   enclose (5)
county (5)   mechanic (6)
diesel (5)   physical (5)
education (5)

■ **Presenting Activity B**
Have a volunteer read aloud the example run-on and the three sentences that are made from it.

Activity B Answers

1) Amanda stayed up too late last night. She was reading an interesting book. All day she kept yawning.   2) Mike has set up another tennis match. He thinks that he and Derek will win. Derek is not so sure.   3) Last year Derek wanted to be a diesel mechanic. Now he likes sports. He is thinking about becoming a physical education teacher.
4) The tennis match was held at noon on Saturday. Mike and Derek lost again. Derek decided to stick to track.   5) Springfield Senior High has a weight room. Every day Laura goes there for an hour. She feels strong and fit.
6) The county track meet will be held next week. Derek wants to set a new record. Everyone hopes that he will win.

APPLICATION

 Career Connection
Have students look again at the three sentences in the Activity B example. Have students tell what kind of letter is probably being written. Discuss the importance of politeness and correctness in a letter from a job applicant.

TEACHER ALERT

Another common way to repair a comma fault is to substitute a semicolon for the comma. Show this alternative fix-up method to students who readily understand the two methods shown on page 118.

Connecting Ideas

Another kind of run-on sentence is made of two or more sentences separated with commas. Do not separate two sentences with a comma. This kind of error is sometimes called a comma fault. Use an end punctuation mark—not a comma—to end a sentence.

> **EXAMPLES**
>
> **Run-on Sentence With Comma Fault**
> Coach Jones is proud of Derek, he hopes that Derek will become county champion.
>
> **Corrected Sentences**
> Coach Jones is proud of Derek. He hopes that Derek will become county champion.

Conjunction

A word used to connect words or phrases or to combine complete ideas in sentences (and, or, but).

Sometimes you may want to show the connection between two related ideas. Turn your run-on sentence into a compound sentence. The two ideas in a compound sentence are separated by a comma followed by a **conjunction**. Notice the conjunction *and* in the compound sentence below.

> **EXAMPLES**
>
> **Run-on Sentence With Comma Fault**
> Coach Jones is proud of Derek, he hopes that Derek will become county champion.
>
> **Corrected Compound Sentence**
> Coach Jones is proud of Derek, and he hopes that Derek will become county champion.

Name _____   Date _____   Period _____ | *Chapter 5* |
| *Workbook Activity* |
| **20** |

Avoiding the Comma Fault

A **comma fault** is using a comma by itself to connect or separate two ideas.
• At the end of a sentence, you must use *end punctuation.*
• Never use a comma to end a sentence.
• Never use a comma by itself to connect two sentences.

> *Wrong:* Carolyn is giving a party, we are all going.
> *Right:* Carolyn is giving a party, **and** we are all going.
> *Right:* Carolyn is giving a party. We are all going.

Commas may be used to separate words in a series.

> *Right:* Victor, Mike, and Tina rode in a helicopter.
> *Right:* Victor liked the ride a little, Mike didn't like it at all,
> and Tina now plans to become a pilot.

Directions: Rewrite these sentences. Correct any errors.

1) Helicopters are fun to ride in, they are also scary.

2) On her first ride Tina fell in love with flying, now she wants to be a pilot.

3) Victor thought flying was OK, Mike made plans to take a bus next time.

4) The fastest a helicopter ever flew was over 200 miles per hour, the pilot was Byron Graham.

5) Byron Graham isn't in the National Aviation Hall of Fame, the Hall of Fame is in Dayton, Ohio, it honors outstanding pioneers.

6) Some of the people in the Hall of Fame are Amelia Earhart, Wiley Post, Orville and Wilbur Wright, also in the Hall of Fame are Charles Lindbergh, and Alexander Graham Bell.

©AGS® American Guidance Service, Inc. Permission is granted to reproduce for classroom use only.   **Basic English Composition**

Workbook Activity 20

Activity C Read each group of words below. Decide whether each group is a correct sentence or a run-on sentence. Write *Correct* or *Run-on* as your answer on your paper.

1) Mike went to the weight room with Derek, and they both worked out.

2) One afternoon Derek and Mike met Laura in the weight room, she was working out, too.

3) A track meet is exciting and suspenseful, have you ever gone to one?

4) Derek's friends want to go to the county meet, and they plan to cheer from the stands.

5) Some people enjoy team sports, and others like to work out by themselves.

6) Tennis is played with rackets and a ball, what other sport uses rackets?

Activity D Each run-on sentence below has a comma fault. Decide how to fix the problem. You may decide to separate the ideas into two complete sentences. If the ideas seem related, add the conjunction *and* after the comma. Rewrite the sentences on your paper.

1) What will you do during your week off, please come to visit us.

2) The main character in this book is a sixteen-year-old boy, he dreams of becoming a fighter.

3) The weight room will be open after school until five, no one will be admitted without permission.

4) The detective tries to figure out who committed the crime, the reader already knows who did it.

5) Derek started out running the mile, then he switched to sprinting.

6) My parents arrived in the United States in 1975, I was born six years later.

Reading Vocabulary
commit (7)   sprint (6)
crime (5)   suspenseful

■ **Presenting Activity C**
Have students go over items 1–6 to tell why each group of words is or is not a run-on sentence. Ask them to tell how to fix the run-on sentences.

Activity C Answers
1) Correct 2) Run-on 3) Run-on
4) Correct 5) Correct
6) Run-on

■ **Presenting Activity D**
After going over the directions with students, have them tell two ways to fix run-on sentences that have comma faults: Write separate sentences, or connect the sentences with a comma followed by a conjunction.

Activity D Answers
Students may be able to justify other responses.

1) What will you do during your week off? Please come to visit us.
2) The main character in this book is a sixteen-year-old boy. He dreams of becoming a fighter.
3) The weight room will be open after school until five. No one will be admitted without permission. 4) The detective tries to figure out who committed the crime. The reader already knows who did it. 5) Derek started out running the mile, and then he switched to sprinting. 6) My parents arrived in the United States in 1975. I was born six years later.

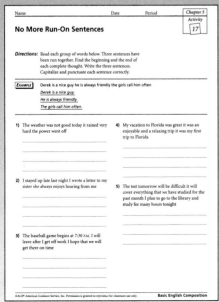

Activity 17

Reading Vocabulary

championship   powerful (6)
guy (6)

■ **Presenting Activity E**

Read the paragraph aloud to students, asking them to listen for separate ideas. Have them tell where the sentences should be separated.

Activity E Answers

Sometimes a song can have a strong effect on a listener. My eyes always fill up with tears when I hear "From Out of My Heart." It is so powerful! Listening to it makes me want to write a sad song, too.

APPLICATION

At Home

Have students bring in a few brochures or other mailings that were delivered to their homes. Ask them to find compound sentences connected with *and*. Students may copy one or more of the sentences. Do classmates agree that the sentence is correctly written and punctuated?

Using Conjunctions Correctly

Another kind of run-on sentence is made with two or more sentences connected with *ands*. Do not use *ands* to connect sentences that should be separated.

> **EXAMPLES**
>
> **Run-on Sentence With Too Many** ands
> The game last Saturday was Johnson's greatest and he'll probably bring the Foxes into the championship and the fans can't wait to see this guy make another touchdown.
>
> **Corrected Sentences**
> The game last Saturday was Johnson's greatest! He'll probably bring the Foxes into the championship. The fans can't wait to see this guy make another touchdown.

Activity E Read the paragraph below. Decide where each complete idea begins and ends. Look for four complete sentences. Write the sentences on your paper. Make sure to use capital letters and end punctuation correctly.

My Favorite Song
by Laura Gonzales

Sometimes a song can have a strong effect on a listener and my eyes always fill up with tears when I hear "From Out of My Heart" and it is so powerful and listening to it makes me want to write a sad song, too.

Separating the Ideas

Chapter 5 Activity 18

Directions: Each paragraph below contains several sentences. Decide where each sentence begins and ends. Rewrite the sentences correctly. Begin each sentence with a capital letter. Add the correct punctuation mark.

Graduation
Graduation takes place after students have completed a course of study people can graduate from a school or college graduates receive a diploma or degree during a ceremony the ceremony connected with graduation is called commencement.

Yearbook
A yearbook editor is a person in charge of producing a yearbook the position involves many responsibilities the editor carries out many duties to meet deadlines many hours are usually spent in drawing layouts, taking pictures, and proofreading pages one of the most important responsibilities is to meet the deadlines missing deadlines will result in a fee and a late publication.

Separating the Ideas

Chapter 5 Workbook Activity 21

Directions: Each group of words below contains several sentences. You must decide where each sentence begins and ends. Rewrite the sentences correctly. Add the correct punctuation.

The Labrador Retriever
The Wilsons got a labrador retriever puppy it was eight weeks old and weighed ten pounds by the time it was three months old the puppy weighed over thirty pounds the veterinarian said the puppy might be over one hundred pounds when he was full-grown Wow said Jane the puppy will weigh more than I do!

Rehoboth Beach
Rehoboth Beach is a little town on the Atlantic Ocean it is in the state of Delaware Rehoboth is a popular summer resort people go there to swim, boat, sunbathe, and fish there is a small boardwalk where people like to walk at night.

Activity 18   **Workbook Activity 21**

Lesson 1 Review

Write your complete ideas as separate sentences. Check your work for run-on sentences, and fix them.

- Begin each sentence with a capital letter. End it with a period, a question mark, or an exclamation point.

- Do not use a comma to separate complete ideas. Fix a comma fault by writing separate sentences. If the ideas are related, make a compound sentence with a comma and a conjunction.

- Avoid connecting separate ideas with *ands*. Write separate sentences instead.

Part A   Read each group of words below. Number your paper from 1 to 5. If the group of words is correct, write *Correct* as your answer. If the group of words is a run-on sentence, rewrite it so that it is correct. There may be more than one way to correct a run-on sentence.

1) Mike went to the tennis courts alone, he practiced his serve.

2) Soon he and Derek would make another challenge, and the next time they would win.

3) Eat at Anna's Restaurant, the pizza is perfect, the sauces are super!

4) I purchased a toaster oven at Riley's Discount Store last November it stopped working last week my sales slip is enclosed.

5) There are too many ideas in a run-on sentence the ideas need to be separated.

Part B   Choose any topic that interests you. Write five sentences about that topic. Include at least one compound sentence that uses *and*. Do not write any run-on sentences.

discount (7)   restaurant (5)
pizza   super
purchase (5)   topic (5)

■ **Lesson Review** Have students use their own words to define the terms *run-on, compound sentence,* and *conjunction.*

Part A Answers

Corrected sentences may vary. Sample answers are given.

1) Mike went to the tennis courts alone, and he practiced his serve.
2) Correct   3) Eat at Anna's Restaurant! The pizza is perfect, and the sauces are super!
4) I purchased a toaster oven at Riley's Discount Store last November. It stopped working last week. My sales slip is enclosed.   5) There are too many ideas in a run-on sentence. The ideas need to be separated.

Part B Answers

Sentences will vary. At least one should be a compound sentence that uses *and*.

Follow-up Activity

Have students take the correctly written sentences from Part B above and rewrite them as a continuous sentence beginning with a capital letter and ending with an end mark of punctuation. Partners then exchange papers and try to write the sentences correctly.

LEARNING STYLES

Auditory/Verbal

Ask each student to create and write down a series of three related and run-on sentences. Then invite volunteers to stand before the class in pairs. Ask one member of the first pair to read aloud his or her run-on sentences without pausing for punctuation. Ask the other partner to step forward each time a point of punctuation is needed to divide the run-ons into three sentences. Then have the partners switch roles. Continue until all the volunteers have read and added punctuation to their sentences.

Lesson at a Glance

Chapter 5   Lesson 2

Overview This lesson teaches how to recognize and repair sentence fragments.

Objectives

- To identify sentence fragments.
- To fix a sentence fragment by adding a missing subject or predicate.
- To fix a sentence fragment by connecting it to another sentence.

Student Pages 122–127

Teacher's Resource Library

Activities 19–20

Workbook Activities 22–23

Reading Vocabulary

clause (7)   phrase (6)

fragment (7)   underline

Teaching Suggestions

- **Introducing the Lesson**
  Write the two items below on the board. Tell students to choose the one that is a complete sentence. When students correctly identify the first one as a sentence, point out that a sentence must express a complete idea. The second group of words is much longer than the first, but it does not express a complete idea.
  - Dogs bark.
  - When the dogs in the neighborhood start barking.

- **Reviewing Skills** Have students look over a page from one of their books to select a few simple sentences. Have them identify the subject and verb in each sentence.

- **Presenting Activity A**
  Discuss each of the pairs in the box of examples on this page. Have students tell why each fragment needs fixing.

Lesson 2   Sentence Fragments

Fragment
A group of words that does not express a complete thought; a phrase or clause incorrectly treated as a sentence.

You have learned that a sentence is a group of words containing a subject and a verb and expressing a complete idea. If the subject or the verb is missing, the sentence is a **fragment**. It fails to express a complete idea. Any group of words that does not express a complete idea is a fragment. Fragments may confuse your readers.

Each fragment below begins with a capital letter and ends with a period. It only looks like a sentence, however. It does not express a complete thought. Notice how each fragment is turned into a complete sentence.

EXAMPLES

Fragment:	Going to the track meet.
Sentence:	Derek is going to the track meet.
Fragment:	The team from Springfield.
Sentence:	The team from Springfield has strong runners.
Fragment:	Because Derek is so fast.
Sentence:	Because Derek is so fast, he may win his race.

Activity A   Read each group of words below. Decide whether each group is a correct sentence or a fragment. Write *Sentence* or *Fragment* as your answer on your paper.

1) Running laps around the track after school.

2) Most of the other members of the track team.

3) A challenging race.

4) Anyone can enjoy running.

5) You should learn to stretch first.

6) Where there are few cars.

Activity B   Make all of the sentence fragments in Activity A into complete sentences. Add words to make each group of words express a complete thought. Underline your added words.

Activity A Answers

1) Fragment   2) Fragment
3) Fragment   4) Sentence
5) Sentence   6) Fragment

- **Presenting Activity B**
  Review the items in Activity A with students before they proceed with Activity B. Ask them to read the directions to Activity B and to use their own words to explain what they are to do.

Activity B Answers

Sentences will vary. Sample sentences are given.

1) Running laps around the track after school <u>is a good way to get exercise.</u>   2) <u>Derek runs with</u> most of the other members of the track team.   3) <u>A marathon is</u> a challenging race.   6) <u>It is safest to run</u> where there are few cars.

Two Parts of a Sentence

The subject of a sentence is the person, place, thing, or idea that a sentence tells about. Every sentence needs a subject. Look at the bold subject in each example sentence.

EXAMPLES
The gas station is open.
Derek and Ms. Lentz have been working there.
He pumps gas.
She fixes cars.

Predicate

The part of a sentence that tells something about the subject; it always contains a verb.

Every sentence also needs a **predicate**. The predicate tells what the subject is or does. Look at the bold predicate in each example sentence.

EXAMPLES
The gas station **is open**. (The verb is *is*.)
Derek and Ms. Lentz **have been working there**. (The verb is *have been working*.)
He **pumps gas**. (The verb is *pumps*.)
She **fixes cars**. (The verb is *fixes*.)

Activity C   Each group of words below is a sentence fragment. Either a subject or a predicate is missing. Decide what part is missing. Then add words to turn the fragment into a complete sentence. Write the complete sentences on your paper. Underline your added words.

1) Enjoys working on cars.

2) Works part-time at the gas station.

3) The owner of the gas station.

4) A job at the gas station.

5) Greeted the customers with a smile.

6) Asked about checking the oil.

7) The gas station on the next corner.

8) The driver of a blue van.

Writing Complete Sentences   Chapter 5   **123**

Reading Vocabulary
attendant (6)   van (6)
predicate

■ **Presenting Activity C**
After students have read the example sentences on this page, have them identify each verb in the first set of examples. Have them identify each subject in the second set of examples.

Activity C Answers
Sentences will vary. Sample sentences are given.

1) <u>Derek</u> enjoys working on cars.
2) <u>He</u> works part-time at the gas station.   3) The owner of the gas station <u>hired Derek</u>.   4) A job at the gas station <u>can be hard work</u>.
5) <u>Derek</u> greeted the customers with a smile.
6) <u>The gas station attendant</u> asked about checking the oil.
7) The gas station on the next corner <u>closes early</u>.   8) The driver of a blue van <u>asked for directions</u>.

APPLICATION

 In the Community
Sentence fragments are common in advertisements. Tell students that advertisers may use sentence fragments on purpose—for emphasis or to express an informal tone. Tell students that a restaurant might have a sign that says, "A great place to gather." Point out that student writers should try to avoid fragments. Have students find sentence fragments on signs and posters and tell how they would turn each into a complete sentence. ("This restaurant is a great place to gather.")

Name _____ **Date** _____ **Period** _____ | Chapter 5 / Activity / 19 |

Correcting Sentence Fragments

Directions: Decide whether each group of words is a sentence or a fragment. Write *Sentence* or *Fragment* on the line provided. Then rewrite each fragment into a complete sentence.

EXAMPLE   *Fragment:*   When he was here.
When he was here, he paid rent monthly.

_____ **1)** I am sorry for not calling you back.

_____ **2)** The store around the corner.

_____ **3)** Wrote a letter yesterday.

_____ **4)** Derek completed his homework assignment.

_____ **5)** Answered the phone all day.

_____ **6)** From my sisters and brothers.

_____ **7)** I cannot wait to go to the beach next week.

_____ **8)** On the computer all day.

_____ **9)** Went to work at eight o'clock.

_____ **10)** The book I read was quite long and detailed.

©AGS® American Guidance Service, Inc. Permission is granted to reproduce for classroom use only.   **Basic English Composition**

Activity 19

Name _____ **Date** _____ **Period** _____ | Chapter 5 / Workbook Activity / 22 |

Repairing Sentence Fragments

A sentence fragment is a part of a sentence. It is a group of words that do not express a complete idea.
Sentence — I just got a new computer.
Fragment — Great machine!

Directions: · Read each group of words.
· Decide whether it is a sentence or a fragment.
· Write *Sentence* or *Fragment* on the line before each sentence.
· Rewrite each fragment into a complete sentence.

_____ **1)** My new computer not so expensive.

_____ **2)** It does so much work for me.

_____ **3)** The computer was a birthday present.

_____ **4)** From my father, mother, and grandparents.

_____ **5)** Word processing, the main use I expect to have for the computer.

_____ **6)** Word processing also called electronic typesetting.

_____ **7)** Also, the computer would balance my checkbook.

_____ **8)** If I had a checkbook, that is!

_____ **9)** Of course, I bought a game or two.

_____ **10)** Looking forward to playing them right after I finish my homework.

©AGS® American Guidance Service, Inc. Permission is granted to reproduce for classroom use only.   **Basic English Composition**

Workbook Activity 22

Writing Complete Sentences   Chapter 5   **123**

Reading Vocabulary

■ **Presenting Activity D** Go over the list of italicized words in the paragraph below the examples. Use each word as the first word of a fragment and of a complete sentence. Have students tell which is the complete sentence. They may then proceed with Activity D.

Activity D Answers

Sentences will vary. Sample sentences are given.

1) Sentence **2)** With luck and hard work, you will succeed.
3) To be the best at everything just is not possible. **4)** When Derek runs, he feels great.
5) The carpenter will have a job repairing porches or a job building houses on Belmont Street. **6)** The visitors came from Chicago, Detroit, and Cleveland. **7)** Because the math course was challenging, the students worked hard in it.
8) Sentence **9)** The storm was wilder than any that had ever been seen before. **10)** Do you know a place where young people can meet?

Incomplete Ideas

A sentence fragment is any incomplete expression. It leaves the reader wondering *who? what? what about it?* Any group of words may be a sentence fragment. Here are more examples of sentence fragments. Compare each fragment with the complete sentence below it.

EXAMPLES		
Fragment:	To go to work.	
Sentence:	It was time to go to work.	
Fragment:	On the bus.	
Sentence:	Everyone rode on the bus.	
Fragment:	When the bus broke down.	
Sentence:	The riders climbed out when the bus broke down.	

Look carefully at any sentence that begins with a word such as *because, when, where, since, that, which, or, if, to, for, from,* or *with.* Make sure that you have written a complete idea.

Activity D Decide whether each group of words below is a complete sentence or a fragment. If it is a sentence, write *Sentence* on your paper. If it is a fragment, add words to make it complete. Write the new sentence correctly.

1) Because it is raining, the game is postponed.
2) With luck and hard work.
3) To be the best at everything.
4) When Derek runs.
5) Or a job building houses on Belmont Street.
6) From Chicago, Detroit, and Cleveland.
7) Because the math course was challenging.
8) If you come to town, please call.
9) That had ever been seen before.
10) Where young people can meet.

Activity E Find the fragments below. Correct them. You may join the fragment with the rest of the sentence. You may add words to turn the fragment into a complete sentence. Write your new sentences on your paper.

Examples:

Fragment: Amanda goes to dancing class. With her mother.

Sentence: Amanda goes to dancing class with her mother.

Sentences: Amanda goes to dancing class. She tap dances with her mother.

1) On a sunny day. Amanda and Laura decided to go to an amusement park.

2) They asked Mike and Derek. To come along.

3) The friends had never been to this park. Which had many thrilling rides.

4) The park was crowded. With long lines of people.

5) Because they knew they would enjoy crashing into one another. They headed for the bumper cars.

6) They took a boat ride. On the lake.

7) The four friends stood in line for the roller coaster. For an hour.

8) When it was time to get on. Derek changed his mind.

9) Laura, Mike, and Amanda begged him. To give it a try.

10) The roller coaster climbed. Derek watched it. From his spot on the ground.

■ **Presenting Activity E** Go over the examples with students, helping them to see that there is more than one way to fix a fragment.

Activity E Answers

Sentences may vary. Sample sentences are given.

1) On a sunny day, Amanda and Laura decided to go to an amusement park.   **2)** They asked Mike and Derek to come along.   **3)** The friends had never been to this park, which had many thrilling rides.   **4)** The park was crowded with long lines of people.   **5)** They headed for the bumper cars because they knew they would enjoy crashing into one another.   **6)** They took a boat ride. It was peaceful sailing on the lake.   **7)** The four friends stood in line for the roller coaster. They waited for an hour.   **8)** When it was time to get on, Derek changed his mind.   **9)** Laura, Mike, and Amanda begged him to give it a try.   **10)** The roller coaster climbed, and Derek watched it from his spot on the ground.

Answering Questions With Complete Sentences

Speakers often use sentence fragments to answer questions. The person who asks the question usually understands the fragment answer. Compare the fragment answer with the sentence answer in each example below.

EXAMPLES

Question:	What do you want for lunch?
Fragment answer:	A hot dog.
Sentence answer:	I would like a hot dog.
Question:	Which ride did you like best?
Fragment answer:	The roller coaster.
Sentence answer:	The roller coaster was my favorite ride.
Question:	Why did you like the roller coaster best?
Fragment answer:	Because I enjoy being scared.
Sentence answer:	I liked the roller coaster because I enjoy being scared.

An answer that is a sentence fragment does not make sense unless the reader knows the question.

Activity F   Answer these questions in complete sentences. The answers should make sense to a reader who does not know what the question is. Do not answer question 10 with just *yes* or *no*.

1) What is your full name?
2) Where were you born?
3) How old are you?
4) What school do you attend?
5) Where is the school located?
6) What is the name of the town or city where you live?
7) How long have you lived there?
8) What is your favorite television program?
9) Why do you like that program?
10) Are all of these answers complete sentences?

Check your writing for sentence fragments. Make sure that each sentence expresses a complete idea. To fix a fragment, you may need to join it to another sentence. You may need to add words to the fragment to turn it into a complete sentence.

Part A   Read each group of words carefully. Decide whether the words express a complete idea. Write either *Sentence* or *Fragment* as your answer on your paper.

1) The trip to the amusement park.

2) Mike, Derek, Laura, and Amanda went together.

3) "The next time I go there."

4) "I might try the roller coaster," said Derek.

5) Mike had eaten five hot dogs.

6) While he was at the park.

7) Derek refused to eat one.

8) He said they tasted terrible.

9) Is watching his diet carefully.

10) When Derek is in training.

Part B   Choose any experience you have had. Write five sentences about that experience. Begin one of the sentences with the word *When*. Check your work to make sure that all of your sentences are complete.

Reading Vocabulary
diet (6)

■ **Lesson Review** If students are unsure of whether a group of words is a sentence or a fragment, have them look back at the examples in this lesson.

Part A Answers
1) Fragment   2) Sentence
3) Fragment   4) Sentence
5) Sentence   6) Fragment
7) Sentence   8) Sentence
9) Fragment   10) Fragment

Part B Answers
Sentences will vary. One sentence should begin with the word *when*. Sentences should be complete.

Follow-up Activity

Write a few sentences on the board. Each sentence should clearly be the answer to a question. (Examples: The capital of France is Paris. Rock-and-roll music first became popular in the 1950s.) Have students tell what question is being answered. (What is the capital city of France? When did rock-and-roll music first become popular?) Then they may write their own complete sentences and have classmates try to name the question each sentence answers.

Completing Sentences

Directions: Label each group of words as a *Sentence*, a *Run-on*, or a *Fragment*. Then rewrite them as complete sentences. Correct the mistakes.

EXAMPLE   Fragment   Laura asked.
Laura asked to go shopping.

1) Amanda will baby-sit, she expects to be paid well.

2) Looking for a job.

3) Brownsville Senior High has an auditorium.

4) The sun was shining we enjoyed the day.

5) While he was doing his homework.

6) My teacher is very proud of me she hopes that I will continue my good study habits.

7) Amanda was upset over the incident.

8) On top of the table.

9) Derek will continue to live at home he wants to get an apartment soon.

10) Being in a good mood.

Activity 20

Writing Complete Sentences

Two common writing mistakes are the run-on sentence and the sentence fragment.
A FRAGMENT is a part of sentence.
A RUN-ON is two or more sentences run together.

Directions: • Read each group of words.
• Identify the words as either a *fragment* or a *run-on*.
• Correct the mistake. Write the corrected sentence or sentences. You may need to add information.

EXAMPLE   Run-on   Thanksgiving is my favorite holiday I love to eat.
Thanksgiving is my favorite holiday because I love to eat.

1) We watch the Super Bowl it's the best game of the year.

2) Last year skiing, next year ice skating.

3) What's your favorite sport, mine's hockey.

4) Rain, wind, lightning, and thunder for hours.

5) Under the chair the dog.

6) In Florida and California sunny skies.

7) Taxes, taxes, and more taxes!

8) The weather was pleasant we enjoyed the day.

9) What's BASIC, it's a computer programming language.

10) A complete sentence is best, don't you agree?

Workbook Activity 23

Chapter 5 Review

The Teacher's Resource Library includes two parallel forms of the Chapter 5 Mastery Test. The difficulty level of the two forms is equivalent. You may wish to use one form as a pretest and the other form as a posttest.

Reading Vocabulary

stew (5)   patience (5)

Part A Answers

Wording of answers will vary.

1) A run-on sentence contains too many ideas that are not clearly separated.   2) One way to fix a run-on sentence is to split it into two or more sentences.   3) An end mark of punctuation must come at the end of every sentence.
4) A writer should watch out for fragments because fragments can confuse a reader.   5) One way to recognize a sentence fragment is to ask whether the subject or predicate is missing.

Part B Answers

Answers will vary. Sample answers are given.

1) Run-on. Victor has a new interest. He is learning to cook.
2) Correct   3) Run-on. I tasted Victor's peanut stew, and it was delicious!   4) Run-on. Cooking takes practice. It requires patience.
5) Correct

Part C Answers

Answers will vary. Sample answers are given.

1) Fragment. Our school basketball team played against a stronger team.   2) Fragment. Most of the other basketball players were more experienced than we were.
3) Fragment. Basketball is a hard game to play well.   4) Correct
5) Correct

Part A   Answer each of these questions with a complete sentence.

1) What is a run-on sentence?

2) What is one way to fix a run-on sentence?

3) What must come at the end of every sentence?

4) Why should a writer watch out for fragments?

5) What is one way to recognize a sentence fragment?

Part B   Read each group of words below. Decide whether each group is a correct sentence or a run-on sentence. Write *Correct* or *Run-on* on your paper. If the sentence is a run-on, rewrite it to make it correct.

1) Victor has a new interest he is learning to cook.

2) Victor's friends can't believe that he wants to spend his time reading cookbooks and chopping vegetables.

3) I tasted Victor's peanut stew, it was delicious!

4) Cooking takes practice, it requires patience.

5) Victor says that food should taste good, and it should look good, too.

Part C   Read each group of words below. Decide whether each group is a correct sentence or a fragment. Write *Correct* or *Fragment* on your paper. If the sentence is a fragment, rewrite it to make it correct.

1) Played against a stronger team.

2) Most of the other basketball players.

3) A hard game to play well.

4) Anyone can play basketball.

5) You should learn to pass the ball.

Chapter 5 Mastery Test A

Name _____ Date _____ Period _____

Chapter 5
Mastery
Test A
page 1

Chapter 5 Mastery Test A

Part A Label each group of words as a *Sentence*, *Run-on* sentence, or sentence *Fragment*.

1) _____ The first king of England was Egbert.

2) _____ For ten years from 829 to 839.

3) _____ The next king, Ethelwulf, for 19 years.

4) _____ Ethelwulf was overthrown by his son, Ethelbald.

5) _____ Ethelbald died soon he was king for only two years.

6) _____ Next, the second son of Ethelbald named Ethelbert.

7) _____ For six years, Ethelbert was king then his third son, Ethelred the First, became king.

8) _____ Ethelred the First only ruled for five years and then his son became king and his son was called Alfred the Great.

9) _____ Alfred the Great for 28 years.

10) _____ Edward the Elder was Alfred's son he unified England, claimed Scotland, and ruled for 25 years.

11) _____ After Edward, Athelstan the Glorious.

12) _____ Two more sons of Edward ruled they were Edmund I and Edred.

13) _____ Then Edwy the Fair, Edgar the Peaceful, and Edward the Martyr.

14) _____ Edward the Martyr was murdered by his stepmother.

15) _____ Ethelred II, also called Ethelred the Unready, ruled next he was king for 37 years.

16) _____ Ethelred II was only 48 when he died.

17) _____ The next kings were Eadmund II, Canute, and Harold I.

18) _____ Next Hardecanute, son of Canute.

19) _____ Then Edward the Confessor ruled from 1042 to 1066.

20) _____ In 1066, Harold II became king he did not last a full year he was killed in an invasion by William the Conqueror.

©AGS® American Guidance Service, Inc. Permission is granted to reproduce for classroom use only.   **Basic English Composition**

Name _____ Date _____ Period _____

Chapter 5
Mastery
Test A
page 2

Chapter 5 Mastery Test A, continued

Part B Add words to make each sentence fragment a complete sentence. Rewrite each new sentence on the blank line.

1) With her mother in the car.

2) When summer comes.

3) Or to dinner and a movie.

4) On a cold and rainy night.

5) For more than 50 people.

Part C Decide how to fix the problem in each run-on sentence. Rewrite the new sentence or sentences on the blank line.

1) Ross went to the apartment, then he went to work.

2) Milk is a source of protein yogurt is a source of protein.

3) My computer doesn't have enough memory I need a new computer.

4) Pat exercises daily she starts her routine with a fast walk.

5) Bruce has fifty CDs he just added ten more to his collection.

©AGS® American Guidance Service, Inc. Permission is granted to reproduce for classroom use only.   **Basic English Composition**

Chapter 5 Mastery Test A

Part D   Read each group of words below. Decide whether it is a run-on sentence or a sentence fragment. Write *Run-on* or *Fragment* on your paper. Then show how you would correct the problem. Write the complete sentences on your paper.

1) I was in the stands with Derek's other friends it was Saturday morning and we all waited for Derek's first race to begin.

2) Derek had trained hard, we were sure he would win.

3) For the 200-meter run, which is one of the fastest of all track-and-field events.

4) Need to burst out like lightning.

5) It's all over in less than half a minute, it's amazingly fast!

6) All the runners exploded out of the blocks, we screamed until we were hoarse.

7) Two runners flew across the ribbon together one of them was Derek.

8) Was first?

9) Our friend, Derek Corelli, we felt so proud to know him.

10) With a trophy to put on his shelf.

Part E   Read the paragraph below. Find the sentence errors. Rewrite the paragraph as five sentences on your paper.

> Laura enjoys singing rounds, she taught her niece and nephew to sing "Row, Row, Row Your Boat" and later the three of them sang "Todos los Pollitos" when everyone sang a different line. All three voices blended together well and several listeners clapped

Test Taking Tip   When you are reading a test question, pay attention to words that are emphasized in bold type or in capital letters. Those words will help you decide how best to answer the question.

Reading Vocabulary

amazingly	nephew (4)
emphasize (7)	niece (5)
meter (6)	trophy (7)

Part D Answers

Corrected sentences will vary. Sample corrections are given.

1) Run-on. I was in the stands with Derek's other friends. It was Saturday morning, and we all waited for Derek's first race to begin.

2) Run-on. Derek had trained hard, and we were sure he would win.

3) Fragment. He had trained for the 200-meter run, which is one of the fastest of all track-and-field events.

4) Fragment. The sprinters need to burst out like lightning.   5) Run-on. It's all over in less than half a minute. It's amazingly fast!   6) Run-on. All the runners exploded out of the blocks. We screamed until we were hoarse.   7) Run-on. Two runners flew across the ribbon together. One of them was Derek.   8) Fragment. Was Derek first?   9) Fragment. Our friend, Derek Corelli, was the winner. We felt so proud to know him.   10) Fragment. Derek went home with a trophy to put on his shelf.

Part E Answers

Corrected paragraph may vary. Sample paragraph is given.

Laura enjoys singing rounds. She taught her niece and nephew to sing "Row, Row, Row Your Boat." Later the three of them sang "Todos los Pollitos." When everyone sang a different line, all three voices blended together well. Several listeners clapped.

Chapter 5 Mastery Test B

Name _____ Date _____ Period _____   Chapter 5 / Mastery Test B / page 1

Chapter 5 Mastery Test B

Part A Label each group of words as a *Sentence, Run-on* sentence, or sentence *Fragment*.

1) _____ Tropical rain forests are home to large numbers of plants and animals.

2) _____ These plants and animals may never be completely cataloged they may never be completely classified.

3) _____ The dense tree canopies are fragile and threatened and the rain forests are irreplaceable.

4) _____ A major source for supplying the earth's oxygen.

5) _____ Tropical rain forests exert a cooling effect worldwide.

6) _____ Through billions of tons of water they release into the air.

7) _____ As much as 400 inches of rain each year.

8) _____ There are tropical rain forests in South America and Africa has rain forests and southeast Asia contains rain forests.

9) _____ Unfortunately, particularly prone to damage.

10) _____ Rain forests are disappearing fast.

11) _____ An estimated rate of 100 acres per minute.

12) _____ Rain forests have thin soil and the topsoil lacks nutrients and it is not very good for growing crops.

13) _____ Unable to support agriculture for more than a few years.

14) _____ Those who burn the forests and cut down trees are creating a problem.

15) _____ They clear the land for planting they clear the land for communities.

16) _____ Destroying ever wider areas of rain forests.

17) _____ Processes of deforestation and erosion have increased this has been happening primarily in recent decades.

18) _____ Destruction of the rain forests is threatening to alter global life radically.

19) _____ The web of life is both complex and delicate.

20) _____ Many people are worried about the rain forests they are afraid for their children and that the animals are disappearing.

©AGS® American Guidance Service, Inc. Permission is granted to reproduce for classroom use only.   **Basic English Composition**

Name _____ Date _____ Period _____   Chapter 5 / Mastery Test B / page 2

Chapter 5 Mastery Test B, continued

Part B Add words to make each sentence fragment a complete sentence. Rewrite each new sentence on the blank line.

1) If things were different.

2) Or find my lost gloves.

3) After the other night.

4) When the sun came up.

5) Since everyone went home early.

Part C Decide how to fix the problem in each run-on sentence. Rewrite the new sentence or sentences on the blank line.

1) The weather was dry the lawn needed to be watered often.

2) Lan brought a birthday present Lan brought birthday treats.

3) It rained on a Saturday in June it rained on another Saturday in June it rained on a third Saturday in June.

4) Juan bought a computer, then he bought software.

5) The book was so exciting that she didn't put it down she read until three in the morning.

©AGS® American Guidance Service, Inc. Permission is granted to reproduce for classroom use only.   **Basic English Composition**

Chapter 6

Planning Guide

Making Each Sentence Count

	Student Text Lesson			
	Student Pages	Vocabulary	Practice Exercises	Lesson Review
Lesson 1 Adding Adjectives and Adverbs	132-143	✔	✔	143
Lesson 2 Using Prepositional Phrases	144-150	✔	✔	150
Lesson 3 Connections and Combinations	151-159	✔	✔	159

Chapter Activities

Teacher's Resource Library

Writing Tip 6: Spicy Adjectives

Community Connection 6: Adjectives and Adverbs in Children's Books

Assessment Options

Student Text

Chapter 6 Review

Teacher's Resource Library

Chapter 6 Mastery Tests A and B

Midterm Mastery Test

	Teaching Strategies							Language Skills			Learning Styles						Teacher's Resource Library		
	Reviewing Skills	Teacher Alert	Follow-up Activity	Career Application	Home Application	Global Connection	Community Application	Identification Skills	Writing Skills	Punctuation Skills	Visual/Spatial	Auditory/Verbal	Body/Kinesthetic	Logical/Mathematical	Group Learning	LEP/ESL	Activities	Workbook Activities	Self-Study Guide
	132	134	143		133	138	142	✔	✔	✔				141			21-22	24	✔
	144	149	150					✔	✔	✔			145				23		✔
	151	152	159	152				✔	✔	✔						155	24	25-28	✔

Writing Tip 6

Spicy Adjectives

Descriptive adjectives can make your writing interesting. Overused adjectives can make your writing boring. Try to spice up your writing. Replace dull adjectives with descriptive ones.

Here is a list of overused adjectives. Beside each word are different words. Look in the dictionary to find any word that is new to you. Then try to use some of these different words when you write.

Overused	Different
boring	dull, unoriginal, pointless, monotonous
fun	pleasant, merry, festive, enjoyable
funny	amusing, comic, humorous, witty
good	beneficial, correct, right, worthy
interesting	amusing, colorful, exciting, fascinating
nice	agreeable, attractive, delightful, pleasant
pretty	attractive, charming, lovely, graceful
tired	exhausted, fatigued, sleepy, weary
bad	mischievous, harmful, evil, unsatisfactory, naughty
big	extensive, overflowing, huge, mature, important

In the spaces below, make a list of words that you use too often. Look for the word in the dictionary. See if you can find different words that mean the same thing. Write them next to your overused word. Try to use some of these new words when you write.

My worn out words   My new choices

Community Connection 6

Adjectives and Adverbs in Children's Books

When you write, make each sentence count. Using **adjectives** and **adverbs** can help to make your sentences more descriptive. How? Adjectives add details to sentences. They describe nouns or pronouns. Adjectives tell what kind, how many, or which ones. Adverbs also add detail. They describe verbs, adjectives, or other adverbs. They often give details about action. For example, they answer questions such as when, how, how often, where, or to what degree.

EXAMPLES   The fat dog was lazy.
            The dog walked slowly and lazily.

Fat and lazy are adjectives because they describe the noun dog. Slowly and lazily are adverbs—they tell how the dog walked.

Authors of children's books use adjectives and adverbs. Because these books are often short, the authors must make their sentences count. Using good adjectives and adverbs makes the sentences stronger. Read through a children's book to see how adjectives and adverbs are used. Follow these steps.

Step 1. Read a children's book to a younger child. As you read, look for adjectives and adverbs. Listen to these words as you read them. See how each word makes the sentence more descriptive.

Step 2. Once you have read the book, go back to the beginning. Look through the book for the adjectives and adverbs you saw when reading. Write down two sentences that use adjectives. Then write down two sentences that use adverbs. Use the space below.

1)

2)

3)

4)

Step 3. Underline each adjective in your sentences. Then circle each adverb.

Step 4. Have your teacher check your work.

Writing Tip 6   Community Connection 6

Making Each Sentence Count

Do you know someone who tells a joke or a story well? That person knows how to hold an audience's attention. A skillful speaker uses just the right words to help listeners picture actions and understand ideas. A skillful speaker makes every sentence count.

When you write, you try to hold your readers' attention, too. You want them to form sharp pictures in their minds. You want them to understand your message clearly.

In this chapter, you will learn how to choose just the right words. You will learn how to make every sentence count.

Goals for Learning

▶ To improve sentences by adding adjectives, adverbs, and prepositional phrases

▶ To combine short, choppy sentences and show clear connections among ideas

▶ To build variety into sentences

131

Reading Vocabulary

adjective	listener
audience (5)	skillful (6)
choppy	speaker
combine (6)	variety (6)
connection (6)	

Introducing the Chapter

Have students examine the introductory photograph accompanying the first page of Chapter 6. Point out the attentive expressions on the faces of the seated people. Ask students to imagine what each person might be thinking and to phrase it as a sentence. (Examples: *That sounds interesting. I've never thought of that before. I think I'm beginning to understand.*) Ask students for words that could describe the speaker at the front of the room. Their suggestions should focus on the speaker's ability to hold an audience's attention.

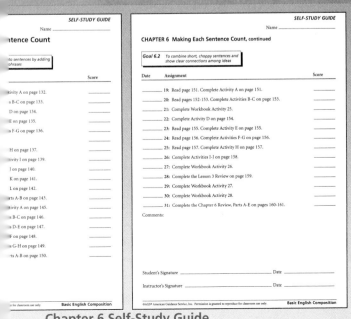

Chapter 6 Self-Study Guide

Lesson at a Glance

Chapter 6   Lesson 1

Overview This lesson focuses on the correct use of adjectives and adverbs as modifiers that add interest and variety to sentences.

Objectives

- To use adjectives to add details to sentences.
- To replace overused or vague adjectives with exact ones.
- To use adverbs to add details to sentences.
- To use adverbs and adjectives correctly.
- To use positive, comparative, and superlative forms of adjectives and adverbs correctly.

Student Pages 132–143

Teacher's Resource Library

   Activities 21–22

   Workbook Activity 24

Reading Vocabulary

describe (5)	**modifier**
detail (5)	**modify (7)**
extinct (8)	motorcycle
furry	noun
fuzzy	pronoun
gulp (5)	student (5)
haircut	yarn (5)

Teaching Suggestions

■ Introducing the Lesson

Point to objects in the room (desk, window, pencil, and so on) and have students name one or two adjectives that could describe each one. Remind students that they can add interest to their writing by using adjectives to describe.

■ Reviewing Skills
Select two or three sentences from a book, and write them on the board without any end punctuation. Have students identify the group of words as a run-on sentence and offer suggestions for repairing it.

Modifier

A word that describes another word in a sentence.

The words in a sentence all have jobs. The main job of some words is to describe, or tell about, other words. Describing words give more information about the other words. Because the describing words change, or modify, meaning, they are also called **modifiers**.

You have learned that an adjective describes a noun or pronoun. An adjective tells how many, what kind, or which ones. Look at the bold adjectives in each list below. Think about the question each one answers.

> **EXAMPLES**   *How many?*
> **one** dog, **few** animals, **nineteen** students
>
> *What kind?*
> **furry** dogs, **extinct** dinosaurs, **curious** students
>
> *Which ones?*
> **those** dogs, **the** animals, **other** friends

Adjectives add details to sentences. Adjectives often appear before the words they modify. Read the sentences below. The adjectives are bold. In the first example sentence, adjectives come before the nouns *man, glass, lemonade,* and *gulps.* In the second example sentence, adjectives come before the nouns *kitten* and *yarn.*

> **EXAMPLES**   **The thirsty** man drank **a tall** glass of **pink** lemonade in **four** gulps.
>
> **A fuzzy black** kitten had wrapped itself in **thick yellow** yarn.

Activity A   Think of an adjective that could describe each noun below. Write the adjective on your paper.

1) _____ tree   4) _____ motorcycle
2) _____ teachers   5) _____ elephants
3) _____ haircut

■ Presenting Activity A
Suggest that students refer to the three questions that adjectives answer as they think of an adjective for each noun listed.

Activity A Answers
Answers will vary. Sample answers are given.

1) tall   2) helpful   3) short
4) powerful   5) African

You may write sentences in which an adjective does not come before the noun. The adjective still modifies the noun, but it comes after the verb. An adjective often follows a form of the verb *to be*. An adjective may follow other state-of-being verbs.

Some Forms of *Be*	Some Other State-of-Being Verbs
am	looks
is	feels
was	seems
has been	appears
should have been	becomes

Notice the bold adjectives after the verbs in these example sentences.

EXAMPLES The winner was **surprised**. She looked **shocked**.
"I am **amazed** and **speechless**," she said.

Activity B Complete each sentence with an adjective. Write the adjective on your paper.

1) The trees were _____.
2) My English teacher seems _____.
3) Movies about romance are _____.
4) I would like to drive a car that is _____.
5) Tests can be _____.

Activity C Add adjectives to each sentence. Write new sentences.

1) The _____ girl did a _____ somersault.
2) Did you order _____ jam on _____ toast?
3) After running _____ miles, Derek said, "I feel _____ and _____!"
4) The _____ dessert made everyone feel _____.
5) The United States is a _____ and _____ country.
6) School subjects that are _____ can also be _____.

■ **Presenting Activity B**
After students read aloud the directions, ask them to identify the verb that will be followed by an adjective.

Activity B Answers
Answers will vary. Sample answers are given.

1) green 2) knowledgeable
3) boring 4) brand new
5) difficult

■ **Presenting Activity C**
Suggest that students read each sentence softly to themselves. They should try to picture what is being described in order to come up with likely adjectives.

Activity C Answers
Answers will vary. Sample answers are given.

1) The small girl did a quick somersault. 2) Did you order grape jam on white toast?
3) After running ten miles, Derek said, "I feel strong and swift!"
4) The rich dessert made everyone feel stuffed. 5) The United States is a large and wealthy country.
6) School subjects that are hard can also be interesting.

APPLICATION

At Home
Ask students to visualize a room at home and to write five sentences to describe the room clearly for a reader. Have them underline the adjectives in their sentences.

Name _____ Date _____ Period _____

Chapter 6
Activity
21

Comparisons

Directions: Choose the correct form of the word in parentheses. Write your answers on the lines provided.

Rule 1: Use the comparative form to compare two people or things.
Laura is *younger* than Shirley is.

Rule 2: Use the superlative form to compare more than two people or things.
This is the *best* cake that I have ever tasted.

1) Of the two pizzas, which do you like _____ ?
(better, best)

2) Out of all the members of the track team, Derek can run the _____ .
(faster, fastest)

3) Chocolate fudge is _____ than an apple.
(more satisfying, most satisfying)

4) Which is the _____ expensive out of those three dresses?
(less, least)

5) The book was _____ than the movie.
(worse, worst)

6) She is _____ than her little sister.
(smaller, smallest)

7) Derek is the _____ person in the group.
(older, oldest)

8) I drive _____ than my dad.
(slower, slowest)

9) In my family, Roger cooks the _____ dinners.
(better, best)

10) Laura received her report card and was _____ than I.
(happier, happiest)

©AGS® American Guidance Service, Inc. Permission is granted to reproduce for classroom use only. **Basic English Composition**

Activity 21

bitter (5)   similar (6)
breezy   software
disobedient   source (6)
exact (6)   spicy
furious (5)   stale (6)
mischievous (6)   stubborn (5)
powerful (6)   sunny
process (6)   **synonym (5)**
reference (6)   **thesaurus**
rotten (5)   vague (5)
sickening   vicious (5)

■ **Presenting Activity D**

Discuss the vague adjectives and sharper synonyms in the box on this page. Have students use each of the sharper synonyms in an oral sentence. Provide a thesaurus for students to refer to as they rewrite the sentences in Activity D.

Activity D Answers

Answers will vary. Sample answers are given.

1) My best friend is thoughtful.
2) The sky looks brilliant.
3) Write a clear sentence.
4) The team had a disappointing game.   **5)** Those flowers are delicate.

TEACHER ALERT

If possible, provide more than one thesaurus for students to examine—with entries arranged alphabetically and with entries arranged by concept. Demonstrate for students how a writer uses a thesaurus to find just the right synonym for an adjective. Advise students to use a synonym only if they know its connotation—the mood or feeling it suggests. Emphasize that "the right" adjective is one that has an appropriate connotation.

Exact Adjectives

You can help your readers to form sharp pictures. Use exact adjectives. Avoid general, vague adjectives such as *good, nice, bad,* and *pretty.* Try to be exact instead.

EXAMPLES		
Vague:	It was a *nice* morning.
Sharper:	It was a *sunny, breezy* morning.
Vague:	The pizza tasted *good.*
Sharper:	The pizza tasted *spicy* and *hot.*
Vague:	Mia painted a *pretty* picture.
Sharper:	Mia painted a *colorful* picture.

Thesaurus
A reference source that lists words and their synonyms.

Synonyms
Words that have a similar meaning. (big *and* large; happy *and* glad)

When you are trying to come up with an exact adjective, a **thesaurus** can help. A thesaurus is a book that lists words with similar meanings, or **synonyms.** You can also find a thesaurus in some word-processing software programs.

Use a thesaurus to choose the synonym that fits best with your meaning. Look at the examples below.

Vague Adjectives	Sharper Synonyms
a *bad* storm	furious, dangerous, threatening, powerful
a *bad* dog	mischievous, disobedient, stubborn, vicious
a *bad* taste	sickening, stale, bitter, rotten

Activity D   Each bold adjective below is not as sharp as it could be. Replace the adjective with a sharper one. Use a thesaurus if you wish. Write the new sentence on your paper.

1) My best friend is **nice.**
2) The sky looks **nice.**
3) Write a **good** sentence.
4) The team had a **bad** game.
5) Those flowers are **pretty.**

Adverbs

An **adverb** is another kind of describing word. Adverbs often give details about actions. Each bold adverb below modifies a verb. Notice the question that each adverb answers.

EXAMPLES

When?
Today we'll shop **early** and eat **later**.

How?
Read **slowly** and **carefully**. Write **clearly**.

How often?
Wages are paid **weekly**. Check in **daily**.

Where?
Put your coat **there**. We'll go **outside**.

Each adverb below modifies an adjective or another adverb. Such adverbs tell about intensity or degree.

EXAMPLE

To what degree?
The girls were **extremely** worried. Benjy ran **too** quickly. He was **almost** lost.

The adverbs of degree include *very* and *quite*, which can be overused. When you check your writing, see whether you have used *very* or *quite* too often. You may be able to cross out these overused words without changing your meaning.

Activity E   Read the sentences below. Decide what question is answered by each bold adverb. Write the question on your paper. Here are the questions to choose from: *When? How? How often? Where? To what degree?*

1) **Immediately**, the door slammed shut.
2) The bell rings **hourly**.
3) Everyone is **very** busy.
4) The baby smiled **happily**.
5) We looked **everywhere** for the keys.
6) The weather **suddenly** turned cold.
7) Derek will run **tomorrow**.

Reading Vocabulary

angrily
dizzily
dizzy (5)
fielder
graceful (5)

parentheses
peacefully
rapid (6)
sunset

■ **Presenting Activity F**

Have students identify the verb in each sentence that will be modified by the adverb they write.

Activity F Answers

1) The boy yawned sleepily.
2) The dog guarded the house bravely. 3) The woman in the painting smiles mysteriously.
4) My aunt sings beautifully.
5) "Ho, ho, ho!" the man laughed merrily.

■ **Presenting Activity G**

Before students proceed with the five sentences, review the corrected examples that appear before Activity G. Have students use their own words to tell why each incorrect example needs fixing.

Activity G Answers

1) The sky at sunset is so colorful.
2) Try to spell all words correctly.
3) The fielder caught the ball easily. 4) We sat here peacefully.
5) "My head feels dizzy," said Mia.

Adjective or Adverb?

You have probably noticed that many adverbs end in *-ly*. You can often change an adjective into an adverb by adding *-ly*. If the adjective ends in *-y*, change the *y* to *i* before adding *-ly*.

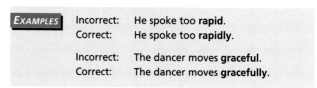

EXAMPLES	**Adjective**	**Adverb**
	Amanda is **careful**.	Amanda works **carefully**.
	We feel **happy**.	We smiled **happily**.
	He gave an **angry** stare.	He stared **angrily**.

Activity F   Change the adjective in parentheses into an adverb. Write the completed sentence on your paper.

1) The boy yawned (sleepy).
2) The dog guarded the house (brave).
3) The woman in the painting smiles (mysterious).
4) My aunt sings (beautiful).
5) "Ho, ho, ho!" the man laughed (merry).

Try to avoid making mistakes with adjectives and adverbs. One common mistake is using an adjective when an adverb is needed. Remember that an adjective cannot modify an action verb. Only an adverb modifies an action verb.

EXAMPLES	Incorrect:	He spoke too **rapid**.
	Correct:	He spoke too **rapidly**.
	Incorrect:	The dancer moves **graceful**.
	Correct:	The dancer moves **gracefully**.

Activity G   Choose the word in parentheses that correctly completes the sentence. Write the completed sentence on your paper.

1) The sky at sunset is so (colorful, colorfully).
2) Try to spell all words (correct, correctly).
3) The fielder caught the ball (easy, easily).
4) We sat here (peaceful, peacefully).
5) "My head feels (dizzy, dizzily)," said Mia.

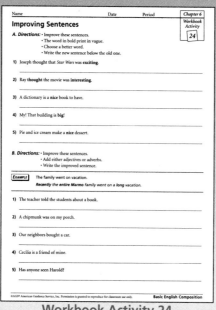

Workbook Activity 24

Placement of Adverbs

Notice the bold adverb in these three sentences:

> **EXAMPLES**   Adverbs **often** move.
>
> **Often**, adverbs move.
>
> Adverbs move **often**.

To add variety to your sentences, try moving your adverbs around. If you decide to place an adverb first in a sentence, add a comma after it to show a pause.

Activity H   Find the adverb in each sentence below. Then rewrite the sentence. Change the placement of the adverb. If you use the adverb as the first word in the sentence, you may need to add a comma.

The Tennis Tournament
by Mike Kaplan

1) I bravely entered the tennis tournament in my neighborhood.

2) I actually thought I might win.

3) These thoughts of grandeur occasionally enter my head.

4) I faced my opponent calmly.

5) My serve has been strong lately.

6) I soon saw that the other player was experienced.

7) "I will certainly win at least a few games," I told myself.

8) I won a few points accidentally.

9) The match was over rapidly.

10) My friends immediately congratulated me for trying.

Reading Vocabulary

accidentally (6)   occasionally
calmly   opponent (7)
comma   placement
congratulate (5)   rewrite
grandeur   tennis (5)
lately   tournament (5)

■ Presenting Activity H

Ask students to say each revised sentence softly to themselves. Listening to a sentence can help them decide whether the adverb placement "sounds right."

Activity H Answers

Answers may vary. One revision is given for each sentence.

1) Bravely, I entered the tennis tournament in my neighborhood. **2)** Actually, I thought I might win.   **3)** These thoughts of grandeur enter my head occasionally.   **4)** I calmly faced my opponent.   **5)** Lately, my serve has been strong.   **6)** Soon I saw that the other player was experienced.   **7)** "Certainly I will win at least a few games," I told myself.   **8)** I accidentally won a few points.   **9)** The match was rapidly over.   **10)** Immediately, my friends congratulated me for trying.

Reading Vocabulary

comparative form
compare (5)
comparison (6)
positive form
superlative form
talented (5)

GLOBAL CONNECTION

Use students' suggestions to make a list on the board of place names around the world. Have them write sentences in which one place is compared to another (using modifiers in the comparative form) and sentences in which one place is compared to all others (using modifiers in the superlative form). Examples: *Minnesota is colder than Florida. Antarctica is the coldest place on Earth.*

Positive form

The basic form of an adjective or adverb. It makes no comparison.

Comparative form

The form of an adjective or adverb used to compare two people, places, things, or actions. It is formed by adding -er to the base word or by using the word more or less. (*small*, smaller; *quickly*, more quickly; less quickly).

Superlative form

The form of an adjective or adverb used to compare more than two people, places, things, or actions. It is formed by adding -est to the base word or by using the word most or least (*small*, smallest; *quickly*, most quickly; least quickly).

Comparisons

You can make comparisons using adjectives and adverbs. Each adjective and adverb has three forms: **positive**, **comparative**, and **superlative**.

1. Use the comparative form when you are comparing just two people, places, things, or actions. Use the comparative form whenever your comparison includes the word *than*.

EXAMPLES

Positive	Comparative
Luis is **tall** and **thin**.	Luis is **taller** and **thinner** than his father.
He walks **quickly**.	He walks **more quickly** than most people.

2. Use the superlative form when you are comparing more than two people, places, things, or actions.

EXAMPLES

Positive	Superlative
Laura sang **beautifully**.	Of all the singers, Laura sang **most beautifully**.
She is **talented**.	She is the **most talented** music student in the class.

3. For most one-syllable words and some two-syllable words, add the ending *-er* to form the comparative. Add *-est* to form the superlative.

EXAMPLES

Positive	Comparative	Superlative
tall	taller	tallest
thin	thinner	thinnest
young	younger	youngest
wise	wiser	wisest
fast	faster	fastest
big	bigger	biggest
happy	happier	happiest

4. With words of more than one syllable, use *more* and *most* to form the comparative and superlative forms.

EXAMPLES	Positive	Comparative	Superlative
	beautiful	more beautiful	most beautiful
	bravely	more bravely	most bravely
	sudden	more sudden	most sudden
	expensive	more expensive	most expensive
	sensible	more sensible	most sensible
	careful	more careful	most careful

Activity I   Copy the following chart on your paper. Fill in the missing positive, comparative, and superlative forms of the words.

	Positive	Comparative	Superlative
1)	big	bigger	_____
2)	slow	_____	slowest
3)	_____	older	oldest
4)	happy	_____	happiest
5)	happily	more happily	_____
6)	ugly	_____	ugliest
7)	bravely	more bravely	_____
8)	lazy	lazier	_____
9)	expensive	_____	most expensive
10)	_____	whiter	whitest
11)	graceful	_____	most graceful
12)	_____	louder	loudest

Reading Vocabulary
lazier   sensible (6)

■ **Presenting Activity I**
Before students write their responses, select words randomly from the ten rows in this activity. Have students use the word correctly in an oral sentence.

Activity I Answers
1) biggest 2) slower 3) old
4) happier 5) most happily
6) uglier 7) most bravely
8) laziest 9) more expensive
10) white 11) more graceful
12) loud

Reading Vocabulary

celery (6)   maple (5)
civilized (5)   misspell
fattening   snail (6)
litter (6)

■ **Presenting Activity J** Go over items 1, 2, and 3 with students, asking them to tell what form of the adjective belongs and why. Students may then proceed with the remaining items.

Activity J Answers

In items 1, 3, 4, 8, and 9, students may be able to justify using forms with the word *least,* in addition to the answers given below.

1) most beautiful   2) less lively
3) faster   4) most often
5) strong   6) more fattening
7) least fattening   8) bigger
9) larger   10) easier
11) smallest   12) most interesting

---

5. Use *less* for the comparative form and *least* for the superlative form with all adjectives and adverbs.

EXAMPLES	Positive	Comparative	Superlative
	new	less new	least new
	expensive	less expensive	least expensive
	often	less often	least often
	civilized	less civilized	least civilized

Activity J   Read each sentence. The positive form of the adjective or adverb is in parentheses. Decide whether the positive, comparative, or superlative form belongs in the sentence. Write the form on your paper.

1) What is the (beautiful) park in the United States?

2) When you are ill, you feel (lively) than usual.

3) A turtle moves (fast) than a snail.

4) Of these ten words, which one do you (often) misspell?

5) Laura is a (strong) person.

6) Cookies are (fattening) than fruit.

7) Celery is probably the (fattening) of any food.

8) This maple tree is (big) than that one.

9) Which of these two trees is (large)?

10) "Running is (easy) than tennis," said Derek.

11) Max was the (small) puppy in the litter.

12) Tell me the (interesting) thing you heard.

Comparing Correctly

A few adjectives and adverbs have irregular comparative and superlative forms. Study the list below.

Positive	Comparative	Superlative
good, well	better	best
bad, badly	worse	worst
many, much	more	most
little	less	least

Make sure that you use only the forms above when you compare with these adjectives and adverbs.

EXAMPLES	Incorrect:	Today I feel even worser than yesterday.
	Correct:	Today I feel even worse than yesterday.

Activity K   Read each sentence below. Write the word that correctly completes the sentence.

1) I have read three books by Tony Hillerman, and I liked *A Thief of Time* (well, better, best).

2) That was the (bad, worse, worst) movie ever made!

3) Ahmed played very (well, better, best) in the chess tournament.

4) (Little, Less, Least) rain fell this month than last month.

5) (Much, More, Most) rain falls in July than in December.

■ **Presenting Activity K** Go over the words in the chart at the top of this page. Before students begin Activity K, have them use each comparative and superlative form in an oral sentence.

Activity K Answers
1) best 2) worst 3) well
4) Less 5) More

LEARNING STYLES

Logical/Mathematical
Divide the class into groups of three. Have each group make four columns on a sheet of paper and give the columns the following headings: *Adjective, Noun, Verb, Adverb.* Provide each group with a colorful magazine picture. Ask the group members to use the picture to create three sentences that follow the pattern on their sheets of paper. Afterward, invite each group to display its picture and to read its three sentences.

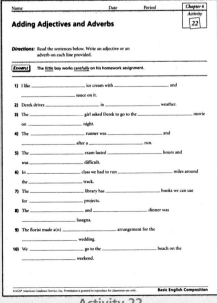

Activity 22

■ **Presenting Activity L**

Before students proceed with these ten items, have them refer to the example sentences above. Ask them to use their own words to explain why each incorrect example needs correcting.

Activity L Answers

1) Today's lunch was better than yesterday's. **2)** Summer is the laziest time of year. **3)** Which of these two brands is cheaper? **4)** The worst storm of the year hit the coast. **5)** Stores hire more people during the busiest shopping season. **6)** Today is the least busy day of the week. **7)** Your painting is better than mine. **8)** Which train arrives sooner? **9)** The friends met less often. **10)** We chose the best day for the party.

APPLICATION

In the Community
Have students give their own ideas about why superlative forms of adjectives are often used by businesses: "**Best** Buys Here," "Area's **Largest** Selection," and so on. Ask students to collect examples of such superlatives from signs and advertisements of neighborhood businesses.

Study this final rule for comparing correctly.

6. Avoid double comparisons. Use either the ending -er or the word *more*—not both. Use either the ending -est or the word *most*—not both. Do not add endings if you are comparing with *less* or *least*.

EXAMPLES		
	Incorrect:	This room is the most cleanest it's ever been!
	Correct:	This room is the cleanest it's ever been!
	Incorrect:	Which car is less noisier?
	Correct:	Which car is less noisy?

Activity L   Find the error in each sentence. Rewrite the sentence correctly.

1) Today's lunch was more gooder than yesterday's.

2) Summer is the most laziest time of the year.

3) Which of these two brands is more cheaper?

4) The more worsest storm of the year hit the coast.

5) Stores hire more people during the most busiest shopping season.

6) Today is the least busiest day of the week.

7) Your painting is more better than mine.

8) Which train arrives more sooner?

9) The friends met less oftener.

10) We chose the most best day for the party.

Adjectives and adverbs are words that describe. Make your sentences clearer and more interesting by adding adjectives and adverbs.

- Use exact adjectives instead of vague ones.
- Use an adverb to modify an action verb.
- Move adverbs to give your sentences variety.
- Use the positive, comparative, and superlative forms correctly.

Part A   These sentences are not as sharp and clear as they could be. Rewrite each sentence. You may change a vague adjective into an exact adjective. You may add adjectives and adverbs. You may also change the word order. Use a thesaurus if you wish.

1) Amanda always looks very nice.
2) Ocean water often feels quite good.
3) I would like to buy a good recording.
4) The weather is bad today.
5) This TV program is usually pretty good.

Part B   Find one error in each sentence below. Rewrite the sentence correctly.

1) Mike's serve is more better than Derek's.
2) Laura can sing highly or low.
3) "Look at what I did," the child said proud.
4) Amanda has several sweaters, but she wears her blue one more often.
5) Victor baked bread careful.
6) Victor's bread smells extremely freshly.
7) Does Computer Village have the most lowest prices?
8) Which of these two computers is least expensive?
9) Ming is older than Mia, but Mia is tallest.
10) "I've just had the horriblest day of my life," announced Yasmin wearily.

Reading Vocabulary

computer (8)   wearily

Part A Answers

Answers will vary. Sample answers are given.

1) Amanda always looks stylish.
2) Ocean water often feels soothing and cool.   3) I would like to buy an up-to-date recording.
4) The weather is steamy today.
5) This TV program is usually action packed and suspenseful.

Part B Answers

1) Mike's serve is better than Derek's.   2) Laura can sing high or low.   3) "Look at what I did," the child said proudly.   4) Amanda has several sweaters, but she wears her blue one most often.   5) Victor baked bread carefully.   6) Victor's bread smells extremely fresh.
7) Does Computer Village have the lowest prices?   8) Which of these two computers is less expensive?
9) Ming is older than Mia, but Mia is taller.   10) "I've just had the most horrible day of my life," announced Yasmin wearily.

Follow-Up Activity

Write the following adjective/adverb pairs on the board. Have students use each pair in one or two oral sentences.

- exact/exactly
- careful/carefully
- extreme/extremely
- good/well

Chapter 6 Lesson 2

Overview This lesson discusses the uses and placement of prepositional phrases in sentences.

Objectives

- To recognize prepositional phrases.
- To understand that a prepositional phrase may function as an adjective or an adverb in a sentence.
- To place a prepositional phrase in a clearly understood position in a sentence.
- To use the prepositions *between* and *among* correctly.

Student Pages 144–150

Teacher's Resource Library

Activity 23

Reading Vocabulary

phrase (6)
predicate
prepositional phrase

Teaching Suggestions

■ **Introducing the Lesson**
Have each student take out a book and a pencil and position them in response to each of these requests:

Put the pencil *on the book.*
Put the pencil *under the book.*
Put the pencil *behind the book.*
Put the pencil *inside the book.*

Students should recognize that only one word changed in each statement. That one word, called a preposition, makes a big difference in meaning.

■ **Reviewing Skills** Write the following questions on the board: *How many? What kind? Which ones? When? How? Where?* Have students tell whether an adjective or an adverb answers each question and give an example of each modifier in a sentence.

Phrase
A group of words that does not contain a subject or predicate, such as a prepositional phrase or a verb phrase.

A group of words in a sentence is sometimes called a **phrase**. Add phrases to your sentences to make your information clearer. A **prepositional phrase** works like an adjective or an adverb in a sentence.

A prepositional phrase begins with a word called a preposition. A preposition shows a connection between a noun or a pronoun and another word. A preposition often shows direction. Some common prepositions are listed below.

Prepositional phrase
A group of words made up of a preposition and its object; it may be used as either an adjective or an adverb (to the store, by the road).

Prepositions		
about	between	near
across	beyond	of
after	by	on
against	during	out
among	for	over
around	from	to
at	in	under
behind	into	with

A prepositional phrase ends with a word called the object. The object of the preposition is a noun or a pronoun. Study these examples.

EXAMPLES		
Preposition	**Object**	**Prepositional Phrase Used in a Sentence**
to	school	He walked to school.
for	him	We bought a present for him.
with	me	Come with me.
from	Karen	I answered the phone call from Karen.

Other words may come between the preposition and the object in a prepositional phrase. A sentence may include more than one prepositional phrase. Read the example sentences below. Notice how the bold prepositional phrases add information to the sentence. The preposition that begins each phrase is underlined.

EXAMPLES   We jumped **into the extremely cold water of the lake**.

A message **from my friend in Denver** appeared **on my computer screen**.

Activity A   Find twenty-five prepositional phrases in these sentences. List them on your paper.

1) The girl in the middle of that photo is my sister.

2) Look for prepositional phrases in this sentence.

3) Benjy hid his bone under the tree in the yard.

4) Derek works at the garage several days a week.

5) The children stared at the storyteller as he told a tale of mystery.

6) For several months, snow covers most of the land.

7) One of the students in the class is absent.

8) The house on the hill belongs to my grandmother.

9) Which of these plays is by Shakespeare?

10) The desk by the window is broken.

11) Stella sat behind Luis during the concert.

12) What begins with a preposition and has an object at the end?

13) Sonia left a message for Vincent on his answering machine.

14) He called her after work.

Making Each Sentence Count   Chapter 6   **145**

Reading Vocabulary
absent (5) storyteller
concert (5) underline
photo

■ **Presenting Activity A**
Have students name each preposition and prepositional phrase in the example sentences. Remind them to refer to the prepositions listed in the box on page 144 as they examine the sentences in Activity A.

Activity A Answers
1) in the middle, of that photo
2) for prepositional phrases, in this sentence   3) under the tree, in the yard   4) at the garage
5) at the storyteller, of mystery
6) For several months, of the land
7) of the students, in the class
8) on the hill, to my grandmother
9) of these plays, by Shakespeare
10) by the window   11) behind Luis, during the concert   12) with a preposition, at the end
13) for Vincent, on his answering machine   14) after work

LEARNING STYLES

Body/Kinesthetic
Ask volunteers to stand and to demonstrate the list of prepositions on page 144. (For example, a student might place a book *over* someone's head, *under* someone's desk, *near* someone's face, *between* two desks, *behind* someone's head, and so on.) Ask the student to announce each preposition he or she is demonstrating. Then have another student silently demonstrate prepositions. Encourage the class to announce the preposition being demonstrated. Challenge the students to come up with a demonstration for each preposition.

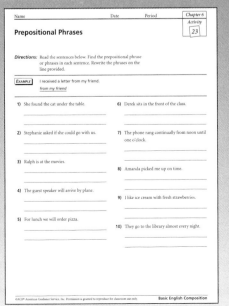

Activity 23

Reading Vocabulary
capital (5)   poem (5)

■ Presenting Activity B

Have students tell what question the prepositional phrase *about kangaroos* answers in the example for this activity. They should recognize that *about kangaroos* answers the question *Which book?* Because the phrase describes the noun *book,* it does the job of an adjective. Have students think about the question each bold adjective phrase answers in order to decide which noun is being modified.

Activity B Answers

1) by Edgar Allan Poe—poem
2) from Karen—letter
3) in Centerville—rodeo
4) near a highway—house
5) with peaches—ice cream

■ Presenting Activity C

Remind students that an adjective phrase, like an adjective, answers the question *Which one?* or *What kind?* Direct them to refer to the listed prepositions on page 144 as they think of phrases to answer either question.

Activity C Answers

Answers will vary. Sample answers are given.

1) George Washington was the first president of the United States.
2) The capital of Indiana is Indianapolis.   3) The man in the red running shorts won the race.
4) The building on Main Street is ten stories high.   5) Amanda received a birthday card from her mother.

Adjective Phrases

A prepositional phrase may do the job of an adjective. It modifies a noun or pronoun in a sentence. Compare the adjective and the adjective phrase in these examples.

| EXAMPLES | Adjective: | The **middle** girl is my sister. |
| | Adjective phrase: | The girl **in the middle** is my sister. |

Activity B   Each sentence contains a prepositional phrase used as an adjective. Write each bold adjective phrase on your paper. Write the word that the adjective phrase describes.

Example   The book **about kangaroos** was missing.
about kangaroos — book.

1) We read a poem **by Edgar Allan Poe**.

2) The letter **from Karen** was short.

3) How often is the rodeo **in Centerville** held?

4) A house **near a highway** can be noisy.

5) Would you like ice cream **with peaches**?

Activity C   Rewrite the sentences below. Add a prepositional phrase after each bold noun. The new phrase must describe that noun.

Example   That **woman** is my aunt.
That woman in the red dress is my aunt.

1) George Washington was the first **president**.

2) The **capital** is Indianapolis.

3) The **man** won the race.

4) The **building** is ten stories high.

5) Amanda received a birthday **card**.

Adverb Phrases

A prepositional phrase may do the job of an adverb. It modifies a verb, an adjective, or another adverb. Compare the adverb and the adverb phrase in these examples. The adverb and the phrase both answer the same question.

EXAMPLES

Adverb:	Sit **nearby**. (sit *where?*)
Adverb phrase:	Sit **near me**. (sit *where?*)
Adverb:	He arrived **later**. (arrived *when?*)
Adverb phrase:	He arrived **in the evening**. (arrived *when?*)
Adverb:	Please drive **carefully**. (drive *how?*)
Adverb phrase:	Please drive **with care**. (drive *how?*)
Adverb:	We are **truly** sorry. (sorry *to what degree?*)
Adverb phrase:	We are sorry **beyond measure**. (sorry *to what degree?*)

Activity D   Each sentence contains a prepositional phrase used as an adverb. Write each bold verb on your paper. Write the adverb phrase that modifies the verb.

Example   The friends **walked** to the store.
            walked — to the store.

1) We **read** the poem by ourselves.
2) Columbus **reached** the island in 1492.
3) The girls **drove** to Centerville.
4) The dog **walked** with a limp.
5) He **arrived** by plane.

Activity E   Use each adverb phrase in a sentence. Make sure that the phrase modifies a verb.

1) across the road
2) by a few inches
3) at the store
4) behind a tree
5) with the principal
6) on time
7) into the pot
8) against my will
9) between four and five o'clock
10) during lunch

■ Presenting Activity D

Have students tell what question the prepositional phrase *to the store* answers in the example for this activity. They should recognize that *to the store* answers the question *Where?* Because the phrase describes the verb *walked*, it does the job of an adverb. Have students think about the questions that adverbs answer as they identify the prepositional phrases in Activity D.

Activity D Answers

1) read—by ourselves
2) reached—in 1492
3) drove—to Centerville
4) walked—with a limp
5) arrived—by plane

■ Presenting Activity E

Help students to understand that a prepositional phrase used as an adverb should answer a question about a verb, not a noun. For contrast, provide these example sentences on the board. Each uses the prepositional phrase from item 1 of this activity:

The house across the road is empty. (adjective phrase modifies the noun *house*)

The chicken walked across the road. (adverb phrase modifies the verb *walked*)

Activity E Answers

Answers will vary. Sample answers are given.
1) An animal ran across the road.
2) A car missed it by a few inches.   3) We bought groceries at the store.   4) The child hid behind a tree.   5) The students spoke with the principal.
6) Please come to class on time.
7) The cook dropped carrots into the pot.   8) "I am being held against my will," said the prisoner.   9) The friends met between four and five o'clock.
10) A guest arrived during lunch.

Reading Vocabulary

advise (5)   physical (5)
confuse (5)   vary (7)
locker

■ **Presenting Activity F**

Read the seven sentences with students. Have them identify the prepositional phrase in each one. Discuss whether the placement of that phrase causes any confusion for a reader.

Activity F Answers

1) The smells are wonderful in Grandmother's kitchen.   **2)** The dog guarded the house for three days.   **3)** The friends talked in the hallway about the party. **4)** The audience left the theater after the first act.   **5)** The apartment with two bedrooms has a big hall closet.   **6)** During a physical exam, a doctor may advise a patient to get more exercise.   **7)** A woman from Sweden spoke to our class.

Placement of Prepositional Phrases

Think about where you place prepositional phrases in your sentences. In general, place an adjective phrase close to the word it modifies. An adverb phrase, like an adverb, can move around in a sentence. Vary your sentences by putting adverb phrases in different positions. Here are examples of correctly placed adverb phrases.

 Amanda went to her locker **between classes**.
Between classes, Amanda went to her locker.

What do you like to do **in your spare time**?
In your spare time, what do you like to do?

Make sure that the phrase is not placed where it may confuse readers.

EXAMPLES		
Unclear:	We learned how to use sunlight to start a fire **in our science class**.
Clear:	**In our science class**, we learned how to use sunlight to start a fire.

Activity F   Find the prepositional phrase in each sentence below. If the sentence is clear, copy the sentence. If the prepositional phrase should be moved, rewrite the sentence correctly.

1) The smells are wonderful in Grandmother's kitchen.

2) The dog guarded the house for three days.

3) The friends talked about the party in the hallway.

4) The audience left the theater after the first act.

5) The apartment has a big hall closet with two bedrooms.

6) A doctor may advise a patient to get more exercise during a physical exam.

7) A woman spoke to our class from Sweden.

Activity G Look again at the sentences you wrote for Activity F. Rewrite three of the sentences by putting the prepositional phrase in a different position. Make sure that the sentence is still clear.

Between or Among

Careful writers know how to choose between the prepositions *between* and *among*. Each word has a different use.

- Use *between* when you are discussing two people or things.

- Use *among* when you are discussing three or more people or things.

> **EXAMPLES** Can you see Laura among all those students?
> Laura is sitting between Mike and Amanda.

Activity H Write *between* or *among* to complete each sentence correctly.

1) When Derek is (between, among) his friends, he is not shy.

2) The members of the group divided the work (between, among) themselves.

3) Some students eat lunch (between, among) third and fourth periods.

4) "Let's split the money (between, among) us," Roy told Arnold.

5) (Between, Among) the two of them, they managed to get the work done.

■ **Presenting Activity G** Go over the sentences students have written for Activity F. Help them to see that only sentences 1–4 contain "movable" adverbial phrases. Students should select three of those sentences for rewriting.

Activity G Answers

All possible sentences are given. Students are required to write only three.

1) In Grandmother's kitchen, the smells are wonderful. (or) The smells in Grandmother's kitchen are wonderful. **2)** For three days, the dog guarded the house. **3)** In the hallway, the friends talked about the party. (or) The friends in the hallway talked about the party. **4)** After the first act, the audience left the theater.

■ **Presenting Activity H** Ask students to use *between* and *among* correctly in oral sentences before they proceed with this activity.

Activity H Answers

1) among **2)** among
3) between **4)** between
5) Between

TEACHER ALERT

Point out to students that an introductory prepositional phrase is often separated from the rest of the sentence by a comma. Use the examples in Activity G, as well as sentences in books on hand, to draw students' attention to the punctuation of introductory prepositional phrases.

Reading Vocabulary

antonym   vocabulary (7)

Part A Answers

1) at a store—adverb; in Springfield—adjective 2) of words—adjective
3) by meanings—adverb 4) with similar meanings—adjective
5) with opposite meanings—adjective 6) of an opposite word—adjective 7) with her—adverb; to English class—adverb
8) During this year—adverb

Part B Answers

Sentences will vary. Sample sentences are given.

1) I waited for a friend at the end of the road. 2) The bus from Chicago arrived during the morning. 3) A tall man sat in the front row. 4) With a big smile, the host greeted the audience. 5) I spoke to the teacher between two classes.

Follow-up Activity

Create word cards using the list of prepositions on page 144 of the student edition. Ask students to name as many nouns as they can think of, and write their suggestions on the board. Distribute the preposition cards to students. Have each student combine a preposition with a noun (adding other words as needed) to create a prepositional phrase. Students may then challenge one another to write sentences containing their prepositional phrases.

Improve your sentences by adding prepositional phrases.

- Use an adjective phrase to describe a noun or a pronoun.
- Use an adverb phrase to describe a verb, an adjective, or an adverb.

Part A Find ten prepositional phrases in these sentences. List them in order on your paper. Label each one *adjective phrase* or *adverb phrase*.

1) Amanda bought a thesaurus at a store in Springfield.

2) A thesaurus has lists of words.

3) The words are listed by meanings.

4) Words with similar meanings are synonyms.

5) A thesaurus may list words with opposite meanings, too.

6) The name of an opposite word is *antonym*.

7) Amanda brings her thesaurus with her to English class.

8) During this year, Amanda has improved her vocabulary.

Part B Write five sentences using all of the prepositional phrases below.

at the end	of the road
with a big smile	for a friend
from Chicago	in the front row
between two classes	during the morning

Show your readers how your ideas are connected. Combine sentences that have related ideas. By combining sentences, you can also avoid short, choppy sentences.

Read the first paragraph below. Notice how it seems to go on forever! The one sentence below it combines all the ideas simply.

| EXAMPLE | Not combined: | Amanda is Laura's friend. Mike is Derek's friend. Derek is Amanda's friend. Amanda is Mike's friend. Laura is Mike's friend. Derek is Laura's friend. |
| | Combined: | Amanda, Laura, Derek, and Mike are all friends. |

The word *and* is an example of a conjunction. Conjunctions are used to show connections among ideas in sentences. Other examples of conjunctions are *but, or, yet,* and *so.*

Activity A Read each pair of sentences. Add the conjunction in parentheses, and combine the sentences. Write each sentence on your paper. Remember to put a comma before the conjunction.

Example Is this statement true? Is it false? (or)
Is this statement true, or is it false?

1) Some sentences can be short. Others can be long. (and)

2) Marcella likes Ahmed. He has never noticed her. (but)

3) You may choose a short story. You may prefer a novel. (or)

4) Mr. Johnson became rich. He never forgot his poor childhood. (yet)

5) Laura was going to have a Spanish test on Monday. She studied all weekend. (so)

Chapter 6   Lesson 3

Overview This lesson provides patterns for sentence-combining with coordinating and subordinating conjunctions.

Objectives

- To understand that conjunctions can show relationships among ideas in sentences.
- To use the conjunction *and* to combine words, phrases, and sentences.
- To use the conjunction *but* to show contrasting ideas.
- To use the conjunctions *or, yet, so, either/or, neither/nor,* and *not only/but also* to connect ideas in sentences.

Student Pages 151–159

Teacher's Resource Library
Activity 24
Workbook Activities 25–28

Reading Vocabulary

childhood (6)	prefer (6)
combination (6)	relate (6)
conjunction	simply
novel (7)	weekend

Teaching Suggestions

- **Introducing the Lesson**
Write the word *conjunction* on the board. Explain that it comes from a Latin word meaning "to join together." Tell students that one example of a conjunction is the word *and*. Have them give their ideas about why *conjunction* is a good label for the word *and*.

- **Reviewing Skills** Ask students to name three adjectives that could describe the noun *weather*. Use their suggestions to create a sentence on the board that contains serial commas and the conjunction *and*. (Example: *Today the weather is sunny, hot, and humid.*) Then have

---

(Reviewing Skills, continued) students create their own sentence using the same pattern and adjectives that modify the noun *sky*.

- **Presenting Activity A**
Before students proceed to turn each pair of sentences into one, discuss the example in this activity. Have students name the capitalization and punctuation changes that were made to create the combined sentence.

Activity A Answers

1) Some sentences can be short, and others can be long.
2) Marcella likes Ahmed, but he has never noticed her.   3) You may choose a short story, or you may prefer a novel.   4) Mr. Johnson became rich, yet he never forgot his poor childhood.
5) Laura was going to have a Spanish test on Monday, so she studied all weekend.

Reading Vocabulary

golf (5)   separate (5)
hockey (5)   series (5)
item (6)

APPLICATION

Career Connection
Write these two items on the board:

- I am hardworking. I am prompt. I am reliable.
- I am hardworking, prompt, and reliable.

Help students to see that combined sentences can make sentences sound more mature and thus appealing to employers. Have students offer their own combined sentences in which they highlight their experience and other job-related qualities.

Using the Conjunction *and*

Use the conjunction *and* to connect words, phrases, and sentences. Study the examples below to see how the conjunction improves sentences.

Choppy:	We planted tomatoes. We planted cabbage. We planted peppers.
Connected words:	We planted tomatoes, cabbage, **and** peppers.
Choppy:	She looked under the bed. She looked in the closet.
Connected phrases:	She looked under the bed **and** in the closet.
Not connected clearly:	Write a good sentence. The world is yours!
Combined sentences:	Write a good sentence, **and** the world is yours!

Study these two rules for using commas with the conjunction *and*.

1. Use a comma to separate a series of three or more words or phrases. Put a comma before the conjunction *and*. If only one item comes before the *and*, do not use a comma.

> **EXAMPLES** We play tennis, hockey, **and** golf.
> We watch football **and** basketball.

2. Use a comma before the conjunction when you combine two or more sentences.

> **EXAMPLE** Laura studied for the Spanish test, **and** she got a high grade.

Activity B Combine each set of three choppy sentences. Use the conjunction *and*. Write each combined sentence on your paper.

1) Monday it rained. Tuesday it rained. Wednesday it rained.

2) I like swimming. I like cooking. I like listening to music.

3) The dog was lost. The dog was tired. The dog was hungry.

4) Charles is late. Rhonda is late. Their daughter is late.

5) We marched up the hill. We marched down the hill. We marched across a field.

Activity C Each sentence has at least one error. Rewrite the sentence correctly.

1) Springfield is a large town and it is growing rapidly.

2) Victor signed up for classes in baking breads, and pies.

3) Jean-Claude speaks English, French and, Creole.

4) Mr. Martin teaches at the high school, and lives a few blocks away.

5) The rodeo events include calf roping bareback riding and barrel racing.

6) Mr. Johnson loves to read and he owns many books.

7) The children swam in the ocean, and played on the beach.

8) Anita plays basketball soccer, and tennis.

9) Chicago New York and Los Angeles are all big cities.

10) The dancers leaped whirled and stepped gracefully.

Using the Conjunction *but*

You have seen that the conjunction *and* connects related ideas. Use the conjunction *but* to point out a difference between ideas. A difference is also called a contrast. Notice the contrasts in the examples on the next page.

■ **Presenting Activity B**
Before students write their responses, have them tell how they plan to combine each set of three sentences.

Activity B Answers
1) Monday, Tuesday, and Wednesday it rained. 2) I like swimming, cooking, and listening to music. 3) The dog was lost, tired, and hungry. 4) Charles, Rhonda, and their daughter are late. 5) We marched up the hill, down the hill, and across a field.

■ **Presenting Activity C**
Have students identify the error or errors in punctuation that need to be repaired in each item. Draw special attention to items 4, 6, and 7; make sure students understand that only item 6 has two complete ideas that should be separated with a comma.

Activity C Answers
1) Springfield is a large town, and it is growing rapidly.
2) Victor signed up for classes in baking breads and pies.
3) Jean-Claude speaks English, French, and Creole. 4) Mr. Martin teaches at the high school and lives a few blocks away.
5) The rodeo events include calf roping, bareback riding, and barrel racing. 6) Mr. Johnson loves to read, and he owns many books. 7) The children swam in the ocean and played on the beach. 8) Anita plays basketball, soccer, and tennis. 9) Chicago, New York, and Los Angeles are all big cities. 10) The dancers leaped, whirled, and stepped gracefully.

Activity 24

Workbook Activity 25

Reading Vocabulary

allergic   lizard (5)
cancel (7)   mammal (7)
chorus (5)

■ **Presenting Activity D** Go over the first few items with students, helping them to consider the meaning of the whole sentence in order to distinguish related ideas from contrasting ideas. Point out that if a negative word, such as *no* or *not* appears in a sentence, the contrasting conjunction *but* may belong.

Activity D Answers

1) Amanda has a dog, but Laura does not.   **2)** Both Amanda and Laura are friends of Derek's.   **3)** Amanda wanted to go to dancing class, but it was canceled.   **4)** Laura sings in the chorus, but she did not sing tonight.   **5)** Springfield has city parks and golf courses.   **6)** Mike likes to play tennis, and he is usually at the courts early Saturday morning.   **7)** The family enjoys hiking, camping, and fishing.   **8)** A dictionary is one useful source for writers, and a thesaurus is another.   **9)** Most deserts are hot, but some are cold.   **10)** The island has birds and lizards but no mammals.   **11)** The drivers honked their horns, but the traffic did not move.   **12)** Most snakes do not harm people, but many people fear snakes anyway.

EXAMPLES

Related ideas:	I like tea **and** coffee.
Contrasting ideas:	I like tea **but** not coffee.
Related ideas:	I enjoy pets, **and** I have two cats.
Contrasting ideas:	I enjoy pets, **but** I am allergic to them.

Activity D   Decide whether each of the following sentences contains related ideas or contrasting ideas. Write each sentence on your paper. Use *and* or *but* to complete each sentence correctly.

1) Amanda has a dog, (and, but) Laura does not.

2) Both Amanda (and, but) Laura are friends of Derek's.

3) Amanda wanted to go to dancing class, (and, but) it was canceled.

4) Laura sings in the chorus, (and, but) she did not sing tonight.

5) Springfield has city parks (and, but) golf courses.

6) Mike likes to play tennis, (and, but) he is usually at the courts early Saturday morning.

7) The family enjoys hiking, camping, (and, but) fishing.

8) A dictionary is one useful source for writers, (and, but) a thesaurus is another.

9) Most deserts are hot, (and, but) some are cold.

10) The island has birds and lizards (and, but) no mammals.

11) The drivers honked their horns, (and, but) the traffic did not move.

12) Most snakes do not harm people, (and, but) many people fear snakes anyway.

Other Conjunctions

You have seen how the conjunctions *and* and *but* are used to connect ideas in sentences. You may also use the conjunctions *or*, *so*, and *yet* to connect ideas. Read the example sentences below. Notice how the bold conjunctions connect words, phrases, or **independent clauses**.

> **EXAMPLES**
>
> I like coffee **or** tea.
>
> Will he travel by car, **or** will he take the bus?
>
> He said he would come by car, **yet** he arrived by bus.
>
> The woman was old **yet** looked young.
>
> The show had begun, **so** everyone hurried.

Look for the commas in the example sentences above. You should see that they follow this rule:

- When you join two independent clauses with the conjunction *and*, *but*, *or*, *yet*, or *so*, use a comma before the conjunction.

Some conjunctions work in pairs: *either...or*, *neither...nor*, *not only...but also*. Notice the bold paired conjunctions below.

> **EXAMPLES**
>
> You may choose to read **either** a poem **or** a story.
>
> **Neither** Amanda **nor** Mike has arrived.
>
> The dog was **not only** lost **but also** wet and muddy.

Activity E List the conjunctions you find in each of the following sentences.

1) The class will read a short story or several poems.

2) It was August, yet the weather grew cold.

3) The winds blew not only from the east but also from the north.

4) I will either phone you tonight or see you tomorrow.

5) The dog had hidden the keys, so Ms. O'Hara never found them.

6) Neither the son nor the daughter looks like the mother.

> **Independent clause**
>
> *A group of words that includes a subject and a verb. It may be written alone as a complete sentence, or it may be combined with another clause.*

- ■ **Presenting Activity E**

Have students list on their paper all the conjunctions they have seen so far: *and, but, or, yet, so, either/or, neither/nor, not only/but also*. They should refer to their list as they read the sentences in Activity E.

Activity E Answers

1) or **2)** yet **3)** not only/but also **4)** either/or **5)** so **6)** neither/nor

---

LEARNING STYLES

LEP/ESL

Invite students for whom English is a second language to print the conjunctions *or, yet, so, and, but,* and *either/or* on the chalkboard in their primary language. Then ask other volunteers to create sentences that use these conjunctions. Encourage the ESL students to point to and say aloud the chalkboard conjunction that goes in each volunteer's sentence.

Reading Vocabulary

dependent clause
doorbell
homework
subordinating conjunction

■ **Presenting Activity F**
Draw students' attention to the conjunction in each partial sentence in this activity. Remind students to think about whether the conjunction signals a contrast, a connection, or a choice.

Activity F Answers

Sentences will vary. Sample sentences are given.

1) Either the doorbell rang, or the kitchen timer went off.
2) The sun is shining, and the air feels warm.   **3)** The room seemed empty, yet something moved behind a curtain.   **4)** We have neither the time nor the money to complete the project.
5) I thought I knew the answer, but I could not explain it clearly.

■ **Presenting Activity G** Go over the directions with students. Do item 2 together to show them how some pairs of sentences may be combined in a number of ways. (*Would you like tea or coffee? Would you like tea, or would you like coffee? Would you like either tea or coffee?*)

Activity G Answers

Sample sentences are given. Students may be able to justify other combinations.
1) Yesterday it was cold and rainy.   **2)** Would you like either tea or coffee?   **3)** We planted peas in our garden, but they did not come up.   **4)** The party was boring, so we left early.   **5)** The runner came in third, yet she seemed pleased.   **6)** You may do your homework before or after dinner.

Activity F   Think of words that could complete each sentence below. Write the completed sentence on your paper.

1) Either the doorbell rang, or
2) The sun is shining, and
3) The room seemed empty, yet
4) We have neither the time nor
5) I thought I knew the answer, but

Activity G   Combine each pair of sentences. Use one of the conjunctions from the box. Rewrite each sentence on your paper. Use commas correctly. (These sentences can be combined in more than one way.)

or	yet	so	and	but	either/or

1) Yesterday it was cold. It was rainy.
2) Would you like tea? Would you like coffee?
3) We planted peas in our garden. They did not come up.
4) The party was boring. We left early.
5) The runner came in third. She seemed pleased.
6) You may do your homework before dinner. You may do it after dinner.

> **Subordinating conjunction**
> *A conjunction that joins a dependent clause to an independent clause (because, when, since).*

> **Dependent clause**
> *A group of related words that contains a subject and a verb but that does not express a complete idea (Before the phone rang).*

Subordinating Conjunctions

Some conjunctions do not connect independent clauses. A conjunction such as *because, although, when, since,* or *until* is called a **subordinating conjunction**. A subordinating conjunction is the first word of a **dependent clause**. A dependent clause cannot stand alone because it is not a complete idea.

Notice the bold dependent clause in each sentence below. Notice that it begins with an underlined subordinating conjunction.

EXAMPLES   The boys played tennis **until it got dark**.
When the car stopped working, we took it to the garage.

When you use a subordinating conjunction, make sure that you have an independent clause in the sentence. If there is only a dependent clause, you have written a sentence fragment.

Activity H   Label each group of words below as *Sentence* or *Fragment*. If it is a fragment, turn it into a complete sentence.

1) Although Ahmed likes to win at chess.

2) Since it was late.

3) Because the sun was shining brightly.

4) When Laura sings, everyone listens.

5) Because the United States was once a British colony.

6) Although Bo is small, he is very strong.

7) Until the movie ended.

8) When the fire began, no one was home.

Follow these two rules for using commas with subordinating conjunctions.

1. If the sentence begins with a dependent clause, put a comma after the clause.

> **EXAMPLE**   **When we arrived,** the game had already begun.

2. Do not use a comma if the dependent clause comes after the independent clause.

> **EXAMPLE**   The game had already begun **when we arrived.**

Reading Vocabulary
fragment (7)

■ **Presenting Activity H**
Remind students that they learned about sentence fragments in Chapter 5. You may want to direct them to Lesson 2 of that chapter for a quick review before they proceed with Activity H.

Activity H Answers
Corrected sentences will vary. Sample sentences are given.

1) Fragment. Although Ahmed likes to win at chess, he feels that he learns a lot by playing against stronger opponents.   2) Fragment. Since it was late, we raced home.
3) Fragment. Because the sun was shining brightly, everyone was wearing sunglasses.
4) Sentence   5) Fragment. Because the United States was once a British colony, Americans speak English.   6) Sentence
7) Fragment. We could not wait until the movie ended.
8) Sentence

Reading Vocabulary

defeat (5)   punctuate (7)
maddening   whenever

■ **Presenting Activity I** Go over the directions with students, making sure they understand that each word is to be used as a subordinating conjunction (*We watched television **after** we ate.*), not as a preposition (*We watched television **after** dinner.*)

Activity I Answers

Answers will vary. Sample answers are given. Students are to use the conjunction first in any four of the sentences.

1) After the sun set, the campers sat around the fire. **2)** Although some rain fell, farmers hoped for more. **3)** Because dogs were barking, people could not sleep. **4)** If you plan to be late, please leave a message. **5)** The game will be played at the park unless it rains. **6)** We will wait until we hear from you. **7)** Please tell us when you will arrive. **8)** I fall asleep whenever I watch that TV program.

■ **Presenting Activity J** Have a volunteer read the paragraph aloud. Discuss ideas in it that could be combined. Then have students proceed with rewriting.

Activity J Answers

One possible eight-sentence paragraph is given.

I lost my first tennis match because I was not playing well. If I expected to improve, I needed to practice every day. When my friend Derek practiced with me, he gave me good pointers. Because the first defeat had been maddening, I entered another tournament. Because I played my best, I won the first match! Although I continued to play well, I lost in the second round. I definitely had improved because the scores were only 6–2 and 6–4. I plan to keep on trying.

Activity I Write each of these subordinating conjunctions in a sentence. In four of the sentences, make the conjunction the first word of the sentence. Check to see that you have used commas correctly.

1) after   **5)** unless

2) although   **6)** until

3) because   **7)** when

4) if   **8)** whenever

Activity J Read the paragraph below. Combine sentences by using these subordinating conjunctions: *when, because, although, until, if.* Write the paragraph in eight sentences. Check to be sure you have punctuated each sentence correctly.

Never Give Up!
by Mike Kaplan

I lost my first tennis match. I was not playing well. I expected to improve. I needed to practice every day. My friend Derek practiced with me. He gave me good pointers. The first defeat had been maddening. I entered another tournament. I played my best. I won the first match! I continued to play well. I lost in the second round. I definitely had improved. The scores were only 6–2 and 6–4. I plan to keep on trying.

Workbook Activity 26

You can combine ideas to make your sentences clear and varied. Use conjunctions to combine ideas.

- Use *and* to combine related ideas. Use *but* to show a contrast.
- Use conjunctions to combine words, phrases, or independent clauses. Use commas when needed.
- Use a subordinating conjunction to connect a dependent clause to an independent clause. If the dependent clause comes first, use a comma to separate it from the rest of the sentence.

Lesson Review   Read the following sentences. Pay attention to the conjunctions and punctuation. Find the mistakes. Rewrite the sentences to show ten correct sentences.

1) I planned to relax last evening but we had visitors.

2) Not only my sister and also her husband and baby came to visit.

3) Tamara Rick and, Michelle stayed for hours.

4) Although my mother was happy to see them. I cannot say that I was.

5) Babies have always seemed noisy, and boring to me.

6) They are always either crying. Or sleeping.

7) Michelle gave me a big smile, whenever she looked at me.

8) She is just one year old. Yet she says lots of words.

9) She not only says "Derek" but she also says "Uncle."

10) Michelle seems smarter than other babies. Because she is my niece.

Making Each Sentence Count   Chapter 6   **159**

Reading Vocabulary

boring   relax (5)
niece (5)

Lesson Review Answers

1) I planned to relax last evening, but we had visitors.   **2)** Not only my sister but also her husband and baby came to visit.   **3)** Tamara, Rick, and Michelle stayed for hours.
4) Although my mother was happy to see them, I cannot say that I was.
5) Babies have always seemed noisy and boring to me.   **6)** They are always either crying or sleeping.
7) Michelle gave me a big smile whenever she looked at me.
8) She is just one year old, yet she says lots of words.   **9)** She not only says "Derek," but she also says "Uncle."   **10)** Michelle seems smarter than other babies because she is my niece.

Follow-up Activity

Have students look through printed materials for sentences that contain one of the conjunctions presented in this lesson. Each student reads aloud one sentence, saying the word *blank* instead of the conjunction. Classmates try to name the conjunction that belongs.

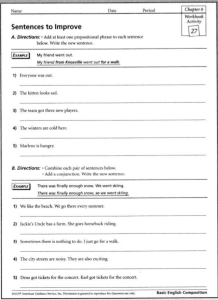

Workbook Activity 27   **Workbook Activity 28**

Chapter 6 Review

The Teacher's Resource Library includes two parallel forms of the Chapter 6 Mastery Test. The difficulty level of the two forms is equivalent. You may wish to use one form as a pretest and the other form as a posttest.

Chapters 1–6 Midterm Mastery Test

The Teacher's Resource Library includes the Midterm Mastery Test. This test is pictured on page 303 of this Teacher's Edition. The Midterm Mastery Test assesses the major learning objectives for Chapters 1–6.

Part A Answers

Answers will vary. Sample sentences are given. Each sentence should include two adjectives.

1) The friends watched a thrilling, action-packed movie.   **2)** The lake is a restful, beautiful place to visit.   **3)** The bread smells fragrant and fresh.   **4)** Your blue sweater is stylish.   **5)** A damaging storm hit the defenseless town.

Part B Answers

Answers will vary. Sample sentences are given. Each sentence should include an adverb or a prepositional phrase.

1) The weather is hot in summer.
2) The dog barked fiercely.
3) We will go on a trip to Arizona.
4) We will go on a trip by car.
5) Arnold arrived extremely late.

Part C Answers

1) The water is less calm today than yesterday.   **2)** "That is the worst music I've ever heard!" said Mr. Noyes.   **3)** Tessa chose the reddest shoes she could find.   **4)** Does Brand X get sheets whiter than Brand Y?   **5)** The bear growled angrily.

Chapter 6 Review

Part A   Rewrite these sentences. Change each bold word into a sharper adjective. Then add one more adjective to the sentence.

Examples   Today is **nice**.
Today is warm and sunny.

1) The friends watched a **good** movie.
2) The lake is a **nice** place to visit.
3) The bread smells **great**.
4) Your sweater is **pretty**.
5) A **bad** storm hit the town.

Part B   Answer each question by adding an adverb or a prepositional phrase to the sentence. Write the new sentence.

1) The weather is hot. (When?)
2) The dog barked. (How?)
3) We will go on a trip. (Where?)
4) We will go on a trip. (How?)
5) Arnold arrived late. (To what degree?)

Part C   Choose the modifier in parentheses that correctly completes the sentence. Write the completed sentence on your paper.

1) The water is (less calm, least calm, less calmer) today than yesterday.
2) "That is the (worstest, most worse, worst) music I've ever heard!" said Mr. Noyes.
3) Tessa chose the (redder, reddest, more redder) shoes she could find.
4) Does Brand X get sheets (whiter, more whiter, most white) than Brand Y?
5) The bear growled (angrily, angry, angriest).

Chapter 6 Mastery Test A

Name _____ Date _____ Period _____   Chapter 6 Mastery Test A page 1

Chapter 6 Mastery Test A

Part A Add an adjective to each sentence. Write it on the blank line.

1) Don is a _____ friend.
2) My _____ sister is moving to Iowa.
3) This _____ dessert will be great for dinner.
4) The _____ kitten ran away and hid.
5) Sharon did a _____ job on her homework.

Part B Add an adverb to each sentence. Write it on the blank line.

1) That train is moving _____ slowly.
2) Buy me that book _____.
3) Judy is _____ bright.
4) Stan went to the beach _____.
5) _____ dinner is served at six o'clock.

Part C Add a prepositional phrase to each sentence. Write it on the blank line.

1) Did you lose a ring _____?
2) The man _____ was here.
3) _____, the construction crew built a house.
4) That family _____ likes their new home.
5) We read a story _____.

©AGS® American Guidance Service, Inc. Permission is granted to reproduce for classroom use only.   **Basic English Composition**

Name _____ Date _____ Period _____   Chapter 6 Mastery Test A page 2

Chapter 6 Mastery Test A, continued

Part D Combine these short sentences into one sentence using a conjunction. Write each new sentence on the blank line.

1) Eggplant is a vegetable. Spinach is a vegetable. Squash is a vegetable.

2) Today there was lightning. Today there was thunder.

3) You may have eaten beets. Have you ever eaten beet greens?

4) I missed the bus. I was late.

5) Tony had not been to Alaska. Paula had not been to Alaska.

Part E Rewrite each sentence in a different word order on the blank line.

1) Often he likes to relax by reading a good book.

2) Cecilia probably will come late to the party.

3) In the summer, I like to hike in the mountains.

4) Bart quickly realized that his shoe was untied.

5) The thunderstorm and high winds developed suddenly.

©AGS® American Guidance Service, Inc. Permission is granted to reproduce for classroom use only.   **Basic English Composition**

Chapter 6 Mastery Test A

Part D Use each of these modifiers correctly in a sentence.

1) highly
2) sometimes
3) harmful
4) gently
5) gentlest

6) daily
7) usually
8) better
9) worse
10) more quietly

Part E Combine the ideas in the sentences below. Use a conjunction. Write the new sentence.

1) Derek would like to be a mechanic. He knows he will work hard.

2) Laura has a clear voice. She has a beautiful voice.

3) Mike plays tennis. He is improving his game.

4) Amanda has known Mike for years. She has never met his brother.

5) Mr. Johnson does not watch TV. He does not go to movies.

6) Is Ahmed playing chess? Is he watching a game?

7) Jean-Claude speaks Creole. His family comes from Haiti.

8) They tried to play soccer. It rained.

9) Basketball is a fast game. Hockey is even faster.

10) Get the necessary ingredients and cooking utensils. Cook your favorite meal.

Test Taking Tip When you have vocabulary to learn, make flash cards. Write a word on the front of each card. Write the definition on the back. Use the flash cards in a game to test your vocabulary skills.

Reading Vocabulary

definition (6)   mechanic (6)
ingredient (7)   utensil (6)

Part D Answers

Answers will vary. Sample sentences are given.

1) The students were highly praised.
2) Sometimes rain falls in the desert.
3) Are the sun's rays harmful?
4) The mother sang gently to her child.   5) A lullaby is the gentlest song that can be sung.   6) Brush your teeth daily.   7) It usually turns warm in the afternoon.   8) Is it better to be rich than poor?
9) My cold is worse today than yesterday.   10) The cat moves more quietly than the dog.

Part E Answers

Answers will vary. Sample answers are given. Each sentence should include a conjunction and correct punctuation.

1) Derek would like to be a mechanic although he knows he will work hard.   2) Laura has a clear and beautiful voice.   3) Mike plays tennis and is improving his game.   4) Amanda has known Mike for years, but she has never met his brother.   5) Mr. Johnson neither watches TV nor goes to movies.   6) Is Ahmed playing chess, or is he watching a game?
7) Jean-Claude speaks Creole because his family comes from Haiti.
8) They tried to play soccer, but it rained.   9) Basketball is a fast game, but hockey is even faster.
10) Get the necessary ingredients and cooking utensils, and cook your favorite meal.

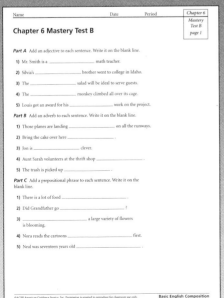

Chapter 6 Mastery Test B

Planning Guide

The Parts of a Paragraph

	Student Text Lesson			
	Student Pages	Vocabulary	Practice Exercises	Lesson Review
Lesson 1 The Topic Sentence	164-168	✔	✔	168
Lesson 2 Developing the Main Idea	169-172	✔	✔	172
Lesson 3 Summaries and Conclusions	173-175	✔	✔	175

Chapter Activities

Teacher's Resource Library
Writing Tip 7: Paragraphs

Community Connection 7: Paragraphs
   in Essays

Assessment Options

Student Text
Chapter 7 Review

Teacher's Resource Library
Chapter 7 Mastery Tests A and B

	Teaching Strategies							Language Skills			Learning Styles						Teacher's Resource Library		
	Reviewing Skills	Teacher Alert	Follow-up Activity	Career Application	Home Application	Global Connection	Community Application	Identification Skills	Writing Skills	Punctuation Skills	Visual/Spatial	Auditory/Verbal	Body/Kinesthetic	Logical/Mathematical	Group Learning	LEP/ESL	Activities	Workbook Activities	Self-Study Guide
	164	166	168		165			✔	✔	✔		167					25-26	29	✔
	169		172				169	✔	✔	✔	170							30-31	✔
	173	173	175	174		175		✔	✔	✔					174		27-28	32-34	✔

Name _____ Period _____ Chapters 7-8 / Writing Tip 7

Paragraphs

The Three Parts of a Paragraph

1) The Topic Sentence
The topic sentence states the main idea in a paragraph. It is usually the first sentence of a paragraph. It lets the reader know what your paragraph is going to be about. The topic sentence should get the reader's attention. It should make the reader want to read the rest of your paragraph.

Ask yourself these questions to help you write your topic sentence:
• What is the purpose of my paragraph?
• What is the main point I want to make?
• Why am I writing this paragraph?
• What will this paragraph be about?

2) The Body
The body of a paragraph is the group of sentences that tell more about your main idea. It supports the point of view of your topic sentence. The body can include:
• Facts
• Details
• Explanations
• Reasons
• Examples
• Illustrations

3) The Conclusion or Summary
The last sentence of a paragraph is a conclusion or a summary. A conclusion is a judgment. It is based on the facts that you presented in your paragraph. Your conclusion must make sense.

A summary is a statement that briefly repeats the main ideas of your paragraph. It repeats your idea or ideas in slightly different words. It does not add new information.

The Purposes of a Paragraph

Every paragraph has one of five purposes. The five purposes are:

1) To give information or facts
Facts are included in all three parts of a paragraph. You may gather facts by reading, listening, or observing.

2) To explain your ideas
You may use this kind of paragraph to:
• Make something clear
• Help someone understand an idea
• Give the meaning of something
• Give reasons for something

3) To ask for information
In this kind of paragraph, make your questions clear and specific. That way, you get specific answers.

4) To persuade
This kind of paragraph helps you to convince someone to act or believe a certain way. You must be sure of what you are saying. Then you can persuade someone.

5) To tell a story
The story you tell in this kind of paragraph can be imaginary or true. A true story should follow the order in which things happened.

©AGS® American Guidance Service, Inc. Permission is granted to reproduce for classroom use only. **Basic English Composition**

Writing Tip 7

Name _____ Date _____ Period _____ Chapter 7 / Community Connection 7

Paragraphs in Essays

A **paragraph** is a group of sentences about one idea or topic. A sentence that states the main idea of a paragraph is a **topic sentence**. The **body** of a paragraph is the part that discusses the main idea. The body includes reasons, facts, examples, or illustrations. Some paragraphs might end with a **summary**. A summary is a statement that briefly repeats the main points of a paragraph. Some paragraphs might also have a **conclusion**. This is a logical judgment based on ideas presented in the body of the paragraph. These parts of a paragraph help to keep paragraphs organized. Readers can more closely follow ideas in paragraphs that are well organized.

All kinds of writing have paragraphs. For example, essays have paragraphs. An essay is a kind of writing about a certain subject from a particular point of view. There are essays about almost anything—government, medicine, sports, and literature. Use an essay to review the parts of a paragraph. Follow these steps.

Step 1. Go to the library. Find an essay in a magazine or book.

Step 2. Write the author's name and the title of the essay on the lines below.

Author: _____

Title: _____

Step 3. Read the essay. Then answer the questions below.

1) What is the author trying to tell the reader about the subject? _____

2) Write the essay's topic sentence. _____

3) Write a sentence from the essay that is a summary or conclusion. _____

4) Do you agree with the author? Why or why not? _____

Step 4. Get into a group with two other classmates. Talk about your essays. Read your answers to one another.

©AGS® American Guidance Service, Inc. Permission is granted to reproduce for classroom use only. **Basic English Composition**

Community Connection 7

Chapter 7

The Parts of a Paragraph

Picture a page of print from a magazine, a newspaper, or any book. Now imagine that the print is NOT broken into separate blocks of type. All the sentences run together. That page would seem hard to read, wouldn't it?

Blocks of type, or paragraphs, make a page easier to read. Paragraphs also have the important job of showing readers how ideas are organized. Do you know how to break your writing into paragraphs? Do you know how to use paragraphs to help your readers follow your ideas?

In this chapter, you will learn how to build a clearly organized paragraph.

Goals for Learning

▶ To write a topic sentence that prepares the reader for the main idea of a paragraph

▶ To write sentences that develop the main idea of a paragraph

▶ To end a paragraph with a conclusion or a summary statement

163

Introducing the Chapter

Have students examine the introductory photograph accompanying the first page of Chapter 7. Tell students that most people do not read every word in a newspaper. Explain that when newspaper readers look at a page, they make decisions about what to read quickly, what to read carefully, and what to skip. The organization of text on a page—with headlines, headings, and text broken into paragraphs—serves as a guide to readers. Have students give their ideas about what the person in the photo might be looking for in the newspaper.

Chapter 7 Self-Study Guide

Lesson at a Glance

Chapter 7 Lesson 1

Overview This lesson provides guidance in using a topic sentence to prepare readers for the main idea of a paragraph.

Objective

- To introduce a paragraph with a topic sentence.

Student Pages 164–168

Teacher's Resource Library

Activities 25–26

Workbook Activity 29

Reading Vocabulary

adjective	**paragraph (4)**
cartoon (6)	produce (5)
film (6)	reread
indent (6)	specific (8)
introduction (6)	studio (6)
lifetime	**topic sentence**

Teaching Suggestions

■ Introducing the Lesson

Before students look at page 164, read aloud the definition of a paragraph, which is given in the margin. Have them tell what term they think is being defined.

■ Reviewing Skills
Write this sentence on the board: *The man worked.* Ask students to suggest additional adjectives, adverbs, and prepositional phrases to add variety to the sentence. Write several new sentences using their additions.

■ Presenting Activity A

Have a student read aloud the boxed paragraph on this page. Briefly discuss how the bold topic sentence prepares the reader for the main idea. Ask: *What do you expect to learn after reading the topic sentence?*

Activity A Answers

Answers will vary. A sample sentence is given.

The right adjective can make a description come alive.

Paragraph

A group of sentences about one idea or topic. It usually has three parts: a topic sentence or introduction, a body, and a conclusion or summary.

A **paragraph** is a group of sentences about one idea or topic. The first sentence of each paragraph is indented on a new line. When you write a new paragraph, your readers expect to find a new idea. You can help them by writing a **topic sentence**. It tells what the paragraph is going to be about.

Since you are the writer of the paragraph, only you know what its main idea should be. Think before writing the first sentence. Here are some questions to ask yourself:

1. What is the purpose of this paragraph?

2. What is the main point I want to make?

3. Why am I writing this paragraph?

4. What will this paragraph be about?

Topic sentence

A sentence that states the main idea in a paragraph; it is often the first sentence.

Read the paragraph below. Think about how the bold topic sentence prepares the reader for the main idea.

> **Adjectives can be words of power.** Writers try to choose exact adjectives that express meaning sharply and clearly. Careful writers avoid adjectives such as *nice* and *bad*, which have little meaning. The best adjective is one that paints a clear picture. An adjective with a specific meaning is a word of power.

Activity A Reread the paragraph about adjectives. Write another topic sentence for it that states the main idea.

Activity B Read the four facts below. Write a topic sentence for these facts. Your topic sentence should state the main idea for a paragraph that includes these facts.

Fact 1: Walt Disney was a film producer.

Fact 2: He produced famous movies, including *Mary Poppins* and *Treasure Island*.

Fact 3: Many of his films were cartoons, such as *Cinderella, Fantasia*, and *Pinocchio*.

Fact 4: The Disney Studio won forty-five Oscars during Walt Disney's lifetime.

■ Presenting Activity B

Have students read the four listed facts and think about what those facts have in common. They may then create the topic sentence that could introduce those facts.

Activity B Answers

Answers will vary. A sample sentence is given.

Walt Disney brought many gifts to the screen.

A topic sentence is a general statement. Examples and details are in the rest of the paragraph. Read the sample paragraph below. The first sentence is the topic sentence. Do you see how it introduces the topic in a general way?

> Springfield is a pleasant place to live. The weather is comfortably warm most of the year. The town has many parks, stores, museums, and restaurants. The townspeople are known for their friendly and helpful attitude. Springfield citizens are proud of their town.

Activity C Read each set of sentences below. Decide which one would work best as the topic sentence of a paragraph. Write the letter of your answer.

1) **a)** Car owners must check their oil.

   b) Car owners must check the air pressure in the tires.

   c) Car owners need to do regular checks.

2) **a)** A topic sentence has two main jobs.

   b) A topic sentence expresses a main idea.

   c) A topic sentence prepares readers for a new idea.

3) **a)** Some students go to college right after high school.

   b) Students have decisions to make.

   c) Some students choose to work after graduation.

Activity D Read the following paragraph. It has no topic sentence. Write a sentence that expresses the main idea of this paragraph.

> A tennis player needs a good forehand. A forehand is used when the ball comes to a right-handed player's right side. The player also needs a backhand. A backhand is used when the ball comes to the player's left side. These two strokes are the ones that a tennis player uses most often.

The Parts of a Paragraph Chapter 7 **165**

attitude (6)   graduation (6)
backhand   pressure (5)
college (5)   restaurant (5)
decision (5)   sample (5)
detail (5)   tennis (5)
forehand   townspeople

■ **Presenting Activity C**

Before students begin Activity C, have them reread the boxed paragraph above it. Briefly discuss how the topic sentence makes a general introductory statement.

Activity C Answers

1) c   2) a   3) b

■ **Presenting Activity D**

Have a student read aloud the boxed paragraph before students decide on a topic sentence.

Activity D Answers

Answers will vary. A sample sentence is given.

Two strokes are basic to the game of tennis.

APPLICATION

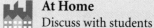

At Home
Discuss with students everyday print materials that are arranged in paragraphs—newspapers, magazines, mailings, and so on. Have students collect samples that show different text arrangements. Students should see that sometimes paragraphs are indented; at other times, paragraphs are separated with extra space or are set off in a frame. Emphasize that regardless of the arrangement, a new paragraph signals a new idea.

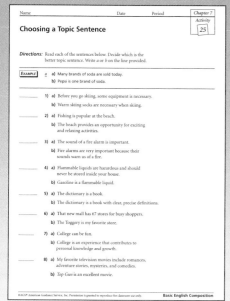

Activity 25

Workbook Activity 29

Reading Vocabulary

■ **Presenting Activity E** To get students started on thinking about topics and topic sentences, have partners brainstorm together. They may jot down all the ideas suggested by each listed general category.

Activity E Answers

Answers will vary. A sample topic sentence is given for each listed topic.

1) If you want excitement, watch hockey. **2)** My third-grade teacher had a strong effect on me. **3)** A person can travel to distant lands with a modem. **4)** Rock Hill Park is a restful place. **5)** TV sitcoms need improvement. **6)** The Volunteers of Springfield organization is doing helpful work.

TEACHER ALERT

To show students model paragraphs from published works, use expository texts, such as informational articles. Preview the work to make sure it contains enough good models. Although it is valuable for student writers to practice writing topic sentences, experienced writers often choose not to place a topic sentence first in the paragraph or not to state it explicitly.

To write a topic sentence, you must start with an idea. Where do ideas for paragraphs come from? Here are some answers:

- Your own experiences
- Reading what others have written
- Information you have received from people

Ideas come from everywhere and from everything that you experience and imagine. Read the examples of topics below. Look at how each topic suggests a topic sentence.

EXAMPLES	Examples of Topics	Possible Topic Sentences
	The fire department	Our local fire department helps the community in many ways.
	Camping	Before you go camping, you will need some equipment.
	Chess	Each of the six chess pieces moves in a different way.

Activity E Practice writing topic sentences. Make a list of five topics on your paper. Choose from the list below, or use topics of your own.

- Sports or other athletic activities
- People
- Hobbies
- Places
- Books, movies, or television programs
- Organizations or clubs

Write a topic sentence about each of your five topics. The examples above can guide you.

Titles and Topic Sentences

The title of a paragraph is like a topic sentence in one way. Both express the main idea. A title and a topic sentence, however, are different. A title is usually a phrase and not a complete sentence. The topic sentence tells the reader more about the topic than the title does.

Compare the title and the topic sentences below. The title only names the topic. A topic sentence sets the tone for the rest of the paragraph. Study the examples below to see the difference between a title and a topic sentence. Do you see how topic sentences 1 and 2 will lead to very different paragraphs?

EXAMPLES		
	Title of Paragraph:	Roller Coasters
	Topic Sentence 1:	A ride on a roller coaster is a thrilling, fascinating, speeding moment in time.
	Topic Sentence 2:	The very word *roller coaster* creates an unforgettable picture in my mind—a picture of sheer terror.

Activity F   Read the paragraph titles below. Write a topic sentence that could prepare the reader for a paragraph with that title.

1) Walt Disney: A Hollywood Genius

2) Why I Enjoy My Garden

3) Five Reasons for Owning a Computer

4) My Future as a Millionaire

5) Beginning a Paragraph

Reading Vocabulary

computer (8)   roller (5)
create (6)   sheer (6)
fascinate (6)   thrilling (5)
genius (6)   tone (6)
millionaire (7)   unforgettable
phrase (6)

■ **Presenting Activity F**

Discuss the two topic sentences in the examples. Have students tell how each topic sentence prepares the reader for a different paragraph. Advise students to think about a paragraph that might be written for each title given in Activity F. Then they may come up with their own topic sentence to introduce that paragraph.

Activity F Answers

Answers will vary. A sample topic sentence is given for each item.

1) Walt Disney was a Hollywood genius.   **2)** My garden is filled with hidden treasures.   **3)** If you are thinking about owning a computer, here are five reasons to go out and buy one.   **4)** I see money in my future—lots of it.   **5)** To begin a paragraph, write a topic sentence.

LEARNING STYLES

Auditory/Verbal
Invite volunteers to call out a topic or paragraph title. Invite other volunteers to turn this topic/title into a topic sentence and to say their sentence aloud. Then divide the class into pairs and have the partners take turns naming a topic and creating a topic sentence. Consider having the students put all these topics and topic sentences on a cassette for use when they begin writing paragraphs and reports.

Name _____ Date _____ Period _____

Chapter 7
Activity
26

Choosing a Title

Directions: Read each paragraph below. Create a title for each paragraph. Write your titles on the lines provided.

Title: _____

1) A person must be eighteen years old to be naturalized as a citizen of the United States. He or she must have been a lawful resident of the United States continuously for five years. Every applicant must pass a comprehensive test on American history and government. In addition, he or she must be able to demonstrate an understanding of the English language, including the ability to read, write, and speak. There is a final hearing before a judge, who administers the oath of allegiance. After completing all of these steps, a person is a naturalized American citizen.

Title: _____

2) The Liberty Bell, an object associated with the historic events of the War of Independence, is located in Independence Hall, Philadelphia. In September of 1752, the bell was cracked while it hung on a beam in the State House yard for testing. The bell was recast and later hung in the State House. It was used while the Continental Congress was in session in the State House. On September 18, 1777, when the British Army was about to occupy Philadelphia, the bell was hidden in Allentown, Pennsylvania, in the Zion Reformed Church. After the British left the city, the bell was moved back to Philadelphia. Each year many thousands of Americans visit Philadelphia to view this wonderful bell.

Title: _____

3) The first American flag had thirteen stripes and thirteen stars—one for each colony. However, the facts of the true history of the Stars and Stripes have become difficult to establish. Although credit is often given to Betsy Ross, no one knows for sure who designed the Stars and Stripes or who made the first flag. No one even knows if this flag ever flew in any sea or land battle of the American Revolution. Although its design has changed several times, the American flag has remained an important symbol of our country.

©AGS® American Guidance Service, Inc. Permission is granted to reproduce for classroom use only.   **Basic English Composition**

Activity 26

Reading Vocabulary

excellent (5)   recipe (6)
ingredient (7)   regularly
purely   source (6)

Part A Answers

Answers will vary. Sample topic sentences are given.

1) Regular maintenance can keep a car going for years.   **2)** If you want to enjoy yourself while learning, pick up a book.   **3)** It is easy to bake cookies.   **4)** Yesterday's storm was violent.   **5)** We planned our picnic well.

Part B Answers

Answers will vary. Sample topic sentences are given.

1) I have watched *The Wizard of Oz* at least fifty times.   **2)** Music that gets me moving is music worth listening to.   **3)** If I were a millionaire, I would do three important things.   **4)** I come from a large family.   **5)** Today I feel like shouting for joy.

Follow-up Activity

Demonstrate for students how to search for a topic that could lead to an interesting paragraph. Start by writing a general category on the board—*Travel*, for example. Then draw lines from it to narrower topics—*Public Transportation, Vacation Spots*, and *Airplanes*, for example. Choose one of those topics, and draw lines to more topics that it suggests. The topic *Airplanes* could suggest *My First Airplane Trip, A Flight to Remember*, and *How an Airplane Flies*. Have students come up with a general category together. Then ask each student to search for a topic of interest.

Begin a paragraph with a topic sentence. Your topic sentence should state the main idea of your paragraph.

Part A   Write a topic sentence on your paper for each set of details below.

1) Car owners should change their oil.
   They should check the hoses for leaks.
   They should also check the air pressure in the tires regularly.

2) Books are excellent sources of information.
   Books can also be read purely for fun.
   People have written thousands of books on every topic you can imagine.

3) First, set the oven temperature.
   Next, gather all the ingredients.
   Finally, follow the steps on the recipe.

4) The wind blew down several trees.
   The electricity was out for two hours.
   The streets were flooded.

5) We packed a big lunch.
   We also took baseball bats, balls, and gloves.
   We took several lawn chairs, too.

Part B   Read the following titles. Write a topic sentence about each title.

1) My Favorite Movie

2) Music I Like

3) If I Were a Millionaire

4) My Family

5) The Way I Feel Today

Body
The part of a paragraph that discusses the main idea; these sentences can include reasons, facts, examples, or illustrations.

What do you do after you have stated your main idea in a topic sentence? Your next job is to develop that main idea. The sentences that tell more about the main idea make up the **body** of a paragraph. Think of the body as a few sentences that support the idea stated in the topic sentence. In the body, you make the main idea clearer to your reader.

Include any of these elements in the body of your paragraph:

- Facts
- Details
- Explanations
- Reasons
- Examples
- Illustrations

Activity A   Practice developing a main idea. Copy the topic sentence shown below on your paper. Then use the details that follow to write three sentences. All of the sentences must be about the main idea stated in the topic sentence.

Topic Sentence: Springfield is a town with many places for recreation.

Recreational Places in Springfield

- 4 city parks
- a sports arena
- a concert hall
- 3 recreational centers
- 2 public swimming pools
- 2 golf courses
- 9 public tennis courts
- a museum
- an amusement park
- 5 movie theaters

Activity B   Read the following topic sentences. Choose the topic that you know the most about. Write at least three sentences that support the topic sentence.

- Everyone needs a hobby.
- Americans are fortunate people.
- Someday, I plan to be a great success in the field of (name of occupation).

APPLICATION

In the Community
Have students work together to make a list of recreational attractions for their own city or town, similar to the list on page 169. They may then use the list to write a paragraph about things to do in their community.

(Activity A Answers, continued)
spend time at the three recreational centers and two public swimming pools. The sports arena and concert hall draw large crowds.

■ **Presenting Activity B**
Make sure students understand they are to choose the topic they feel most comfortable writing about. Use the bulleted list at the top of the page to discuss the kinds of supporting details that they could include.

Activity B Answers
Answers will vary. Students should write at least three sentences that support the topic sentence.

Lesson at a Glance

Chapter 7   Lesson 2

Overview This lesson provides guidance in developing the body of a paragraph.

Objective
■ To develop the body of a paragraph with sentences that support the main idea.

Student Pages 169–172

Teacher's Resource Library
Workbook Activities 30–31

Reading Vocabulary

arena (6)   include (5)
body (3)   occupation (6)
concert (5)   public (5)
element (6)   recreation (6)
illustration (6)   theater (6)

Teaching Suggestions

■ **Introducing the Lesson**
Write the following topic sentence on the board: *There are many reasons to live in a city.* Ask students what they would expect to find in the rest of the paragraph. They should be able to tell that the writer needs to provide the reasons that would support that topic sentence.

■ **Reviewing Skills** Write the following sentences on the board, and have students combine the ideas in them using the conjunctions *or* and *and*: *We are planning a trip to Springfield. We may visit an amusement park. We may visit a museum.*

■ **Presenting Activity A** Tell students that they need not include all the recreational places listed when they write their three supporting sentences.

Activity A Answers
Answers will vary. A sample development is shown.

   Springfield is a town with many places for recreation. People of all ages can enjoy walking among flowers and trees at any one of four city parks. Young people

Reading Vocabulary

bizarre (11)　　　revenge (6)
confess (5)　　　rewrite
crime (5)　　　　springtime
lazily　　　　　　suitable (6)
murder (7)　　　surf (6)
narrator (6)　　　theme (6)
plot (5)　　　　　tourist (5)
poem (5)　　　　vacationer
publish (6)

■ Presenting Activity C

Discuss the off-the-topic sentence in the boxed paragraph on this page before students proceed with Activity C.

Activity C Answers

1) His most famous poem was "The Raven."

This sentence tells about a poem, but the paragraph is about Poe's short stories.

LEARNING STYLES

Visual/Spatial
Have each student print a topic word in the middle of a sheet of paper—for example, *cars, flowers, TV shows, songs, singers, school.* Encourage the students to create a web of related facts, feelings, details, examples, and thoughts about the topic. Suggest that they let these new words race into their minds and onto their pages. Ask them to draw lines from the topic word to their new words and then from the new words to other thoughts. Demonstrate on the chalkboard how this creates a web of information that they could use to expand a topic sentence into a paragraph or essay.

Sticking to the Topic

The sentences in the body of a paragraph support the main idea. Sometimes, you may find one or two sentences that are off the topic. Take those sentences out of your paragraph, or rewrite them so that they fit better with the topic.

Read the following paragraph. Look for one sentence that is off the topic.

> Summer is the best time of year for vacations. Children do not have to go to school. Freedom from classes allows time for sleeping late on sunny mornings. Usually the pleasant weather is suitable for outdoor hobbies: tennis, running, gardening, or just lying lazily in the yard. Sometimes, spring is also a good time for a vacation. In summer, the beaches and the mountains have many activities for tourists. Vacationers can surf or swim, hike or explore, for hours on end. It is no wonder that vacation spots do big business in summer.

Did you find the sentence that was off the topic? All the sentences support the main idea that summer is the best time for vacations. Only one sentence tells about a different topic: *Sometimes, spring is also a good time for a vacation.* That sentence about springtime vacations belongs in a different paragraph.

Activity C　Read each paragraph below and at the top of the next page. Copy the one sentence that does not belong in the body of each paragraph. Write a sentence on your paper that tells why it does not belong.

1)
> Edgar Allan Poe is famous for his bizarre short stories. One of his most famous stories is "The Tell-Tale Heart." In this story, the narrator is drawn to kill and later to confess his crime. Poe also published a collection of stories called *Tales of the Grotesque and Arabesque.* Many of his stories involve plots of revenge and murder. The fear of death, especially of being buried alive, is a common theme. His most famous poem was "The Raven." Many people have enjoyed reading Poe's horrifying tales.

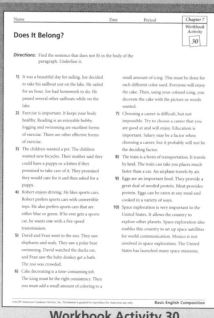

Workbook Activity 30

2) Regular exercise keeps a person fit. People who exercise feel better and probably live longer. Exercise also helps people to maintain a healthy weight. It stimulates the heart and lungs. After a person exercises, he or she will probably be sore and tired. Everyone should try to exercise every day.

3) Our camping trip was simply awful! We froze at night and chased bugs away all day. No one caught a single fish! We enjoyed hiking through the woods. It took us an hour to start a fire, and the dinner burned. The strong winds overturned one canoe and blew down two tents. On top of it all, it rained. I am sure that we will never plan another camping trip.

Combining Paragraphs

The number of sentences in the body of a paragraph will vary. Sometimes you may find that you have written two or three short paragraphs about the same main idea. Combine those paragraphs into one longer one.

Activity D   Read the two short paragraphs below. Both are about the same topic. Combine the two paragraphs into one longer paragraph. Follow these steps:

1) Write a new topic sentence.
2) Use details and facts from both paragraphs to write new sentences.
3) Write the new paragraph on your paper. Remember to indent the first word of the topic sentence.

Springfield used to be a small town. The population is growing. Springfield is now larger than some cities.

Many people are moving to Springfield. Older people find that it is a quiet and pleasant place to live. Many recreational activities attract young, active families. Jobs are plentiful. Large, older homes are affordable. Someday, Springfield may become a city.

Reading Vocabulary

active (6)	overturn
affordable	plentiful (6)
attract (5)	population (5)
combine (6)	stimulate (10)
lung (5)	vary (7)
maintain (6)	

(Activity C Answers, continued)
2) After a person exercises, he or she will probably be sore and tired.

This sentence tells something negative about exercise, but the paragraph is about the benefits of exercise.

3) We enjoyed hiking through the woods.

This sentence tells about an enjoyable event, but the paragraph is about all the things that went wrong.

■ Presenting Activity D

Have a student read aloud the two paragraphs in the box for Activity D. Then read and discuss the three steps that should be taken to combine the paragraphs.

Activity D Answers

Answers will vary. A sample paragraph is given.

Springfield is a growing town. It used to be small, but now its population is greater than in some cities. Older people are moving to Springfield because it is a quiet and pleasant place to live. Many recreational activities attract young, active families. Jobs are plentiful. Large, older homes are affordable. Someday, Springfield may become a city.

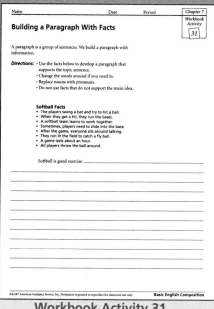

Workbook Activity 31

Reading Vocabulary

clue (5)   refresh (8)
conversation (5)   relax (5)
informative   vitamin (7)

■ **Lesson Review**   Have students use their own words to tell how they can check their written paragraphs to make sure they have developed the body well.

Part A Answers

1) Ms. Lentz owns a gas station.

This sentence does not support the main idea that Ms. Lentz is likable.

2) She also goes to dancing class with Amanda.

This sentence is not about reading, which is the topic of the paragraph.

3) Too much sugar is not good for you.

This sentence is not about what makes lemonade a refreshing drink.

Part B Answers

Sentences will vary. Students should write at least three sentences that support the topic sentences.

Follow-up Activity

Have students offer a list of topics they know something about. (Topics listed for the Follow-up Activity after Lesson 1 may be used here.) Under each topic, list some facts that students already know about the topic. Discuss ways to get more information. Have students write sentences containing details to support the main idea of a paragraph on one of the topics.

Lesson 2 Review

Use the body of a paragraph to develop your main idea.

- The body is the middle part of a paragraph.
- The body is made of one or more sentences.
- The sentences of the body support the main idea of the paragraph.
- The body of a paragraph can include facts, details, explanations, reasons, examples, and illustrations.

Part A   Read the three paragraphs below. Copy the one sentence that does not support each paragraph. Explain why this sentence does not belong with the rest of its paragraph.

1) You would like my friend, Ms. Lentz. She is almost always cheerful and friendly. Ms. Lentz owns a gas station. I like to stop by her home to visit. She invites me in for a snack. We always have fascinating conversations. A visit to Ms. Lentz brightens my day.

2) Amanda's mother likes to read. She also goes to dancing class with Amanda. Her favorite books are mysteries. She enjoys hunting for clues. Sometimes she likes to read short stories. They allow her to visit other times and places without leaving her house. She says that reading is relaxing, informative, and fun.

3) Lemonade is a refreshing drink. If freshly squeezed lemons are used, lemonade has vitamin C. We add sugar to our lemonade. Too much sugar is not good for you. Lemonade tastes best on a hot summer day.

Part B   Choose one of the sample topic sentences below, or write a topic sentence of your own. Then write three sentences that support the topic. Be sure to indent the first line.

- A funny thing happened today before school.
- Before buying a computer, think about these three points.
- Daily exercise is important for good health.

Summary
A statement that briefly repeats main points, often as the last sentence of a paragraph or the last sentences of an essay.

How will you bring your paragraph to a close? You might write a sentence that gives a **summary**. A summary is a statement that briefly repeats the main idea of the paragraph. A summary sentence does not add information to the paragraph. It repeats the main idea using slightly different words. A summary is to a paragraph what a period is to a sentence. They both announce, "The end."

Read this paragraph. Notice how the last sentence repeats the main idea in slightly different words. The last sentence is a summary.

> Track has become Derek's favorite activity. He runs five miles every day and goes to practice regularly. He has won three races already. Derek will continue to improve his time, according to his coach. Derek is working hard at track and enjoying it, too.

Conclusion
A logical judgment based on evidence; often presented at the end of a paragraph or an essay.

Another way to end a paragraph is with a **conclusion**. A conclusion is a judgment based on the facts or evidence that you presented in the paragraph. A conclusion must be logical. It must make sense.

The paragraph above could end with a conclusion instead of a summary sentence. This conclusion could replace the last sentence: *Derek has a good chance to win a college scholarship in track.*

Activity A   Read each paragraph. Write a summary sentence for each one.

1) In today's world, education must never stop. New scientific discoveries appear almost daily. The jobs that must be done keep changing. The amount of new information that people need to know is increasing rapidly!

2) Springtime is my favorite season of the year. The air has a pleasant scent. Flowers and trees are budding. Birds are nesting. The world seems suddenly colorful. I feel like spending more time outdoors.

The Parts of a Paragraph   Chapter 7   **173**

Lesson at a Glance

Chapter 7   Lesson 3

Overview This lesson provides guidance in bringing a paragraph to a satisfying close.

Objective

- To end a paragraph with a sentence that gives a summary or a conclusion.

Student Pages 173–175

Teacher's Resource Library

Activities 27–28

Workbook Activities 32–34

Reading Vocabulary

briefly	increase (5)
bud (5)	judgment (6)
conclusion (6)	logical (8)
daily (5)	scholarship
education (5)	scientific (6)
essay (6)	slightly
evidence (5)	**summary (8)**

Teaching Suggestions

- **Introducing the Lesson**
  Tell students that a period at the end of a sentence has the same job as the last sentence of a paragraph. Ask students what that same job might be. Help them to see that a period and a final sentence both bring ideas to an end, and both help readers follow a writer's ideas.

- **Reviewing Skills** Ask students to write a sample topic sentence to introduce a paragraph about how to choose a pet.

- **Presenting Activity A**
  Have students take turns reading aloud the discussions and boxed paragraph on this page. Discuss the similarity between the topic sentence and the last sentence in the boxed paragraph. Make the point that a final summary sentence should not be worded too similarly to the topic sentence. Then have students proceed with Activity A.

Workbook Activity 32

Activity A Answers
Answers will vary. Sample summary sentences are given.

1) Education is becoming ever more important.   **2)** The best time of year is spring.

> ## TEACHER ALERT
>
> The distinction between a summary and a conclusion is a subtle one that not all students may grasp. Emphasize instead that if a paragraph seems to be left hanging, a final sentence (sometimes called a clincher) can bring the main idea to a satisfying close.

Parts of a Paragraph   Chapter 7   **173**

Reading Vocabulary
forecast (6)   postpone (7)
percent (6)   routine (7)

■ Presenting Activity B
Before students proceed with this activity, have them tell what they think a logical conclusion is.

Activity B Answer
A sample response is given.

Paragraph 1 has the logical conclusion. It makes sense to postpone a picnic when the weather forecast calls for rain, but it makes no sense to say that a useful computer was a waste of money.

■ Presenting Activity C
Have one student read aloud the boxed paragraph on page 173. Have another student read it again, substituting the conclusion (given below the box on page 173) for the summary sentence. Discuss how a conclusion differs from a summary.

Activity C Answers
1) Conclusion
2) Summary

APPLICATION

Career Connection
Tell students that if they are writing a letter to apply for a job, they may include a paragraph telling why they are qualified. Have students give examples of conclusions that a job applicant might write to wrap up such a paragraph.

LEARNING STYLES

Interpersonal/Group Learning
Divide the class into groups of five. Ask each group to create a paragraph by composing a topic sentence, three middle sentences that develop this topic, and a concluding or summary sentence. Have the groups read their paragraphs to the class.

Activity B   Read the two paragraphs below. Study the last sentence of each. Does paragraph 1 or paragraph 2 have a logical conclusion? Write a sentence on your paper to give a reason for your choice.

1) Amanda and Laura wondered whether Saturday would be a good day for a picnic. Most of their friends were going away. The weather forecast called for rain. All week the weather had been cold. They decided to postpone the picnic until some other time.

2) Last year Amanda's mother bought a computer for Amanda. Amanda and her mother enjoyed playing computer games. Ms. O'Hara used the computer to keep track of spending. Amanda used the computer to learn Spanish. The computer had been a waste of money.

Activity C   Read both of the paragraphs below. Read the last sentence of each paragraph carefully. Decide whether that ending sentence is a summary or a conclusion. On your paper, write *Summary* or *Conclusion*.

1) Every day, Ms. Lentz listens to the weather report. Then she looks outside. One day the report called for sunny skies. The chance of rain was only ten percent. When Ms. Lentz looked outside, she saw that it was raining. She decided that the weather report was wrong.

2) Ms. Lentz does the same thing every morning. She gets up, takes a shower, gets dressed, and then reads her newspaper. While she eats her breakfast, she reads. When she has finished the paper, she leaves for work. Ms. Lentz follows this routine every day.

Name	Date	Period	Chapter 7 Activity 27

Building a Paragraph With Facts

Directions: A paragraph is a group of sentences about one idea or topic. Build a paragraph with information. Use the facts below to develop a paragraph that supports the topic sentence. Arrange these facts in a logical order. Change the words around or add words if necessary. Replace nouns with pronouns. Do not use any facts that do not support the main idea. Write a conclusion or summary sentence at the end of your paragraph.

Skiing Facts
- Skiing takes a lot of coordination and balance.
- Learning to ski takes a lot of time and effort.
- Skiers need to purchase or rent equipment suitable for their size and skill level.
- People's ability to ski changes as they practice.
- Skiing is good exercise.
- Good snow conditions will have a major effect on how people ski.
- Skiers must dress warmly in cold weather.
- Skiing is a very expensive sport.
- Various slopes are open in many states.
- Skiing is fun.

Skiing is a popular sport. _____

_____

_____

_____

_____

_____

©AGS® American Guidance Service, Inc. Permission is granted to reproduce for classroom use only.   **Basic English Composition**

Activity 27

Name	Date	Period	Chapter 7 Activity 28

Writing a Paragraph

Directions: A paragraph has three parts: a beginning, a middle, and an end. Follow the steps below to write a paragraph on a topic of your choice. Indent the first sentence of the paragraph. After you have completed your paragraph, write an interesting title on the line provided.

Step 1: The beginning of the paragraph is called the topic sentence. It states the main idea of a paragraph. Decide what subject you want to write about. Write a topic sentence that tells the reader what your paragraph is about.

Step 2: The middle of the paragraph is the body. The body tells about the subject. It includes examples, details, and explanations. Write three or four sentences about the subject in your paragraph.

Step 3: The end of the paragraph is the conclusion. The last sentence of the paragraph should summarize the main idea. Write the conclusion to your paragraph.

Title: _____

_____

_____

_____

_____

©AGS® American Guidance Service, Inc. Permission is granted to reproduce for classroom use only.   **Basic English Composition**

Activity 28

Lesson 3 Review

You can bring a paragraph to a close by writing a final sentence. The sentence can be a summary or a conclusion.

- A summary states the main idea again but with different words.
- A conclusion is a logical judgment based on the details in the paragraph.

Part A Read each paragraph below. End the first paragraph with a summary statement. End the second with a conclusion.

1) Have you ever found a writer who makes you laugh out loud? I read everything I can find by Dave Barry. Every week, I read his column in the newspaper. If it is especially funny, I cut it out and save it. I have also bought two of Dave Barry's books.

2) The Summer Olympics includes a contest called the decathlon. The decathlon is actually ten events. Athletes from all over the world try to run fastest in the 100-meter, the 400-meter, and the 1,500-meter races. They run a high hurdle race. They throw the discus, the javelin, and the shot put. They leap in the high jump and the long jump. They also aim high in the pole vault.

Part B Read the paragraphs below. Write either a summary or a conclusion for each paragraph.

1) Last month, Derek met a girl on the track team. She runs the mile. She told him that she has played sports all her life. She also teaches an exercise class. She and Derek share many interests. Her name is Shirley.

2) Amanda and Laura are worried about their friend Derek. Now that he has met Shirley, he looks dreamy all the time. He has stopped doing his homework. His old friends hardly ever see him.

Reading Vocabulary

athlete (6)   hurdle (5)
column (5)   javelin
decathlon   meter (6)
discus (5)   Olympic
dreamy   shotput
homework   vault (6)

Part A Answers

Answers will vary. Sample sentences are given.

1) Whenever I need a chuckle, I reread Dave Barry's writings.
2) It is no surprise that the winner of a decathlon is sometimes called the greatest athlete in the world.

Part B Answers

Answers will vary. Sample sentences are given.

1) Derek may be falling in love with Shirley.   2) Amanda and Laura are wishing that the old Derek would return.

Follow-up Activity

Have students refer to the topic sentence and supporting sentences they worked on in the Follow-up Activity after Lesson 2. Ask them to develop a complete paragraph using those sentences. Remind them to bring the paragraph to a close with a summary or a conclusion.

GLOBAL CONNECTION

Use item 2 in Part A to stimulate discussion of the Olympics. Help students to use an almanac to look up information about the Olympic Games. Have them list facts about recent Olympic winners and their countries of origin. Work together to develop a paragraph about the Olympic Games.

Workbook Activity 33

Name _____ Date _____ Period _____ | Chapter 7 Workbook Activity 33

Paragraph Writing Practice

Directions: • Use each group of sentences to build a paragraph.
• The first sentence must express the main idea.
• The body must support the main idea.
• The last sentence must be a conclusion or a summary.

A. A Fire Protection Engineer

1) Builders consult these engineers to be sure the building follows the fire safety codes.
2) Most people have never heard of a fire protection engineer.
3) Communities hire fire protection engineers to decide where fire hydrants should be placed.
4) A fire protection engineer does an important job in a community.
5) After a fire, these engineers investigate to find out the cause.

B. Being Letter Perfect

1) Are you neat or sloppy?
2) Every paper that you write in school says something more than words.
3) A reader can tell many things about a writer.
4) Are you careful or careless?
5) Do you think before you speak or write?
6) Your writing says something about you.

©AGS® American Guidance Service, Inc. Permission is granted to reproduce for classroom use only.   **Basic English Composition**

Workbook Activity 34

Name _____ Date _____ Period _____ | Chapter 7 Workbook Activity 34

Writing a Paragraph

A paragraph has three parts: a beginning, a middle, and an end.

Directions: • Follow the steps listed below.
• Write your own paragraph on a topic of your choice.
• Indent only the first sentence of the paragraph.
• Write an interesting title for the paragraph.

Step 1: The beginning of the paragraph is called the **topic sentence**. It states the main idea of a paragraph.
Decide what subject you want to write about. Write a topic sentence that tells the reader what the paragraph is about.
Step 2: The middle of the paragraph is the **body**. The body tells about the subject. It has examples, details, and explanations.
Write three or four sentences about the subject.
Step 3: The end of the paragraph is the **conclusion**. The last sentence of the paragraph should summarize the main idea.
Write the conclusion to your paragraph.

Title _____

©AGS® American Guidance Service, Inc. Permission is granted to reproduce for classroom use only.   **Basic English Composition**

Chapter 7 Review

The Teacher's Resource Library includes two parallel forms of the Chapter 7 Mastery Test. The difficulty level of the two forms is equivalent. You may wish to use one form as a pretest and the other form as a posttest.

Reading Vocabulary

atlas (7)　　raft (6)
connect (5)　research (6)
personal (6)　tax (5)
process (6)　value (5)

Part A Answers

Answers will vary. Sample topic sentences are given.

1) Ironworkers probably have the most dangerous jobs in the world. **2)** A loving family is more valuable than gold. **3)** I dream of driving a Corvette. **4)** In the future, there will be no need for students to go to a classroom. **5)** I would not like to be famous.

Part B Answers

Answers will vary. Sample paragraphs are given.

1) Personal computers have many uses. Word processing is probably the most popular use. More and more people are also using computers with modems to access computer networks. Students do research using CD-ROM disks and on-line databases. Working people use computers to track their finances and do their taxes. Personal computers are part of daily life in the United States. **2)** The Grand Canyon is a popular tourist spot. Tens of thousands of visitors come to gaze at the steep canyon walls. Many tourists take rafting trips down the Colorado River. They may also reach the bottom of the canyon by riding on mules or by hiking the trails. There is no place in the world quite like the Grand Canyon. **3)** Researchers can find many resources at the library. An encyclopedia gives general information. A dictionary gives word meanings and word histories. An atlas contains maps. The reference room of the library has all these sources and more.

Part A　Write a topic sentence that could introduce a paragraph on each topic below.

1) A dangerous job
2) Something of value
3) The perfect car
4) Schools of the future
5) Fame

Part B　Read each set of four facts below and on the next page. Use each set of facts to write a paragraph. Add more information if you wish. Start your paragraph with a topic sentence. End your paragraph with a summary or a conclusion.

1) People use personal computers for word processing.

   Personal computers connect users to other computers.

   Students do research using personal computers.

   People do their taxes on personal computers.

2) Visitors want to see the steep canyon walls.

   Rafting trips down the river are popular.

   Mules take riders to the bottom of the canyon.

   There are many hiking trails.

3) An encyclopedia gives general information.

   A dictionary gives word meanings.

   A dictionary also gives word histories.

   An atlas contains maps.

Chapter 7 Mastery Test A

Name _____ Date _____ Period _____

Chapter 7 Mastery Test A page 1

Part A　Write a topic sentence for each of these titles.

1) My Favorite Book

2) My Idea of a Perfect Vacation

3) The Job I Would Like Most

4) The Holiday I Like Best

5) The Person I Most Admire

6) My Favorite Musician

Part B　Pick one title from Part A. Copy the topic sentence you wrote for it. Write three sentences to support your topic sentence.

Topic Sentence _____

1) _____

2) _____

3) _____

©AGS® American Guidance Service, Inc. Permission is granted to reproduce for classroom use only.　**Basic English Composition**

Name _____ Date _____ Period _____

Chapter 7 Mastery Test A page 2

Chapter 7 Mastery Test A, continued

Part C　Choose the better summary or conclusion for each paragraph. Circle A or B.

1) Wintertime in Alaska is very strange. There are only a few hours of sunlight each day. People go to school and work in the dark. They also go home in the dark.
   A) During the winter in Alaska, a day is mostly night.
   B) During the summer, the opposite is true.

2) Your ears are a marvelous thing. Ears let you know when someone is calling you. They hold up your eyeglasses. Ears help you to keep your hair out of your face. Your ears are a place to put earrings.
   A) Eyes are important, too.
   B) Ears help you in more ways than just hearing.

3) Reading a book can be habit forming. You get wrapped up in the story. You become involved with the people you are reading about. The only thing that matters is finding out what happens next.
   A) The power of a good book can be amazing.
   B) Good books often make good movies.

4) There are several reasons for being a vegetarian. Some people think it is heartless to eat animals. Other people think that a meatless diet is healthier for their body. Weight control can be easier when meat is dropped from the diet.
   A) Then again, some people just can't pass up a good steak.
   B) A vegetarian diet may be right for you.

5) What is your favorite way to cook an egg? Fried eggs are a traditional favorite. Poached eggs are a healthy choice. Eggs Benedict is delicious. Scrambled eggs are fast and easy.
   A) Choosing a favorite egg dish is hard.
   B) Eggs are used in desserts, too.

6) Most successful people make sacrifices. When others are playing or resting, these people are working. Playing and resting are not as important to them as pleasure in completing their work.
   A) Personal sacrifices lead to success for some people.
   B) Successful people never have any fun.

©AGS® American Guidance Service, Inc. Permission is granted to reproduce for classroom use only.　**Basic English Composition**

Chapter 7 Mastery Test A

4) First roll out the dough for the crust.

Place the dough in a pie plate.

Next prepare the filling.

Pour the filling into the crust.

5) Snow began *falling* at midnight.

It continued to fall for 36 hours.

Snow piled high in the streets.

No cars were allowed downtown.

Part C   Read the paragraphs below. Write a summary or a conclusion for each paragraph.

1) Mike's little brother, Tim, loves tennis. Although he is very young, Tim is strong. He moves quickly around the court. He has developed a spin serve. His two-handed backhand is steady.

2) There are six children in Mike's family. Mike is the oldest. Next in line is his sister, Karen. The middle kids are twins. Their names are Jack and Joe. Number five is Kathy. The youngest child is Tim.

Part D   Write a five-sentence paragraph on this topic: *The three parts of a paragraph.*

Test Taking Tip   Look over a test before you begin answering questions. See how many parts there are. See what you are being asked to do on each part.

Reading Vocabulary

crust (5)	downtown
dough (5)	

(Part B Answers, continued)

4) It is simple to bake a pie. First roll out the dough for the crust. Then place the dough in a pie plate. After that, prepare the filling. You can use fresh fruit or canned filling. Pour the filling into the crust. Put the pie in the oven. Baking a pie is easy, and eating it is even easier.

5) Last week we had an amazing storm! Snow began falling at midnight on Sunday. It continued to fall for 36 hours. Snow piled high in the streets. No cars were allowed downtown. Schools and public buildings were closed. Weather can certainly change people's lives.

Part C Answers

Answers will vary. Sample sentences are given.

1) Tim may someday be a professional tennis player.

2) By modern American standards, Mike's family is huge.

Part D Answers

Answers will vary. A sample paragraph is given.

A paragraph has three main parts. The topic sentence introduces the main idea of the paragraph. The body of the paragraph develops the main idea. The body is made of several sentences with supporting facts, examples, and reasons. The last sentence of a paragraph may be a conclusion or a summary.

Chapter 7 Mastery Test B

Chapter 8

Planning Guide

The Purpose of a Paragraph

	Student Text Lesson			
	Student Pages	Vocabulary	Practice Exercises	Lesson Review
Lesson 1 Information and Explanations	180-183		✔	183
Lesson 2 The How-To Paragraph	184-187	✔	✔	187
Lesson 3 Asking for Information	188-190		✔	190
Lesson 4 The Art of Persuasion	191-193	✔	✔	193
Lesson 5 Telling a Story	194-197	✔	✔	197

Chapter Activities

Teacher's Resource Library

Writing Tip 7: Paragraphs

Writing Tip 8: Checklist for Proofreading and Revising

Community Connection 8: Finding the Purpose of Paragraphs

Assessment Options

Student Text

Chapter 8 Review

Teacher's Resource Library

Chapter 8 Mastery Tests A and B

	Teaching Strategies							Language Skills			Learning Styles						Teacher's Resource Library		
Reviewing Skills	Teacher Alert	Follow-up Activity	Career Application	Home Application	Global Connection	Community Application	Identification Skills	Writing Skills	Punctuation Skills	Visual/Spatial	Auditory/Verbal	Body/Kinesthetic	Logical/Mathematical	Group Learning	LEP/ESL	Activities	Workbook Activities	Self-Study Guide
180		183	182	183			✔	✔	✔						182			✔
184	185-186	187				184	✔	✔	✔				185					✔
188		190					✔	✔	✔	189						29	35	✔
191		193			192		✔	✔	✔		193							✔
194		197					✔	✔	✔					195		30-32	36-37	✔

Writing Tip 7

Name _____ Period _____   Chapters 7-8 / Writing Tip 7

Paragraphs

The Three Parts of a Paragraph

1) The Topic Sentence
The topic sentence states the main idea in a paragraph. It is usually the first sentence of a paragraph. It lets the reader know what your paragraph is going to be about. The topic sentence should get the reader's attention. It should make the reader want to read the rest of your paragraph.

Ask yourself these questions to help you write your topic sentence:
• What is the purpose of my paragraph?
• What is the main point I want to make?
• Why am I writing this paragraph?
• What will this paragraph be about?

2) The Body
The body of a paragraph is the group of sentences that tell more about your main idea. It supports the point of view of your topic sentence. The body can include:
• Facts
• Details
• Explanations
• Reasons
• Examples
• Illustrations

3) The Conclusion or Summary
The last sentence of a paragraph is a conclusion or a summary. A conclusion is a judgment. It is based on the facts that you presented in your paragraph. Your conclusion must make sense.

A summary is a statement that briefly repeats the main ideas of your paragraph. It repeats your idea or ideas in slightly different words. It does not add new information.

The Purposes of a Paragraph

Every paragraph has one of five purposes. The five purposes are:

1) To give information or facts
Facts are included in all three parts of a paragraph. You may gather facts by reading, listening, or observing.

2) To explain your ideas
You may use this kind of paragraph to:
• Make something clear
• Help someone understand an idea
• Give the meaning of something
• Give reasons for something

3) To ask for information
In this kind of paragraph, make your questions clear and specific. That way, you get specific answers.

4) To persuade
This kind of paragraph helps you to convince someone to act or believe a certain way. You must be sure of what you are saying. Then you can persuade someone.

5) To tell a story
The story you tell in this kind of paragraph can be imaginary or true. A true story should follow the order in which things happened.

©AGS® American Guidance Service, Inc. Permission is granted to reproduce for classroom use only.   **Basic English Composition**

Writing Tip 8

Name _____ Period _____   Chapter 8 / Writing Tip 8

Checklist for Proofreading and Revising

Use this checklist to proofread and revise your papers.

Check your paper:
____ Do I have a meaningful title?
____ Do I have a conclusion or a summary at the end?

Check your paragraphs:
____ Do I start every paragraph on a new line?
____ Is the first line of every paragraph indented?
____ Does my first sentence (topic sentence) in every paragraph explain the main idea of my paragraph? Does it attract my reader's attention well?
____ Do the sentences in the middle of my paragraphs (body) support the main idea?
____ Do I include facts, details, explanations, reasons, examples, or illustrations to support my main idea?
____ Do I need to take out any sentences that do not relate to my main idea?

Check your sentences:
____ Do I capitalize the first word of every sentence?
____ Do I end every sentence with the correct punctuation mark?
____ Do I express a complete idea in every sentence?
____ Do my pronouns all have clear antecedents?
____ Do I have any run-on sentences that I need to correct?
____ Can I improve my sentences?
____ Can I add specific and vivid adjectives, adverbs, or prepositional phrases?
____ Can I combine short, related ideas into longer, more varied sentences?

Check your verbs:
____ Do I have a subject and a verb in every sentence?
____ Do my subject and verb agree in every sentence?
____ Is my verb tense logical in every sentence?
____ Is my verb tense consistent in every sentence?
____ Are my irregular verbs correct?

Check your punctuation and capitalization:
____ Did I capitalize all my proper nouns and proper adjectives?
____ Did I capitalize and punctuate all my direct quotations correctly?
____ Did I use a comma to separate words in a series?

Check your spelling:
____ Did I choose the correct spelling for each homonym?
____ Did I use an apostrophe only in contractions and possessive nouns?
____ Did I spell every plural noun correctly?
____ Did I spell all words with *ie* or *ei* correctly?
____ Did I drop the final silent *e* before adding an ending beginning with a vowel?
____ Did I double the final consonant before adding an ending according to the rules?

(Use the index on pages ___ of the textbook to locate any topic in this checklist.)

©AGS® American Guidance Service, Inc. Permission is granted to reproduce for classroom use only.   **Basic English Composition**

Community Connection 8

Name _____ Date _____ Period _____   Chapter 8 / Community Connection 8

Finding the Purpose of Paragraphs

When reading, think about why something was written. Was it to inform or to explain? Was it to tell how to do something? It might have been asking for information. Maybe it was trying to persuade. It even could have been telling a story. Review these purposes of paragraphs. Follow these steps.

Step 1. Find at home or at the library some magazines, newspapers, advertisements, catalogs, how-to manuals, letters, and books. Then look at the list of paragraph purposes. Find a paragraph that is an example of each purpose.

Step 2. Fill in the chart below. Write where you found the five paragraphs. Then write what each paragraph is about.

Purposes of Paragraphs
1) to inform or explain
2) to tell how to do something
3) to ask for information
4) to persuade
5) to tell a story

Purpose	Where paragraph was found	What paragraph is about
Informs or explains		
Tells how to do something		
Asks for information		
Persuades		
Tells a story		

Step 3. Have your teacher check your work.

©AGS® American Guidance Service, Inc. Permission is granted to reproduce for classroom use only.   **Basic English Composition**

Chapter 8

The Purpose of a Paragraph

Think about the purpose of your last piece of writing. Were you writing to explain an idea? Maybe you were asking for information. Maybe you were giving directions. You might have been writing to express your opinion.

You write for all sorts of purposes. No matter what your purpose is, you use paragraphs to organize your ideas. Paragraphs make your ideas clear to your readers.

In Chapter 8, you will learn about common purposes of paragraphs. You will practice writing paragraphs for different purposes.

Goals for Learning

▶ To write a paragraph that informs and explains

▶ To write a paragraph that explains how to do something

▶ To write a paragraph that makes a request

▶ To write a paragraph that persuades

▶ To write a paragraph that tells a story

179

Introducing the Chapter

Have students examine the introductory photograph accompanying the first page of Chapter 8. Ask students to imagine that the person in the photograph is a traveler exploring a city she has never seen before. Have students tell what they think tourists read and write about when visiting a new place. Students may suggest examples such as writing directions, writing a postcard, and writing in a travel diary. Discuss the main purpose of each kind of writing they mention.

Chapter 8 Self-Study Guide

Lesson at a Glance

Chapter 8   Lesson 1

Overview This lesson focuses on the general purpose of an expository paragraph: to inform and explain.

Objectives

- To write a topic sentence that prepares readers for the information or explanation.
- To support the main idea with facts and reasons.
- To end the paragraph with a conclusion or a summary.
- To write a paragraph based on a definition.
- To write a paragraph that answers a question.

Student Pages 180–183

Reading Vocabulary

checkbook	personal (6)
computer (8)	summary (8)
conclusion (6)	topic (5)
detail (5)	

Teaching Suggestions

■ Introducing the Lesson

Ask students whether they have recently had to write a paragraph in response to a question. They may mention that they have taken an essay test or filled out an application that required an explanation. Briefly discuss the importance of writing a clearly organized paragraph when giving information.

■ Reviewing Skills
Write these two sentences on the board: *When threatened, the hognose snake can play dead./Animals have varied ways of defending themselves.*

Have students tell which sentence could be the topic sentence of a paragraph and give reasons for their choice. (They should recognize that the second sentence is the better topic sentence because it is more general; the first sentence gives a detail that belongs in the body of a paragraph.)

When you write to inform and explain, you give your readers facts about a topic. In your paragraph, you aim for one or more of these goals:

- To make something clear
- To help someone understand an idea
- To give the meaning of something
- To give reasons for something

Your topic sentence prepares your readers for your main idea. The body of your paragraph is made of sentences that give facts and other supporting details. Your final sentence may be a summary or a conclusion.

Activity A   This paragraph gives information. Read it. Then write answers to the questions on your paper.

> **The Personal Computer**
>
> Personal computers are appearing in more and more homes. Even the smallest personal computers are more powerful than the room-sized computers of the 1960s. Computers have become easy and fun to use. Families use computers to find information, write letters, play games, draw pictures, save a mailing list, and keep track of checkbook balances. Someday soon, people will not remember a time when they did not have computers in their homes.

1) What is the main idea of this paragraph? Use your own words to state the main idea.

2) What facts and reasons does the writer give to support the main idea?

3) What conclusion does the writer give? Use your own words to state the conclusion.

■ Presenting Activity A
Read aloud the paragraph "The Personal Computer" as students follow along. They may then proceed to analyze its parts by answering the questions. Remind students to use complete sentences in their answers.

Activity A Answers
Wording of answers will vary. Sample answers are given. Answers should be complete sentences.

1) Personal computers are becoming more popular. 2) Computers have become fun and easy to use. Families find many uses for computers. Some of the uses are research, writing, games, art, and tracking addresses and finances. 3) Computers will someday be a part of every household.

Paragraphs Based on Definitions

You may write a paragraph that develops a definition. Use details from dictionaries and encyclopedias to write a paragraph that informs and explains.

Compare the definition below with the paragraph that is based on it.

EXAMPLES

Definition:

Killiecrankie *(n.)* a mountain pass in Scotland; the place where a battle was fought in 1689.

Paragraph:

Have you ever heard of Killiecrankie? Killiecrankie is the name of a place in Scotland. It is a mountain pass. In 1689, a famous battle was fought there. Killiecrankie would be an interesting place to visit.

Activity B Read the following words and meanings. Use each definition to write a short paragraph about the word. Start with a topic sentence. End your paragraph with a summary or a conclusion.

1) **glockenspiel** *(n.)* an instrument with flat level bars, formerly bells or tubes, set in a frame; the metal bars are tuned to produce bell-like tones when struck with two small hammers. It is a percussion instrument.

2) **paisley** *(adj.)* a type of cloth with a colorful pattern of flowers or designs; originally used to make soft wool shawls. This pattern is named after Paisley, Scotland, where it was first made.

3) **leotard** *(n.)* a tight-fitting garment made of a stretchy fabric. It is worn by dancers, gymnasts, and people who are exercising. It is named for a nineteenth-century French acrobat, Jules Léotard, who wore the garment and made it famous.

4) **doodle** *(v.)* to wander aimlessly or without purpose; also, to scribble designs on a piece of paper. To doodle originally meant to play a bagpipe.

a bagpipe. Maybe people once thought that playing a bagpipe was a mindless, silly way to pass the time.

Reading Vocabulary

aimlessly	gymnast
bagpipe	leotard
definition (6)	originally
doodle	paisley
fabric (7)	percussion
garment (5)	scribble (6)
glockenspiel	stretchy

■ **Presenting Activity B** Use the example definition and paragraph to help students see how the details in the definition are expanded to sentences that fill out a paragraph. Provide dictionaries so that students can find out more about each term if they wish.

Activity B Answers

Answers will vary. Sample paragraphs are given.

1) A glockenspiel is a percussion instrument. Like all percussion instruments, it makes its music by being struck. Glockenspiels used to be made of bells or tubes. Today a glockenspiel is made of flat level bars that are hit with two small hammers. The notes of a glockenspiel sound like bells. A glockenspiel resembles a more familiar percussion instrument, the xylophone. **2)** If you would like to see paisley, look at men's ties and women's scarves. Paisley is a pattern that originated in Paisley, Scotland. Paisley was originally a cloth used to make soft wool shawls. Today paisley designs come in many colors and fabrics. **3)** When you exercise wearing a stretchy one-piece outfit, do you ever wonder why it is called a leotard? The first leotard was worn by a French acrobat more than one hundred years ago. He invented a garment that he could move around in easily. His name was Jules Léotard. **4)** Do you find yourself drawing designs or silly pictures when you talk on the telephone? Many people doodle while talking on the telephone or sitting at a meeting. Doodling is a way to occupy your hands when your mind is elsewhere. To doodle originally meant to play

Reading Vocabulary

false (6)	regret (5)
informative	revenge (6)
innocent (5)	smother (5)
prefer (6)	undo

■ Presenting Activity C

Emphasize the connection between the question *why* and answers that explain causes. After students have written their paragraph, suggest that they reread it to make sure that they have given reasons that tell why something is true.

Activity C Answers

Answers will vary. Students should select only one of the questions to write a paragraph response to.

APPLICATION

Career Connection
Have students make up a *why* question about a job or a career they are considering. (Examples: *Why do I want to become a nurse? Why should Woodrow's hire me as a salesperson?*) They then develop reasons in a clearly organized paragraph. Some students may want to read their paragraphs aloud to the group.

LEARNING STYLES

LEP/ESL
Encourage the students for whom English is a second language to create questions in their primary language that ask for information and explanation about something new to them. Encourage them—one by one—to ask their questions in their primary language and then in English. Ask volunteers to speak or write answers in paragraph form.

Answering Questions

Informative paragraphs can answer questions. If a question asks *why*, you can answer it with an explanation. Your paragraph tells about causes. You give statements to prove the idea is right.

Read the question below. Notice how the paragraph gives an explanation to answer the question.

> **EXAMPLE**
>
> Question:
>
> Why did Othello kill Desdemona?
>
> Paragraph answer:
>
> In Shakespeare's play, Othello killed his wife, Desdemona, because of a mistake. Othello's false friend, Iago, lied to him. Iago told Othello that Desdemona was in love with another man. Othello was in a rage. To get revenge, he smothered his innocent wife. Othello found out that he was wrong. But it was too late to undo the terrible mistake.

Activity C   Choose one of the questions below. Write a paragraph to answer it.

- What is your favorite sport, and why do you prefer it?
- Why is a good education important for everyone?
- What is your favorite television show, and why do you like it?
- Why do people do things that they later regret?
- Why is it important to be on time?

You may write a paragraph to give information or explain an idea.

- Make your main idea clear in a topic sentence.
- Use the body of the paragraph to give facts and reasons.
- End with a conclusion or a summary.

Part A   Read the paragraph below. Then answer the questions that follow it on your paper.

Who's Who

When you write a report, you may want to get information from *Who's Who*. This commonly used reference book lists the names of famous living people. The names are listed in alphabetic order. A short paragraph is included about each person. This paragraph is a brief biography and gives a few facts about the person's life. A little information about many people can be found in *Who's Who*.

---

1) What is the main idea of this paragraph?

2) What information would you find in *Who's Who?*

3) What are three facts about *Who's Who?*

4) What is the purpose of the last sentence?

Part B   Write a paragraph on one of the topics listed below. State the main idea in the first sentence. Write three sentences that give facts and reasons to support the main idea. End with a summary or conclusion. Your completed paragraph should have five sentences.

- Uses for a dictionary
- What is a friend?
- What makes a good movie?
- The meaning of *silhouette*

Reading Vocabulary

alphabetic (6)   reference (6)
biography (7)   silhouette (10)
brief (6)

Part A Answers

Wording of answers will vary. Sample answers are given.

1) *Who's Who* is a reference book used to find out information about famous living people. **2)** *Who's Who* contains short paragraphs of biographical information.
3) Students can list any three facts: Report writers might want to use a *Who's Who*.   The names are listed alphabetically.   A short paragraph is provided about each person. The people are still living.   **4)** The last sentence sums up the information in the paragraph.

Part B Answers

Answers will vary. Students should select one topic and write a five-sentence paragraph of information or explanation.

Follow-up Activity

Provide dictionaries and reference sources about word origins. Have students select words that intrigue them and write paragraphs discussing the word's meaning and history.

APPLICATION

 At Home
Students may look through magazines and newspapers for question-and-answer features: "Ask the Money Manager," "Ask the Auto Expert," and so on. Have them clip examples of one-paragraph answers written in response to a question. Can they identify the main idea of the paragraph?

Lesson at a Glance

Chapter 8 Lesson 2

Overview This lesson focuses on the expository paragraph that explains how to do or make something. The lesson also includes a checklist for proofreading and revising.

Objective

- To develop a how-to paragraph that is well organized and clearly written.

Student Pages 184–187

Reading Vocabulary

blowout	hazard (8)
brake (5)	lessen (8)
gently (6)	swerve (8)

Teaching Suggestions

■ Introducing the Lesson

Ask students to imagine that they are at a familiar location in town (in front of the library, for example, or on a particular corner of a major intersection). Then have them suppose that a visitor asks them for directions to another site, some distance away. Name both locations, and ask volunteers to demonstrate how they would give oral directions to the visitor. The group can evaluate the effectiveness of the directions: Would the visitor be able to find the site? Make the connection to writing: Why is it important to be precise when writing a paragraph that tells how to do something?

■ Reviewing Skills Choose

sentences from a newspaper or book. Write them on the board, introducing errors in capitalization and punctuation. Ask students to find and fix the errors.

■ Presenting Activity A

Have a volunteer read aloud the paragraph "Blowout!" Ask students if anything in the paragraph needs clarifying before having them answer the three questions in this activity.

The shelves of libraries are filled with how-to books. They tell readers how to do something or how to make something. You can tell your readers how to do or make something, too. Write a paragraph that clearly explains the steps to follow.

In a how-to paragraph, your topic sentence should tell readers what they will be doing or making. The body of the paragraph takes them through the steps with words such as *first, next, when,* and *finally.* Your final sentence can be a conclusion or a summary.

Activity A   Read the how-to paragraph below. Then answer the questions that follow on your paper.

Blowout!

If your car tire suddenly loses air while you are driving, what should you do? The first thing to do is stay calm. The car may be swerving, but do not step on the brake. Instead, keep your foot steady on the gas pedal. At the same time, hold the steering wheel firmly. Next, turn on your hazard lights. When the swerving lessens, slowly take your foot off the gas pedal. Finally, steer gently to the shoulder of the road. Your goal is to get the car off the road safely.

---

1) What is the main idea of this paragraph?

2) What words help the reader know when to take certain steps?

3) What is another way of stating the final sentence?

Activity B   You have invited a friend home for dinner. Write a paragraph that gives him or her directions from school to your home.

Activity A Answers

Wording of answers will vary. Sample answers are given.

1) If you get a flat tire while driving, take several steps to protect yourself.   **2)** Words that help the reader with the steps are *first, at the same time, next, when, finally.*   **3)** A safe stop at the side of the road is most important.

■ Presenting Activity B

Before students begin their paragraph, discuss the kinds of direction and distance words (*north, left, blocks, miles, yards, and so on*) they should probably include.

Activity B Answers

Answers will vary. Students' paragraphs should clearly state the departure and arrival points.

APPLICATION

In the Community
Collect a variety of brochures, advertisements, and coupons in which local businesses provide maps of their locations. Have students examine the maps and the accompanying text. They may use the information to practice writing a paragraph that tells what the business offers and how to find the store.

Proofreading and Revising Paragraphs

Proofread
To look for mistakes in spelling, grammar, punctuation, and other things.

Revise
To correct errors or to make changes.

Rewrite
To write again.

After you have written a paragraph, look for ways to improve it. To **proofread** your paragraph, look for mistakes in spelling, grammar, and punctuation. To **revise** your paragraph, correct any errors. Make other improvements. You may need to **rewrite** your paragraph.

Use this checklist when you look over your paragraphs.

Checklist for Proofreading and Revising a Paragraph

1. Do you have a meaningful title?

2. Is the first line of your paragraph indented? Does it start on a new line?

3. Does your topic sentence prepare the reader for the main idea of your paragraph?

4. Do the sentences in the body of the paragraph support the main idea? Have you included facts, details, explanations, reasons, examples, or illustrations? Have you taken out any sentences that do not relate to your main idea?

5. Do you have a conclusion or a summary at the end?

6. Read each sentence carefully. Does each sentence have a capital letter and a correct end punctuation mark? Does each sentence have a subject and a verb? Does each sentence express a complete thought? Correct any run-on sentences.

7. Can you improve your sentences? Can you add specific and vivid adjectives, adverbs, or prepositional phrases? Can you combine short, related ideas into longer, more varied sentences?

8. Check the following items in your paragraph. Correct any errors that you find. (You can look up these topics in the index of this book.)

   • Spelling

   • Punctuation

   • Capitalization of proper nouns

   • Subject-verb agreement

   • Agreement of pronouns and antecedents

   • Tenses and spellings of irregular verbs

   • Spellings of plurals and possessives

Reading Vocabulary

adviser (8)　　labor (5)
combine (6)　　proofreader
drainage　　　successful (5)
fertilize　　　suggestion (5)
guarantee (7)　sunshine

■ Presenting Activity C

Spend time discussing each of the eight entries in the checklist on page 185. Review terms such as *subject, verb, run-on sentence, plurals,* and *possessives.* Then have students read the directions to Activity C.

Activity C Answers

Revisions of the paragraph will vary. These errors should be corrected.

1) successful (spelling)
2) harvest. (end punctuation)
3) choose (verb tense)　**4)** right spot. The garden (run-on sentence)　**5)** It's (contraction)
6) The sequence of steps should be re-ordered: (a) buy good seeds and (b) plant them. The steps of fertilizing, watering, and weeding can follow in any order.

■ Presenting Activity D

Have students look back through their writings to find a paragraph that has not been corrected. They may select that paragraph to exchange with a partner.

Activity D Answers

Students should provide before-and-after paragraphs, to show the results of proofreading and revision.

Activity C　Practice using the checklist in this lesson. Read the how-to paragraph below. Proofread for mistakes. Revise by changing the order of some sentences. You may want to combine short sentences into longer ones. Rewrite the improved paragraph on your paper.

How to Have a Successful Garden

To have a succesful garden you must do several things. Following all of these steps will guarantee you a rich harvest First, you must chose the right spot, the garden will need plenty of sunshine. It helps to have a slight slope for good drainage. Its also a good idea to fertilize. Be sure to buy good seeds. Water and weed your garden. Plant your seeds. Later, you will be able to enjoy the fruits of your labor.

Activity D　Sometimes a friend can be a helpful proofreader and adviser. Choose one of the paragraphs you have written so far in this chapter. Then take these steps:

1) Exchange paragraphs with a partner.

2) Proofread each other's paragraphs.

3) Offer suggestions for revising.

4) Rewrite your own paragraph.

A how-to paragraph explains to readers how to do or make something. Your paragraph should include these three main parts:

- topic sentence

- body

- conclusion or summary

Part A   The following facts tell how to become more physically fit. Use the facts to write a how-to paragraph. Start with your own topic sentence. Rewrite the sentences below. Use words such as *first* and *finally* to make the steps clear. Add a conclusion or a summary at the end of your paragraph. Use the checklist on page 185 to proofread and revise your paragraph.

1) Build the activity into your schedule.

2) Start with a short walk around the block.

3) Take the walk several times a week.

4) Gradually increase your walking speed.

5) Work up to a fast mile-and-a-half walk three times a week.

Part B   Think of something that you know how to do. Write a paragraph about that topic. Follow these directions:

1) Write no more than seven sentences.

2) Make the first sentence a topic sentence.

3) Make the last sentence a summary.

Use the checklist on page 185 to proofread and revise your paragraph.

Reading Vocabulary

increase (5)   schedule (6)
physically

Part A Answers

Paragraphs will vary. A sample paragraph is given.

How to Become Physically Fit

Would you like to build your physical fitness? The most important thing to do is to make physical activity a regular part of your schedule. Start with a short walk around the block. Take the walk the next day or the day after. Try to take the walk several times a week. After you are used to the walk, gradually increase your walking speed. Finally, work up to a fast mile-and-a-half walk three times a week. You will see a big improvement in your fitness level.

Part B Answers

Paragraphs will vary. Students' how-to paragraphs should have no more than seven sentences, include a title, a topic sentence, a summary sentence, and clearly organized steps.

Follow-up Activity

Use students' suggestions to list on the board varied sources that include how-to paragraphs: cookbooks, repair manuals, software manuals, health journals, financial guides, and so on. Ask students to locate examples of the sources. Together, look over the printed materials to find features discussed in this lesson, such as topic sentences that tell readers what they will learn and sequence words that advise readers what to do first, next, and finally.

Lesson at a Glance

Chapter 8 Lesson 3

Overview This lesson focuses on a paragraph that asks for information.

Objective

- To write a clear, specific paragraph when requesting information.

Student Pages 188–190

Teacher's Resource Library

Activity 29

Workbook Activity 35

Reading Vocabulary

cruise (6)	sincerely (5)
equipment (5)	stereo
madam (5)	subscription (7)
publish (6)	video
seek (5)	

Teaching Suggestions

- **Introducing the Lesson**
Write on the board this sentence starter: *I would like some information about. . . .* Brainstorm with students about how that sentence might be completed.

- **Reviewing Skills** Write on the board the sentence: *I would like to buy shoes.* Ask students to add specific details to the sentence by adding adjectives and a prepositional phrase. (Example: *I would like to buy up-to-the-minute athletic shoes at Marty's Shoe Store.*)

- **Presenting Activity A**
Have a volunteer read aloud the letter of request shown before students proceed with this activity.

Activity A Answers
Wording of answers will vary.

1) Amanda wants to learn about Video View magazine.   **2)** She wants to know how often it is published, its subscription price, and where she can find a copy.
3) She ends the paragraph with a thank-you.

You may write a paragraph to ask for information. Use the body of the paragraph to explain the main idea of your request. Read this sample letter.

Dear Sir or Madam:

Please send me information about *Video View* . How often is this magazine published? What is the price of a subscription? I would like to look at a copy of the magazine. Where can I find one? Thank you for your help.

Sincerely,

Amanda O'Hara

Amanda O'Hara

Activity A   Answer the following questions about this letter.

1) What is the main idea of this paragraph?
2) What exactly does Amanda want to know about the magazine?
3) How does Amanda end the paragraph?

Activity B   Write a paragraph asking for specific information. Choose one of the topic sentences below. Add three sentences that explain the request in more detail. Think carefully about the specific information that you would need to know. Add a conclusion.

- I am seeking information about vacations on a cruise ship.
- Please tell me more about your party.
- Please send me information about your stereo equipment.
- I need some information about growing vegetables.

- **Presenting Activity B**
Review the directions with students. Tell them that they may prefer to choose a topic of their own.

Activity B Answers
Paragraphs will vary. If they wish, students may model their paragraphs after the letter shown on this page. They should choose one of the topic sentences listed (or make up one of their own) and add three sentences that give specific details. Their conclusion can be a thank-you.

Name	Date	Period	Chapter 8 Activity 29

Asking for Information

Directions: Imagine that you are shopping for each of the items below. Write three specific questions that you would ask the salesperson about these items. Write your questions in complete sentences on the lines provided.

EXAMPLE   You are buying a suit.
   a) *What are your alteration prices?*
   b) *Can the suit be returned?*
   c) *Do you have a layaway plan?*

1) You are buying a ring.
   a) _____
   b) _____
   c) _____

2) You are selecting a stereo.
   a) _____
   b) _____
   c) _____

3) You are buying a camera.
   a) _____
   b) _____
   c) _____

4) You are renting an apartment.
   a) _____
   b) _____
   c) _____

©AGS® American Guidance Service, Inc. Permission is granted to reproduce for classroom use only.   **Basic English Composition**

Activity 29

Clear, Specific Requests

When you are writing to request information, be specific. If your question is vague, the response may be incomplete.

Suppose that someone is asking Derek about his new friend, Shirley. A vague question may produce a vague answer.

> **EXAMPLE** Vague question: Who is Shirley?
>
> Vague answer: She's a girl I know.

Compare the more specific request with the more complete response.

> **EXAMPLE** Specific request:
>
> I would like to know about your new friend, Shirley. Where did you meet her? What does she like to do? Tell me about her family. I would like to hear all about Shirley.
>
> Specific answer:
>
> Shirley is the most wonderful girl I have ever met. We are both on the track team. She runs the mile. Shirley has one older brother. Her mother works at the supermarket. Her dad is a carpenter. You will like Shirley when you meet her.

Activity C   Choose a partner in your class. Then follow these directions.

1) Write a paragraph requesting information about your partner. Be specific in your request.

2) Exchange paragraphs with your partner.

3) Write a second paragraph that answers the questions your partner asked. Be specific in your answers.

Reading Vocabulary
incomplete (7)   vague (5)
supermarket

■ Presenting Activity C
Discuss the specific request and answer in the example. Help students to form partnerships. Make the point that not everyone likes to reveal personal information, so partners should try to avoid private topics. Afterward, some students may volunteer to read aloud their paragraphs.

Activity C Answers
Requests and responses will vary. Students should write two paragraphs each.

LEARNING STYLES

Visual/Spatial
Ask the class a question such as "What is your favorite sport?" or "Who is a special person in your life?" or "What is your favorite type of music?" Invite each student to draw two pictures. One should represent a vague answer with no details; one should represent a specific answer with details. Afterward, display each set of pictures and ask the class which is vague and which is specific.

Name _____ Date _____ Period _____

Chapter 8
Workbook Activity
35

Asking for Information

Directions: • Imagine that you are shopping for each of the items below.
• Write three specific questions that you would ask the salesperson about these items.
• Write your questions in complete sentences.

A. You are renting an apartment.
   1) _____
   2) _____
   3) _____

B. You are buying a new car.
   1) _____
   2) _____
   3) _____

C. You are selecting a new telephone.
   1) _____
   2) _____
   3) _____

D. You are buying a puppy at a pet store.
   1) _____
   2) _____
   3) _____

©AGS® American Guidance Service, Inc. Permission is granted to reproduce for classroom use only.   **Basic English Composition**

Workbook Activity 35

Reading Vocabulary

canister   vacuum (5)
deluxe

Part A Answers

Answers will vary. Sample questions are given.

1) What is the weather like in northern Mexico in December? **2)** Do you sell the 123X Rell PC with 1 gigabyte hard drive and 4-speed CD-ROM? **3)** Does Springfield have a good library and recreational facilities for young people? **4)** How do I get to the used car dealer that is on the east side of Centerville? **5)** Can you tell me more about the job for a driver advertised in the Sentinel on Sunday, March 4?

Part B Answers

Answers will vary. A sample paragraph is given.

    I am responding to the ad in the July 2 Telegram for a 3-room apartment on Winter Street. What is the rent? Does the rent include heat and hot water? Are pets allowed? Is there a parking space for one car? Please call 423-5165 anytime and leave a message on the machine. Thank you.

Follow-up Activity

Have students list products and services they are most interested in purchasing. Ask them to generate a list of four specific questions that they would like answered before they make a purchasing decision.

When you ask for information, be specific. Ask a clear question, and you will get a clear answer.

Part A   Each of these questions is vague. Rewrite each one to ask a more specific question.

Example   Vague question: What is the price of your vacuum cleaner?

             Specific question: What is the price of the Model 4150 Deluxe Canister vacuum cleaner?

1) What is Mexico like?

2) Do you have any information about computers?

3) Is Springfield a good place to live?

4) How do I get to Centerville?

5) What is the job?

Part B   Rewrite this paragraph so that the request is clear and specific.

> I saw your ad for an apartment. I am interested in renting it. Please tell me more about it.

Persuade
To write or talk in a convincing way; to give reasons and facts that convince others to act or believe in a certain way; to appeal to feelings in order to convince.

Do you have a good idea? Would you like to convince someone else that your idea will work? Then write to **persuade**. When you persuade readers, they will believe what you tell them. They will act in the way you suggest.

To write a persuasive paragraph, keep these points in mind:

- State your position or your request clearly.
- Use logical reasons to support your position.
- Use facts to support your position.
- Think about your reader's doubts. Try to overcome those doubts.

Suppose that Derek is applying for a scholarship to Western College. The application form includes a question asking why he thinks he deserves a scholarship. Read the paragraph that Derek writes in response to that question.

> I believe that I deserve a scholarship to Western College. I participate fully in school events. My major activity at Springfield High School is the track team. I intend to continue running track in college. I know that Western College has high academic standards, and I look forward to the opportunity to learn. Although I was only a fair student when I began high school, I began to challenge myself at the end of my sophomore year. My grades have improved steadily. I work hard and take my studies seriously. I need this scholarship to continue my education. I hope you agree that I would be a successful and involved student at Western College.

Activity A   Answer these questions about Derek's paragraph.

1) Whom is Derek trying to persuade in this paragraph?

2) What is he trying to persuade his readers to do?

3) What objection has he noted and overcome in his paragraph?

Activity A Answers
1) Derek is trying to persuade the scholarship committee of Western College.   **2)** He wants the committee to award him a scholarship.   **3)** He has noted that his grades were not always high. He tries to overcome objections by saying that he has been steadily improving and working hard at his studies.

Lesson at a Glance

Chapter 8   Lesson 4

Overview This lesson provides pointers on writing a persuasive paragraph.

Objective

- To write a clearly organized paragraph to persuade readers to take a particular action or position.

Student Pages 191–193

Reading Vocabulary

academic (8)	opportunity (5)
application (8)	overcome (7)
apply (6)	participate (7)
challenge (5)	**persuade (4)**
convince (5)	persuasion
involve (6)	persuasive
logical (8)	scholarship
major (6)	sophomore (8)
objection (6)	standard (6)

Teaching Suggestions

- **Introducing the Lesson**
  Ask students what these four forms of writing all have in common: (1) a brochure asking you to vote for a political candidate; (2) a letter asking you to send money to a charity; (3) a newspaper advertisement about a once-a-year sale; and (4) a letter to the editor of a newspaper in which the writer makes an argument about an issue in the news. Students may recognize that all the writings share the purpose of persuading readers to do something or think a certain way.

- **Reviewing Skills** Write the word pairs *its/it's, theirs/there's,* and *we're/were* on the board. Have students write sentences in which each word is used correctly.

- **Presenting Activity A**
  Have a volunteer read aloud the sample paragraph on this page. Briefly discuss Derek's purpose before students proceed to answer the three questions.

■ Presenting Activity B

Discuss the six reasons on Mike's list. Ask students for ideas about how to list the reasons in paragraph form. Point out that many persuasive writers like to end with their strongest reason.

Activity B Answers

Answers will vary. Each paragraph should begin with a topic sentence in which Mike states his goal—persuading Derek to join him in the next tournament. Each paragraph should also include the reasons from the boxed list and a sentence that summarizes or concludes.

■ Presenting Activity C

Have students offer ideas about why Derek, who prefers track to tennis, might not want to play in another tournament with Mike.

Activity C Answers

Answers will vary. Each paragraph should include a topic sentence, facts and logical reasons, a summary or conclusion, and a title.

GLOBAL CONNECTION

Discuss some of the international issues that are currently in the news. Have students look over editorial and op-ed pages of newspapers to find opinion essays and letters on one of the issues. Together, identify the writer's position. Evaluate the effectiveness of the written arguments.

Suppose that Mike believes that he and his friend Derek can win the next tennis tournament. Listed below are the reasons that Mike will give to persuade Derek to play in the tournament.

Mike's Reasons

1. I have been practicing.
2. I have developed a better serve.
3. I will practice with Derek every day.
4. We both have had experience; we will not be as nervous as we were last time.
5. The other players are not very good.
6. I have a strong wish to enter the tournament.

Activity B   Pretend that you are Mike. Use the reasons above to write a persuasive paragraph. Try to persuade Derek to join you as a partner in the next tennis tournament.

1) Start with a topic sentence. State your request or position.

2) Include the reasons in the body of your paragraph.

3) End the paragraph with a summary or conclusion.

4) Proofread, revise, and rewrite your paragraph. Use the checklist on page 185.

Activity C Derek wants to persuade Mike to find another partner. Write a paragraph for Derek. Follow the directions below.

1) Be sure that your paragraph begins with a topic sentence.

2) Think of logical reasons why Mike should find another partner. Be convincing. Give facts. Be creative.

3) End your paragraph with a summary or a conclusion.

4) Add a title to your paragraph.

5) Proofread, revise, and rewrite your paragraph. Use the checklist on page 185.

Sometimes you want your readers to act or to believe in a certain way. Write a paragraph of persuasion.

- State your main idea in a topic sentence.
- Use facts and reasons to support your main idea.
- Use your last sentence to sum up your case.

Lesson Review Write a paragraph of persuasion. Follow the directions.

1) Choose one of these topics. Use it as the title of your paragraph. You may make up your own topic instead.

- Why Every School Should Have a Technology Center
- Why Everyone Should Exercise
- Summer: The Best Season of the Year
- Why I Should Be Hired for the Job of (Name of Job)

2) Write your paragraph. State your main idea in a topic sentence. Persuade by giving reasons and facts in the body of your paragraph. End your paragraph with a summary or a conclusion.

3) Finally, proofread, revise, and rewrite your paragraph. Refer to the checklist on page 185.

Reading Vocabulary
technology

Lesson Review Answers
Answers will vary. Students may choose one of the topics listed or make up one of their own. They should proofread, revise, and rewrite to make sure they have met the requirements listed in the second step.

Follow-up Activity

With the group, list topics for which students have opinions. Select two or three topics. Have partners interview each other to determine the interviewee's position on the topic and the facts and experiences that have led to the position. Discuss the results of the survey with the group.

LEARNING STYLES

Auditory/Verbal
On slips of paper, print things a student might want to persuade someone to do—for example, play golf; bake bread; vote for the Independent Party candidate; spend $5 on a raffle ticket; join the drama club; buy a new prom dress. Ask volunteers to draw a slip and then to present to the class a persuasive argument for the chosen topic. After each persuasive speech, encourage students to offer other persuasive elements the student could have used.

Chapter 8 Lesson 5

Overview This lesson provides guidance in developing narratives.

Objectives

- To write a paragraph of personal narrative.
- To use dialogue to develop a narrative.
- To tell about events in chronological order.

Student Pages 194–197

Teacher's Resource Library

Activities 30–32

Workbook Activities 36–37

Reading Vocabulary

anecdote (9)   nonfiction
assume (6)   personal
basic (7)   narrative
comment (5)   unforgettable
fiction (7)   viewpoint
narrator (6)

Teaching Suggestions

■ Introducing the Lesson

Ask students for their ideas about the difference between a paragraph that tells a story and a paragraph that gives information. Then ask for thoughtful responses to this question: Can a paragraph that tells a story also give information?

■ Reviewing Skills Write the following bits of conversation on the board. Have students proofread and show correct punctuation and capitalization.

"Did you hear a knock on the door asked Terell?"

Yes said Frank. "but I'm not expecting anyone."

■ Presenting Activity A

Have a volunteer read aloud the paragraph "The Day I Almost Drowned." Students may then proceed to answer the questions about it.

Anecdote
A very short story about an interesting or amusing happening.

Fiction
An imaginary story; writing based largely on the writer's imagination.

Nonfiction
Writing that expresses facts and ideas; a true story, rather than an imaginary one.

Personal Narrative
A true story told from the viewpoint of the narrator.

When you write a story, you are answering a basic question: "What happened?" Stories come in different sizes. A story may be one thousand pages long. A story may be only one paragraph long. A story that short is sometimes called an **anecdote**.

Stories can be **fiction**, or based on an author's imagination. Stories can be **nonfiction**, or based on actual events and real people. A true story that uses the pronouns *I* and *me* is called a **personal narrative**.

Activity A Read the following paragraph. Write your answers to the questions that follow it on your paper.

The Day I Almost Drowned
by Laura Gonzales

When I was eight years old, I almost drowned in the Gulf of Mexico. My cousin Julio and I were playing with a raft. Suddenly, he let go. The raft started to drift out to sea. It was a windy day, but I did not want to lose the raft. As I swam toward the raft, the wind took it out farther and farther. Soon I was out too far. I could not get back to shore. People were yelling, but I could not hear them. A man on shore saw me and swam out to rescue me. When I got back to the beach, my mom and Julio were crying. We all thanked the man who had saved me from drowning. Almost drowning was an unforgettable experience!

---

1) Who is the "I" of this story?
2) Who are the other characters or people in this story?
3) What event does this paragraph tell about?
4) Assume that Laura is a real person. Is her story fiction or nonfiction?

Activity B Write a paragraph that tells a story about something that happened to you.

1) Begin with a topic sentence.
2) Use the body to tell the beginning, middle, and end of your story.
3) End the paragraph with a comment on your feelings about your experience.

Activity A Answers

1) The "I" of the story is the narrator, Laura Gonzales.
2) The other people in the story are the narrator's mother, her cousin Julio, and the man who rescued her. **3)** The event that the paragraph tells about is the day that Laura almost drowned trying to swim to a raft. **4)** If Laura is a real person, then the story is nonfiction.

■ Presenting Activity B

Tell students that one way to come up with a topic for a personal narrative is to list quickly as many experiences as one can think of. An experience that makes a good topic for a paragraph is one that is straightforward and can be recounted easily.

Activity B Answers

Answers will vary. Paragraphs should include a beginning, a middle, and an end.

Dialogue

Stories often include dialogue, the exact words spoken by people or characters. If you include dialogue in your story, then you will set up the paragraphs differently. Remember that each time the speaker changes, you must begin a new paragraph. Remember to enclose the speaker's exact words in quotation marks.

Activity C   Read the story below. Then write your answers to the questions that follow it on your paper.

My Luckiest Day

By Marta Gonzales

"Laura! Laura! Let the raft go! You are out too far!" I screamed to my daughter.

"I'm sorry, Aunt Marta," Julio cried.

"Do you want me to go out and get her?" asked a stranger.

"Oh, yes," I said. The man jumped into the water at once. In a few minutes, Laura and the man were back on the shore.

"Thank you!" I cried. Then I ran to hug Laura.

When I looked around a moment later, the man was gone. I wish that I could have thanked him more.

---

1) Who is telling this story?

2) How many paragraphs are there?

3) How many times does Marta Gonzales speak?

4) How many times does Julio speak?

5) What are the exact words spoken by the stranger?

6) How is this second story different from the one titled "The Day I Almost Drowned" on page 194?

■ **Presenting Activity C**
Have a volunteer read aloud the passage before students proceed to answer the questions.

Activity C Answers
1) Marta Gonzales is telling this story.   **2)** There are six paragraphs.   **3)** Marta Gonzales speaks three times.   **4)** Julio speaks once.   **5)** The stranger says the words, "Do you want me to go out and get her?"   **6)** This is the same story as "The Day I Almost Drowned," but the narrator is different. That story was told by Laura, and this one is told by Laura's mother.

LEARNING STYLES

Interpersonal/Group Learning
Divide the class into groups of three. Invite each group to write a story that contains dialogue between two characters. Encourage each group to brainstorm before it begins to write and to create two interesting characters, an interesting setting, and an event that has some drama or mystery to it. Afterward, invite volunteer groups to act out their stories with two students reading the dialogue for the two characters and one student reading the narrative, or the "glue" words that hold the dialogue together.

Reading Vocabulary

chronological order   recent

■ **Presenting Activity D**

Have a volunteer read aloud the paragraph "How I Met Shirley." Point out the words *last month, at the same moment, immediately, after practice,* and *soon,* telling students that these words signal the sequence of events.

Activity D Answers

1) The meeting took place one day last month.   **2)** Right after they bumped into each other, they both fell down.   **3)** They both started laughing when they saw each other's surprised face.   **4)** They decided to meet for practice after school three days a week.

■ **Presenting Activity E**

Review the bulleted items with students. Have them tell which event happened first, second, third, and last.

Activity E Answers

Answers will vary. A sample paragraph is given.

The History of St. Paul, Minnesota

The modern city of St. Paul began as a settlement named "Pig's Eye." The name came from its first European settler, Pierre "Pig's Eye" Parrant. In 1841, Father Lucien Galtier built St. Paul's Chapel. That was when the settlement's name was changed to St. Paul. Eight years later, St. Paul became a town. In 1854, it became a city.

Chronological order	
Arrangement according to time, usually from oldest to most recent.	

Chronological Order

When you write paragraphs to tell a story, you must think about the order of events. Often, you will tell about events in **chronological order,** the order in which they happened. You may start with the oldest event and end with the most recent.

Notice the chronological order in this paragraph about an event.

> ### How I Met Shirley
> #### by Derek Corelli
>
> One day last month, I was running laps at the track. I wasn't watching where I was going. I bumped into another runner. We really bumped! We both fell. Each of us saw the other's surprised face at the same moment and started laughing. I noticed immediately that the other runner had a beautiful smile. She told me her name was Shirley. After practice, we started talking. Soon we decided to meet for practice after school three days a week.

Activity D   Write the answers to these questions about Derek's paragraph.

1) When did the event take place?

2) What happened right after Derek and Shirley bumped into each other?

3) Why did they both start laughing?

4) What was the last thing that happened?

Activity E   Write a paragraph about historical events. Read the list of events below. Use them to tell the story of St. Paul, Minnesota. Start with the oldest event and end with the most recent.

- St. Paul became a city in 1854.
- The name of the settlement was changed to St. Paul in 1841, when Father Lucien Galtier built St. Paul's Chapel.
- It became a town in 1849.
- The settlement was first named "Pig's Eye" after its first European settler, Pierre "Pig's Eye" Parrant.

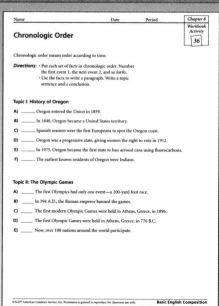

Activity 30   **Workbook Activity 36**

Paragraphs that tell a story answer the question, "What happened?"

- A story may be fiction or nonfiction.
- A story has a beginning, a middle, and an end.
- Think about chronological order. Report events in the order in which they happened.

Part A   Read the paragraph below. Then write your answers to the questions that follow on your paper.

> My life began in Springfield about seven years ago. I had three sisters, but they were all sold. Amanda and her mother wanted to keep me, so I wasn't sold. Now I spend my days eating, sleeping, and barking. Whenever I get a chance, I jump the fence and run away. Everyone chases me and yells, "Benjy!" It is a lot of fun. All in all, I'm a happy guy.

1) What words point out chronological order in this paragraph?

2) What is the purpose of the final sentence?

3) What would be a good title for this paragraph?

Part B   Read each of the sentences below. Think about stories that each one suggests. Then choose one idea for a story. Develop and write a story of one paragraph or more. Use dialogue if you wish. Remember to proofread, revise, and rewrite your story. Refer to the checklist on page 185.

- I had a weird experience.
- Did I do the right thing?
- Some moments are unforgettable.
- The incident made everyone laugh.

The Purpose of a Paragraph   Chapter 8   **197**

Reading Vocabulary

guy (6)   weird (6)
incident (6)

Part A Answers

Answers to question 3 will vary.

1) Words that signal time order are *about seven years ago, now,* and *whenever.*   **2)** The final sentence sums up the main idea of the paragraph.   **3)** A good title might be "Living Like a Dog."

Part B Answers

Answers will vary. Students should choose one of the listed ideas. Each narrative should be developed in one or more paragraphs. If dialogue is used, it should include correct punctuation. Suggest that students come up with their own topic if they prefer.

Follow-up Activity

Students have seen how the point of view of the narrator changes the way the story is told. They may enjoy retelling a well-known story from the viewpoint of a different character. Suggest that they rewrite a folktale or a fairy tale and present it to a young reader.

Activity 31

Activity 32

Workbook Activity 37
The Purpose of a Paragraph   Chapter 8   **197**

Chapter 8 Review

The Teacher's Resource Library includes two parallel forms of the Chapter 8 Mastery Test. The difficulty level of the two forms is equivalent. You may wish to use one form as a pretest and the other form as a posttest.

Reading Vocabulary

ability (5)	overdo
drummer	weekend
girlfriend	workshop

Part A Answers

1) to tell a story 2) to make a request 3) to persuade 4) to inform or explain 5) to inform or explain

Students should select one of the five topic sentences as an introduction to their own paragraph. Their paragraph should include at least three sentences in the body and should close with a conclusion or summary sentence.

Part B Answers

The following errors should be corrected in students' rewritten paragraphs.

1) activities (spelling)
2) Ms. Lentz's (possessive)
3) Friday (capitalization)
4) I (capitalization) 5) My mother keeps saying, "Aren't you overdoing things, Derek?" (punctuation of dialogue)

Part A Each topic sentence below could lead into a paragraph. Write what main purpose each paragraph would serve. Choose from these purposes:

- to inform or explain
- to persuade
- to make a request
- to tell a story

1) Last Friday evening began like any other Friday evening.

2) I would like information about the drummers' workshop being offered by Driscoll College.

3) Karli Lane deserves your vote for council president.

4) You can learn the right way to wash a car.

5) Basketball players need special abilities.

Now choose one of the five topic sentences. Write a paragraph that begins with that topic sentence. Add at least three sentences to the body of the paragraph. End the paragraph with a conclusion or a summary. Then proofread and revise your paragraph.

Part B Proofread the paragraph below to find errors. Rewrite the paragraph correctly on your paper.

> ### My Busy Life
> #### by Derek Corelli
>
> Lately, it is hard to fit in all of my activites. Three days each week, I work for a few hours in the evening at Ms. Lentz' gas station. Every day from Monday to friday, I go to school. After school I have track practice. My girlfriend Shirley and I run some evenings as well on the weekends. Often I get up early to do homework before i leave for school. My mother keeps saying aren't you overdoing things, Derek?

Chapter 8 Mastery Test A

Name _____ Date _____ Period _____

Chapter 8 / Mastery Test A / page 1

Chapter 8 Mastery Test A

Part A Write a five-sentence paragraph explaining one of these topics. Write the main idea in the topic sentence. Write three sentences that support the main idea. Write a summary or conclusion as the last sentence.

- What is a good meal?   • What is a family?   • Uses for a computer

Part B Think of something that you know how to do. Write a five-sentence paragraph telling how to do it. Make the first sentence the topic sentence. Make the last sentence a summary.

©AGS® American Guidance Service, Inc. Permission is granted to reproduce for classroom use only.   **Basic English Composition**

Name _____ Date _____ Period _____

Chapter 8 / Mastery Test A / page 2

Chapter 8 Mastery Test A, continued

Part C Write a paragraph asking for specific information about one of these topics. Write a topic sentence. Write three sentences that explain what you need to know. Write a conclusion.

- Applying to a college or school of your choice   • Setting up a stereo system   • Volunteering at the hospital

Part D Write a paragraph of persuasion about something you want someone to do. State your main idea in a topic sentence. Write three sentences using facts and reasons to support your main idea. Write a final sentence to sum up your case.

Part E Write a personal story telling about your most memorable weekend. Write a topic sentence. Write four sentences in the order in which the vacation events happened.

©AGS® American Guidance Service, Inc. Permission is granted to reproduce for classroom use only.   **Basic English Composition**

Chapter 8 Mastery Test A

Part C   Read the five sets of directions below. Choose **three** of them to follow. Write three paragraphs. Remember to proofread and revise.

1) Write a paragraph that gives information about a person, animal, place, or thing. You may use one of these topics if you wish.

   - A sports hero
   - A popular place
   - An unusual bird
   - The ideal room
   - The climate in your region

2) Write a paragraph that tells a reader how to make or do something. You may use one of these topics if you wish.

   - How to change the oil in a car
   - How to write a paragraph
   - How to celebrate a birthday
   - How to solve a problem
   - How to cook a certain food

3) Write a paragraph in which you ask for information. You may be asking about a product, a service, a place, or anything you wish. Be specific in your request.

4) Write a paragraph in which you persuade your reader to give you something that you want. Start by thinking about what you want. For example, you might want an *A* in English, a car, a new coat, or a scholarship. Then think about the person you wish to convince. Persuade this person that you deserve the item you have selected.

5) Write a paragraph that tells a story. The story may be fiction or nonfiction. Tell what happened by putting the events in chronological order.

Test Taking Tip   When a test item asks you to write a paragraph, make a plan first. Jot down the main idea of your paragraph. List the supporting details you can include. Then write the paragraph.

Part C Answers
Answers will vary. Students should choose three of the five categories listed in order to write three paragraphs. Each paragraph should begin with a topic sentence and be developed according to the directions given.

Chapter 8 Mastery Test B

Name _____ Date _____ Period _____   Chapter 8 Mastery Test B page 1

Part A Write a five-sentence paragraph explaining one of these topics. Write the main idea in the topic sentence. Write three sentences that support the main idea. Write a summary or conclusion as the last sentence.

- What is a home?
- What is a friendship?
- Importance of good driving

Part B Think of something that you can teach a friend how to do. Write a five-sentence paragraph telling the friend how to do it. Make the first sentence the topic sentence. Make the last sentence a summary.

©AGS® American Guidance Service, Inc. Permission is granted to reproduce for classroom use only.   **Basic English Composition**

Name _____ Date _____ Period _____   Chapter 8 Mastery Test B page 2

Chapter 8 Mastery Test B, continued

Part C Write a paragraph asking for specific information about one of these topics. Write a topic sentence. Write three sentences that explain what you need to know. Write a conclusion.

- The year's schedule for your favorite professional sports team
- Tickets to a concert
- Vacations in your state

Part D Write a paragraph of persuasion about something you want to convince someone about. State your main idea in a topic sentence. Write three sentences using facts and reasons to support your main idea. Write a final sentence to sum up your case.

Part E Write a personal story telling about the most memorable event in your childhood. Write a topic sentence. Write four sentences in the order in which the events happened.

©AGS® American Guidance Service, Inc. Permission is granted to reproduce for classroom use only.   **Basic English Composition**

Chapter 8 Mastery Test B

Chapter 9

Planning Guide

Improving Your Paragraphs

	Student Text Lesson			
	Student Pages	Vocabulary	Practice Exercises	Lesson Review
Lesson 1 Improving Topic Sentences	202-204	✔	✔	204
Lesson 2 Sentence Variety	205-207	✔	✔	207
Lesson 3 Transitions	208-210	✔	✔	210
Lesson 4 Making Comparisons	211-215	✔	✔	215

Chapter Activities

Teacher's Resource Library

Writing Tip 9: Ways to Improve Your Paragraphs

Community Connection 9: Improving Your Paragraphs

Assessment Options

Student Text

Chapter 9 Review

Teacher's Resource Library

Chapter 9 Mastery Tests A and B

	Teaching Strategies							Language Skills			Learning Styles						Teacher's Resource Library		
Reviewing Skills	Teacher Alert	Follow-up Activity	Career Application	Home Application	Global Connection	Community Application	Identification Skills	Writing Skills	Punctuation Skills	Visual/Spatial	Auditory/Verbal	Body/Kinesthetic	Logical/Mathematical	Group Learning	LEP/ESL	Activities	Workbook Activities	Self-Study Guide
202		204			203		✔	✔	✔				204			33	38	✔
205		207				206	✔	✔	✔			207						✔
208	208	210	209				✔	✔	✔						210	34	39-40	✔
211		215		214			✔	✔	✔	215						35-36	41-43	✔

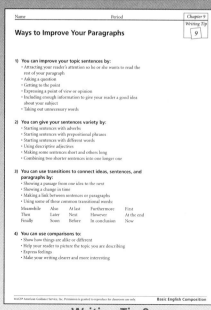

Name _____ Period _____

Chapter 9
Writing Tip
9

Ways to Improve Your Paragraphs

1) You can improve your topic sentences by:
- Attracting your reader's attention so he or she wants to read the rest of your paragraph
- Asking a question
- Getting to the point
- Expressing a point of view or opinion
- Including enough information to give your reader a good idea about your subject
- Taking out unnecessary words

2) You can give your sentences variety by:
- Starting sentences with adverbs
- Starting sentences with prepositional phrases
- Starting sentences with different words
- Using descriptive adjectives
- Making some sentences short and others long
- Combining two shorter sentences into one longer one

3) You can use transitions to connect ideas, sentences, and paragraphs by:
- Showing a passage from one idea to the next
- Showing a change in time
- Making a link between sentences or paragraphs
- Using some of these common transitional words:

Meanwhile	Also	At last	Furthermore	First
Then	Later	Next	However	At the end
Finally	Soon	Before	In conclusion	Now

4) You can use comparisons to:
- Show how things are alike or different
- Help your reader to picture the topic you are describing
- Express feelings
- Make your writing clearer and more interesting

©AGS® American Guidance Service, Inc. Permission is granted to reproduce for classroom use only.   **Basic English Composition**

Writing Tip 9

Name _____ Date _____ Period _____

Chapter 9
Community Connection
9

Improving Your Paragraphs

Writing a paragraph is one thing. Improving a paragraph takes a little more work. When you write a paragraph, study it. Ask yourself these questions:

1. Is my topic sentence good? Are there unnecessary words that get in the way?

2. Have I used good sentence variety? Can I vary the length of my sentences? Can I make some of my sentences begin with adverbs or prepositional phrases?

3. How are my **transitions**? Transitions are words that help readers see how ideas relate.

| EXAMPLE | at last | furthermore | first | in addition |

4. Have I made any comparisons? Have I explained how things are alike or different? Have I used **metaphors** or **similes**? A metaphor is a direct comparison between two things. A simile is an indirect comparison that uses the words *like* or *as*.

| EXAMPLE | Tom was a giant. (metaphor) |
| | Tom was as big as a giant. (simile) |

If you can answer *yes* to these questions, you probably have a good paragraph. Practice using these tips for improving a paragraph. Follow the steps below.

Step 1. Take this paper and a pencil. Go somewhere in your neighborhood. Examples are a park, library, or shopping area.

Step 2. Study what you see. On the back of this paper, write a paragraph about what you see. Use at least one transition and one comparison. Try to use good sentence variety. Be sure to write a topic sentence.

Step 3. Underline your topic sentence. Circle any comparison sentences and transition words.

Step 4. Have your teacher check your work.

©AGS® American Guidance Service, Inc. Permission is granted to reproduce for classroom use only.   **Basic English Composition**

Community Connection 9

Improving Your Paragraphs

Reading Vocabulary

appeal (5)   uncommon
style (5)   vary (7)
topic (5)

S uppose that you hear about a person who always "does things with style." That person probably uses imagination. That person probably tries to do things in lively, uncommon ways. A person with style is interesting to meet.

Be a writer who "does things with style." Your writing will be interesting to read. Give your paragraphs style by making them lively. Use words and sentences in varied, appealing ways.

You have learned about writing clear, correct paragraphs. Now you can try making those paragraphs even better. In this chapter, you will learn how to improve your paragraphs.

Goals for Learning

▶ To improve topic sentences

▶ To use sentence variety

▶ To make smooth transitions between sentences

▶ To make comparisons

Introducing the Chapter

Have students examine the introductory photograph accompanying the first page of Chapter 9. Write the words *style* and *stylist* on the board. Have students use the word *style* in a sentence that might be spoken by the customer in the photograph. (Example: *I'd like my hair cut in a glamorous style.*) Ask students why people want haircuts, cars, clothes, and other things that have "style." Discuss students' ideas about whether people can have style, too.

201

Chapter 9 Self-Study Guide

Lesson at a Glance

Chapter 9   Lesson 1

Overview This lesson discusses topic sentences that grab a reader's attention.

Objectives

- To write a topic sentence that is clear, concise, and imaginative.
- To express a point of view in a topic sentence.

Student Pages 202–204

Teacher's Resource Library

Activity 33

Workbook Activity 38

Reading Vocabulary

cologne	product (5)
fragrant (6)	rewrite
liquid (5)	translate (6)
perfume (5)	unnecessary

Teaching Suggestions

■ Introducing the Lesson

Ask students why someone might want a speaker or writer to get to the point. Briefly discuss the meaning of the expression "to get to the point."

■ Reviewing Skills
Write the following title on the board: *A Speedy Sport*. Have students give their ideas about the topic of a paragraph that could fit with the title. They may suggest auto racing, track, speed skating, hockey, or any other appropriate topic. Select one topic and ask for students' ideas about topic sentences that might introduce a paragraph on that topic.

■ Presenting Activity A

Contrast the poor example with the improved topic sentence. Have students identify unnecessary words ("Let me begin by telling"). Ask for their ideas about why the second example is stronger. They may express their understanding that it makes the reader want to discover why New Orleans is a "one-of-a-kind city."

You have learned that a topic sentence prepares your reader for the main idea of your paragraph. A topic sentence can also get a reader's attention. A lively topic sentence makes the reader want to find out more.

To improve a topic sentence, get to the point. Take out unnecessary words. Add information that will grab the reader's attention. Compare the topic sentences below.

EXAMPLE

Poor: Let me begin by telling about New Orleans, which is an interesting place to visit.

Better: New Orleans is a one-of-a-kind city that offers visitors experiences they will never forget.

Activity A   These topic sentences need improvement. Rewrite them by taking out unnecessary words. Add words that will grab a reader's attention.

1) This paragraph is about our family vacation in Arizona.

2) I think I will begin this paragraph by telling you that I just got a new CD player.

3) Let me tell you about what I want to be someday, which is a musician.

4) I am going to write about the trip my friends and I took to a museum last Saturday.

One way to get your reader's attention is by asking a question. Notice the topic sentence in the paragraph below. It asks a question.

> **Cologne**
>
> Have you ever wondered how cologne got its name? Cologne is a fragrant liquid that is used like perfume. It was first made in a city in Germany over 200 years ago. The name of the city is Cologne! Its famous product became known by the French name *Eau de Cologne*, which translates as "water of cologne." The name has been shortened to *cologne*.

Activity A Answers

Answers will vary. Sample answers are given.

1) Our family vacation in Arizona was unforgettable.   2) My brand-new CD player is the machine of my dreams.   3) Someday, I'll be onstage making music.   4) As I discovered last Saturday, the Museum of Transportation is an amazing place.

Name _____ Date _____ Period _____

Rewriting Topic Sentences

Directions: Improve these topic sentences.

1) You have to do things like practice and concentrate if you want to be good at baseball.

2) Novels that tell why people do things are good very often.

3) Old things that you can find in attics are interesting.

4) Different spices go into a lot of gourmet foods.

5) If one wants a good job then he should have skills for it.

6) Swimmers ought to know rules which will help them be safe.

7) If you want to enjoy something, look at a sunset.

8) Insects do things that human beings often do.

9) Children who watch a television can have their attitudes influenced by television.

10) I know a guy named Charles who is always forgetting something.

11) There are things about tennis and baseball that are the same.

12) Even though Jill and Jean were twins, they were not the same.

13) There are a lot of things you can do with old newspapers.

14) Kittens can make you laugh with the things they do.

©AGS® American Guidance Service, Inc. Permission is granted to reproduce for classroom use only.   **Basic English Composition**

Workbook Activity 38

Activity B Read each pair of questions below. Decide which one is better as a topic sentence. Write *a* or *b* as your answer. Be ready to give reasons for your choice.

1) **a)** Would you like me to tell you something about my cat?
   b) Have you met Harold, our family cat?

2) **a)** Aren't some plants interesting?
   b) Have you ever heard of a meat-eating plant?

3) **a)** Would you like to live next door to a volcano?
   b) What is a volcano?

Activity C Write a short paragraph. Choose your own topic. Begin your paragraph with a question. The topic sentence should get to the point. It should get a reader's attention.

Point of View

You may use your topic sentence to express your opinion. Give your readers your **point of view**. Help them to see your way of looking at the topic.

Include enough information in your topic sentence. Your topic sentence should lead your reader into the body of your paragraph. The body gives supporting details about your point of view.

> **Point of view**
> An opinion; the way in which something is looked at.

EXAMPLE	Poor:	Some television shows are boring.
	Better:	Television shows about roommates are all alike.

Activity D Write a topic sentence for each topic below. Express a point of view. Include enough information to lead the reader into your paragraph.

1) Going to the doctor
2) Eating pickles
3) Thanksgiving dinner
4) Poison ivy
5) Oatmeal
6) Personal computers

■ **Presenting Activity B**
Discuss the paragraph "Cologne" on page 202. Help students to see that the introductory question makes readers say, "I'd like to find out more about how cologne got its name." Readers are prepared for the answer given in the body of the paragraph.

Activity B Answers
In addition to identifying the better topic sentence in each pair, students may be able to give a reason orally for their choice. The better sentence gives more specific information and uses livelier language.

1) b   2) b   3) a

■ **Presenting Activity C** If students need support to come up with a topic, suggest that they look back at Chapter 8 for models of paragraphs that serve different purposes.

Activity C Answers
Paragraphs will vary. Each topic sentence should be a question.

■ **Presenting Activity D**
Briefly discuss various opinions people might have about each of the six topics listed. Students may find that they agree with one of the opinions or are stimulated to come up with their own viewpoint.

Activity D Answers
Answers will vary. Sample topic sentences are given.

1) A visit to an optometrist can be an eye-opening experience.
2) There is only one right way to eat pickles.   3) The best holiday of the year is Thanksgiving.
4) Have you ever wondered what is good about poison ivy?   5) If you think oatmeal is boring, you've never tasted my special oatmeal surprise.   6) Personal computers have made our lives less personal.

Name _____ Date _____ Period _____ | Chapter 9 Activity 33 |

Improving Topic Sentences

Directions: Write a topic sentence for each topic below. Let the reader know how you view the topic. You may also explain what your opinion of the topic is. A topic sentence may ask a question. It may express a point of view. It should get to the point! It should also make the reader want to read the rest of the paragraph. Write your topic sentences on the lines provided.

EXAMPLE **Topic:**
  Watching a movie
  Topic Sentence:
  Watching a well-made movie can be both fun and exciting.

1) A birthday party   6) Eating crabs
2) Homework   7) Summer vacation
3) Going shopping   8) Getting a letter
4) Valentine's Day   9) Halloween
5) Playing a sport   10) Exercise

©AGS® American Guidance Service, Inc. Permission is granted to reproduce for classroom use only.   **Basic English Composition**

Activity 33

GLOBAL CONNECTION

Review the paragraph "Cologne" on page 202. Students may write a similar paragraph about a word taken from a place name. They may use encyclopedias, dictionaries, and books of word origins to investigate one of the following words or find one of their own: *denim, jersey, jeans, hamburger, frankfurter,* and *dalmatian.*

Reading Vocabulary

bore (5)   tragedy (8)
cigarette (6)   weapon (5)
motorcycle

Part A Answers

In addition to identifying the better topic sentence in each pair, students should write a reason for their choice. Their responses should show that they recognize the importance of being specific, eliminating extra words, and grabbing a reader's attention with lively language.

1) b   2) b   3) a   4) a   5) a

Part B Answers

Answers will vary. Sample sentences are given.

1) Last Friday I saw a movie that gave me nightmares.   2) Have you ever laughed yourself awake from sleep?   3) I can't understand how people can watch hours of boring daytime television.   4) Ms. Jefferson believes every student is a scientist.   5) *Motorcycle Mania* is filled with fascinating facts.

Follow-up Activity

As students read their own books and magazines, have them take note of especially interesting topic sentences. They may copy the sentences to read aloud to the group. Spend some time discussing the author's craft. Why does each topic sentence grab the reader's attention?

Lesson 1   Review

A topic sentence prepares a reader for the main idea of a paragraph. A lively topic sentence grabs the reader's attention. He or she wants to read on to find out more.

- A topic sentence should get to the point.
- A topic sentence may ask a question.
- A topic sentence may express a point of view.

Part A   Read each pair of topic sentences below. Which one is better? Write *a* or *b* as your answer. Write a short explanation for your choice.

1) a) This paragraph is going to be about my cat.
   b) Our cat, Harold, rules our home with an iron paw.

2) a) Derek Corelli is a student who runs track at Springfield High School.
   b) Meet Derek Corelli, a shining star of Springfield High's track team.

3) a) Have you ever read a book with 1,037 pages?
   b) *Gone With the Wind* is about the Civil War.

4) a) Cigarettes are weapons of death.
   b) Cigarette smoking is bad for your health.

5) a) One day at the beach, a terrible tragedy almost took place.
   b) I'm going to tell you about a dangerous experience I had at the beach.

Part B   Each topic sentence below needs improvement. Rewrite each one to make it better.

1) We saw a movie not long ago.

2) Let me tell you about a funny dream I had once.

3) Do you know what is really boring?

4) Science can be an interesting subject.

5) The book I read was about motorcycles.

> Variety's the very spice of life,
> That gives it all its flavor.
> —William Cowper

Variety
A number or collection of many different things.

Spice up your paragraphs by giving your sentences **variety**. Sentences with variety are more interesting to read. Here are some ways to add variety to sentences:

- Start sentences with adverbs.
- Start sentences with prepositional phrases.
- Make your sentences different lengths. Some can be short. Others can be long.

Activity A   Rewrite the sentences below. Combine each pair of sentences into one longer sentence. Use a conjunction. Add necessary punctuation. If you wish, review the lesson on combining sentences, on pages 151–159.

Example   Two sentences: Mike was excited about the tennis match. Derek was worried.

         Combined: Mike was excited about the tennis match, but Derek was worried.

1) After the tennis match, Mike was happy. Derek was tired.

2) Derek wanted to go home. Mike wanted to celebrate.

3) Mike wants to play in another tournament. Derek does not.

4) Derek and Mike are good friends. Derek just does not like tennis.

Lesson at a Glance

Chapter 9   Lesson 2

Overview This lesson shows how variety can be added to sentences, making them more interesting to read.

Objectives

- To add variety to sentences by starting them with adverbs or prepositional phrases.
- To vary sentence length.

Student Pages 205–207

Reading Vocabulary

adverb	punctuation (7)
combine (6)	spice (5)
conjunction	tennis (5)
prepositional phrase	tournament (5)
	variety (6)

Teaching Suggestions

- **Introducing the Lesson**
  Read aloud the quotation at the top of this page of the student book. Tell students that William Cowper was an English poet who lived more than two hundred years ago. Briefly discuss the meaning of the common expression, "Variety's the spice of life," helping students to understand how spices and flavors of foods are compared to experiences.

- **Reviewing Skills** Write the word *conjunction* on the board, and have students name examples of conjunctions. (They may refer to Lesson 3 of Chapter 6.) Have them use each listed conjunction in an oral sentence.

- **Presenting Activity A**
  Have a volunteer read aloud the two sentences and the combined sentences in the example. Help students to see how the conjunction *but* points out a contrast and is thus helpful to readers.

Activity A Answers

Answers may vary. Sample answers are given.

1) After the tennis match, Mike was happy, but Derek was tired.
2) Derek wanted to go home, but Mike wanted to celebrate.
3) Although Mike wants to play in another tournament, Derek does not. 4) Derek and Mike are good friends, but Derek just does not like tennis.

Reading Vocabulary

director (7)   punctuate (7)
forehand   surprisingly
livelier   trophy (7)
opponent (7)

■ Presenting Activity B

Go over the directions and examples with students. Remind students that an adverb or a prepositional phrase used as an adverb often answers the question *How? Where?* or *When?* They should think about the answers to those questions as they follow the directions to add variety to sentences 1–5.

Activity B Answers

Answers will vary. Sample sentences are given.

1) Fortunately, Mike's tennis serve is better.   **2)** With loud voices, their friends cheered when Mike and Derek won.
3) After the match, the tournament director gave them a trophy.   **4)** Proudly, Mike has been showing everyone the trophy.   **5)** Now Derek hopes that this tournament is his last.

■ Presenting Activity C

Have a volunteer read aloud Mike's paragraph. Have students give a few ideas about improvements they can make by following the three directions below it.

Activity C Answers

Answers will vary. A sample paragraph is given.

   Would you like to hear about a memorable tennis match? At noon, the match began. The sun blazed overhead. All our friends had high hopes that Derek and I would win. Because our opponents were weak and out of shape, this match ended differently from the others. This time, the victory was ours!

Activity B   Rewrite these sentences. Begin each sentence with an adverb or a prepositional phrase. If you wish, review the lessons on pages 132–150.

Examples   Sentence: Derek has the better forehand.

   Improved: Surprisingly, Derek has the better forehand. (adverb added)

   Improved: Of the two friends, Derek has the better forehand. (prepositional phrase added)

1) Mike's tennis serve is better.

2) Their friends cheered when Mike and Derek won.

3) The tournament director gave them a trophy.

4) Mike has been showing everyone the trophy.

5) Derek hopes that this tournament is his last.

Activity C   Read Mike's paragraph below. Then improve it by taking the steps that follow. Rewrite the paragraph with your changes.

The Tennis Match

   The story that I am about to tell is about an important tennis match. The match began at noon. The sun was very hot that day. The hopes were high that Derek and I would win. The opponents were weak and out of shape. The match ended differently from the others. The victory this time was ours!

---

1) All the sentences start with the same word, *The.* Vary the sentence beginnings.

2) Add or change words to make the sentences livelier.

3) Combine two short sentences into a longer sentence. Use a conjunction. Punctuate the new sentence correctly.

APPLICATION

In the Community

Have students obtain the sports pages of a local newspaper. Have students examine the articles for sentence variety. Students may list the words or phrases that begin the sentences within a paragraph. Do students agree that the sentences begin in varied and pleasing ways?

Lesson 2 | Review

When you read over your paragraphs, look for ways to add variety. Make your sentences more interesting for your readers.

- Begin your sentences with different words, including adverbs and prepositional phrases.

- Combine some short sentences to make longer ones.

Part A Read the news item below. Then rewrite it on your own paper. Add variety to the sentences.

> ### KAPLAN AND CORELLI WIN TENNIS TOURNAMENT
>
> The Annual Springfield Tennis Tournament had a surprise ending. The Harris twins were the defending champions. The guys looked tired and out of shape. The challengers were a new pair named Mike Kaplan and Derek Corelli They took command immediately. The final scores were 6–0 and 6–2.

Part B Choose one of the suggested topics below, or use one of your own topics. Write a paragraph about your chosen topic. Aim for sentence variety!

- Describe a recent sporting event.

- Tell about your favorite sport or hobby.

- Explain why you prefer a particular kind of music.

- Write a review of a movie that you have seen recently.

Reading Vocabulary

annual (6)   item (6)
challenger   prefer (6)
describe (5)   recent (6)
guy (6)

Part A Answers

Answers will vary. A sample paragraph is given.

Yesterday, the Annual Springfield Tennis Tournament had a surprise ending. Although the Harris twins were the defending champions, the guys looked tired and out of shape. The challengers were a new pair named Mike Kaplan and Derek Corelli. From the start, they took command, and the final scores were 6–0 and 6–2.

Part B Answers

Answers will vary. Students should write a paragraph in which sentences begin with different words and are of different lengths. They may choose one of the listed topics or come up with an original topic.

Follow-up Activity

Students may enjoy using sentences of varying lengths to capture action. Read aloud this paragraph to get them started:

The batter waits. Pitch one comes in. It's high. He swings. He misses. Another pitch whizzes in. It's over the plate. He doesn't swing. Strike two! Here comes another pitch. He swings. He connects! Like a low-flying arrow, the ball crashes toward right field, and in moments the grinning batter is standing safely on first base!

LEARNING STYLES

Body/Kinesthetic
Divide the class into a number of groups of varying sizes—from two to ten. Ask each group to make a sentence that has the same number of words as the group size. Have the groups stand as each member says his or her sentence word. Afterward, invite groups to combine or separate to form larger and shorter sentences.

Chapter 9   Lesson 3

Overview This lesson introduces transitions, expressions that connect related ideas within and between sentences.

Objectives

- To use transitions to show relationships in time.
- To use transitions to point out similarities or contrasts.
- To use transitions to point out cause-effect relationships.

Student Pages 208–210

Teacher's Resource Library

Activity 34

Workbook Activities 39–40

Reading Vocabulary

conclusion (6)   relate (6)
connection (6)   thundercloud
consequently (8)   **transition (11)**
expression (5)

Teaching Suggestions

■ Introducing the Lesson

Say the following sentences, asking students to listen for the one word that differs: *The package arrived before I got home. The package arrived after I got home.* Ask students why the words *before* and *after* can make a big difference to readers and writers.

■ Reviewing Skills
Write the following compound sentences on the board. Ask students whether *and* or *but* belongs on each blank and to give reasons for their choice:

Alaska is the largest state, _____ it ranks forty-ninth in population.

Alaska is the northernmost state, _____ it is sometimes called the Land of the Midnight Sun.

Transition

An expression that connects ideas, sentences, or paragraphs (however, therefore, on the other hand, in the meantime).

You can improve your paragraphs by making smooth, clear connections among the ideas in your sentences. Try using words such as *as a result, finally, on the other hand,* and *meanwhile.* Such words and expressions are called **transitions.** They help your reader see how your ideas are related.

Use these transitions to show connections in time.

While	Later
Meanwhile	Soon
Then	At last
Finally	Next
In the meantime	Before
At the end	First

EXAMPLE
Connection not clear:
No rain fell for three months. Thunderclouds appeared.

Connection clear with transition:
No rain fell for three months. At last, thunderclouds appeared.

Study the list of transitions below. Transitions such as *also* and *in addition* point out how things are alike. Transitions such as *however* and *on the other hand* point out differences. Transitions such as *in conclusion* and *therefore* point out causes and results. All transitions show connections among ideas.

However	In conclusion
For example	As a result
Also	Consequently
Furthermore	Therefore
In addition	

TEACHER ALERT

Point out that some transitions have a formal tone and may sound too stiff for everyday writing. Formal transitions should probably be reserved for reports or nonfiction articles. Examples of formal transitions are *in conclusion, consequently, moreover, accordingly,* and *nevertheless.*

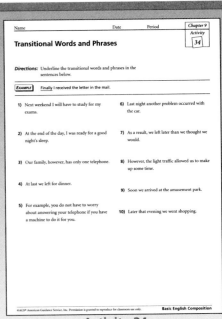

Activity 34

> **EXAMPLE** Connection not clear:
> A personal computer has many uses. Children use software to learn math and reading.
>
> Connection clear with transition:
> A personal computer has many uses. For example, children use software to learn math and reading.

Activity A Read the paragraph below. Notice how transitions make connections smooth and clear. List the transitions that you find. (Not every sentence will have one.)

Cable TV Comes Home!
by Amanda O'Hara

For a long time, I have wanted cable television. After much discussion, my mother agreed to sign up. At last it is here! We used to get seven television channels. Now we get 70! Our family, however, has only one television set. Therefore, every evening we have long talks about what to watch. Sometimes it is hard for us to agree on one channel. Cable television has both advantages and disadvantages for my family.

Activity B Practice using transitions. Rewrite the paragraph below. Improve it by adding some of the transitions listed on page 208.

A Good Night's Sleep

Would you like to improve the quality of your sleep? Give yourself a bedtime routine. Do something relaxing. Read a book. Listen to soothing music. Take a bath. Go to bed at the same time. Wake up at the same time. You will feel more rested.

Reading Vocabulary
advantage (5)	quality (5)
bedtime	relax (5)
channel (5)	routine (7)
disadvantge	software
discussion (6)	soothe (5)

■ Presenting Activity A
Have a volunteer read aloud the paragraph "Cable TV Comes Home." Tell students to think about chronological order, similarities, contrasts, and causes as they look for words that show transitions.

Activity A Answers
1) For a long time 2) After
3) At last 4) Now 5) however
6) Therefore 7) Sometimes
8) both

■ Presenting Activity B
Have a volunteer read aloud the paragraph "A Good Night's Sleep." Help students to understand that the short, choppy sentences do not clearly show connections among ideas. Have students give their ideas about transitions to add, along with sentences that could be combined.

Activity B Answers
Answers will vary. A sample paragraph is given.

Would you like to improve the quality of your sleep? Then give yourself a bedtime routine. First, do something relaxing. Read a book, for example, or listen to soothing music. You may also take a bath. In addition, go to bed at the same time every night, and wake up at the same time every morning. As a result, you will feel more rested.

APPLICATION

Career Connection
List on the board a variety of careers suggested by students. Ask them to choose one career and write a paragraph in which they tell about its advantages and disadvantages. They should use transitions such as *but*, *on the other hand*, and *however*.

Workbook Activity 39

Name ___ Date ___ Period ___ *Chapter 9* Workbook Activity **39**

Transitional Words and Phrases

Directions: · Find 20 transitional words and phrases in the puzzle. The words and phrases are across, down, diagonal, and backwards.
· List them in the spaces below the puzzle.
· Use each one in a sentence.
· To review transitional words, see textbook, page 208.

```
I F E T R F A S A R E S U L T U Q
N N D F U R T H E R M O R E T H E
C V T V I R R T H E R E F O R E T
O B H H D R A R A H G F V B R D S
N E E E E L S Q W W O A A A N N A
C C Y Y Y M M T T R T W W E O O L
L W L W T T E Z X V B Z E E O O T
U E L I H W N A E M M H H V S X A
S Q A Q E O Q L N N T T E N E R R
I N N R W W Q S Q T H P R N N R W
O O I I E F Q O A A I Q O G L L Q
N W F W F Z I X X T X M F T H E N
D Y W O R R O M O T L Q E E X Q U
S F O R E X A M P L E E B W H L N
```

· Fill in these lines with your answers.

1) A _ _ _ _ _
2) A _ _ _ _
3) A _ _ _ _ _
4) A _ _ _ _
5) B _ _ _ _ _
6) F _ _ _ _ _ _
7) F _ _ _ _
8) F _ _ _ _ _ _ _
9) F _ _ _ _ _
10) H _ _ _ _ _ _

11) I _ _ _ _ _ _ _ _ _ _ _
12) I _ _ _ _ _ _
13) L _ _ _ _
14) M _ _ _ _ _ _ _ _
15) N _ _ _
16) N _ _
17) S _ _ _ _ _ _
18) T _ _ _
19) T _ _ _ _ _ _ _
20) T _ _ _ _ _ _ _

©AGS® American Guidance Service, Inc. Permission is granted to reproduce for classroom use only. **Basic English Composition**

Workbook Activity 40

Name ___ Date ___ Period ___ *Chapter 9* Workbook Activity **40**

Using Transitional Words

Directions: Rewrite these paragraphs. Add some transitional words or phrases such as *then, first, meanwhile, later, next, before, finally, also.*

Anthony walked onto the tennis court. He was ready to serve. He tossed the ball into the air. He hit it hard. He really wanted to win the match.

_____
_____
_____
_____
_____
_____

Computers do many things to help us. They keep banking records. They do difficult problems in math. They even change traffic lights in big cities.

_____
_____
_____
_____
_____
_____
_____
_____

Suzanne watched the waves coming in. She looked around for her parents. She saw them. She decided to hold their hands. The ocean looked too rough today.

_____
_____
_____
_____

Pete studied the pitcher carefully. It was his turn to bat. A solid hit would bring in the winning run. He stepped up to the plate. His eyes followed the ball right until it met his bat. He knew he helped win the game.

_____
_____
_____
_____
_____
_____

©AGS® American Guidance Service, Inc. Permission is granted to reproduce for classroom use only. **Basic English Composition**

Part A Answers
1) First   2) At least once a day
3) Then   4) Lately   5) Finally
6) At last   7) Tomorrow

Part B Answers
Answers will vary. Paragraphs should be on the topic of a recent local event and should include at least three transitions.

Follow-up Activity

Make a card for each of the transitions listed on page 208 of the student book, and distribute the cards to students. Have pairs of students work together to use their transitions in one to three sentences on any topic they choose. Partners may read aloud their sentences; classmates listen for the transitions and then name them.

LEARNING STYLES

LEP/ESL
Ask the students for whom English is a second language to write on the chalkboard in their primary language the transition words from the two boxes on page 208. Then ask a volunteer to begin a sentence. Encourage an ESL volunteer to step forward and add to the sentence an appropriate transition word from the chalkboard list. Ask another volunteer to complete the sentence.

Lesson 3   Review

Transitions are words that connect ideas in sentences. Use transitions to take your reader smoothly from one idea to another.

- Use transitions to show changes in time.
- Use transitions to show how things are alike and how they are different.
- Use transitions to point out causes and results.

Part A   Read the paragraph below. Find seven transitions. List them on your paper.

> **Shirley**
> by Derek Corelli
>
> Everyone I know wants to meet Shirley. First there is my mom. At least once a day, she asks me when she will meet Shirley. Then there are my friends, Laura and Amanda. Lately all they talk about is Shirley. Finally, there is my best friend, Mike, who keeps asking, "When, Derek, when?" At last their lucky day is almost here! Tomorrow, at the last track meet of the year, they will all meet Shirley.

Part B   Practice using transitions. Write a paragraph about a recent event in your town or city. Include at least three of the transitions from the lists on page 208. Remember to use sentence variety, too!

Comparison
A statement about how two or more things are alike or different.

Compare
To point out ways in which two or more things are alike or different.

Whenever you tell how things are alike or different, you are making a **comparison**. When you write, you often **compare** people, places, things, or ideas.

The sentences below all show common ways to make comparisons.

EXAMPLES   Shirley is as tall as Laura.
Shirley's hair is shorter than Amanda's.
Shirley's time for the mile is the best on the team.

You can also use less common comparisons to add interest to your sentences. Notice the bold comparisons in Derek's sentences below.

Why I Run
by Derek Corelli

I feel **as if I'm flying**.
The track **is made of sky**.
I am **like a bird**.
My legs are **as strong as an eagle's wings**.

Activity A   On your paper write an ending to each of the comparisons below. Use your imagination.

1) A day without ice cream is like

2) The lake was as clear as

3) A book is like a

4) Before the tournament, Derek was as nervous as

5) The cat's purring sounded like

6) The elephant looked as big as

7) My computer is like

helps readers to picture Derek's sense of freedom and speed.

Activity A Answers
Answers will vary. Sample answers are given.

1) A day without ice cream is like a week of gray clouds. **2)** The lake was as clear as a window. **3)** A book is like a visit to another land. **4)** Before the tournament, Derek was as nervous as a rabbit in a doghouse. **5)** The cat's purring sounded like a lawnmower. **6)** The elephant looked as big as a truck. **7)** My computer is like a window to the world when I surf the Internet.

Lesson at a Glance

Chapter 9   Lesson 4

Overview This lesson treats direct comparisons, or metaphors; indirect comparisons, or similes; and exaggeration.

Objectives
- To use direct and indirect comparisons to help readers form interesting and vivid pictures.
- To enliven language with exaggeration.

Student Pages 211–215

Teacher's Resource Library
Activities 35–36
Workbook Activities 41–43

Reading Vocabulary
compare (5)   comparison (6)

Teaching Suggestions

- **Introducing the Lesson**
Students may be familiar with words that are frequently used to complete the comparisons below. Say each one; have students provide the common ending (or any ending they wish); and discuss the meaning of the comparison:

    as big as a . . .
    as cool as a . . .
    as quiet as a . . .
    as sharp as a . . .

- **Reviewing Skills** Write the terms *positive, comparative,* and *superlative* on the board. Students may recall from Lesson 1 of Chapter 6 that these are the forms used for comparing adjectives and adverbs. List the words *bad, fast, happy,* and *happily* on the board. Have students name the comparative and superlative form of each one.

- **Presenting Activity A**
Discuss the comparisons in "Why I Run" on this page. Point out that each sentence contains a comparison that is not literally true but

Reading Vocabulary

direct
  comparison
graceful (5)
indirect comparison

metaphor
similar (6)
simile (11)

■ **Presenting Activity B**

Discuss the distinction between an indirect comparison (simile) and a direct comparison (metaphor). Tell students that the word *as* or *like* signals an indirect comparison.

Activity B Answers

1) Direct 2) Indirect
3) Indirect 4) Direct
5) Indirect

Direct comparison

An expression showing that two things have similar qualities; also called a **metaphor.**

Indirect comparison

An expression using like *or* as *to show that two things are like each other in a certain way; also called a* **simile.**

Direct and Indirect Comparisons

You may want to use a **direct comparison** to help your readers form a sharp, interesting picture. A direct comparison is also called a **metaphor**.

EXAMPLE | **Direct Comparison**

When she runs, Shirley is a deer.
(Shirley is directly compared to a deer. The reader can picture a fast, graceful runner.)

You may also point out how different things are alike with an **indirect comparison**. An indirect comparison uses *like* or *as*. An indirect comparison is also called a **simile**.

EXAMPLES | **Indirect Comparisons**

Shirley runs like a deer.
When she is in a race, Shirley is as fierce as a tiger.

Activity B Each of the sentences below contains a comparison. The comparison is a familiar saying. Decide whether the comparison is direct or indirect. Write *Direct* or *Indirect* as your answer. Be ready to discuss the meaning of each familiar saying.

1) The woman is a puzzle to me.

2) The man eats like a horse.

3) That sentence is as clear as mud.

4) Shirley is a breath of fresh air.

5) Shirley is as sweet as honey!

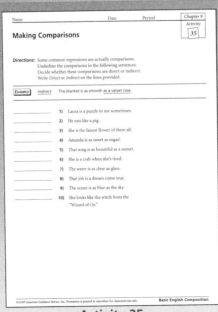

Activity 35

Activity C   Now try to make indirect and direct comparisons that are NOT familiar sayings. Rewrite each sentence below. Include an interesting comparison in it.

1) When I stood before the audience, I felt nervous.
2) Derek talks about Shirley constantly.
3) Basketball players are tall.
4) The TV announcer spoke fast.
5) Laura has a beautiful singing voice.

Exaggerations

Exaggerate

To overstate; to say that something is greater than it is.

When you **exaggerate**, you say that something is greater than it is. An exaggeration is a comparison that helps readers understand your feelings. An exaggeration can entertain your readers. Notice the exaggerations in each of these sentences.

> **EXAMPLES**   Shirley is the most beautiful girl that ever lived.
>
> Your smile is brighter than any star in the sky!
>
> When the roller coaster reached the top of the first hill, I looked down. The bottom was at least one thousand feet below me!

Activity D   Complete the following statements on your paper. Write a beginning for each exaggeration.

Example   . . . more honest than George Washington.

How could I lie? I've always been more honest than George Washington.

1) . . . worth a million dollars to me.

2) . . . flew as high as an astronaut.

3) . . . more frightened than a mouse.

4) . . . like a sudden clap of thunder.

5) . . . as tall as a tree.

6) . . . blew up like a volcano!

Reading Vocabulary
announcer   exaggerate (7)
audience (5)   exaggeration
constantly   roller coaster
entertain (5)

■ **Presenting Activity C**   Go over the directions with students. Explain that writers try to invent imaginative comparisons and to avoid the overused comparisons that are often called clichés.

Activity C Answers

Answers will vary. Sample answers are given.

1) When I stood before the audience, I felt as if the earth were shaking beneath my feet.
2) When Derek starts talking about Shirley, he's like a runaway train.   3) Basketball players are telephone poles.   4) The TV announcer spoke like a tape recorder set on fast forward.
5) Laura's singing voice is as beautiful as a shimmering sunset.

■ **Presenting Activity D**

Review the examples on this page and within this activity before having students proceed with their own exaggerations.

Activity D Answers

Answers will vary. Sample answers are given.

1) Getting into college is worth a million dollars to me.   2) When I got the college acceptance notice, I flew as high as an astronaut.   3) When Melvin stayed alone in the dark house, he was more frightened than a mouse.   4) The announcement of the award came like a sudden clap of thunder. Luann was so startled, she fell out of her chair.
5) How can Raymond drive that tiny car? He is as tall as a tree!
6) When my brother Thomas heard that I broke his CD player, he blew up like a volcano.

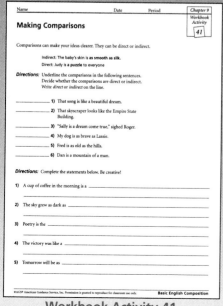

Workbook Activity 41

Reading Vocabulary

annoy (6) energetic (8)
behavior (5) task (5)

■ Presenting Activity E

Read through the ten items with students, and brainstorm comparisons that could sound fresh and entertaining.

Activity E Answers

Answers will vary. Sample answers are given.

1) When I looked up at the building, I was sure it was touching the sun. 2) Tasting that cake was like falling in love. 3) That job was like counting grains of sand on a beach. 4) By the end of that day, I was dancing on the ceiling. 5) That song was so touching, it could make a stone cry. 6) Ashley had more energy than a power station. 7) The meal was as tasty as a dusty carpet. 8) When I won first prize, my head swelled up as big as a blimp. 9) People who talk in movie theaters are as popular as whining mosquitoes. 10) The night on Greenpoint Mountain was as much fun as sleeping in a freezer.

APPLICATION

 At Home
Exaggeration and other humorous comparisons are a staple of television sitcoms. Discuss the sitcoms that students watch. Suggest that they select one program to watch with a notepad. They may jot down the jokes that depend on humorous comparisons. Set aside time for students to share their findings.

Activity E Write a sentence that describes each of the items below. Include a comparison that exaggerates.

Example The most boring person you have ever met
Spending the day with him was like spending a day watching the hands move around a clock.

1) The tallest building that you have ever seen

2) The most delicious dessert that you have ever eaten

3) The most difficult task that you have ever completed

4) The most exciting day of your life

5) The most beautiful song that you have ever heard

6) The most energetic child that you have ever met

7) The worst meal that you have ever tasted

8) The proudest moment that you have ever experienced

9) A behavior that annoys you

10) An experience that you would never want to have again

Name	Date	Period	Chapter 9

Comparisons

Activity 36

Directions: Write a sentence that describes each of the items below.
Use a direct or indirect comparison.

EXAMPLE The most exciting place you have ever visited
Visiting Paris was a dream come true.

1) The most beautiful thing you have ever seen

2) The longest day of your life

3) The hardest job you have ever completed

4) The most important event of your life

5) The most delicious food you have ever eaten

6) The most expensive car you have ever seen

7) The funniest thing you have ever done

8) The most exciting day of your life

9) The most daring thing you have ever done

10) The shortest event of your life

©AGS® American Guidance Service, Inc. Permission is granted to reproduce for classroom use only. **Basic English Composition**

Activity 36

Lesson 4 | Review

Use comparisons to show how two or more things are alike or different. Use imaginative comparisons such as exaggerations to make your ideas clear and lively.

Part A   Match each sentence beginning at the left with a sentence ending at the right. Write the completed sentence on your paper. Be ready to explain what each comparison means.

Column 1

I was so nervous that my hands

Snowflakes were

An unexpected compliment

Riding in Mike's old car

We settled down as happily as

Column 2

as large as cotton balls.

was like being inside a bouncing ball.

chicks in a nest.

is like a rainbow appearing suddenly overhead.

fluttered like frightened butterflies with no safe place to land.

Part B   Write five sentences that compare someone you like to other people or things. Exaggerate if you wish.

Reading Vocabulary
compliment (5)   unexpected (6)
rainbow

Part A Answers

1) I was so nervous that my hands fluttered like frightened butterflies with no safe place to land.
2) Snowflakes were as large as cotton balls.   3) An unexpected compliment is like a rainbow appearing suddenly overhead.
4) Riding in Mike's old car was like being inside a bouncing ball.
5) We settled down as happily as chicks in a nest.

Part B Answers

Answers will vary. Students' five sentences should include any of the figurative comparisons treated in this lesson.

Follow-up Activity

Provide poetry anthologies. Have students select poems they like. Ask them to look in the poems for unusual, vivid comparisons. Some students may want to read their poems aloud.

LEARNING STYLES

Visual/Spatial
Challenge the students to create pictures to represent the five comparisons in Activity B on page 212 and the five in Part A on page 215. Encourage each student to select one comparison and to draw a picture to illustrate it. Afterward, invite the students—one by one—to display the pictures. Ask the class to guess which comparison has been illustrated.

Workbook Activity 42

Name _____ Date _____ Period _____ | Chapter 9 Workbook Activity 42

Improving a Paragraph

Directions: Read the following paragraph carefully. Proofread the paragraph for mistakes. Make corrections. Then write it correctly on the back of this paper or on your own paper.

For You to Do:

1) Improve the topic sentence.
2) Be sure the body supports the main idea.
3) Improve the summary sentence.
4) Add sentence variety and transitions.
5) Check for run-on sentences and fragments.
6) Check spelling. Correct any errors.
7) Check punctuation and capitalization.
8) Check verbs for errors.

Reference Sources

Do you know what reference sources are. They are books and also files that helps us to find lots of information. The library has most of them but cant be tooken home. A library catalog is a list of all books a library got. If you know the title and author you can find it easy. The dictionary atlas and encyclopedia are other reference books, maybe you never heard of *who's who in america*. it has names of famous people and tells about them. If you dont know what a thesaurus *Readers' Guide* and almanac is used for, you oughta find out, they can help with your schoolwork.

©AGS® American Guidance Service, Inc. Permission is granted to reproduce for classroom use only.   **Basic English Composition**

Workbook Activity 43

Name _____ Date _____ Period _____ | Chapter 9 Workbook Activity 43

Proofreading Practice

Directions: • Read the paragraph below very carefully. Circle these kinds of mistakes:
    Spelling
    Capitalization
    Punctuation
    Sentence errors
  • Correct the mistakes.
  • Rewrite the improved paragraph below.

Why I Quit Bowling

For many years, I enjoyed bowling. Too year ago I quit my team and this be the reason why. The name of my team were the starframers. A starframe in bowling means that everyone gots a spare or a strike in that frame. We was great, everyones averages kept improving. Naturally, we was in first place all year. Finally it was the last nite of the season, my team had went into the final position round three games ahead of the second place team. Confidence was our middle name that Night! We only had to win one game to take home the first place trophy. All I can says is that I is looking right now at a second place trophy. Yes, we lost all four games, surely, no more needs to be said.

_____
_____
_____
_____
_____
_____
_____
_____

©AGS® American Guidance Service, Inc. Permission is granted to reproduce for classroom use only.   **Basic English Composition**

Chapter 9 Review

The Teacher's Resource Library includes two parallel forms of the Chapter 9 Mastery Test. The difficulty level of the two forms is equivalent. You may wish to use one form as a pretest and the other form as a posttest.

Reading Vocabulary

medical (6)   retirement
retire (6)   spectacular (7)

Part A Answers

Answers will vary. Sample answers are given.

1) Even if you love desserts, you can still choose healthy ingredients.
2) Listen to jazz and let your spirit soar.   **3)** An emergency medical technician has a job that is hard, scary, and wonderful.   **4)** Baby-sitting for the Florio twins was a night to remember!   **5)** Did you know that George Washington once stayed on Forrest Street here in Northboro?   **6)** If you're looking for something fascinating to read, pick up a dictionary.   **7)** Have you ever seen an elephant in a supermarket?

Part B Answers

Answers will vary. Revised paragraphs should include modifiers, transitions, and sentences of varied lengths.

Part A   Each topic sentence below needs improvement. Rewrite it so that it grabs a reader's attention.

1) This paragraph will be about eating healthy foods.

2) Some kinds of music are great.

3) I think it would be good to have a job in the medical field.

4) Let me tell you about an interesting experience.

5) I am going to write about the history of our town.

6) A dictionary is a useful book.

7) Do you know what I saw last week?

Part B   Three paragraphs follow. They all need improvement. Read each paragraph. Then think about how to make it more interesting to read. Vary the sentence beginnings. Add adjectives, adverbs, or prepositional phrases. Combine some of the ideas into longer sentences. Use transitions to make clear connections. Write the improved paragraph on your paper.

1)

My Retirement
by Derek Corelli

Mike and I played in several tennis tournaments. We lost the first ones. We did improve. We found really bad tennis players. We won our last tournament. We even got a trophy. It was over. I decided not to play again. I am just too busy for tennis.

2)

The Grand Canyon

Have you ever seen the Grand Canyon? The canyon is a national park in Arizona. Thousands of people visit it. The people come mainly in the summer. The Colorado River formed this canyon. The canyon is 277 miles long. It is 4 to 14 miles wide at the rim. It is the most spectacular canyon in the United States.

Chapter 9 Mastery Test A

Part A Improve these topic sentences. Rewrite each sentence by taking out unnecessary words. Use different words if it will help.

1) This paragraph is going to be about a camping trip that I took when I was seven and got poison ivy.

2) I think becoming a millionaire would be an interesting thing to do.

3) I would like to move to the country after I work for a while and save some money.

4) Being a collector of special treasures is fun, but you need lots of space for your collections.

5) I'll bet working at an ice-skating rink would be fun because you could skate all the time for free.

Part B Rewrite these sentences to give them variety. Begin each sentence with an adverb or a prepositional phrase.

1) I enjoyed our visit last week.

2) I found your family to be very likable.

3) I hope that we can get together again.

4) I'd like to come back.

5) I'll call you to plan another visit.

Part C Rewrite this paragraph. Improve it by adding five transitional words or phrases. Use *meanwhile, surprisingly, at last, finally, later, at first, for a moment, however, or then.*

Ruth once visited the Statue of Liberty in New York. She was fifteen. She climbed and climbed. She reached the top. She was able to see the view of the city and the harbor. It was spectacular! She always remembered that trip.

Part D Write an ending to each of the comparisons below.

1) A thing of beauty is

2) The tornado sounded like

3) The moon looked as white as

4) Jody is as happy as

5) The morning hours are like

Chapter 9 Mastery Test A

3)

> **The Right Amount of Sleep**
>
> How much sleep does a person need? Some people need ten hours a night. Some people need only four. Figure out how much sleep you need. Choose three days when you don't need to get up at a particular time. Go to bed at the same time each of those three nights. Notice what time you wake up in the morning. By the third morning, you should know how much sleep your body needs.

Part C Read each sentence below. Notice the common comparison that is in it. Think about the meaning of the sentence. Rewrite the sentence to include a different comparison. Try to make your comparison lively.

1) Mike is as strong as an ox.

2) Derek looks like a million bucks today!

3) The math problem is as clear as mud.

4) That house is as old as the hills.

5) Passing the test was as easy as pie.

Test Taking Tip When studying for a test, write your own test problems with a partner. Then complete each other's test. Double-check your answers.

Part C Answers

Answers will vary. Sample answers are given.

1) Mike is as strong as ten trucks. **2)** Derek looks as if he just won a free trip around the world. **3)** The math problem is like a two-million-piece jigsaw puzzle. **4)** That house is a prehistoric fossil. **5)** Passing the test was as easy as spelling my name.

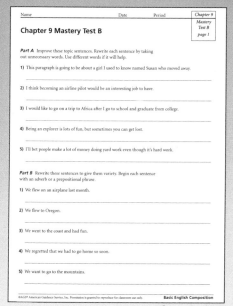

Chapter 9 Mastery Test B

Planning Guide

Answering Questions

Chapter Activities

Teacher's Resource Library
Community Connection 10:
   Answering Essay Questions

Assessment Options

Student Text
Chapter 10 Review

Teacher's Resource Library
Chapter 10 Mastery Tests A and B

Teaching Strategies							Language Skills			Learning Styles						Teacher's Resource Library		
Reviewing Skills	Teacher Alert	Follow-up Activity	Career Application	Home Application	Global Connection	Community Application	Identification Skills	Writing Skills	Punctuation Skills	Visual/Spatial	Auditory/Verbal	Body/Kinesthetic	Logical/Mathematical	Group Learning	LEP/ESL	Activities	Workbook Activities	Self-Study Guide
220		222				221	✔	✔	✔		222					37-39	44	✔
223	225	227	223		224		✔	✔	✔				227			40	45-46	✔

Name _____ Date _____ Period _____   Chapter 10
Community
Connection
10

Answering Essay Questions

An **essay** is a short piece of writing about a single subject or topic.
Essay questions usually begin with the words *describe, compare,*
explain, or *discuss.*

EXAMPLE   *Explain the difference between a noun and a verb.*

An essay answer is one or more paragraphs. It has a topic sentence, a
body, and a summary or conclusion. Two kinds of essay questions are
descriptions and discussions. A description essay asks you to
tell about something. A discussion essay question asks you to tell more
than one point of view about the subject.

Writing good essay answers takes practice. Follow these steps to
practice answering essay questions.

Step 1. Think of something that interests you that you would like to
learn more about. Examples are sports, hobbies, places, or jobs.

Step 2. Think of two essay questions about this subject. Make sure
that you do not know the answers to the questions. Write one
of the questions so that it asks for a description. Write the other
question so it asks for a discussion. Write the questions below.

1) _____

2) _____

Step 3. Find answers for your questions. Interview someone who
knows something about the subject. You can also find
information by looking in encyclopedias, books, and
magazines at the library.

Step 4. Use the back of this paper to answer your essay questions. Be
sure to include a topic sentence. Write a body that supports
your topic sentence. Then write a summary or conclusion.

Step 5. After you write each essay answer, underline the topic
sentence.

Step 6. Share your essay questions and answers with the class.

©AGS® American Guidance Service, Inc. Permission is granted to reproduce for classroom use only.   **Basic English Composition**

Community Connection 10

Answering Questions

Reading Vocabulary
organize (6)   require (6)
properly (5)

Introducing the Chapter

Have students examine the introductory photograph accompanying the first page of Chapter 10. Have them tell what the scene shows. (Students are taking a test.) Ask: What goals do the students have in this scene? What does the teacher probably hope to gain from this test?

Write two headings on the board: *Writing for Tests* and *Writing for Other Purposes*. Briefly discuss how writing for tests is different from other forms of writing.

How do you feel about taking tests? If you're like most students, you would rather be doing something else. Tests may never be fun, but there are ways to make them easier to take. The most important thing to do is to prepare. You will feel more sure of yourself if you have studied well.

You can also improve your test scores if you learn how to answer questions properly. Some test questions require short answers, usually complete sentences. Some test questions require longer answers—one or more paragraphs.

In Chapter 10, you will learn how to give written answers to test questions.

Goals for Learning

▶ To answer test questions in complete sentences

▶ To write answers to essay test questions in well-organized paragraphs

---

SELF-STUDY GUIDE

Name _____

CHAPTER 10: Answering Questions

Goal 10.1 *To answer test questions in complete sentences*

Date	Assignment	Score
_____	1: Read pages 219-220. Complete Activity A on page 220.	_____
_____	2: Read page 221. Complete Activities B-C on page 221.	_____
_____	3: Complete the Lesson 1 Review, Parts A-B on page 222.	_____
_____	4: Complete Workbook Activity 44.	

Comments:

SELF-STUDY GUIDE

Name _____

CHAPTER 10 Answering Questions, continued

Goal 10.4 *To write answers to essay test questions in well-organized paragraphs*

Date	Assignment	Score
_____	5: Read page 223. Complete Activity A on page 223.	_____
_____	6: Read page 224. Complete Activities B-C on page 224.	_____
_____	7: Read page 225. Complete Activities D-E on page 225.	_____
_____	8: Complete Workbook Activity 45.	
_____	9: Read page 226. Complete Activity F on page 226.	_____
_____	10: Complete the Lesson 2 Review, Parts A-B on page 227.	
_____	11: Complete Workbook Activity 46.	
_____	12: Complete the Chapter 10 Review, Parts A-D on pages 228-229.	

Comments:

Student's Signature _____ Date _____

Instructor's Signature _____ Date _____

Chapter 10 Self-Study Guide

Chapter 10   Lesson 1

Overview This lesson provides guidance in using complete sentences to answer test questions.

Objectives

- To determine the details to provide in response to a short-answer test question.
- To write answers in complete sentences.

Student Pages 220–222

Teacher's Resource Library

Activities 37–39

Workbook Activity 44

Reading Vocabulary

accomplish (6)   numerous (6)

almanac (7)   predicate

capital (5)   proficient (10)

feature (6)   reference (6)

geologic   sample (5)

geyser (7)   subject (5)

governor (5)

Teaching Suggestions

■ Introducing the Lesson

Ask students to tell what kind of test they expect to see if a teacher announces a "short-answer" test. They may note such test formats as fill-in-the-blanks, matching, and multiple choice. Explain that this lesson will focus on the kinds of short answers that are given in complete sentences.

■ Reviewing Skills Write the

following fragments and sentences on the board. Have students identify each and then offer ideas for turning each fragment into a complete sentence:

North of Georgia in the eastern United States. (fragment)

Robins eat worms. (sentence)

Use an almanac for recent information. (sentence)

President of the United States. (fragment)

Use a complete sentence to answer a test question. Remember that a complete sentence expresses a complete idea. It must include both a subject and a predicate. Study the sample short answers to the questions below.

EXAMPLES

Question:	Who was William Bradford?
Answer:	William Bradford was a Pilgrim and the second governor of Plymouth Colony.
Question:	What unusual geologic features can be found in Yellowstone National Park?
Answer:	Yellowstone National Park is famous for its numerous geysers and hot springs.

Activity A Write one or two sentences to answer each of the questions below. You may use a reference book. The answers can be found in a dictionary, an encyclopedia, or an almanac. Be sure that your answers are in complete sentences.

1) Why is Galileo famous?

2) Who was Frederick Douglass?

3) Why are pictures of Cupid often included on valentines?

4) Where is Denali National Park?

5) What is a Nobel Prize?

6) Where is Pearl Harbor?

7) What is the capital of Colorado?

8) What did Marie Curie accomplish?

9) At what temperature on the Fahrenheit scale will water boil?

10) What is a caterpillar?

11) Describe a Persian cat.

12) What does the word *proficient* mean?

■ Presenting Activity A

Provide the reference sources named in the directions, or give students the opportunity to do this activity in the library.

Activity A Answers

Wording of answers will vary. Sample sentences are given.

1) Galileo is famous for his work in astronomy, including the discovery of four of Jupiter's moons.   2) Frederick Douglass was an African American writer, abolitionist, and former slave. 3) Cupid was the ancient Roman god of love.   4) Denali National Park is in Alaska.   5) A Nobel Prize is an international award given each year for major achievements in science, medicine, literature, economics, and world peace.   6) Pearl Harbor is on the southern coast of Oahu, Hawaii.   7) Denver is the capital of Colorado. 8) Marie Curie made many discoveries in physics and chemistry, especially with radioactivity.   9) Water boils at 212 degrees Fahrenheit.   10) A caterpillar is the larva of a moth or butterfly.   11) A Persian cat has long, silky fur, short legs, and a stocky body.   12) The word *proficient* means "expert and skillful."

Identify

To tell the most important characteristics of something; these characteristics make the person, place, or thing different or recognizable.

Identifications

Test items may ask you to **identify** certain people, places, or things. Your answer should state the most important characteristics of the person, place, or thing. Ask yourself, "What makes this person famous? What is unusual about this place? What are the special characteristics of this thing?"

Both sentences below are answers to the same test item. Do you see why the second answer is stronger?

EXAMPLES

Test item:	Identify Mammoth Cave.
Poor answer:	Mammoth Cave is a big cave that has many visitors.
Better answer:	Mammoth Cave is a national park in Kentucky; it has 336 miles of underground passages.

Activity B Identify each of the following. You can find information in this book by looking on the page given in parentheses. Write your answers in complete sentences.

1) St. Paul (page 196)

2) Othello (page 182)

3) *Who's Who* (page 183)

Activity C Choose five of the people listed below. Identify these people in complete sentences. You can find information in a reference book.

- Sandra Day O'Connor
- Rosa Parks
- Robert E. Lee
- Joe Louis
- Jim Thorpe
- Nelson Mandela
- Robin Hood
- Florence Nightingale
- Edgar Allan Poe
- I. M. Pei

Reading Vocabulary

characteristic (6)	parentheses
identification (8)	passage (5)
identify (6)	recognizable
mammoth (5)	underground

■ **Presenting Activity B**

Help students to find the relevant information on the page cited.

Activity B Answers

1) St. Paul is a city in Minnesota. It is named for St. Paul's Chapel, which was built on the site in 1841. **2)** Othello is the main character in Shakespeare's play of the same name. In a jealous rage, Othello mistakenly kills his wife. **3)** Who's Who is a reference book that gives information about living people. A short paragraph is included about each person.

■ **Presenting Activity C**

Review the names on the list, asking students for any information they already know. Discuss the characteristics that are probably most important to include in response to a test identification question.

Activity C Answers

Answers will vary. Students should choose five names and write five responses, each of at least one sentence.

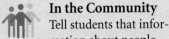

APPLICATION

In the Community
Tell students that information about people, past and present, can be found in specialized sources, including *Who's Who*. Write the term *biographical dictionary*. Have volunteers investigate the reference room of a library for biographical dictionaries. Ask students to copy the title of each source and its call number and to report to the group about the kinds of information it contains.

Name ___ Date ___ Period ___ | Chapter 10 Activity **37**

Writing Short Answers

Directions: Write short answers for each of these questions. You may use a reference book for information. Be sure that your answers are in complete sentences.

1) What did Ben Franklin invent?

2) Where is Yellowstone National Park?

3) Who was Edgar Allan Poe?

4) Where was the first permanent English colonial settlement in America?

5) Which planet is closest to the sun?

6) What is the capital of the United States?

7) Who was Christopher Columbus?

8) Why is Walt Disney famous?

9) When did the Japanese bomb Pearl Harbor?

10) Who was the first president of the United States?

©AGS® American Guidance Service, Inc. Permission is granted to reproduce for classroom use only. **Basic English Composition**

Activity 37

Name ___ Date ___ Period ___ | Chapter 10 Activity **38**

Identifying People, Places, and Things

Directions: To *identify* means to tell the most important characteristics about something. Identify each person, place, or thing below. Write one complete sentence stating the characteristics that make each person, place, or thing different or recognizable. Use a dictionary if necessary.

1) Joseph Stalin

2) posology

3) Hong Kong

4) melton

5) scatterbrain

6) Theodore Roosevelt

7) NASA

8) observation car

9) trackwalker

10) riot

©AGS® American Guidance Service, Inc. Permission is granted to reproduce for classroom use only. **Basic English Composition**

Activity 38

Reading Vocabulary

burden (5)   llama (5)
domesticate   mythology (8)
glacier (5)   source (6)

Part A Answers

1) No 2) No 3) Yes 4) Yes
5) Yes

Part B Answers

Wording of answers will vary.
Each answer must be a complete
sentence. Sample answers are given.

1) A capybara is a large South
American rodent that lives near
water. 2) Austin is the capital of
Texas. 3) Francis Scott Key was the
author of the anthem of the United
States, "The Star-Spangled Banner."
4) Eleanor Roosevelt was a human-
rights supporter and the wife of
President Franklin D. Roosevelt.
5) Glacier National Park is a
national park in northern Montana;
it covers over one million acres and
has many glaciers and lakes.

Follow-up Activity

Write the questions *Who? What?
Where?* and *When?* on the board. Say
a sentence that gives a fact, and have
students tell what question is being
answered. Example sentences:

Albany is the capital city of New
York State. (Question: *What is
Albany?*)

Alexander the Great was a military
leader of ancient times. (Question:
Who was Alexander the Great?)

The Gulf of Mexico lies on Florida's
western coast. (Question: *Where is
the Gulf of Mexico?*)

The American colonies declared
independence in 1776. (Question:
*When did the American colonies
declare independence?*)

LEARNING STYLES

Auditory/Verbal
Ask volunteers to read
aloud the questions and
answers in Part A on page 222 and
to compose and read aloud
complete sentences for #1 and #2.

Lesson 1 Review

When a test item requires short answers, write your answers in
complete sentences.

Part A Read each question and the answer below. Decide
if the answer is a complete sentence. Write *Yes* or *No* for
each answer.

1) How many rooms are in your home?
   Three bedrooms, a living room, dining room, and
   kitchen.

2) Why is there a picture of Cupid on many valentines?
   Because Cupid was the god of love in Roman mythology.

3) Identify Zachary Taylor.
   Zachary Taylor was an American general and the twelfth
   president of the United States.

4) Identify Annapolis.
   Annapolis is the capital of the state of Maryland.

5) What is a llama?
   A llama is a domesticated animal used in the Andes as a
   beast of burden and as a source of wool.

Part B Identify the following items. Write each answer in a
complete sentence. Use a reference book if necessary.

1) What is a capybara?

2) Identify Austin, Texas.

3) Identify Francis Scott Key.

4) Identify Eleanor Roosevelt.

5) Identify Glacier National Park.

Completing Sentences

Name _____ Date _____ Period _____   Chapter 10 Activity 39

Directions: Read each question. The answer has been given as a
fragment. Rewrite each answer into a complete sentence.

EXAMPLE Question: Who was the first U.S. president?
         Fragment: George Washington
         Sentence: George Washington was the first U.S.
                    president.

1) What city has the largest population?
   New York City

2) Who sailed across the Atlantic Ocean to
   America in 1492?
   Christopher Columbus

3) What is the capital of the United States?
   Washington, D.C.

4) What document was adopted by the
   Continental Congress on July 4, 1776?
   The Declaration of Independence

5) What is the oldest national park?
   Yellowstone

6) Who invented the lightning rod and bifocal
   eyeglasses?
   Benjamin Franklin

7) What naval site did the Japanese attack and
   bomb on December 7, 1941?
   Pearl Harbor, Hawaii

8) In what state is the Grand Canyon located?
   Arizona

9) What are the two tallest buildings in the
   United States?
   The World Trade Center in New York and the
   Sears Tower in Chicago

©AGS® American Guidance Service, Inc. Permission is granted to reproduce for classroom use only.   **Basic English Composition**

Activity 39

Identifying People, Places, and Things

Name _____ Date _____ Period _____   Chapter 10 Workbook Activity 44

To **identify** means to tell the most important
characteristics about something.

Directions: • Identify each person, place, or thing.
• Write one complete sentence stating
the characteristics that make them
different or recognizable.
• Use a dictionary as needed.

1) Neapolitan ice cream _____

2) Naugahyde _____

3) haberdasher _____

4) Winston Churchill _____

5) Carson City _____

6) Casablanca _____

7) bighorn _____

8) Thanksgiving _____

9) rya rug _____

10) trinket _____

11) trilogy _____

12) NATO _____

©AGS® American Guidance Service, Inc. Permission is granted to reproduce for classroom use only.   **Basic English Composition**

Workbook Activity 44

Essay
A short piece of writing about a single subject or topic.

The directions in an **essay** question usually begin with a word such as *describe, compare, explain,* or *discuss.* An essay answer is one or more paragraphs. To write an essay answer, organize your information well. Start with a topic sentence that states the main idea of your essay. Include your information in the body. End with a summary or conclusion.

Make sure that your topic sentence clearly identifies the subject of your essay. Avoid the vague pronoun *it* or a vague reference to the subject. Study this example.

EXAMPLE

Test item:	What qualities made George Washington a great leader?
Poor topic sentence:	This person had many great qualities.
Better topic sentence:	George Washington showed many qualities of leadership.

Activity A   Read each test item below. Choose the better topic sentence in each case. Write the letter of each answer on your paper.

1) Describe Glacier National Park.
   a) It is a large park in northern Montana.
   b) Glacier National Park is in northern Montana.

2) Discuss the activities people do in the spring.
   a) It is a season for doing things outdoors.
   b) Spring is a season for doing things outdoors.

3) Discuss the advantages and disadvantages of having a garden.
   a) Having a garden involves some advantages and disadvantages.
   b) Here are some good and bad things.

4) Compare a short answer and an essay answer.
   a) One is shorter, and the other has more details.
   b) The main difference between a short answer and an essay answer is the amount of detail.

Answering Questions   Chapter 10   **223**

Activity A Answers
1) b   2) b   3) a   4) b

APPLICATION

Career Connection
Help students to come up with hypothetical questions that a job interviewer might ask. Examples: *Why do you think you will make a contribution to this company? What kind of work are you especially good at? Where did you get your training?* Have students try to turn each question into a statement that would lead to a fuller answer.

Lesson at a Glance

Chapter 10   Lesson 2

Overview This lesson discusses strategies for writing a paragraph in response to an essay test item.

Objectives
- To identify the subject of the essay in a topic sentence.
- To respond appropriately to questions that require describing or discussing a topic.

Student Pages 223–227

Teacher's Resource Library
   Activity 40
   Workbook Activities 45–46

Reading Vocabulary

advantage (5)	leadership (6)
conclusion (6)	pronoun
detail (5)	quality (5)
disadvantage	summary (8)
essay (6)	vague (5)

Teaching Suggestions

- **Introducing the Lesson**
   Tell students that an essay test question requires an answer of at least one paragraph. Ask them for their ideas about what would make a good essay answer. They may note such features as full and relevant details, clear organization, and correct usage and punctuation.

- **Reviewing Skills** Write the terms *topic sentence, body,* and *conclusion or summary* on the board. Have students identify them as labels of parts of a paragraph. Have them tell what purpose each part serves.

- **Presenting Activity A**
   Point out that the topic sentence of a paragraph written for a test should come right to the point. One way to start is to restate the information in the test question, as in the example.

■ Presenting Activity B

Read the test question to students. Have them suggest their own topic sentences in response to the question before reading the three choices given.

Activity B Answer

Choice b is the correct answer.

■ Presenting Activity C

Ask students how Americans celebrate Valentine's Day. List on the board phrases that students suggest. Students may then refer to the list as they develop their paragraphs.

Activity C Answer

Students' paragraphs will vary. A sample paragraph is given.

Valentine's Day is celebrated in many ways in the United States. Sending cards is probably the most common custom. Cards can be made by hand or bought in a store. They may be funny and rude, or they may be romantic and sentimental. A card can be sent to one's sweetheart, but cards are also sent to teachers, relatives, and friends. In addition to cards, people give each other candy, especially chocolates. Men and women may send each other flowers, too. A couple may go to a restaurant for a romantic dinner. Whatever method people use, Valentine's Day is a time to show others that they are cared for and appreciated.

GLOBAL CONNECTION

Discuss with students holidays that are celebrated by different cultural groups, within the United States and in other countries. Students choose a holiday to write about and do research if necessary. They may model their paragraph on the one they have written about Valentine's Day in this lesson.

Activity B   Read the question below. Then read each of the three topic sentences. Decide which topic sentence is best. Write the reason for your choice.

Question: How do people in the United States celebrate Valentine's Day?

Topic sentences:

a) There are many ways to celebrate this day.

b) Valentine's Day is celebrated in many ways.

c) It is a day for giving cards and having parties.

Activity C   Write a one-paragraph essay about the different ways in which people celebrate Valentine's Day. Use the best topic sentence from Activity B, or write one of your own. Include the details of your answer in the body of your paragraph. End your paragraph with a conclusion or a summary.

Descriptions

Sometimes an essay question will ask you to describe a topic. *To describe* means "to tell about" or "to make a picture with words."

Read the sample description below. The details help readers picture the place.

EXAMPLE

Test item: Describe the Grand Canyon.

Description: The Grand Canyon is an extremely deep gorge of the Colorado River. The Grand Canyon is 277 miles long. It is from four to eighteen miles wide. It is one mile deep. This spectacular canyon in Arizona is a national park. Every year, thousands of visitors come to the Grand Canyon. They stand at the rims and gasp at the vast scene before them.

Activity D Write a paragraph to describe each place below. Include facts about each item that will help your readers picture it.

1) Your house or apartment

2) Your school or your classroom

3) A park in your town or city

Discussions

Sometimes an essay test item will ask you to discuss a topic. To **discuss,** tell about what is good and what is bad about the topic. A discussion often includes opinions. Study the example.

EXAMPLE

Test item: Discuss jogging.

Discussion answer:

To *jog* means "to run slowly." Usually, jogging is good exercise. Because it is an aerobic exercise, jogging stimulates the heart and lungs. Still, doctors recommend that joggers get physical checkups before beginning an exercise program. Jogging is a cheap and easily available form of exercise. No special equipment, other than proper shoes, is needed. Although jogging can be done year-round, it is not so enjoyable in hot, cold, or stormy weather. However, because of its numerous benefits, many people are jogging to improve their physical fitness.

Activity E Choose one of the topics below. Think of a smaller topic within it. (For example, if you choose *Television*, think about one kind of program or a particular program.) Write at least one paragraph about this topic. Remember to include both good and bad characteristics of this topic.

- Television
- Movies
- Music
- Sports
- Vacations
- Education

■ **Presenting Activity D** Ask students to name the descriptive details in the paragraph about the Grand Canyon, on page 224. Suggest that they think about similar details as they write the three paragraphs in this activity.

Activity D Answers

Answers will vary. Students should write one descriptive paragraph for each of the three places named. Each paragraph should begin with a topic sentence that names the place and should include details that help readers picture the setting.

■ **Presenting Activity E** Review the paragraph that discusses jogging, on this page. Have students point out the advantages and the disadvantages that are noted by the writer.

Activity E Answers

Answers will vary. Students should write one paragraph on one of the listed topics or any subtopic it suggests. Their paragraph should begin with a topic sentence and include both favorable and unfavorable characteristics of their topic.

TEACHER ALERT

Tell students that contrast words such as *however, although, on the other hand, still,* and *but* are common in paragraphs that discuss a topic or issue. Suggest that as they discuss their topic, students use such words to point out the contrast between an advantage and a disadvantage.

Reading Vocabulary

achievement (5)   reelect
balcony (5)   specific (8)
exact (6)

■ Presenting Activity F

Read each test item with students, asking them how the question should be answered. They may then proceed with reading the "wrong" responses and developing their critiques.

Activity F Answers

Wording of answers will vary. Sample answers are given.

1) This paragraph does not tell how Valentine's Day was celebrated <u>long ago.</u> Instead, it tells general information about Valentine's Day today.   **2)** This paragraph tells who Millard Fillmore was, but it does not give any information about his achievements.   **3)** This paragraph does not include enough details to help readers picture the Grand Canyon. The only descriptive words are <u>very beautiful</u> and <u>very crowded,</u> but more specific information is needed in a description.   **4)** The topic sentence sticks to the subject, but the other sentences do not tell why planting a vegetable garden is popular.

Read Carefully!

Always be sure to read the essay question carefully. Follow the exact directions. Even if an answer contains correct information, it will be marked wrong if it does not answer the specific test question.

Activity F   Read each of the test items and answers below. None of the answers is correct. Give a reason why each answer below would be marked wrong. Write your reasons in complete sentences.

1) Tell how Valentine's Day was celebrated long ago.

> Valentine's Day in the United States is celebrated by sending cards. These cards often ask the person to "Be My Valentine." Someone's valentine is a special friend. People usually enjoy receiving valentines.

2) Discuss the achievements of Millard Fillmore.

> Millard Fillmore was the thirteenth president of the United States. He became president after Zachary Taylor died in office. Fillmore had been the vice president. He was not reelected to a second term.

3) Describe the Grand Canyon.

> Many people visit the Grand Canyon every year. They sometimes walk on the trails all the way to the bottom of the canyon. It is a very beautiful place. In the summer, the Grand Canyon is very crowded.

4) Why do many people plant vegetable gardens?

> Planting a vegetable garden is becoming more popular every year. In a small area, people can grow vegetables as well as flowers. Even people in apartments often have a small garden. Tomatoes can be grown in flower pots on a balcony.

Lesson 2 Review

An essay is a piece of writing about a single subject or topic. An essay answer is made up of one or several paragraphs. Remember these points when you answer an essay test item:

- Read the question carefully.

- Be sure that your first sentence clearly identifies the subject of the essay.

- Be sure that your essay specifically answers the question asked.

Part A   Choose one of the topics listed below. Write an essay answer on your paper.

- Discuss a popular musician.

- Describe a house you would like to own someday.

- Tell about an unusual animal.

- Explain why summer is a busy time of year.

Part B   Proofread, revise, and rewrite your essay. Refer to the checklist on page 185. Check spelling, punctuation, capitalization, sentence variety, and verb tense.

Reading Vocabulary

capitalization	tense (6)
clearly	variety (6)
punctuation (7)	verb
specifically	

Part A Answers

Answers will vary. Students should write one or two paragraphs on one of the listed topics.

Part B Answers

Students should show that they have proofread and revised the drafts of the essays from Part A.

Follow-up Activity

Have the group create a poster checklist of five or six elements to look for in well-written essays: a topic sentence that identifies the subject of the essay, complete sentences, details that support the main idea, and so on. They may title their checklist "An Essay Should . . ."

LEARNING STYLES

Logical/Mathematical
Divide the class into groups of five. Invite each group to pick an essay topic to brainstorm. Suggest that each group create a web of related words, ideas, facts, comparisons, descriptions, explanations, and so on. Ask each group to divide the words in their web into five subgroups. Have them use different colors to highlight or underline the words in each subgroup. Afterward, ask the groups to read aloud their subgroups. Have the class guess what the main topic is.

Workbook Activity 46

Chapter 10 Review

The Teacher's Resource Library includes two parallel forms of the Chapter 10 Mastery Test. The difficulty level of the two forms is equivalent. You may wish to use one form as a pretest and the other form as a posttest.

Reading Vocabulary

author (6)   public (5)
career (6)   pueblo
kudu   recently (5)

Part A Answers

Answers will vary. Each response should be one or two complete sentences.

Part B Answers

Wording of answers will vary. Reference sources to consult are a dictionary, an almanac, and an encyclopedia. Sample sentences are given.

1) Acadia National Park is located in the state of Maine.   **2)** Thomas Edison made over one thousand inventions, including the stock ticker, the incandescent lamp, and the phonograph.   **3)** Astronauts first landed on the moon in July 1969.   **4)** The first woman to win a Nobel Prize in science was Marie Curie, whose first Nobel Prize was awarded in 1903.   **5)** Hawaii is about 2,400 miles from San Francisco, California.   **6)** A kudu is a large antelope of Africa. It has a brown coat with white stripes.   **7)** Toni Morrison is a prize-winning American novelist.   **8)** Palau is a nation of about 200 islands in the Pacific Ocean, about 500 miles southeast of the Philippines.
9) William Shakespeare wrote his plays in the late 1500s and early 1600s.   **10)** The Zuñi Pueblo is located in the western part of the present state of New Mexico.

Part A   Answer these questions in complete sentences.

1) What is your favorite dessert?
2) Where do you like to go for a vacation?
3) What time do you usually get to school?
4) What kind of music do you like best?
5) Who teaches your English class?
6) Who is a sports star today?
7) Who is the author of a book you have read recently?
8) Who is a government leader in the news?
9) Where is the public library nearest your home?
10) What job or career seems interesting to you?

Part B   Use a reference source to find the answer to each question below. Write each answer in one or two complete sentences.

1) Where is Acadia National Park?
2) What did Thomas Edison invent?
3) When did astronauts first land on the moon?
4) Who was the first woman to win a Nobel Prize in science?
5) How far is Hawaii from San Francisco, California?
6) What is a kudu?
7) Who is Toni Morrison?
8) Where is Palau?
9) When did William Shakespeare write his plays?
10) Where is the Zuñi Pueblo located?

Chapter 10 Mastery Test A

Name _____ Date _____ Period _____

Chapter 10 Mastery Test A

Part A The answer to each question is given as a fragment. Rewrite the answer in a complete sentence. Use sentence variety.

Question	Answer
1) What is Canada's largest river?	St. Lawrence River
2) In what state is Niagara Falls?	New York
3) Where is the Mojave Desert?	In California
4) What prize did Jane Addams win?	The Nobel Peace Prize
5) What animal can run at speeds over 60 miles per hour?	The cheetah
6) What does GOP stand for?	Grand Old Party
7) How often are presidential elections held in the United States?	Every four years
8) What is a cyclops?	A mythological giant with one eye
9) What is the longest national park in the United States?	Blue Ridge Parkway
10) Which lake is the world's largest?	The Caspian Sea

Name _____ Date _____ Period _____

Chapter 10 Mastery Test A, continued

Part B Write a five-sentence essay paragraph that describes the planet Jupiter. Use the facts listed below. Begin your paragraph with a topic sentence.

Facts • The largest planet
         • 88,000-mile diameter
         • Eleven times bigger than Earth
         • Has at least sixteen moons
         • Takes almost twelve Earth years to travel once around the sun

Part C Write a five-sentence essay paragraph on one of the topics below.
         • Describe your favorite relative.
         • Compare summer and winter weather in your area.
         • Discuss the advantages of a good education.
         • Explain the difference between jazz and rock music.

Chapter 10 Mastery Test A

Part C Read each test item. Then read the topic sentence that follows. The topic sentence is supposed to lead into the rest of the essay. If you think the topic sentence is a good one, write *Correct*. If the topic sentence is poor, rewrite it to make it better.

1) Discuss the use of fuel oil as an energy source.
   Fuel oil is a source of energy that has advantages and disadvantages.

2) Describe the planet Mars.
   It is a planet that is close to Earth.

3) Tell about the first moon landing.
   This was an event that amazed everyone.

4) Explain the origin of Mother's Day.
   The American holiday of Mother's Day was suggested by a woman in Philadelphia.

5) What qualities did Thomas Edison have that made him successful?
   Thomas Edison was a famous inventor.

Part D Choose one of the topics below. Write a one-paragraph essay on the topic. Remember to start your essay with a topic sentence.

- Tell about the characteristics of an ideal friend.
- Describe your favorite vacation place.
- Give a brief history of an American holiday.
- Discuss an Olympic sport.

Test Taking Tip When you read over your written answer, imagine that you are someone reading it for the first time. Ask yourself if the ideas and information make sense. Revise and rewrite to make the answer as clear as you can.

Reading Vocabulary

brief (6)	inventor (5)
energy (6)	Olympic
fuel (5)	origin (6)
ideal (6)	successful (5)

Part C Answers

Wording of revised answers will vary. Sample answers are given.

1) Correct 2) The planet Mars is Earth's neighbor and is like Earth in several ways. 3) The first moon landing captured the world's attention. 4) Correct 5) Thomas Edison had unusual qualities that made him an extremely successful inventor.

Part D Answers

Answers will vary. Students should choose one of the listed topics and write a one-paragraph essay on it. The paragraph should begin with a sentence that restates the topic, include supporting details, and end with a summary or a conclusion.

APPLICATION

At Home
Have students use a television guide to create five "TV quiz" questions that can be answered in complete sentences. Each question should begin with the word *When, Who, Where,* or *What* and may cover such topics as broadcast times, channels, names of programs, and names of performers. Students should bring in their guides so that group members can refer to them as they try to answer one another's questions.

Chapter 10 Mastery Test B

Chapter 10 Mastery Test B
page 1

Name _____ Date _____ Period _____

Part A The answer to each question is given as a fragment. Rewrite the answer in a complete sentence. Use sentence variety.

Question	Answer
1) What is the largest South American country?	Brazil
2) What title was given to ancient Egyptian rulers?	Pharaoh
3) When did the United States gain possession of the Louisiana Purchase?	1803
4) What general was defeated at the Battle of Little Big Horn?	General Custer
5) Who was John Jay?	First chief justice of the U.S. Supreme Court
6) What was the Boston Tea Party?	A protest against the British tea tax
7) What is Acapulco famous for?	Beautiful beaches
8) How did the Blackfoot Indians get their name?	Wearing moccasins dyed black
9) What causes the disease beriberi?	A vitamin deficiency
10) When is the Bering Strait usually frozen?	Between October and June

©AGS® American Guidance Service, Inc. Permission is granted to reproduce for classroom use only. **Basic English Composition**

Chapter 10 Mastery Test B, continued

Chapter 10 Mastery Test B
page 2

Name _____ Date _____ Period _____

Part B Write a five-sentence essay paragraph that describes the planet Pluto. Use the facts listed below. Begin your paragraph with a topic sentence.

Facts	• Ninth planet from the sun
	• About 2,000-mile diameter
	• Discovered in 1930 by Clyde Tombaugh
	• One known moon, Charon
	• Thought to have a thin methane atmosphere

Part C Write a five-sentence essay paragraph on one of the topics below.
- Describe your best friend.
- Compare spring and fall in your area.
- Discuss the advantages of refusing to use tobacco, alcohol, and other drugs.
- Explain the difference between movies and television.

©AGS® American Guidance Service, Inc. Permission is granted to reproduce for classroom use only. **Basic English Composition**

Chapter 10 Mastery Test B

Planning Guide

Messages and Memorandums

	Student Text Lesson			
	Student Pages	Vocabulary	Practice Exercises	Lesson Review
Lesson 1 Writing Messages	232-234	✔	✔	234
Lesson 2 Writing Memos	235-237	✔	✔	237

Chapter Activities

Teacher's Resource Library
Writing Tip 10: Writing Messages and Memos

Community Connection 11: The Parts of a Memo

Assessment Options

Student Text
Chapter 11 Review

Teacher's Resource Library
Chapter 11 Mastery Tests A and B

Teaching Strategies							Language Skills			Learning Styles						Teacher's Resource Library		
Reviewing Skills	Teacher Alert	Follow-up Activity	Career Application	Home Application	Global Connection	Community Application	Identification Skills	Writing Skills	Punctuation Skills	Visual/Spatial	Auditory/Verbal	Body/Kinesthetic	Logical/Mathematical	Group Learning	LEP/ESL	Activities	Workbook Activities	Self-Study Guide
232		234		233		234	✔	✔	✔		232					41-42	47	✔
235		237	236				✔	✔	✔						238	43-44	48-50	✔

Writing Messages and Memos

Writing Tip 10

Messages

Messages are any kind of written or spoken communication. When you write messages, you usually write them by hand. To make messages helpful, you should write neatly so they are readable. You can help the person the message is for by including:

- Time you wrote the message
- Date you wrote the message
- Name of the person who called or gave you the information
- Information that the person who gets the message needs to know
- Your name, to show who wrote the message

Reread your message to:

- Make sure the information is complete
- Make sure nothing is missing
- Make sure the information is correct
- Make sure it is written neatly

Memos

A **memo**, or memorandum, is an informal message written in a special form. It is not usually sent in the mail. A memo is usually for people who work in a company.

The purpose of a memo may be to include:

- Brief information
- Advice
- Directions
- A reminder

Below is a sample of the special form for memos. Use it to write a memo to yourself. Remind yourself about the information to include in a memo.

Reread your memo to:

- Make sure the information is complete
- Make sure nothing is missing
- Make sure the information is correct
- Make sure the information is clear

```
                    MEMO
  Date: _____
  To: _____
  From: _____
  Subject: _____
  _____
  _____
  _____
  _____
```

©AGS® American Guidance Service, Inc. Permission is granted to reproduce for classroom use only.   **Basic English Composition**

The Parts of a Memo

Community Connection 11

A **memorandum**, or memo for short, is an informal message written in a special form. It is used most often by businesses. At the top of most memos are four bits of information: who the memo is to, who it is from, the date, and the subject.

Learning how to read and write memos is an important skill to have when you begin to work. A memo is the main way to communicate for most companies. Writing an unclear memo or not reading a memo correctly can cause mistakes.

To get an idea of what memos look like, study actual memos. Follow the steps below.

Step 1. Get at least two copies of memos from a friend or family member who works. You could also ask for a copy of a memo from a local business.

Step 2. Answer the questions below about the two memos.

1) Who are the memos to? _____

2) Who are the memos from? _____

3) What is the subject for each memo? _____

4) What information is being communicated in the body of each memo? _____

5) Do the memos ask for someone to do something? _____

Step 3. Have your teacher check your answers.

©AGS® American Guidance Service, Inc. Permission is granted to reproduce for classroom use only.   **Basic English Composition**

Writing Tip 10   **Community Connection 11**

Messages and Memorandums

11

Reading Vocabulary

annoy (6)
communication (6)
confuse (5)
entrance (5)
include (5)
mixup
occur (6)
situation (5)

I magine this situation. You are waiting at the entrance to a store. You had told your friend to meet you there at three o'clock. It is now three-thirty. Where is your friend? You are worried. Why hasn't your friend arrived? You are also annoyed. "How much longer should I wait?" you ask yourself.

When these mixups occur, the cause is often a missed communication. Maybe your friend left a message for you, but you never got it. Maybe you forgot to tell your friend exactly where to meet you. Missed or confused communications can cause all sorts of problems.

In Chapter 11, you will learn one way to avoid missed communications. You will learn how to write clear, complete messages.

Goals for Learning

▶ To write clear messages

▶ To include all necessary information in messages and memorandums

Introducing the Chapter

Have students examine the introductory photograph accompanying the first page of Chapter 11. Together, invent a situation for the woman in the photograph: Who is she? Where is she? Why is she looking at her watch? What is she thinking and feeling? Call on volunteers to take turns developing a short narrative that tells what has happened so far.

231

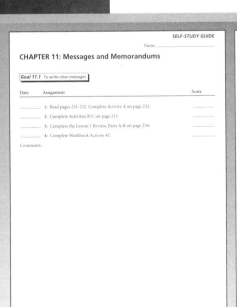

SELF-STUDY GUIDE

Name

CHAPTER 11: Messages and Memorandums

Goal 11.1 *To write clear messages*

Date	Assignment	Score
	1: Read pages 231–232. Complete Activity A on page 232.	
	2: Complete Activities B–C on page 233.	
	3: Complete the Lesson 1 Review, Parts A–B on page 234.	
	4: Complete Workbook Activity 47.	

Comments:

©AGS® American Guidance Service, Inc. Permission is granted to reproduce for classroom use only.   **Basic English Composition**

SELF-STUDY GUIDE

Name

CHAPTER 11 Messages and Memorandums, continued

Goal 11.2 *To include all necessary information in messages and memorandums*

Date	Assignment	Score
	5: Read page 235. Complete Activity A on page 235.	
	6: Complete Activities B–C on page 236.	
	7: Complete the Lesson 2 Review, Parts A–B on page 237.	
	8: Complete Workbook Activity 48.	
	9: Complete Workbook Activity 49.	
	10: Complete Workbook Activity 50.	
	11: Complete the Chapter 11 Review, Parts A–E on pages 238–239.	

Comments:

Student's Signature _____ Date _____

Instructor's Signature _____ Date _____

©AGS® American Guidance Service, Inc. Permission is granted to reproduce for classroom use only.   **Basic English Composition**

Chapter 11 Self-Study Guide

Overview This lesson focuses on written messages that include all necessary information.

Objective

- To write a clear, complete message.

Student Pages 232–234

Teacher's Resource Library

Activities 41–42

Workbook Activity 47

Reading Vocabulary

element (6)   member (5)
handwritten   **message (3)**
handwriting   readable

Teaching Suggestions

- **Introducing the Lesson**
Have students imagine that they have answered the phone in the school office and are taking down a message for a teacher. Ask them what information they should include in order for the message to be complete.

- **Reviewing Skills** Select five or six words from the "Spelling Demons" list on page 109 of the student book. Have volunteers come to the board to write each word correctly in a sentence.

- **Presenting Activity A**
Have a volunteer read aloud the sample message shown on this page. Students should refer to it as they answer questions 1–5. Direct students to write their answers in complete sentences.

Activity A Answers

1) Amanda called at three o'clock in the afternoon. **2)** Laura's mother took the message.
3) Laura will get this message.
4) Laura should call Amanda before 4:30 or after 5:30.
5) Amanda is not yet home.

> **Message**
> *Communication,
> either written
> or spoken.*

A **message** is any kind of communication. Friends and family members often leave messages to inform one another of plans. Taking messages is an important job in many offices.

Messages may be spoken or written. A written message is more often handwritten than typed. Be careful to make your handwriting readable. Also be sure to include all necessary information.

This list shows the main elements to include in any message:

- The time and date that you wrote the message
- The name of the person who told you the information
- The information needed by the person who gets the message
- Your name, to show who wrote the message

Read the message below. It is written completely and correctly. The person receiving the message has been given all the information she needs to know.

> 3:00 P.M. Monday
> Laura,
> Amanda called at 3:00 P.M. Call her at home if you get home before 4:30. She'll be at her dancing class until 5:30. Then she'll be home.
>   Love,
>   Mom

Activity A   Use the message above to answer the following questions. Write your answers on your paper.

1) What time did Amanda call?

2) Who took this message?

3) Who is to get this message?

4) What is Laura supposed to do?

5) It is now 5:00 P.M. Is Amanda home?

LEARNING STYLES

Auditory/Verbal
Write down a three-to-five-line message you want to give to the class. Then whisper this message into the ear of the student nearest you. Ask that student to whisper the same message into the ear of the next student. Continue around the room until everyone has listened to the message. Ask the last student who heard the message to write it on a slip of paper. Then compare your written message with the one the student wrote down. If differences occur between the two messages, discuss why this happened.

Activity B Read each message below. Decide what important information has been left out. Write the missing information on your paper.

Mom, I'm going out. I'll be home later.
Amanda

Laura, Derek called. Call him back.
Mom

MIKE, YOU ARE SUPPOSED TO PLAY TENNIS.   TIM

Dad, someone called about the car.

Mr. Martin, I stopped by during second period to ask about my homework. I'll be back.
Amanda

Ms. Lawson, I NEED AN APPOINTMENT TO TALK TO YOU. I'LL BE BACK AT THREE O'CLOCK.

Activity C Imagine that you have answered the phone at home. You need to write a message for a family member. List at least five kinds of information that you would want to include in such a message.

Name _____ Date _____ Period _____ | Chapter 11 Activity 41 |

Messages

If you take a message, be sure that it is complete. A message should include the following information:
• The time and date that you wrote the message
• The name of the person who called or who told you the information
• The information you want the person who gets the message to know
• Your name, to show that you wrote the message

Directions: Write what is missing from each message below.

EXAMPLE   Dad, I'm going to the movies. I'll see you later.
time, date, when he or she will be back, and who left the message

1) Derek, we were supposed to go to the movies. Laura.

2) Mom, my teacher called. She'll call back later. Derek.

3) Coach Jones, I won't be able to be at practice today. I'll talk to you later.

4) Amanda, Derek called. Mom.

5) Mr. Smith, I need help with my homework. I'll stop by later.

6) Laura, Amanda called. She wants you to go shopping. Call her back.

7) Dad, your boss called.

©AGS® American Guidance Service, Inc. Permission is granted to reproduce for classroom use only.   **Basic English Composition**

Activity 41

---

appointment (6)   tennis (5)
homework

- **Presenting Activity B** Tell students to use their imagination in order to complete the information in each message. Refer them to the list on page 232 of their book.

Activity B Answers
The missing information is given below.

1) Add the date and the time. Be more specific about the time "later." **2)** Add the date and the time. **3)** Add the date, the time, the name of the person who called, and more specific information about where and when the tennis game is being held. **4)** Add the date, the time, the name of the caller, and the caller's phone number. **5)** Add the date and a detail about when Amanda will be back. **6)** Add the date and the message writer's name.

- **Presenting Activity C** Review the directions with students. Make sure they understand they are to write categories of information rather than details of any particular call.

Activity C Answers
Answers may vary. A sample answer is given.

1) Name of person receiving message **2)** Date and time **3)** Name and phone number of caller **4)** Most important details of message **5)** Name of person taking message

APPLICATION

At Home
Ask students whether any of them have sure-fire methods at home for taking messages completely and accurately. Students may offer ideas for making sure all the people who share a household receive the information they need.

Reading Vocabulary

addition (5) education (5)
anytime   neatly
dialogue (7) physical (5)

Part A Answers

Answers will vary. A sample message is given.

January 4, 4 P.M.

Sheila,

I've gone to Mahoney's. I'll be back by six, in time for dinner.

Davis

Part B Answers

Wording of answers will vary. A sample message is given.

April 5, 2:30 P.M.

Coach Jones:

Ms. Handley of Springfield Sporting Goods Company called. The ten bats you ordered are ready. You can pick them up between 9 A.M. and 6 P.M. any day except Sunday. If you have questions, call her at 577-8900.

Derek Corelli

Follow-up Activity

Provide samples of message forms used by businesses. ("While You Were Out" message pads are common.) Have students practice filling out the forms with information you provide.

APPLICATION

In the Community
Have students tell where they have seen message boards in their neighborhoods: Laundromats, supermarkets, libraries, and so on. Ask students to look more closely at these boards the next time they are in one of those locations. They may report back to the group on ways in which people post information about services or products that are wanted or are for sale. Have students describe postings they think are particularly effective.

Lesson 1 Review

When you take a message, remember to include all necessary information. In addition to the message itself, include the time and date, the name of the caller, and your name. Remember to write neatly, too.

Part A Write a message to a member of your family. Explain that you went to the store and will be home in time for dinner. Include these five elements in your message.

1) Date
2) Time
3) Name of person who is receiving the message
4) Message
5) Your name

Part B Read the telephone dialogue below. Then write the message that Derek should write for Coach Jones. Include all necessary information. Use today's date.

Derek is walking past the coach's office at 2:30 P.M. The telephone rings. He answers it.

Derek: Hello. This is the Springfield Physical Education Department. The coach isn't here. May I help you?

Woman: Yes, this is the Springfield Sporting Goods Company. Coach Jones ordered ten baseball bats.

Derek: Yes. What should I tell him?

Woman: Tell him that the bats are ready. He can pick them up anytime between 9 A.M. and 6 P.M. except on Sunday.

Derek: Who should I say called?

Woman: My name is Ms. Handley. If he has any questions, he can call me at 577-8900.

Derek: OK. I've got the message.

Woman: Thank you. Good-bye.

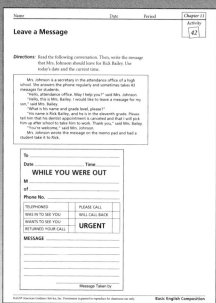

Activity 42

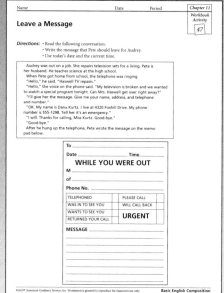

Workbook Activity 47

Memorandum

An informal message written in special form and frequently used in the business world; often shortened to memo.

A **memorandum** is often called by its shorter name—*memo*. A memo is a special kind of written message. It seems like a letter, but it is less formal. Unlike a letter, a memo is not usually sent by mail. Instead, a memo may be delivered to the employees of a company. Memos are common in business settings.

Read the sample memo below. It gives brief information about an event.

MEMO

Date: May 3, 20–
To: Ms. Hall
From: Ms. Lawson, Chairperson, Awards Committee   *ACL*
Subject: Awards Assembly

The Awards Assembly will be held on Monday, June 10, at 2:00 P.M. Because of lack of space in the auditorium, the committee decided that only the seniors would be invited to attend. If these plans are all right, please let me know.

The next meeting of the Awards Committee will be held on May 12 at 3:30 P.M. in room 216. We will discuss the decoration of the stage and the program for the assembly.

Activity A Write the answers to these questions. Use the information in the sample memo above.

1) What four words are printed on most memo forms?

2) There is no address included on this memo. Why not?

3) Does the writer sign his or her name on a memo?

4) What did the committee decide?

5) What will happen on Monday, June 10, at 2:00 P.M.?

6) What will happen on May 12 at 3:30 P.M.?

7) In what room will the meeting be held?

8) What will be discussed at this meeting?

9) Who sent this memo? Who received it?

10) After reading the memo above, what would you say is the purpose of a memo?

Lesson at a Glance

Chapter 11   Lesson 2

Overview This lesson provides practice in writing memos, the specialized messages often used in businesses.

Objective

- To write a clear, complete memo.

Student Pages 235–237

Teacher's Resource Library

Activities 43–44

Workbook Activities 48–50

Reading Vocabulary

assembly (7)	formal (6)
attend (5)	frequently
auditorium (5)	informal (7)
award (5)	lack (5)
brief (6)	memo
decoration (6)	**memorandum (8)**
discuss (5)	senior (6)
employee (6)	unlike

Teaching Suggestions

- **Introducing the Lesson**
  Ask students who have jobs whether they have ever written or received a memo at work. If so, ask them to explain what its purpose was.

- **Reviewing Skills** Write the following message on the board, as is, and have students rewrite it with correct punctuation and capitalization:

  i have gone to chicago with marie we will be back next friday

- **Presenting Activity A**
  Have a volunteer read aloud the sample memo. Tell students to refer to it to answer the ten listed questions.

Activity A Answers

1) The four words that appear on most memos are <u>Date</u>, <u>To</u>, <u>From</u>, and <u>Subject</u>. **2)** Because memos usually travel within an organization, there is no need to

---

(Activity A Answers, continued) include an address. **3)** The writer may initial the memo after the typed name. **4)** The committee decided that only seniors would be invited to attend the Awards Assembly. **5)** On Monday, June 10, at 2:00 P.M., the Awards Assembly will be held in the auditorium. **6)** The next meeting of the Awards Committee will take place on May 12, at 3:30 P.M.

7) The meeting will be held in room 216. **8)** The committee will discuss the decoration of the stage and the program for the assembly. **9)** The memo was sent by Ms. Lawson, who is chairing the Awards Committee. It is being sent to Ms. Hall. **10)** The purpose of a memo is to come right to the point with necessary information.

Reading Vocabulary

colon	rewrite
computer (8)	sincerely (5)
principal (5)	sufficient (6)
promptly	weekend
request (6)	

■ Presenting Activity B

Review the four directions with students before they proceed with choosing their topic.

Activity B Answers

Answers will vary. Students should write one memo that includes all necessary information and the four words *Date, To, From,* and *Subject,* each on a separate line and followed by a colon.

■ Presenting Activity C

Have a volunteer read aloud the message shown. Briefly discuss how this note differs from a memo before students proceed to rewrite it as a memo.

Activity C Answers

Answers will vary. A sample memo is given.

MEMO

Date: (Students should write today's date.)

To: Coach Jones

From: Ms. B. Hall, Principal (initials)

Subject: Baseball Bats

Have the ten new bats from the Springfield Sporting Goods Company arrived? Will ten bats be sufficient for both the boys' and girls' teams?

Please give me the bill for the bats when they arrive. I will see that it is paid promptly.

APPLICATION

Career Connection

Many businesses have replaced paper memos with electronic mail. Have students share any experiences with e-mail, and discuss the advantages and disadvantages of e-mail communications. If possible, provide printouts of e-mail messages.

Activity B Practice writing a memo. Start by writing the heading *Memo* at the top of a sheet of paper. Then take the following steps.

1) List these words: *Date, To, From,* and *Subject.*

2) Put a colon (:) after each of the listed words.

3) Choose one of the topics below.

4) Write a memo. Give all necessary information.

- Write a memo to a parent. Make a request for something you need.
- Write a memo to your teacher. Explain why you should not have homework on the weekend.
- Write a memo to someone in your class. Ask to borrow a computer game.

Activity C Read the message below. Rewrite it in memo form. Include all necessary information. Use today's date.

> Dear Coach Jones,
>
> Several weeks ago you spoke to me about ordering ten new baseball bats from the Springfield Sporting Goods Company.
>
> Have these new bats arrived? Will ten bats be sufficient for both the boys' and girls' teams?
>
> Please give me the bill for the bats when they arrive. I will see that it is paid promptly.
>
> Sincerely,
>
> Ms. B. Hall,
> Principal

Name	Date	Period	Chapter 11 Activity 43

More About Memos

A. Directions: Write a memo to a family member. Tell them about a telephone message that you received for them.

B. Directions: Write a memo to your mom or dad. Ask for permission to go away for the weekend with a friend whose family is going to a lake. Include information about the family and the trip. Tell them when you will leave and when you will arrive home.

MEMO

Date:
To:
From:
Subject:

MEMO

Date:
To:
From:
Subject:

©AGS® American Guidance Service, Inc. Permission is granted to reproduce for classroom use only.   **Basic English Composition**

Activity 43

Name	Date	Period	Chapter 11 Activity 44

Writing Memos

Directions: Read the two messages below. Rewrite each one into memo form. Use the current year.

September 10, 20—
Dear Mrs. Smith,
    Please excuse John Hall today at 1:00 P.M. He has a doctor's appointment this afternoon at 1:30 P.M.
Mrs. K. Hall

May 5, 20—
Dear Mr. White,
    The student body would like to see more school spirit and involvement. We would like to plan a special Brownsville High Sports Day. Would you please help us in any way that you can?
Elizabeth Proctor

MEMO

Date:
To:
From:
Subject:

MEMO

Date:
To:
From:
Subject:

©AGS® American Guidance Service, Inc. Permission is granted to reproduce for classroom use only.   **Basic English Composition**

Activity 44

A memo is a message written in a special form. Memos are common in business settings. Memos must include all necessary information.

Part A   Read the memo below. Then answer the questions that follow.

MEMO

Date: May 7, 20–
To: Ms. Hall
From: Coach Jones   *HMJ*
Subject:

   I have attached to this memo the bill for the ten new baseball bats. The boys' team has a sufficient number of bats. These ten new baseball bats are for the girls' team. This year is the first year for the girls' team, we needed these bats to complete our stock of new equipment.

---

1) What information is missing from this memo?

2) Should Coach Jones have signed his name?

3) Why is an address not included on this memo?

4) What is the sentence error? Correct it on your paper.

Part B   Read the message below. Rewrite it in memo form. Include all necessary information. Use today's date.

Dear Coach,

We have paid the bill for the new baseball bats from the Springfield Sporting Goods Company. Thank you for ordering this equipment for the girls' team.

Sincerely,

Ms. B. Hall
Principal

Messages and Memorandums   Chapter 11   **237**

Reading Vocabulary

attach (5)   error (6)
equipment (5)   stock (5)

Part A Answers

1) Information about the subject of the memo is missing.   2) No, it is not necessary to sign your name on a memo.   3) No address is usually needed on a memo.   4) The run-on sentence needs to be corrected. This year is the first year for the girls' team. We needed these bats to complete our stock of new equipment.

Part B Answers

MEMO

Date: (Students should write today's date.)

To: Coach Jones

From: Ms. B. Hall, Principal (initials)

Subject: Baseball Bats

We have paid the bill for the new baseball bats from the Springfield Sporting Goods Company. Thank you for ordering this equipment for the girls' team.

Follow-up Activity

Students may be learning to use word-processing software. If possible, have them design a memo form by selecting fonts, creating borders, and laying out the standard headings and rules.

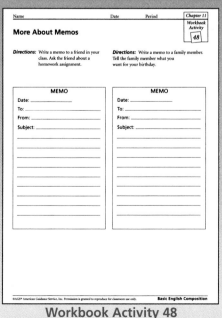

Workbook Activity 48

Workbook Activity 49

Workbook Activity 50

Chapter 11 Review

The Teacher's Resource Library includes two parallel forms of the Chapter 11 Mastery Test. The difficulty level of the two forms is equivalent. You may wish to use one form as a pretest and the other form as a posttest.

Reading Vocabulary
baby-sitting   conversation (5)

Part A Answers

(date), 3 P.M.

Shirley,

Derek has gone to work and will meet you at seven at school.

Ms. Corelli

Part B Answers

Date, time, message taker's name, and wordings will vary. A sample message is given.

May 4, 8 P.M.

Ms. Jefferson,

Denise Stith called to say she cannot meet you tomorrow evening. She is sorry about the change in plans and will try to call you tomorrow.

Francesca

Part C Answers

Students' memos will vary.

Part A Read the following conversation between Derek and his mother. Write the message that is to be given to Shirley. Use complete sentences.

Derek: It is nearly three o'clock. I have to go to work. Tell Shirley that I'll be home by six. I'll meet her at school.

Ms. Corelli: You'll have to eat dinner before you go out.

Derek: OK. Tell her I'll meet her at seven.

Ms. Corelli: I'll give her your message.

Part B Imagine that you are baby-sitting for little Tanya at the Jefferson home this evening. You answer the telephone and explain that Ms. Jefferson has gone out for the evening. This is the information the caller gives you:

- "My name is Denise Stith."
- "I am Tanya Jefferson's aunt."
- "I cannot meet Ms. Jefferson tomorrow evening."
- "I will try to call Ms. Jefferson tomorrow."
- "Tell Ms. Jefferson I'm sorry about the change in plans."

Use the information to write a message for Ms. Jefferson, Tanya's mother. Include all necessary information.

Part C Copy the parts of the memo below onto your paper. Write a message to your teacher, a friend, or a family member. Choose any subject you wish. Include all necessary information. Use today's date.

> **MEMO**
>
> Date:
> To:
> From:
> Subject:

Chapter 11 Mastery Test A

Name ___ Date ___ Period ___ | Chapter 11 Mastery Test A page 1

Chapter 11 Mastery Test A

Part A List five things that you should include when you write a message.

1) ___
2) ___
3) ___
4) ___
5) ___

Part B Write a message on the lines below asking a friend to meet you tonight for dinner at your favorite restaurant. Include the five elements you listed in Part A.

MESSAGE

___

©AGS® American Guidance Service, Inc. Permission is granted to reproduce for classroom use only.   **Basic English Composition**

Name ___ Date ___ Period ___ | Chapter 11 Mastery Test A page 2

Chapter 11 Mastery Test A, continued

Part C Read the information below. Then write a memo using the information. Use today's date.

Howie is responsible for telling Eileen about a safety committee meeting that she must attend. The meeting will be held tomorrow at 10 A.M. in Room 8. Susan must bring a copy of her financial report to the meeting.

MEMO

To: ___
From: ___
Date: ___
Subject: ___

___

©AGS® American Guidance Service, Inc. Permission is granted to reproduce for classroom use only.   **Basic English Composition**

Part D Rewrite the message below. Put it into memo form.
Use today's date.

> 11:00 A.M., Tuesday
>
> Luis,
>
> The chess club is meeting in room 111 tomorrow.
> Mr. Harris says he has an important announcement.
> Try to come early, before three o'clock.
>
> Mia

Part E Find five errors in the following memo. List them on
your paper.

> **MEMO**
>
> **Date:** April 3, 20–
> **To:** Mr. Henry Tso
> **Subject:** Vacation days
>
> I have received your request to take five days of vacation
> from Monday, June 12, through Friday, June 16, the request
> has been approved. I hope you have a great time in arizona!
>
> Best wishes,
>
> Fred Lamont

Test Taking Tip When you read test directions, try to restate them in your own
words. Tell yourself what you are expected to do. That way,
you can make sure your answer will be complete and correct.

Reading Vocabulary

announcement   chess (7)
approve (6)   restate

Part D Answers

MEMO

Date: (Students should write
today's date.)

To: Luis

From: Mia

Subject: Chess club meeting

The chess club is meeting in room
111 tomorrow. Mr. Harris says he
has an important announcement.
Try to come early, before 3 P.M.

Part E Answers

Students should find the following
five errors.

1) Fred Lamont should have put his
name after the heading "From" at
the top of the memo, not at the
end. **2)** There should be a period
after June 16 to end the first
sentence. **3)** The first word of the
next sentence ("The request . . .")
should be capitalized. **4)** Capitalize
Arizona. **5)** The closing "Best
wishes," should be deleted.

GLOBAL CONNECTION

Have students imagine that
a visitor is coming from
another country. Their job
is to make sure the visitor is met at
the nearest airport. List the critical
information to include on a message to the person who is meeting
the visitor: date and time of
arrival, airline, flight number, and
any other important details. Have
students create a message that is
complete and concise.

Chapter 11 Mastery Test B

Name _____ Date _____ Period _____

| Chapter 11 Mastery Test B |
| Mastery Test B page 1 |

Chapter 11 Mastery Test B

Part A List five things that you should include when you write
a memo.

1) _____
2) _____
3) _____
4) _____
5) _____

Part B Write a message on the lines below to your sister, Nicki. Tell
her that her friend Bud called today to cancel a date scheduled for this
Friday night. Include the five elements of any message.

MESSAGE

_____
_____
_____
_____
_____
_____
_____

Name _____ Date _____ Period _____

| Chapter 11 Mastery Test B |
| Mastery Test B page 2 |

Chapter 11 Mastery Test B, continued

Part C Read the information below. Then write a memo using the
information. Use today's date.

Louise is the assistant manager at a restaurant where Taylor works.
Louise is responsible for telling Taylor to attend a training session this
Saturday at 9 A.M. in the main dining room of the restaurant. Taylor
must wear his uniform to the training session.

MEMO

To: _____
From: _____
Date: _____
Subject: _____

_____
_____
_____
_____
_____
_____
_____

Chapter 12

Planning Guide

Writing Letters

	Student Text Lesson			
	Student Pages	Vocabulary	Practice Exercises	Lesson Review
Lesson 1 The Personal Letter	242-248	✔	✔	248
Lesson 2 The Business Letter	249-255	✔	✔	255

Chapter Activities

Teacher's Resource Library
Writing Tip 11: Sample Letters

Community Connection 12: Writing a Letter

Assessment Options

Student Text
Chapter 12 Review

Teacher's Resource Library
Chapter 12 Mastery Tests A and B

Teaching Strategies							Language Skills			Learning Styles						Teacher's Resource Library		
Reviewing Skills	Teacher Alert	Follow-up Activity	Career Application	Home Application	Global Connection	Community Application	Identification Skills	Writing Skills	Punctuation Skills	Visual/Spatial	Auditory/Verbal	Body/Kinesthetic	Logical/Mathematical	Group Learning	LEP/ESL	Activities	Workbook Activities	Self-Study Guide
242	246	248		245		243	✔	✔	✔					244		45-47	51	✔
249	254	255	252		250		✔	✔	✔		252					48	52-54	✔

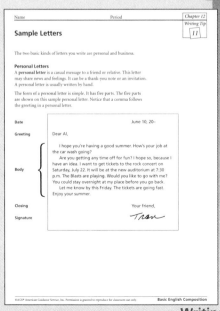

Name   Period   *Chapter 12*

Writing Tip 11

Sample Letters

The two basic kinds of letters you write are personal and business.

Personal Letters

A **personal letter** is a casual message to a friend or relative. This letter may share news and feelings. It can be a thank-you note or an invitation. A personal letter is usually written by hand.

The form of a personal letter is simple. It has five parts. The five parts are shown on this sample personal letter. Notice that a comma follows the greeting in a personal letter.

Date — June 10, 20—

Greeting — Dear Al,

Body — I hope you're having a good summer. How's your job at the car wash going?
Are you getting any time off for fun? I hope so, because I have an idea. I want to get tickets to the rock concert on Saturday, July 22. It will be at the new auditorium at 7:30 p.m. The Blasts are playing. Would you like to go with me? You could stay overnight at my place before you go back.
Let me know by this Friday. The tickets are going fast. Enjoy your summer.

Closing — Your friend,

Signature — Tran

©AGS® American Guidance Service, Inc. Permission is granted to reproduce for classroom use only.   **Basic English Composition**

Writing Tip 11

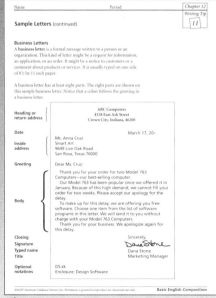

Name   Period   *Chapter 12*

Writing Tip 11

Sample Letters (continued)

Business Letters

A **business letter** is a formal message written to a person or an organization. This kind of letter might be a request for information, an application, or an order. It might be a notice to customers or a comment about products or services. It is usually typed on one side of 8½ by 11 inch paper.

A business letter has at least eight parts. The eight parts are shown on this sample business letter. Notice that a colon follows the greeting in a business letter.

Heading or return address — **ABC Computers**
4328 East Ash Street
Crown City, Indiana, 46200

Date — March 17, 20—

Inside address — Ms. Anna Cruz
Smart Art
9649 Live Oak Road
San Rosa, Texas 76000

Greeting — Dear Ms. Cruz:

Body — Thank you for your order for two Model 763 Computers—our best-selling computer.
Our Model 763 has been popular since we offered it in January. Because of this high demand, we cannot fill your order for two weeks. Please accept our apology for the delay.
To make up for this delay, we are offering you free software. Choose one item from the list of software programs in this letter. We will send it to you without charge with your Model 763 Computers.
Thank you for your business. We apologize again for this delay.

Closing — Sincerely,
Signature — Dana Stone
Typed name — Dana Stone
Title — Marketing Manager

Optional notations — DS:zk
Enclosure: Design Software

©AGS® American Guidance Service, Inc. Permission is granted to reproduce for classroom use only.   **Basic English Composition**

Name   Date   Period   *Chapter 12*

Community Connection 12

Writing a Letter

There are two main kinds of letters: a **personal letter** and a **business letter**. A personal letter is an informal message to a friend or relative. A personal letter has five parts: the date, salutation, body, closing, and signature. A business letter is more formal. It is a message to a person or organization. Business letters have eight parts: the heading (or return address), date, inside address, salutation (or greeting), body, closing (or complimentary close), handwritten signature, and the typed name and title of the person writing the letter.

Envelopes for personal and business letters are similar. Both have the return address, or the address of the person sending the letter, in the top left corner. The mailing address, or the person and place where the letter is being sent, is in the center of the envelope and a little to the right.

Often the return and mailing addresses are typed on a business envelope.

Now that you know what to do to write and send letters, practice doing so. Follow the steps below.

Step 1. Think of a company or person that you could write a letter to. For example, maybe you have a question for a company or community organization. Or maybe you would like to write a personal letter to a relative or friend.

Step 2. On the back of this paper, write a business letter to that company or a personal letter to that person.

Step 3. In the box below, write how you would address the envelope for your letter.

Step 4. Have your teacher check your work.

©AGS® American Guidance Service, Inc. Permission is granted to reproduce for classroom use only.   **Basic English Composition**

Community Connection 12

Writing Letters

H ave you ever written a thank-you note for a gift? Have you ever received a long letter from a family member far away? Have you ever written a letter to a complete stranger? What are some other kinds of letters you can think of?

Whether you write a personal letter or a business letter, remember to express your ideas clearly. Use correct sentences and well-organized paragraphs, and your reader will appreciate your message.

Chapter 12 discusses several purposes and kinds of personal letters. You will also learn two standard styles for business letters.

Goals for Learning

▶ To know the parts of a letter

▶ To write business and personal letters

▶ To address an envelope

241

Reading Vocabulary

appreciate (5)   organize (6)
clearly   personal (6)
discuss (5)   standard (6)
member (5)   style (5)

Introducing the Chapter

Have students examine the introductory photograph accompanying the first page of Chapter 12. Ask students what the woman appears to be doing and what her mood seems to be. They should recognize that the woman is responding happily to a letter. Ask students why people write letters, and list their reasons on the board.

Chapter 12 Self-Study Guide

SELF-STUDY GUIDE

Name _____

CHAPTER 12: Writing Letters

Goal 12.1 To write personal letters

Date	Assignment	Score
____	1: Read pages 241-242. Complete Activity A on page 242.	____
____	2: Read page 243. Complete Activity B on page 243.	____
____	3: Read page 244. Complete Activity C on page 244.	____
____	4: Read page 245. Complete Activities D-E on page 245.	____
____	5: Complete Workbook Activity 51.	____
____	6: Read page 246. Complete Activities F-G on page 246.	____
____	7: Read page 247. Complete Activity H on page 247.	____
____	8: Complete the Lesson 1 Review, Parts A-B on page 248.	____

Comments:

Goal 12.2 To know the parts of a letter

Date	Assignment	Score
____	9: Read page 249. Complete Activity A on page 250.	____

Comments:

©AGS® American Guidance Service, Inc. Permission is granted to reproduce for classroom use only.   **Basic English Composition**

SELF-STUDY GUIDE

Name _____

CHAPTER 12 Writing Letters, continued

Goal 12.3 To write business letters

Date	Assignment	Score
____	10: Read pages 250-251. Complete Activity B on page 251.	____
____	11: Complete Workbook Activity 52.	____
____	12: Read page 252. Complete Activities C-D on page 253.	____
____	13: Complete Workbook Activity 53.	____

Comments:

Goal 12.4 To address an envelope

Date	Assignment	Score
____	14: Read page 254. Complete Activities E-F on page 254.	____
____	15: Complete the Lesson 2 Review, Parts A-B on page 255.	____
____	16: Complete Workbook Activity 54.	____
____	17: Complete the Chapter 12 Review, Parts A-D on pages 256-257.	____

Comments:

Student's Signature _____ Date _____

Instructor's Signature _____ Date _____

©AGS® American Guidance Service, Inc. Permission is granted to reproduce for classroom use only.   **Basic English Composition**

Chapter 12 Self-Study Guide

Lesson at a Glance

Chapter 12   Lesson 1

Overview This lesson discusses the purposes and format of a personal, or friendly, letter.

Objectives

- To use a standard format when writing an informal letter to a friend or a relative.
- To address an envelope correctly.

Student Pages 242–248

Teacher's Resource Library

Activities 45–47

Workbook Activity 51

Reading Vocabulary

format	salutation
informal (7)	sample (5)
personal letter	signature (6)
punctuation (7)	tennis (5)
relative (5)	

Teaching Suggestions

■ Introducing the Lesson

Ask students what kinds of things arrive in the mail that they are happy to find. Students may mention invitations, letters from relatives, and other items that fit in the category of "personal letter." List those items on the board, and discuss the writers' purposes.

■ Reviewing Skills
Write the following common nouns on the board, and have students give a corresponding example of a proper noun. Have a volunteer come to the board to write the proper noun with correct capitalization. An example is shown in parentheses.

- my uncle (Uncle James)
- southwestern state (Arizona)
- football team (New York Giants)
- high school (Peabody High School)

■ Presenting Activity A
Have a volunteer read aloud the sample personal letter before

---

Personal letter

An informal message written to a friend or a relative.

When you write a **personal letter**, you share news and feelings with a friend or family member. A personal letter is also called a friendly letter. It has a simple five-part format. Study the five parts of the personal letter below.

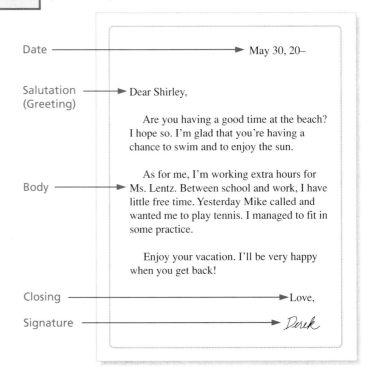

Date — May 30, 20–

Salutation (Greeting) → Dear Shirley,

Are you having a good time at the beach? I hope so. I'm glad that you're having a chance to swim and to enjoy the sun.

Body → As for me, I'm working extra hours for Ms. Lentz. Between school and work, I have little free time. Yesterday Mike called and wanted me to play tennis. I managed to fit in some practice.

Enjoy your vacation. I'll be very happy when you get back!

Closing — Love,

Signature — Derek

Activity A Use the sample letter above to answer these questions.

1) What mark of punctuation follows the salutation?

2) What closing does Derek use in this letter?

3) What mark of punctuation follows the closing?

4) Which part of a letter contains the message?

5) What part of a letter is also called the greeting?

---

students proceed to answer the questions about it. If you wish, direct students to use complete sentences in their answers.

Activity A Answers

1) A comma follows the salutation.   **2)** Derek uses the closing "Love."   **3)** The closing is followed by a comma.   **4)** The message is contained in the body. **5)** The salutation is also called the greeting.

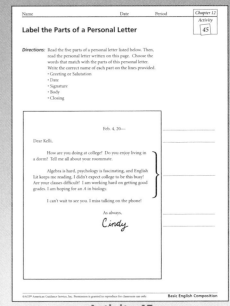

Activity 45

Invitations

You may write a friendly letter to invite someone to join you at an event. An invitation should include all necessary facts:

> • Description of the event
> • Details about when and where the event is taking place
> • Transportation, prices, special clothing, and so on

The sample letter below includes all necessary details. As you read the letter, look for the details.

May 18, 20–

Dear Joan,

Hi! I've got wonderful news. John and I were able to rent the cabin at the lake for two weeks in July. There is plenty of room for your family and ours, so we hope that you can join us as our guests. The children will have a wonderful time.

The cabin is furnished, including linens, pots and pans, and dishes. I'll send you a map with directions to the cabin. All that is needed for a great time is for our two families to be there!

The exact dates are from July 6 to July 20. If you can arrange to be there, please write me as soon as possible. Isn't this a tricky way to get a letter from you?

Michelle

Activity B Write an invitation to someone you know. Choose one of the topics below. Use the five-part format shown in this lesson. Include all necessary information: event, location, time, date, cost, and so on. Remember to write neatly!

• An invitation to a sporting event
• An invitation to a party
• An invitation to a movie, a play, or a concert
• An invitation to a school event that will be held soon
• An invitation to your teacher to attend a school or community event in which you are participating

attend (5)	invitation (5)
concert (5)	linen (5)
description (6)	location (6)
detail (5)	participate (7)
exact (6)	topic (5)
furnish (5)	transportation (5)
include (5)	tricky

■ Presenting Activity B

Have a volunteer read aloud the sample letter. Have students name the details in it that correspond to each of the three bulleted items in the box above the letter.

Activity B Answers

Answers will vary. Students should select one of the listed topics, think of a recipient, and write an invitation that includes the five parts of a personal letter.

APPLICATION

In the Community
Ask students whether and where they have bought standard party invitations produced by greeting card companies. Briefly discuss how a written invitation, such as the one shown on page 243, differs from a greeting card. When might a letter be more appropriate than a pre-printed invitation?

Reading Vocabulary

comment (5)   positive (6)
describe (5)   specific (8)
perfectly   thoughtful

■ Presenting Activity C

Have students jot down names of potential recipients of a thank-you letter before they begin their writing.

Activity C Answers

Answers will vary. Students' letters should include specifics about the gift or favor. The format should have the five basic parts of a personal letter.

LEARNING STYLES

Interpersonal/Group Learning

Divide the class into pairs. Give each pair a catalog with pictures. Invite the partners to page through the catalog and find something they would each like to receive as a gift. Ask the pair members to imagine that their partner has given them the catalog item. Then ask each partner to write a thank-you letter to the other partner. Suggest that the partners describe the catalog gift with some detail and also tell how or when they will use the item.

Thank-You Letters

It is always polite to say thank you for a gift or a favor. It is even more thoughtful to say it in a letter. Read the sample letter below. Notice that the writer has described the gift in detail. Such personal comments show that the gift was truly appreciated.

> August 6, 20—
>
> Dear Aunt Marie,
>
> I want to thank you for the wonderful soft sweater that you sent. It was so thoughtful of you to remember my birthday. How did you ever guess that the sweater was exactly what I wanted? It fits perfectly. Blue is my favorite color, too.
>
> The rest of the family says hello. I am looking forward to seeing you soon.
>
> Love,
>
> Carolyne

Activity C   Write a thank-you letter to someone who has given you a gift or done a favor for you. Be specific. Make positive comments. (You may want to mail this letter.)

Envelopes

Address your envelope clearly and correctly. Then your letter will arrive on time. Study the information in the sample at the top of the next page.

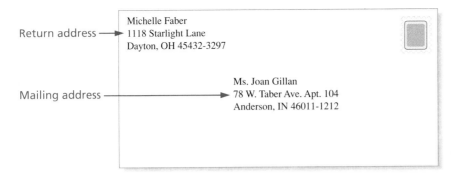

Return address → Michelle Faber
1118 Starlight Lane
Dayton, OH 45432-3297

Mailing address →
Ms. Joan Gillan
78 W. Taber Ave. Apt. 104
Anderson, IN 46011-1212

Use the proper abbreviation for the state followed by the ZIP code. Use the complete ZIP+4 code if you know it. Write as clearly as you can. The US Postal Service recommends that if you are writing by hand, print in all capital letters.

Activity D Write your answer to the following questions in complete sentences. Refer to the sample envelope above.

1) What is a return address?

2) What is a mailing address?

3) What is usually written on the first line of an address?

4) What is usually written on the second line of an address?

5) What is usually written on the third line of an address?

6) What punctuation mark is used between the city and the state?

Activity E Read the following three sample addresses. Find the error in each one. Rewrite all three addresses correctly on your paper.

1) Thomas, Dottie
4398 First Avenue
Rosedale, MD 20840-3129

2) Carlos Riverez
60 Harris St.
01060-2224 Hampton, MA

3) BETH SIMMINS
HARGATE, TN 37752-4008
RTE 2, BOX 407

Writing Letters *Chapter 12* **245**

■ **Presenting Activity D**
Point out the abbreviations on the sample envelope, and ask students to define an abbreviation using their own words. Briefly discuss the reasons for standard abbreviations on envelopes (the address can be read efficiently by machine or by a human operator).

Activity D Answers

1) The return address is the address of the person sending the letter.   **2)** The mailing address is the address of the person receiving the letter.
3) The first line of an address is usually a person's name.   **4)** The second line is the street number.
5) The third line is the city, state, and ZIP code.   **6)** A comma separates the city from the state.

■ **Presenting Activity E**
Have students identify the one error in each address before they rewrite the three addresses.

Activity E Answers
Errors are noted below. Students should rewrite the addresses correctly.

1) First and last names have been reversed. The first line should be *Dottie Thomas*.   **2)** The ZIP code should follow the state abbreviation. The last line should be *Hampton, MA 01060-2224*.
3) The second and third lines have been reversed. The last line should be *HARGATE, TN 37752-4008*.

APPLICATION

At Home
Have students bring in examples of envelopes addressed to their homes. They may examine elements such as postmarks, stamps, meter marks, placement of return addresses, and variations in methods of writing addresses.

Activity 46 (workbook sheet)

Name _____ Date _____ Period _____ Chapter 12 / Activity 46

Addresses

Directions: The sample addresses below are all written incorrectly. Rewrite them correctly on the lines provided.

1) Jones, Christopher
1528 Pikestown Rd.
Daytona Beach
FL 32018

2) Melissa Thomas
Box 561
Rt. 1 Annapolis
MD 21401

3) Mr. John Kennedy
Chula Vista, CA 92013
1976 East Gate Way

4) Paul Jacobs Apt. 6
12 Ocean Drive
San Francisco, CA
94101

5) Ms. Beth Hall
Box 1
Columbus, OH 43085
Rt. 5

6) Mary Moran
Hollywood, MD
20636
1375 Maryland Way

7) Tom Smith
Salt Lake City
UT, 84110
612 Tenth Avenue

©AGS® American Guidance Service, Inc. Permission is granted to reproduce for classroom use only. **Basic English Composition**

Workbook Activity 51 (workbook sheet)

Name _____ Date _____ Period _____ Chapter 12 / Workbook Activity 51

Addressing an Envelope

Addressing an envelope correctly is important. If we go to the trouble of writing a letter, we want to be sure it gets to the right place.

Return Address → Christy Walker
3212 Harrigut Avenue, Apt. 201
Dayton, OH 45442

Mailing Address →
Ms. Bland Pearson
23 Tralee Way
San Rafael, CA 94903

Directions: • Below are some sample addresses. They are all wrong in some way.
• Rewrite them correctly.
• Use the examples above as a guide.

1) Tony Pierce
Dartmouth Ct 17
Trenton, NJ 08601

2) Janet Lahney
Apt. 13
92 Westland Drive
College Park, MD 20740

3) Valerie Armstrong
67 Tulip Drive
19050 Lansdowne, PA

4) Marty Jo Golato
Sartoga avenue 4210
95129
CA San Jose

5) taffy clayton
Cumberland MD 21502
517 Louisville Lane

6) Jill Edmonds
43 main street apt 101
Poughkeepsie NY 12603

©AGS® American Guidance Service, Inc. Permission is granted to reproduce for classroom use only. **Basic English Composition**

Activity 46   **Workbook Activity 51**

■ Presenting Activity F

Students may write their envelope samples on notebook paper within envelope-sized frames.

Activity F Answers

Students should show two envelopes with correctly written mailing and return addresses.

■ Presenting Activity G

Review the bulleted topics listed on this page. Tell students that these ideas are prompts to get their own thinking started. Topics for personal letters should come from their own experiences and interests.

Activity G Answers

Answers will vary. Students should show the name of one or more potential recipients and several possible writing topics.

TEACHER ALERT

Emphasize to students that the word *personal* refers to the informal tone of the letter and does not necessarily mean "private" or "secret." Another name for a personal letter is "friendly letter."

Activity F Practice addressing envelopes correctly.

1) Address an envelope to someone you know. Use your address as the return address.

2) Address an envelope to yourself. Use your school address as the return address.

Letters to Keep in Touch

A good reason for writing a personal letter is just to keep in touch with friends and family members. Even everyday events can be of interest to the person who receives your letter.

Here are some topics that you could write about:

- Tell about a book, a movie, a song, or a television program.

- Tell about school. What are you studying? Do you have a report that is due soon? What are your teachers like? Are you active in a program, a team, or a club?

- Tell about something you did that was fun or boring. Tell about something you plan to do.

- Tell about vacations or vacation plans.

- Tell about what has happened in your life since you saw the person.

- Tell about a hobby or a sport.

Activity G Think of a friend or a relative who would like to receive a letter from you. Jot down some of the topics you might tell this person about.

Name _____ **Date** _____ **Period** _____ | **Chapter 12** |
| **Activity** |
| **47** |

Writing a Personal Letter

Directions: Write a personal letter to a friend or a relative. This letter may be an invitation, a thank-you, or just a letter to keep in touch. Remember to do these things when writing a personal letter:
- Date your letter.
- Include a salutation or greeting. (Dear Tim)
- Write a message. (The body of the letter)
- Add a closing. (Sincerely,)
- Sign your name.

©AGS® American Guidance Service, Inc. Permission is granted to reproduce for classroom use only.   **Basic English Composition**

Activity 47

Read this sample letter. Notice that it includes some of the topics suggested on page 246.

May 3, 20–

Dear Richard,

I bet you're surprised to get this letter from me. Well, I had to do a letter for my English class. I decided to write to you because I thought that you might write me back.

School is going well. I'm spending a lot of time in the technology center. I'm getting to be an expert at upgrading personal computer systems. My computer course is my favorite. Guess what else? Only 40 days until graduation! Did you think I could do it?

I've also been busy outside of school. I won a tennis tournament. Lately, I've been playing softball. I had a single and a double last night. I had to slide into second, but I made it! Oh, yes, I'm jogging five miles a day now. Sometimes I jog with Derek.

Write soon.

Your friend,

Mike

Activity H   Look at the topics you listed in Activity G. Think about the friend or relative who will receive your letter. Add any other topic that would interest this person. Write the letter. Follow the form for a personal letter given in this lesson. Include all necessary parts. Write neatly. Address the envelope correctly. Then stamp and mail your letter.

Reading Vocabulary
computer (8)   system (5)
double (5)   technology
graduation (6)   tournament (5)
jog (5)   upgrade
softball

■ **Presenting Activity H**
Have students review the possible topics they have listed and choose the recipient before they proceed with letter writing.

Activity H Answers
Answers will vary. Students' letters and envelopes should include all necessary parts. Some students may wish to mail their letters.

generous (5)

Part A Answers

1) The letter needs a date. **2)** A comma should follow the greeting. **3)** The closing should be placed above the signature.

Part B Answers

Answers will vary. Students' letters and envelopes should include all necessary parts. Some students may wish to mail their letters.

Follow-up Activity

Students may agree that people like to receive personal letters more than they like to write them. Have students write a persuasive paragraph titled "Why a Personal Letter Is Worth Writing." Their paragraph should include a topic sentence. The body of the paragraph should give reasons why a letter has advantages over other forms of communication.

Lesson 1   R e v i e w

Personal letters are an informal way to share news and feelings with a friend or a relative. When you write a personal letter, remember these points:

- Date your letter.
- Include a salutation or greeting. (Dear Joan,)
- Write your message in the body of the letter.
- Add a closing. (Yours,)
- Sign your name.
- Address the envelope correctly.
- Stamp and mail the letter.

Part A   Read this sample thank-you letter. Find three format errors. List the errors on your paper.

> **D**EREK
>
> Dear Aunt Harriet
>
> It was so thoughtful of you to remember my birthday. You are so generous! I really needed the money. I need new running shoes for the next track meet. Thanks! Love,
>
> Derek

Part B   Write a personal letter to a friend or a relative. It may be an invitation, a thank-you, or just a letter to keep in touch. After your teacher returns the letter to you, put it into an envelope and mail it.

Business letter
A formal message written to a person or an organization.

You may write a **business letter** to request information from an organization. You may also write to discuss a product or service, or to apply for a job. A business letter is more formal than a personal letter.

Here are the other main differences between the two letters:

- Stationery for personal letters comes in many sizes and colors. The standard size for a business letter is $8\frac{1}{2} \times 11$ inches. White or off-white paper is usually preferred for a business letter.

- A personal letter may be handwritten. A business letter should be typed.

- Both sides of the paper may be used for a personal letter. Only one side of the paper is used for a business letter.

- A personal letter has five main parts. A business letter has eight main parts.

Read about the eight parts of a business letter.

---

1. **The heading, or return address,** gives the address of the sender. Business stationery often has an imprinted heading that includes the company name.

2. **The date** helps businesses keep track of correspondence.

3. **The inside address** shows who is receiving the letter.

4. **The salutation, or greeting,** includes the title and last name of the person being addressed. A colon comes after the salutation. Here are some examples of business letter salutations:

       Dear Dr. Jackson: Dear Sir or Madam: Dear Editor:

5. **The body** contains the message, usually in several paragraphs.

6. **The closing, or complimentary close,** is more formal than the closing in a personal letter. Only the first letter of the first word is capitalized. A closing always ends with a comma. Here are some examples of business letter closings:

       Yours truly,   Sincerely,   Respectfully yours,
       Very truly yours,   Sincerely yours,   Cordially,

7. **The handwritten signature** appears above the typed name.

8. **The typed name and title** appear four lines below the closing.

Writing Letters   *Chapter 12*   **249**

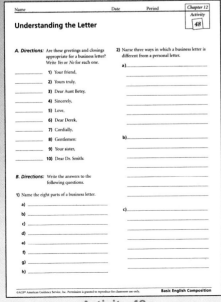

Activity 48

Reading Vocabulary

additional (6)	notation (11)
advantage (5)	opportunity (5)
attach (5)	optional
available (6)	purchase (5)
brief (6)	quality (5)
brochure	recently (5)
enclosure (8)	request (6)
indicate (6)	secretary (5)
label (6)	shipment
manager (6)	value (5)

■ Presenting Activity A

Review the eight parts of a business letter listed on page 249.

Activity A Answers

1) A heading is in a business letter but not in a personal letter. The heading shows the name of the business sending the letter.
2) An inside address is in a business letter but not in a personal letter. The inside address shows where the letter is being sent.
3) A typed name and title appear only in a business letter. They tell who has sent the letter.

GLOBAL CONNECTION

Discuss with students the various means people now have to send messages and longer documents almost anywhere in the world. Students may mention networked computers and telecommunications satellites, faxes, and mailings that travel by land, sea, and air. Students who have received airmail letters from abroad may bring in the envelopes so that the group can look at the address and foreign stamps.

Activity A Compare the eight parts of a business letter with the five parts of a personal letter. (See page 242.) What three parts are in a business letter that are *not* in a personal letter? List each part and write a brief description of its purpose.

Study the eight parts of this sample business letter. Notice the two additional parts at the bottom of the letter. They are labeled *Optional notations*. The first notation shows that Lynda Handley did not type her own letter. It was typed by her secretary, Cindy King. The second notation shows that a brochure is included in the envelope with this letter.

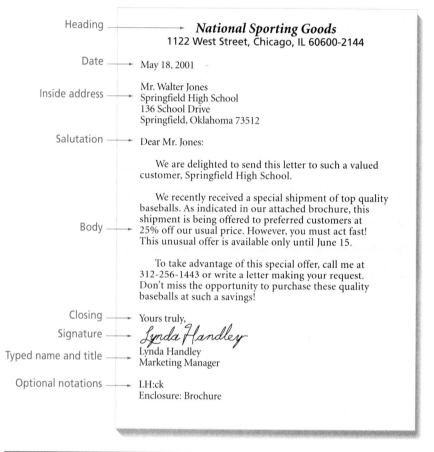

Heading → **National Sporting Goods**
1122 West Street, Chicago, IL 60600-2144

Date → May 18, 2001

Inside address → Mr. Walter Jones
Springfield High School
136 School Drive
Springfield, Oklahoma 73512

Salutation → Dear Mr. Jones:

Body → We are delighted to send this letter to such a valued customer, Springfield High School.

We recently received a special shipment of top quality baseballs. As indicated in our attached brochure, this shipment is being offered to preferred customers at 25% off our usual price. However, you must act fast! This unusual offer is available only until June 15.

To take advantage of this special offer, call me at 312-256-1443 or write a letter making your request. Don't miss the opportunity to purchase these quality baseballs at such a savings!

Closing → Yours truly,

Signature → *Lynda Handley*

Typed name and title → Lynda Handley
Marketing Manager

Optional notations → LH:ck
Enclosure: Brochure

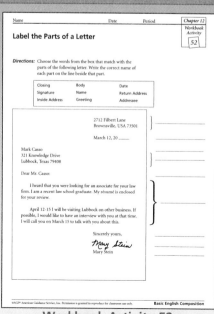

Workbook Activity 52

Activity B Write your answers to these questions about the sample letter on page 250.

1) Notice that the heading (the return address) is printed on the stationery in a different type. What part is added just below the heading?

2) Did someone from National Sporting Goods or Springfield High School write this letter? How can you tell?

3) What punctuation mark is used after the salutation?

4) Read the body of the letter. What does Lynda Handley want Coach Jones to do?

5) Give one reason why Coach Jones might want to do this.

6) What closing is used in this letter? What are three other closings that could be used in a business letter?

7) Why is Lynda Handley's name typed on the letter below her signature?

8) What is Lynda Handley's job title?

9) What do the letters *LH:ck* mean? Why are they typed on this business letter?

The sample letter on page 250 is typed in *block style*. Block style is the most formal style. It is often used when the business stationery has a letterhead. All parts of the letter begin at the left margin. The paragraphs are not indented.

Another style to use for business letters is the *modified block style*. Several lines begin near the middle of the page: the return address, the date, the closing, the handwritten signature, and the typed name. All the other parts begin at the left margin. Each paragraph of the body is indented. The sample letter on page 252 is typed in modified block style.

Reading Vocabulary
indent (6)   margin (7)
letterhead   modify (7)

- ## Presenting Activity B
Have a volunteer read aloud the sample business letter on page 250 before students proceed to answer questions about it. Suggest that they write answers in complete sentences.

Activity B Answers
1) The date appears just below the heading. **2)** Because a letterhead shows the name and address of the writer, this letter was written by someone from National Sporting Goods.
3) A colon follows the salutation.
4) Lynda Handley wants Coach Jones to buy baseballs. **5)** Coach Jones might want to take up her offer if the school needs baseballs at a lower-than-usual price.
6) The closing in this letter is *Yours truly.* Other closings are *Cordially, Sincerely, Sincerely yours, Respectfully yours,* and *Very truly yours.* (Students may note any three closings from the chart on page 249.) **7)** Lynda Handley has typed her full name so that the reader knows exactly whom to call or write. People's signatures are not always easy to read. **8)** Lynda Handley is the Marketing Manager of National Sporting Goods. **9)** The letters are the initials of Lynda Handley and her secretary, Cindy King. Cindy King did the final typing of the letter.

Reading Vocabulary

advertisement (6)
agent (5)
available (6)
cash (6)
consider (5)
employ (6)
industry (6)
interview (6)
plaza
register (6)
response (6)
temporary (8)

APPLICATION

Career Connection
Briefly discuss with students the many jobs that require making sure that letters and packages get to the right address. Such jobs occur in mailrooms, shipping departments, and companies that specialize in shipping packages to their destination within a specified time. Tell students that the United States Postal Service provides a handy list of standard abbreviations to use when writing addresses, as well as other postal information. One or two volunteers may visit the post office to bring back reference items to share with the group.

LEARNING STYLES

Auditory/Verbal
Call on volunteers to read aloud the business letter on page 252. Use this activity to review the parts of a business letter. For example, ask Volunteer #1 to read the heading; #2, the date; #3, the inside address; #4, the salutation; #5, the body of the letter; #6, the closing; #7, the signature; and #8, the typed name. If time permits, do this same activity for the letter on page 250.

---

18 Silver Lane
Springfield, OK 73510
May 12, 20–

Mr. Paul Elliott
Western Industries
One Western Plaza
Centerville, Texas 79408

Dear Mr. Elliott:

This letter is in response to your advertisement in the *Daily News*. I would like to apply for the position of ticket agent. I understand that this position is temporary and will last only during the rodeo season.

For the past year, I have been employed at a gas station. My duties included selling parts and using a cash register. I believe I have the experience necessary to be a ticket agent.

I will call you on May 20. You may reach me at 405-234-7766 before then. I am available any Saturday for an interview.

Thank you for considering me for this position.

Sincerely,

Derek Corelli

Derek Corelli

Activity C   Refer to the sample letter on page 252. Write your answers to these questions in complete sentences.

1) What punctuation mark is used after the salutation?
2) What punctuation mark is used after the closing?
3) What are the numbers *79408*?
4) How is the style of this letter different from the style of the sample letter on page 250?
5) What is the main purpose of this letter?
6) A business letter should come to the point quickly. Has Derek come to the point quickly? Has he included all necessary information? Explain your answer.

Activity D   Choose one of these topics for a business letter.

- Write a letter to a local museum. Request information about an exhibit. Include a reason for wanting this information.

- Write to a local radio or television station. Express your opinion about a program. Include facts to back up your opinion.

- Write to a local business. Ask about summer employment. Include facts about your job experiences, educational background, and personal qualifications. Make the company want to hire you!

- Write a letter to the editor of a local newspaper. Express your opinion about a recent event in your city. Include facts to back up this opinion.

After you have chosen a topic, use the telephone directory to find addresses. Use your own return address. Type or write a business letter. Organize the body of your letter in this way:

1) In paragraph 1, introduce yourself or briefly explain why you are writing the letter.
2) In paragraph 2, request the information or state your opinion. Be specific. What do you want this person or organization to do for you? Include all necessary information.
3) In paragraph 3, express your thanks.

Check your letter to make sure you have included all eight parts correctly.

background
directory (7)
educational
employment (6)
exhibit (5)
local (6)
qualification
(7)

■ Presenting Activity C

Have a volunteer read aloud the sample letter on page 252 before students proceed to answer the questions about it.

Activity C Answers

1) A colon is used after the salutation.   **2)** A comma is used after the closing.   **3)** The numbers 79408 are the ZIP code of the person receiving the letter.
4) This letter has some parts beginning near the middle of the page. Each paragraph is also indented. The block letter on page 250 shows all parts beginning at the left margin, including the first lines of paragraphs.
5) The main purpose of this letter is to apply for a job.
6) Derek has come to the point quickly and has included all necessary information. He has told Mr. Elliott exactly what job he is interested in, what his qualifications are, and how he and Mr. Elliott will get in touch.

■ Presenting Activity D

Read through the directions and topic choices with students. Direct them to use the model on page 252 when they are ready to proofread their letters.

Activity D Answers

Letters will vary. Each letter should include the eight parts of a business letter and three paragraphs that are organized according to the directions at the bottom of page 253.

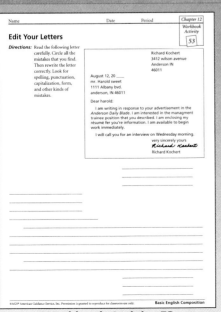

Workbook Activity 53

Reading Vocabulary

crease (7)   insert (6)
fashion (5)   postage (5)
flair (9)

■ Presenting Activity E

Have students compare the two sample envelopes to find differences. Tell students to use complete sentences as they explain which envelope is correct.

Activity E Answer

Envelope A is addressed completely and correctly. It includes the state abbreviation for Arizona in the return address. The fourth line of the mailing address correctly shows the city, state, and ZIP code.

■ Presenting Activity F Ask

students where on the envelope they will put the inside address from the business letter they wrote for Activity D.

Activity F Answers

Answers will vary. Students should address the envelope correctly in preparation for mailing the business letter. They may choose to add postage and mail it.

TEACHER ALERT

Students may be able to use word-processing software to address envelopes. If possible, have students choose a readable typeface and print out an envelope with their return address and the mailing address in correct positions.

Mailing a Business Letter

Before you insert your business letter into an envelope, fold it in thirds. Follow these steps:

1. Place the letter face up on the desk.
2. Fold a little less than a third of the sheet from the bottom toward the top and crease.
3. Fold the top third down to one-fourth inch from the first crease.
4. Insert the last fold into the envelope first.

A standard business envelope is $4\frac{1}{8}$ inches by $9\frac{1}{2}$ inches. To prepare a business envelope for mailing, follow these steps:

1. Write or type the complete return address in the top left corner.
2. Write or type the complete mailing address in the center of the envelope, a little to the right.
3. Write or type the person's name first. If you do not know the person's name, you may write the person's title or position.
4. Put the correct postage on the letter.

Activity E Which of these two envelopes is addressed completely and correctly? Explain the reasons for your choice.

Envelope A	Envelope B
D. Diamond 1234 Archmore Rd Tucson, AZ 85727-2254	D. Diamond 12324 Archmore Road Tucson 85727-2254
Editor Fashion Flair Magazine 112 Center St Gainesville, FL 32602-2903	Fashion Flair Magazine Della Lyons, Editor Gainesville, FL 32602-2903 112 Center Street

Activity F Use the business letter you wrote for Activity D. Fold it and insert it into a business envelope. Address the envelope correctly. If you wish, add a stamp and mail your letter.

A business letter is more formal than a personal letter. When you write a business letter, remember to include all eight parts:

- Return address, or heading
- Date
- Inside address
- Salutation, or greeting, followed by a colon
- Body
- Formal closing
- Signature
- Name (and title, if appropriate)

Be clear, correct, and complete when addressing the envelope. The envelope will be the first thing that is noticed. Be sure that it is letter-perfect!

Part A Read the salutations and closings below. Is each one appropriate for a business letter? Write *Yes* or *No* for each number.

1) Dear Mr. Levin: 5) Love,

2) Hi, Harry,   6) Very truly yours,

3) Dear Manager: 7) Cordially,

4) To Whom It May Concern: 8) Take care,

Part B Write answers to the following items.

1) List the eight parts of a business letter.

2) List two appropriate closings for a business letter.

3) Write the amount of postage that is needed to mail a first-class letter.

4) List three ways in which a business letter is different from a personal letter.

5) Write your complete mailing address.

Reading Vocabulary
appropriate (6)   concern (5)

Part A Answers
1) Yes 2) No 3) Yes 4) Yes
5) No 6) Yes 7) Yes 8) No

Part B Answers
1) return address or heading, date, inside address, salutation or greeting, body, formal closing, signature, name or name and title
2) Answers will vary. Two correct closings are: *Very truly yours,* and *Sincerely yours,* 3) Students should name the current price of a first-class stamp. 4) Answers may vary. A sample answer is given. A business letter is more formal than a personal letter. A business letter has an eight-part format, and a personal letter has five parts. A business letter is often written to a stranger, and a personal letter is almost always written to a friend or relative.
5) Answers will vary. Students should write their complete mailing address.

Follow-up Activity

A current almanac is another reference students can use to find ZIP codes and postal rate information. An almanac may also contain a model letter of complaint provided by the United States Office of Consumer Affairs. Provide this or any other model complaint letter, and have students write their own letters of complaint about an imaginary product or service.

Workbook Activity 54

Chapter 12 Review

The Teacher's Resource Library includes two parallel forms of the Chapter 12 Mastery Test. The difficulty level of the two forms is equivalent. You may wish to use one form as a pretest and the other form as a posttest.

Part A Answers

Answers will vary. The error(s) in each sample address is given below. Students should correct the error as they rewrite the five addresses.

1) The second line should read *78 Kentmill Rd., Apt A.*   **2)** The third line should read *DELRAY BEACH, FL 33445.*   **3)** The third line should read *Annapolis, MD 21401-2218.*
4) The name of the addressee and the department should come first in the address, together on line 1 or separately on line 1 and line 2.
5) A street address and a city name are missing. Students should make up the missing information.

Part B Answers

Answers will vary. Students' letters and envelopes should include all necessary parts.

Part A   Read the following five sample addresses. Each one contains at least one error. Rewrite all five addresses correctly on your paper. (Use your imagination if you need to add information.)

1) Chris Gillan Apt. A
   Kentmill Rd.
   78
   Oakville, PA 15139

2) NORMA STOOPS
   1580 ETON WAY
   DELRAY BEACH 33445
   FLORIDA

3) Mr. Frank Chung
   Box 800
   Maryland
   Annapolis 21401-2218

4) Handy Pencil Company
   123 Broadway
   Sanford, GA 31402-2435
   Eugenia Tillots
   Customer Service

5) Student Art Contest
   WBTM Radio
   Massachusetts 02154-3214

Part B   Write a personal letter to someone who lives near you. Share some news about what you are doing in school. Make sure your letter includes the five basic parts. Then address an envelope. Use your home address as the return address. Use the person's home address as the mailing address. Have your teacher review your letter and envelope. Then add a stamp and mail your letter.

Chapter 12 Mastery Test A

Part C Find the five format errors in the business letter below. List each error on your paper. Show how it could be corrected.

Janine Wittson
421 Dover Street
West Oakley, NY

Ms. Carla Marcos
Consumer Complaint Department
XYZ Greeting Card Company
Claymore, WA 98259

Dear Ms. Marcos,

On September 30, I ordered three boxes of greeting cards: items 1327, 1459, and 2346 from your autumn catalog. I enclosed a check for $43.59, including shipping and handling. I have received the canceled check. Although three months have gone by, I have not received the greeting cards.

I am enclosing a copy of my canceled check and a copy of my order form. I would like to receive the greeting cards as quickly as possible. If they cannot be sent, I would like my money back.

Thank you for your attention to this matter. I look forward to your reply. I can be reached at the address above or by phone at 914-332-6789.

Janine Wittson

Janine Wittson

Enclosures

Part D Write a business letter to anyone you choose. Include the eight main parts. Make sure that your paragraphs are well organized and contain all necessary information. Be sure that your spelling, capitalization, and punctuation are perfect. Refer to the checklist on page 185.

Test Taking Tip When a teacher announces a test, listen carefully. Write down the topics that will be included. Write down the names of any specific readings the teacher says to review.

Reading Vocabulary

cancel (7)   complaint (6)
catalog (6)   consumer (7)

Part C Answers

1) The name *Janine Wittson* should be deleted from the return address. **2)** A date should appear below the return address. **3)** A street number should be added to the inside address. **4)** The salutation should be followed by a colon, not a comma. **5)** A closing such as *Sincerely yours,* needs to be added above the signature.

Part D Answers

Answers will vary. Students' letters and envelopes should include all necessary parts.

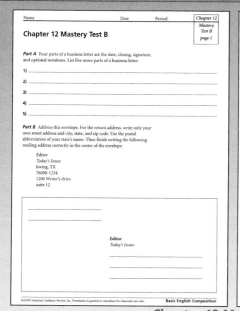

Chapter 12 Mastery Test B

Name _____ Date _____ Period _____ | Chapter 12 / Mastery Test B / page 1

Chapter 12 Mastery Test B

Part A Four parts of a business letter are the date, closing, signature, and optional notations. List five more parts of a business letter.

1) _____
2) _____
3) _____
4) _____
5) _____

Part B Address this envelope. For the return address, write only your own street address and city, state, and zip code. Use the postal abbreviation of your state's name. Then finish writing the following mailing address correctly in the center of the envelope:

Editor
Today's Issues
loving, TX
76000-1234
1200 Writer's drive
suite 12

Editor
Today's Issues

Name _____ Date _____ Period _____ | Chapter 12 / Mastery Test B / page 2

Chapter 12 Mastery Test B, continued

Part C Read the information below. Then write a business letter to the editor of the magazine using the information given. Use today's date. Include the eight parts of a personal letter. Indent each new paragraph.

You sent a copy of a story you wrote to a magazine called *Today's Issues*. You sent the story to the Editor at the address in Part B of this test. You have not had a response yet. You want to write a letter asking if the story is being considered for publication. You are enclosing another copy of the story.

Planning Guide

Writing a Report

	Student Text Lesson			
	Student Pages	Vocabulary	Practice Exercises	Lesson Review
Lesson 1 Planning a Report	260-263	✔	✔	263
Lesson 2 Finding Information	264-275	✔	✔	275
Lesson 3 Getting Organized	276-280	✔	✔	280
Lesson 4 Writing the Report	281-285		✔	285
Lesson 5 Preparing a Bibliography	286-289		✔	289

Chapter Activities

Teacher's Resource Library
Writing Tip 12: Planning and Writing
    Reports
Community Connection 13: Library
    Research

Assessment Options

Student Text
Chapter 13 Review

Teacher's Resource Library
Chapter 13 Mastery Tests A and B
Final Mastery Test

Teaching Strategies							Language Skills			Learning Styles						Teacher's Resource Library		
Reviewing Skills	Teacher Alert	Follow-up Activity	Career Application	Home Application	Global Connection	Community Application	Identification Skills	Writing Skills	Punctuation Skills	Visual/Spatial	Auditory/Verbal	Body/Kinesthetic	Logical/Mathematical	Group Learning	LEP/ESL	Activities	Workbook Activities	Self-Study Guide
260	260	263	261				✔	✔	✔			262				49		✔
264	270, 274	275		268		265	✔	✔	✔			266				50	55-56	✔
276		280			278		✔	✔	✔				277			51	57-58	✔
281		285					✔	✔	✔	284								✔
286	288	289					✔	✔	✔					288		52	59	✔

Writing Tip 12

Name _____ Period _____   Chapter 13 / Writing Tip 12

Planning and Writing Reports

A **report** is an organized summary of information that you have gathered about a topic. Following these five steps will help you to write a report.

1) Plan the Report
 • Choose a broad subject you would like to explore
 • Select a topic in that subject area
 • Find out how much information is in the library about your topic
 • Limit your topic so that you have enough information to write a complete report
 • Write a title for your report
 • List your subtopics, or the parts of your larger topic

2) Find Information
 • Go to the library to find information on your topic
 • Look in the library catalog for books that have useful information
 • Check almanacs, encyclopedias, atlases, or other sources in the library reference section
 • Check *The Readers' Guide to Periodical Literature* for magazines with information you could use
 • Take notes on the information you find
   – Use index cards
   – Start each card with this information about the source you find facts in:
       authors' names
       book or article and magazine title
       page numbers
       volume numbers
       date of publication
   – Copy all the information that you may need
   – Copy any quotations exactly as they are printed
   – Use a different card for each source

3) Get Organized
 • Put your note cards in order by topic and subtopic
 • Do not use notes that may not fit anywhere
 • List your main topics
 • Choose an order that seems suitable for your topics
 • Write a final topic outline

4) Write Your Report
 • Write your report using your note cards and outline
 • Begin your report with a topic paragraph that states the main idea
 • Use your own words to write the ideas you found in your sources (**paraphrase**)
 • Write an author's exact words if you use direct quotations
 • Name the author or source of any direct quotations you use
 • Repeat your main ideas in a summary paragraph at the end
 • Proofread your report
 • Revise and rewrite it as needed
 • Include a title page at the front of your report

5) Prepare a Bibliography
 • Use the bibliographic information on your note cards
 • Put your cards in alphabetical order
 • Study Chapter 13 Lesson 5 for information you need to include in each kind of entry
 • Include a blank page after your bibliography

©AGS® American Guidance Service, Inc. Permission is granted to reproduce for classroom use only.   **Basic English Composition**

Community Connection 13

Name _____ Date _____ Period _____   Chapter 13 / Community Connection 13

Library Research

To write a report, you need to do **research**. This means that you need to find information about a topic. You can use periodicals and books to do research. You can also research a topic by observing something or asking questions of an expert. The more you know about how to do research, the better your report will be. A well-researched report has a good amount of current facts and information.

Research is done most often at the library. Follow the steps to see how a library can be helpful for doing research.

Step 1. At your local or school library, look for the following:

 • library catalog
 • reference books section
 • periodicals section
 • *Reader's Guide to Periodical Literature*

Step 2. Once you find each item, answer the questions below. Write where you found the item. Then write how it is organized. Is it organized alphabetically? By subject? By author? Is there a decimal system? Ask a librarian to help you.

Library catalog

Where did you find it? _____

How is it organized? _____

Reference books section

Where did you find it? _____

How is it organized? _____

Periodicals section

Where did you find it? _____

How is it organized? _____

Reader's Guide to Periodical Literature

Where did you find it? _____

How is it organized? _____

Step 3. Share with the class what you found out.

©AGS® American Guidance Service, Inc. Permission is granted to reproduce for classroom use only.   **Basic English Composition**

Chapter

13

Writing a Report

When a teacher assigns a report, do you know how to get the most out of the experience? First of all, try not to think of a report as a difficult chore. Think of it as a chance to learn about something that interests you.

Choose a topic that you are curious about. Track down information. Think about the information. Organize it. Write about it. When you do all those things, you may discover that you have gained valuable understandings.

In Chapter 13, you will learn how to plan and write a report.

Goals for Learning

▶ To make a plan for a report

▶ To find information and take notes

▶ To organize information and make an outline

▶ To write, proofread, revise, and rewrite

▶ To prepare a bibliography

▶ To hand in a good report on time

259

Writing a Report Chapter 13 **259**

Reading Vocabulary

assign (6)	rewrite
organize (6)	topic (5)
proofread	valuable (5)
revise (8)	

Introducing the Chapter

Have students examine the introductory photograph accompanying the first page of Chapter 13. Tell students that the woman in the photograph has been given a report to write. Ask them why she is making this stop in the library. Briefly discuss what students know about on-line catalogs and library resources. Then have students give questions that could best be answered at a library; write their suggested questions on the board.

Chapter 13 Self-Study Guide

Lesson at a Glance

Chapter 13   Lesson 1

Overview This lesson points out the steps in report writing and the importance of selecting a topic of just the right size.

Objectives

- To choose a report topic within a broad subject area.
- To do some preliminary research to determine whether the topic is a practical and interesting one.

Student Pages 260–263

Teacher's Resource Library

Activity 49

Reading Vocabulary

atom (6)	sample (5)
career (6)	science (5)
computer (8)	source (6)
culture (7)	subject (5)
energy (6)	technology
geography (5)	**term paper**
literature (6)	thesis (11)
orchestra (6)	transportation (5)
report (4)	

Teaching Suggestions

■ Introducing the Lesson

Tell students that their final goal is to hand in a good report on time. Ask for their ideas about four or five steps they will need to take to reach that goal. They may then compare their ideas with the five steps listed on this page.

■ Reviewing Skills Write these
transition words on the board: *however, on the other hand, in addition, for example.* Ask students to use each transition in one or two oral sentences on an informational topic.

■ Presenting Activity A

Read the bulleted list of twelve general subject areas with students. Briefly discuss topics that fall in each area. Tell students to choose the subject area of greatest interest

---

Lesson 1   Planning a Report

Report

An organized summary of information about a topic that has been researched; a report may be written or spoken.

Term paper

A formal report in which a writer tries to prove a thesis or an idea about a chosen topic.

Your final goal is to write a well-organized, fact-filled, interesting **report** or **term paper**. Spend some time making a careful plan that will lead you to that final goal. Here are the steps you will follow:

Step 1	Choose a topic.
Step 2	Find information and take notes.
Step 3	Organize your information and make an outline.
Step 4	Write the report; proofread, revise, and rewrite.
Step 5	Prepare the bibliography.
Final Goal	Hand a good report in on time!

Take the first step. Think of topics that interest you. You might start with a subject area and list topics that fall within it. Look at these sample lists.

Science	History	Music
Energy sources	The American Revolution	Popular dances
The atom	Early computers	The orchestra
Earthquakes	Transportation	African music

Activity A   Choose one of the subject areas listed below. Then list topics that fall within that subject. List as many topics as you can think of. Finally, circle any topics that you think might be interesting to learn about.

• Science	• Geography	• Music
• History	• Literature	• Art
• Cultures	• Mathematics	• Technology
• Sports	• Travel	• Careers

---

to them. They may explore more than one subject area in their search for a report topic.

Activity A Answers

Answers will vary. Students should show that they have thought about a variety of possible topics. They should be able to give reasons for circling the ones that seem best.

TEACHER ALERT

This chapter will take students through the writing of a report. Advise them to make a folder in which they can keep track of all their research. The first item to put in the folder is their list of possible topics from Activity A.

Suppose that you have chosen the topic *Transportation* within the subject *History*. Here are just some of the questions that could be asked about that topic:

Subject: History
Topic: Transportation

- What were the earliest wheeled vehicles?
- When were motorcycles invented?
- What were the first airplanes like?
- Who invented and improved the automobile?
- What animals have been used in the past for transportation?

You can see that the history of transportation is a broad topic— *too* broad. Try to narrow your topic to one that you can handle in a report. Find **subtopics** within your topic. You may need to find subtopics within your subtopics, too. A report on the history of transportation would be too long and hard to manage. A report on the history of motorcycles, however, may be just the right size.

Subtopic

A division or a part of a larger topic. Video games is one subtopic under the main topic Computers, for example.

The best topic for a report is neither too broad nor too narrow. If the topic is too broad, there will be too much information to choose from. If the topic is too narrow, you will not find enough information.

Activity B   In each pair below, identify the topic that is broad and the topic that is narrow. Write *Broad* or *Narrow* on your paper.

1) a) Growing vegetables
   b) Growing root vegetables

2) a) Computers from past to present
   b) The first computers

3) a) Schools in the United States
   b) High schools in the United States

4) a) Sun spots
   b) The sun

5) a) The history of Mexico
   b) The Mexican War with the United States

Reading Vocabulary
broad (5)   **subtopic**
identify (6)   vehicle (5)
motorcycle   video

■ **Presenting Activity B**
Ask students to tell how a topic, a subtopic, and a sub-subtopic differ. Go over item 1 with students, asking them why the narrow topic would be better for a report.

Activity B Answers
1) a) Broad
   b) Narrow
2) a) Broad
   b) Narrow
3) a) Broad
   b) Narrow
4) a) Narrow
   b) Broad
5) a) Broad
   b) Narrow

APPLICATION

Career Connection
Many libraries have special career guidance sections containing various handbooks and other print materials relevant to job seekers. If the local library has such a section, ask for volunteers to spend some time looking over the publications. Have them report back to the group to describe materials that seemed especially useful or interesting.

Name   Date   Period   Chapter 13
                                                   Activity
                                                   49
Choosing a Topic

Directions: Read each pair of topics below. Decide which one is broad and which one is narrow. Write *Broad* or *Narrow* on the lines provided.

EXAMPLE   *Broad*   a) Cancer
           Narrow   b) Treatment for Cancer

_____   1) a) The first president, George Washington
_____   b) A president

_____   2) a) Judges of the Supreme Court—How they are elected
_____   b) Judges

_____   3) a) Nutrition
_____   b) Vitamin deficiencies

_____   4) a) Risk factors of smoking
_____   b) Smoking

_____   5) a) United States history
_____   b) The discovery of America

_____   6) a) Computers
_____   b) Selecting a computer

_____   7) a) The historical sites in Washington, D.C.
_____   b) Washington, D.C.

_____   8) a) Education
_____   b) Funds from the federal government for education

©AGS® American Guidance Service, Inc. Permission is granted to reproduce for classroom use only.   **Basic English Composition**

Activity 49

Reading Vocabulary

atmosphere (5)   magnify (5)
available (6)   microfiche
catalog (6)   public (5)
film (6)   truly
item (6)

■ Presenting Activity C

Help students to plan a visit to a library, a large one if possible, in order to investigate each listed subject.

Activity C Answers

Students should list a number for each item, telling how many books are available on that subject. Students' answers may vary from the ones given below.

1) Too Broad **2)** Too Broad (or Just Right) **3)** Too Narrow
4) Too Broad (or Just Right)
5) Just Right **6)** Too Broad
7) Too Narrow **8)** Too Broad
9) Too Narrow

■ Presenting Activity D

Have students refer to their circled topics from Activity A in this lesson as they do preliminary research in the library catalog.

Activity D Answers

Students should write down the name of their report topic. Have them tell why they think it would be an interesting topic to research and write about.

Catalog
A list of items arranged in a special way.

One way to find out whether your topic is too broad or too narrow is to do a quick check at the library. Use the library **catalog** to look up subjects. A library catalog lists every book, magazine, and recording in that library.

The catalog is on a computer in most public libraries. In some libraries, the catalog is still arranged on cards in drawers. In a few libraries, the catalog is on sheets of film called microfiche. Microfiche is read through a special magnifying machine.

Activity C   Go to the library catalog to look up each of the subjects below. Write down how many books are available on that subject. Then write whether you think the topic is *Too Broad, Too Narrow,* or *Just Right.*

1) Computers

2) Computers—history

3) Video games

4) Motorcycles

5) Motorcycle racing

6) Solar system

7) Venus—atmosphere

8) Gardening

9) Carrots—gardening

Activity D   Look over your own possible report topics. (You listed them in Activity A.) Locate your topics among the subject listings in the library catalog. Decide on the topic you think is best. To decide on your topic, ask yourself these questions:

- Am I truly interested in learning about this topic? (Your answer should be yes.)
- Is the topic too broad? (Narrow it.)
- Is the topic too narrow? (Make it broader.)

Write down the name of your report topic.

You have completed the first step in writing your report: You have chosen your topic. You may still change your mind, however. As you work on your report, you may decide to do any of these things:

- Change your topic completely.
- Make your topic broader.
- Make your topic narrower.

Part A Write your answers to the following questions in complete sentences.

1) Would *Science* be a good topic for a report? Explain why or why not.

2) Why might it be hard to find information on some topics? Give two reasons.

3) Why should you check subject records in the library catalog *before* you choose a topic?

4) What is an example of a topic that is too broad? What is an example of a topic that is too narrow?

5) What is the difference between a main topic and a subtopic?

Part B Each row contains one main topic and three subtopics. Identify the main topic. Write the main topic on your paper.

1) Vegetables	Turnips	Beans	Carrots
2) Literature	Poetry	Short Stories	Novels
3) Poodles	Dogs	Collies	Terriers
4) Roses	Daisies	Flowers	Marigolds
5) Robins	Crows	Blue Jays	Birds
6) French	Spanish	Languages	English
7) Mars	Venus	Earth	Planets
8) Gardening	Fertilizing	Planting	Weeding
9) Hurdles	Marathon	Long Jump	Olympics
10) Football	Hockey	Sports	Volleyball

Reading Vocabulary

collie (5)	novel (7)
fertilize	Olympic
hockey (5)	poetry (6)
hurdle (5)	poodle
marathon	terrier
marigold	volleyball

Part A Answers

Answers may vary. Sample answers are given.

1) The topic *Science* would be too broad for a report.   **2)** It might be hard to find information about a person, a place, or an event that is not widely known. Some topics are too recent, and the only information would be in newspapers and current magazines, not in books.   **3)** If you know that not enough or too much has been written about a topic, then you can change your topic before you have spent time trying to research it.   **4)** An example of a topic that is too broad is "Animals." An example of a topic that is too narrow is "How to Feed a Cat."
5) A main topic is broader than a subtopic.

Part B Answers

1) Vegetables   2) Literature
3) Dogs   4) Flowers   5) Birds
6) Languages   7) Planets
8) Gardening   9) Olympics
10) Sports

Follow-up Activity

Play a game of Categories with students. Name a category, such as *Cities in the United States* or *Team Sports*. Students have one minute to write down as many topics as they can think of within that category. Vary the activity by having partners or small groups work together to list one topic for each letter of the alphabet; the time limit could be ten or fifteen minutes.

Reading Vocabulary

agriculture (5)   **investigate (6)**
alphabetically   observe (5)
alphabetize   **research (6)**
author (6)   thoroughly
chemistry (5)   title (5)
file (5)

Teaching Suggestions

- **Introducing the Lesson**
  Display any nonfiction book from the public library. Point out the call number on the spine. Ask students to tell everything they know about the call number: what it means, how a researcher can find it, and how to use it to find books on library shelves.

- **Reviewing Skills** Remind students that when they are asked to identify a person, place, or thing, they should think about its special characteristics. Have students use a dictionary to find each of the following entries and then write one or two sentences that identify the thing: *cowrie, Boxing Day, sombrero, femur, kabuki.*

Research
To look for information about a topic by reading books and periodicals, by observing events, or by questioning experts.

You have chosen a topic. Now you are ready to find information, or **research** your topic. You will need to keep track of your sources. You will need to take notes as you **investigate** your topic. Where should you begin?

The library catalog is always the best place to begin. If your library has a card catalog, you will find three kinds of cards: title, author, and subject.

Investigate
To search thoroughly; to examine.

- If you know the author's name, look for an author card. It is filed alphabetically by last name. *(Patent, Dorothy Hinshaw)*
- If you know the book title, look for a title card. It is filed alphabetically by the first important word (not *A, An,* or *The*).
- For research, subject cards are probably most useful. Look for a subject card filed alphabetically by the first important word of your topic. If your subject is a person, look for the last name first *(Lincoln, Abraham).*

The drawers of a card catalog have guide letters on them. The letters show which alphabetized cards are in each drawer. This sample shows six drawers from a card catalog.

A - Am   An - Bo   Br - Ce   Ch - Cy   Da - Ez   Fa - Fy

Activity A Notice the guide letters on the six drawers above. Write the letters of the drawer containing cards on each subject below.

1) Canyons   **5)** Chemistry

2) Ants   **6)** Agriculture

3) Earthquakes   **7)** Business

4) Dinosaurs   **8)** Frederick Douglass

- **Presenting Activity A**
  Point out that each of the eight listings is a subject, so students should imagine themselves looking for subject cards in the drawers shown.

Activity A Answers
1) Br–Ce 2) An–Bo 3) Da–Ez
4) Da–Ez 5) Ch–Cy 6) A–Am
7) Br–Ce 8) Da–Ez

Each of the three kinds of cards in the card catalog has the same information. The arrangement is slightly different. Here are three sample cards:

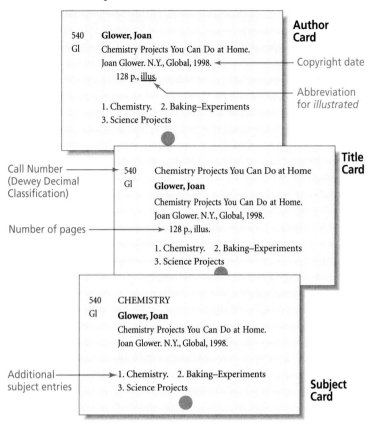

Author Card

540
Gl
Glower, Joan
Chemistry Projects You Can Do at Home.
Joan Glower. N.Y., Global, 1998. ← Copyright date
128 p., <u>illus.</u> — Abbreviation for *illustrated*

1. Chemistry.   2. Baking–Experiments
3. Science Projects

Call Number (Dewey Decimal Classification) →

Title Card

540
Gl
Chemistry Projects You Can Do at Home
Glower, Joan

Chemistry Projects You Can Do at Home.
Joan Glower. N.Y., Global, 1998.

Number of pages → 128 p., illus.

1. Chemistry.   2. Baking–Experiments
3. Science Projects

540
Gl
CHEMISTRY
Glower, Joan

Chemistry Projects You Can Do at Home.
Joan Glower. N.Y., Global, 1998.

Additional subject entries →

1. Chemistry.   2. Baking–Experiments
3. Science Projects

Subject Card

Activity B   Study the information in the sample cards above. Write your answers to the following questions.

1) Why is it important to write down the call number of a book you will look for on the library shelves?
2) In what year was the book by Joan Glower published?
3) What subject did a researcher look for to find this card?
4) Does this book have chemistry projects involving foods? Explain your answer.

abbreviation (8)   entry (6)
additional (6)   illustrate (7)
classification (8) project (5)
copyright (8)   slightly
decimal (6)

■ **Presenting Activity B** Go over each of the labeled elements in the sample cards. You may want students to use complete sentences in their answers to questions 1–4.

Activity B Answers

1) Nonfiction books are organized by subject, and the call number tells you where on the shelves to look.   **2)** This book was published in 1998.   **3)** The researcher looked for the subject "Chemistry."   **4)** Yes, this book has chemistry projects involving food. One of its additional subjects is "Baking—Experiments."

APPLICATION

In the Community
Have students investigate the largest public library within fifteen miles of their location. If transportation is a problem, let students know that they can gather this information by calling the library. Together, compile a list of questions that students can try to answer about the library. Topics to consider include special exhibits and collections; electronic resources; reference specialists; availability of periodicals; and rules for borrowing software, CDs, and videos.

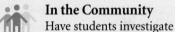

Name _____ Date _____ Period _____ | Chapter 13 |
                                               | Workbook Activity |
Library Catalog Entries | 55 |

The catalog in a library lists every book the library has. Each book has at least three records: title, author, subject.

Directions: • Put the list below in alphabetic order the way each entry would be in a library catalog.
• Identify each one as a subject, an author, or a title.

John Steinbeck	The Writer's Handbook	history
Olympics, history	Pearl Buck	The Red Pony
Gone With the Wind	William Shakespeare	Hamlet
Russia	psychology	S. E. Hinton
Joyce Carol Oates	The Outsiders	art

List the entries here.   Identify each one here.

1) _____   _____
2) _____   _____
3) _____   _____
4) _____   _____
5) _____   _____
6) _____   _____
7) _____   _____
8) _____   _____
9) _____   _____
10) _____   _____
11) _____   _____
12) _____   _____
13) _____   _____
14) _____   _____
15) _____   _____

©AGS® American Guidance Service, Inc. Permission is granted to reproduce for classroom use only.   **Basic English Composition**

Workbook Activity 55

■ Presenting Activity C

Show students how each element in the computer catalog entry on page 266 corresponds to an element on a card from a card catalog shown on page 265. You may want students to use complete sentences in their answers to questions 1–4.

Activity C Answers

1) The author's last name is Leonard. **2)** The title of the book is *Motorcycle Classics*. **3)** The abbreviation "ill." means the book is illustrated. **4)** The copyright date tells when the book was published. If researchers want up-to-date information, then they should look for books with recent copyright dates.

■ Presenting Activity D

Remind students that they may look up a title, an author, or a subject regardless of what kind of cataloging system a library uses.

Activity D Answers

1) Subject: Einstein, Albert
2) Author: Lauber, Patricia
3) Subject: Motorcycles
4) Subject: Antarctica
5) Subject: Bulldogs
6) Title: *Long March*

Most libraries have computer catalogs. Instructions appear on the screen to tell you what steps to take. You can pull up a listing by typing the author's name, the title, or the subject.

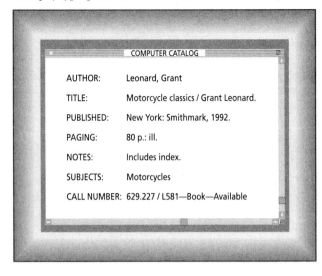

COMPUTER CATALOG

AUTHOR: Leonard, Grant

TITLE: Motorcycle classics / Grant Leonard.

PUBLISHED: New York: Smithmark, 1992.

PAGING: 80 p.: ill.

NOTES: Includes index.

SUBJECTS: Motorcycles

CALL NUMBER: 629.227 / L581—Book—Available

Activity C   Study the information in the computer catalog entry above. Write your answers to the following questions.

1) What is the last name of the author of this book?
2) What is the title of this book?
3) How can you tell that this book has pictures in it?
4) Why would the copyright date of a book be important to a researcher?

Activity D   Read about each situation below. Write what you would look up in the library catalog.

1) You are writing a report about Albert Einstein.
2) You would like to look at science books written by Patricia Lauber.
3) You are looking for books about motorcycles.
4) You are looking for books about the exploration of Antarctica.
5) You are looking for a book about bulldogs.
6) You would like to find a book about Chinese history called *The Long March*.

Inside Books

The library catalog has led you to a book that might be useful to you. You have used the call number to find the book on the shelf. Now, how can you tell whether the book contains the information you need? Look inside.

The **table of contents** is in the front of the book. It gives you a general sense of the information inside. This is part of a table of contents from a book about transportation.

——————— Contents ———————

The **index** gives more detail about information in the book. The index entry on the left is from the same book about transportation.

Activity E   Use the samples on this page to answer the following questions. Write your answers on your paper.

Ocean liners, 25-29
  largest, 26, 28
  speeds of, 29
  See also Ships

1) On which page of the book about transportation would you find information about how fast ocean liners travel?

2) Which chapter of the book tells about submarines?

3) On which page does the chapter about submarines begin?

4) If your research topic is motorcycles, would this book be useful to you? Why or why not?

5) What other topic could you look up in the index to find out about ocean transportation?

■ **Presenting Activity E**
Make sure students understand that the numbers in a table of contents indicate the number of the chapter and the page on which a chapter begins. A number in an index is the page on which specific information is found.

Activity E Answers
1) page 20   2) Chapter 3
3) page 32   4) This book would be useful for research about motorcycles because Chapter 4 is "Unicycles, Bicycles, and Motorcycles."   5) Ships

Reading Vocabulary

almanac (7)   reference (6)
atlas (7)   region (5)
biographical   statistics (11)
generally (5)   volume (6)
issue (6)

■ Presenting Activity F

Provide examples of the four
reference sources discussed so that
students can familiarize themselves
with the organization of and general
contents of each.

Activity F Answers

Students need name only one
reference source for each
question.

1) almanac 2) atlas
3) almanac 4) atlas, almanac,
encyclopedia 5) almanac,
encyclopedia, biographical
dictionary 6) encyclopedia
7) encyclopedia 8) almanac
9) atlas, encyclopedia, almanac
10) encyclopedia, biographical
dictionary

APPLICATION

At Home
As a home assignment,
have students go to their
local library to find the four reference sources discussed. They
should use the reference sources to
find the answer to each question
in Activity F. They may also use
the four references to create "who,
what, when, where" questions that
will challenge classmates.

Reference Books

The library catalog lists all books, including those in the
reference section of the library. There are many kinds of
reference books on all sorts of subjects. Generally, reference
books cannot be checked out.

An almanac is published every year. Almanacs contain facts,
statistics, and records for current and past years. Major topics
covered include sports, inventions, states and nations, and
current issues in the news.

An encyclopedia has many volumes. Encyclopedia articles cover
a huge range of topics. Use an encyclopedia to get general
information on your topic.

An atlas is a book of maps. Atlases also contain facts about
cities, states, countries, and world regions.

A biographical dictionary contains information about famous
people. Examples are *The International Who's Who* or *Who Was
Who in America*.

Activity F   Read each question below. Write in which
reference book you would find information on that topic:
almanac, atlas, encyclopedia, biographical dictionary. (There may
be more than one correct answer.)

1) Who is the mayor of El Paso, Texas?
2) What major highways cross Montana?
3) How many people visit the Grand Canyon each year?
4) What climates are in Australia?
5) Who was Albert Einstein?
6) What were the first computers like?
7) How should tomatoes be planted?
8) On what day will New Year's Day fall in the year 2050?
9) Where is Malaysia?
10) What plays did Lorraine Hansberry write?

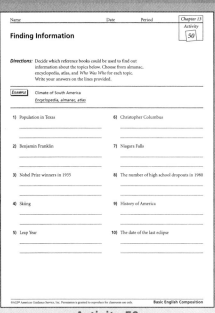
Activity 50

Periodicals

As you research, look for information in magazines and newspapers. Librarians can help you find articles in current and back issues of **periodicals**.

First find out what articles you need. Computer catalogs often contain records for periodicals. Suppose you are researching the history of the Olympic Games. Here is a record from a computer catalog that appears for the subject *Olympics*.

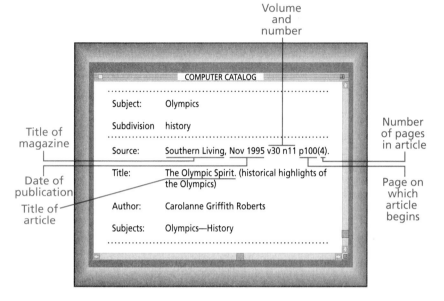

Activity G Study the sample entry above. Answer the following questions on your paper.

1) What is the name of the magazine shown on this computer screen?

2) How long is the article "The Olympic Spirit"?

3) Suppose you want to read the article. What issue of the magazine should you ask the librarian for?

4) Suppose you are researching the most recent Olympic records in swimming. Would this article be useful to you? Explain your answer.

■ **Presenting Activity G**
Review the material shown in the computer record before students proceed to answer questions 1–4.

Activity G Answers

1) The magazine is *Southern Living*. **2)** The article is four pages long. **3)** The issue is November 1995 (volume 30 number 11). **4)** This article would probably not be useful to me if I were looking for recent records. The description is "historical highlights of the Olympics," so the information is about the past.

Reading Vocabulary

abyss (9)	**key words**
geographic	sperm
humpback	wildlife
jot	

■ Presenting Activity H

Review the features of the *Readers' Guide* entries before students proceed with answering the two questions.

Activity H Answers

1) To locate the article, the librarian needs to know the title of the magazine, *National Geographic;* the date of publication, November 1995; and possibly the page numbers, 56–73. **2)** The article about humpback whales is in the October/November 1995 issue of *National Wildlife,* volume 33.

You can also find magazine articles using the *Readers' Guide to Periodical Literature.* It is an index to articles in popular magazines.

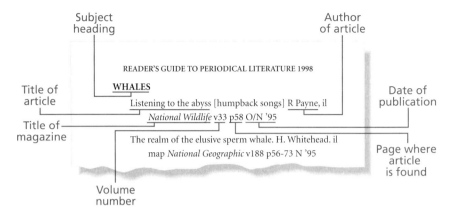

Activity H Study the sample entries above. Answer the following questions on your paper.

1) Suppose you want to read the article in *National Geographic.* You should jot down a few items so that the librarian can help you find the article. What information from the *Readers' Guide* is most important to jot down?

2) In what issue of the magazine *National Wildlife* will you find an article about humpback whales?

Knowing What to Look Up

As you start researching your topic, list questions that you will try to answer in your report. Then think about how to find answers to your questions in books, reference sources, and periodicals. Use **key words** to find the information you need.

> **Key words**
> The words you look up to find information on a topic. They name what your question is about.

Suppose you are trying to answer this question: *How did Valentine's Day begin?* The key words in that question are *Valentine's Day.* You could look up those words in a library catalog. You could also look them up in an encyclopedia and in the index to a book about holidays.

Suppose this is your question: *What mammals are in danger of becoming extinct?* Key words might be *extinction* or *endangered animals.*

Activity I   Read each question below. Write what key word or key words would be likely to lead you to the answer.

1) What kinds of birds live in Hawaii?

2) Are any lizards poisonous?

3) What were the earliest computers like?

4) What are the rules for the game of lacrosse?

5) What languages are spoken in the Philippines?

Activity J   Write a list of questions for your own report topic. Then list key words that you think will be most useful in leading you to information.

Taking Notes

Think about your report topic and the questions you hope to answer. Make a list of main topics you can start searching for.

Mike is preparing a report on vegetable gardening. He has listed four possible main topics to include.

Report topic: Growing Vegetables

Main topics:

1. How to choose seeds

2. How to prepare the soil

3. When to plant each vegetable

4. When to harvest each vegetable

As Mike does his research, he may change some of his main topics. He will add subtopics. But his list will help him to take notes in an organized way.

■ **Presenting Activity I** Go over the first question with students, helping them to understand that the key word *Hawaii* is narrower than *Birds*. Point out that the subject *Hawaii* in a library catalog will probably have subdivisions. Students may see a subject such as *Hawaii—Wildlife,* which will be even more helpful.

Activity I Answers

1) Hawaii   **2)** Lizards
3) Computers   **4)** Lacrosse
5) Philippines

■ **Presenting Activity J** Have students take out their report folders to find the report topic they chose in Activity D.

Activity J Answers

Answers will vary. Students should write questions they think are important to try to answer in their report. They then list key words that will lead them to likely subject listings in the library catalog.

■ Presenting Activity K

Students should look at the list of questions they wrote for Activity J. Tell them to select the most important questions to turn into main topics for their report. Refer them to the model on page 271.

Activity K Answers

Answers will vary. Review students' main topics to make sure that they cover main ideas rather than details. Emphasize that these main topics are starting points only and can change as the research proceeds.

Activity K   Think about your own report topic. Write your own list of main topics to research.

Bibliography
A list of books and periodicals that have been used to find information.

Use one set of index cards to keep track of your sources. Use a separate card for each source. These cards will help you make a **bibliography**.

For a book, write the author's last name first. Underline the book title. Give the place of publication, the publisher, and the date of publication.

Sample bibliography card for book:

Jones, Robert C. *Your Vegetable Garden.*
New York: Tellmore Book Company,
1996.

For a magazine article, write the author's last name first. Use quotation marks around the title of the article. Underline the name of the magazine. Include the volume number, date, and page numbers.

Sample bibliography card for magazine article:

Ling, Marla. "Tips for City Gardeners."
Gardening Today 10 (May 5, 1995)
12–14.

Use a separate set of index cards for your notes. On each note card, list a main topic or subtopic. Then write information that fits with that topic. If you copy any exact words from your source, put quotation marks around them. On each note card, tell where you found the information.

Study these sample note cards. Notice how a main topic or subtopic is written at the top. Notice how the source is listed in a shortened form. The long form is on the bibliography card.

> Choosing Seeds
> Quality matters. "Home gardeners will reduce the chance of disappointment if they choose high quality seeds." (p. 81)
> It's important to read the information on the packages.
> Jones, p. 81

> Garden Locations
> People in cities can grow food. City gardeners can grow many vegetables in pots on windowsills and balconies.
> Examples: tomatoes, radishes, herbs.
> Ling, p. 12

Activity L Use Mike's cards above and on page 272 to answer these questions. Write your answers on your paper.

1) At the bottom of one of the note cards is *Jones, p. 81.* What does that mean?

2) Why has Mike written GARDEN LOCATIONS at the top of one of his note cards?

3) What did Robert C. Jones write?

4) In what magazine did Mike find Marla Ling's article?

5) Why did Mike put quotation marks around one of the sentences in his first note card?

Reading Vocabulary

balcony (5)   reduce (6)
herb (5)   shorten
quality (5)   windowsill
radish (6)

■ **Presenting Activity L**
Review the sample bibliography cards on page 272 and the sample note cards on page 273 before students answer questions 1–5. You may want students to use complete sentences in their answers.

Activity L Answers

1) The information came from page 81 of the book by Robert C. Jones. **2)** One of the main topics or subtopics in Mike's report is "Garden Locations." **3)** Robert C. Jones wrote the book *Your Vegetable Garden.* **4)** Mike found Marla Ling's article in the magazine *Gardening Today.* **5)** Quotation marks show that the author's exact words have been copied.

Reading Vocabulary

advance (5)   resist (6)
century (5)   resource (8)
delete (9)   sustain (7)
evidence (5)   synonym (5)
paraphrase (12)   twentieth
quantity (6)   variety (6)
rearrange

■ Presenting Activity M

Read item 1 aloud to students. Then think aloud about how to put it into your own words to model the process of coming up with a paraphrase.

Activity M Answers

Answers will vary. Sample answers are given.

1) Seeds from expert growers are best to use in most cases.
2) Order seeds many weeks before you will plant them.
3) Order only enough seeds for one growing season.   **4)** Today seeds are varied and are less prone to disease.   **5)** Although some seeds can live up to five years, others will not grow after one year.

■ Presenting Activity N

Discuss each of the four steps listed in this activity. Students should find their list of main topics in their report folders and may already have begun to list sources.

Activity N Answers

Answers will vary. Each student should show a correctly annotated bibliography card and several cards with notes from that source. Each note card should be labeled with a main topic or a subtopic and should have a reference to the source.

Paraphrase

To express someone else's ideas in your own words.

Paraphrasing

As you take notes, use quotation marks around a writer's exact words. The other words in your notes should be your own. Instead of copying words and sentences, **paraphrase** the ideas you read about.

> **EXAMPLE**
>
> Author's Words: By the late twentieth century, some population experts were warning of dangers. They pointed to evidence that planet Earth no longer had the agricultural and energy resources to sustain its enormous human population.
>
> Paraphrase: Scientists of the late twentieth century were studying population changes. Some warned that there were too many people in the world. Because food and fuel were running out, many lives were in danger.

Activity M   Paraphrase the information in these sentences. Rearrange ideas. Use synonyms. Add or delete words. Rewrite each sentence on your paper.

1) A gardener should buy seeds from expert growers except in special cases.
2) Seeds should be ordered well in advance of the planting season.
3) A gardener should order only the quantity of seeds needed for that growing season.
4) Most seeds now come in many varieties and can resist disease.
5) Some seeds live for as long as five years, but others are not good after only one year.

Activity N   Prepare to take notes on your report topic. Follow these steps.

1) Find a book or a magazine with information on your topic.
2) Prepare a bibliography card for that source.
3) Take notes on index cards. Write a main topic or a subtopic at the top of each card. If you copy words directly, put quotation marks around them. Paraphrase other information.
4) On the note card, write information about your source.

TEACHER ALERT

Help students to understand why information should be paraphrased rather than copied word for word. Paraphrasing requires thinking about the information, so the researcher is learning about the topic. Paraphrasing also means that the researcher has not plagiarized another writer's work. Briefly discuss why plagiarizing is illegal.

Lesson 2 Review

Find information for your report in an organized way.

- Use the library catalog to find books, magazines, and other reference books.
- Use index cards to keep track of your sources.
- Take notes on index cards. Each card should be labeled with a main topic or a subtopic.

Part A Write your answer to each question in a complete sentence.

1) You want to find a book in the library catalog. What are three pieces of information you may use to look up the book?

2) You are writing a report about Albert Einstein. Should you look up *Albert* or *Einstein*?

3) Mike wants to find a book with information about turnips. He cannot find that subject in the library catalog. What should he do?

4) What reference book should you use to find out when the next leap year will be?

5) Where can you find information about an event that happened two months ago?

6) What kind of information does an atlas contain?

7) What are two kinds of periodicals?

8) You are writing a report about animal life in Alaska. You find a book called *Learning About Alaska*. How can you find out if this book has the information that you want?

9) Why are index cards often used for taking notes?

10) Why must you make a bibliography card for every source you use?

Part B Continue researching your report topic. Remember to use bibliography cards. Remember to use note cards labeled with main topics and subtopics.

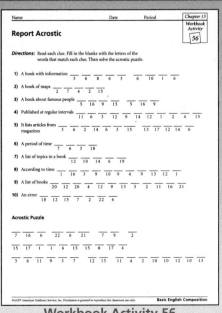

Workbook Activity 56

Part A Answers

Answers may vary. Sample answers are given.

1) To find a book in the library catalog, I can look up Subject, Author, or Title. **2)** For information about Albert Einstein, look up Einstein. **3)** Mike should broaden the subject to Vegetables or Roots to find information about turnips. **4)** An almanac would tell when the next leap year will be. **5)** Information about events from two months ago are in periodicals. **6)** An atlas contains maps and other geographical information. **7)** Two kinds of periodicals are magazines and newspapers. **8)** I can check the table of contents and the index to find out what kinds of information are in the book. **9)** Index cards can be rearranged in any order so that a researcher can put ideas together in different ways. **10)** Researchers need to tell where facts and ideas come from, so they must keep track of all the sources they use.

Part B Answers

Students should proceed with their research. Set aside time for check-ins, when you can review students' note cards and provide any necessary guidance.

Follow-up Activity

Provide an array of nonfiction books, informational articles, and reference sources such as almanacs, biographical dictionaries, and encyclopedias. Randomly select a short passage from one of the sources and have students practice paraphrasing the information orally. Students may then take turns selecting passages for classmates to paraphrase.

Chapter 13   Lesson 3

Overview This lesson offers guidance in organizing information in preparation for report writing.

Objectives

- To sort notes by main topics and subtopics.
- To choose a logical order for organizing the information of a report.
- To write an outline.

Student Pages 276–280

Teacher's Resource Library

Activity 51

Workbook Activities 57–58

Reading Vocabulary

framework   outline (6)

Teaching Suggestions

- **Introducing the Lesson**
  Display any informational article or content-area textbook chapter, and point out the headings and subheadings. Tell students that these headings show how the writer has organized information. Ask students why such headings are helpful to readers.

- **Reviewing Skills** Choose words with *ie* or *ei* spellings (see page 99 of the student book). Write each word on the board, using a blank for the two missing vowels. Have students come to the board to show the correctly spelled word.

Outline

A list of information arranged by main topics and subtopics. An outline is a plan. An outline provides a framework for a report.

When you have finished finding information, you will have many note cards. Before you write your report, you must sort the note cards, or put them in order. Start by listing your main topics. Then choose an order to put them in. Finally, you will be able to write an **outline**. An outline will guide you in the writing of your report.

Here are the steps to follow in sorting your note cards.

1. Look at the topic or subtopic listed at the top of each card. Put the notes on the same topics together.

2. If you have only one card on a topic, see if it fits with one of the other topics.

3. If you have a large pile of cards on one topic, you may need to separate them into subtopics.

4. Some of your notes may not fit anywhere. You do not have to use all of the information that you found when you researched your topic.

Mike is writing a report about growing vegetables. He divided his note cards into five groups.

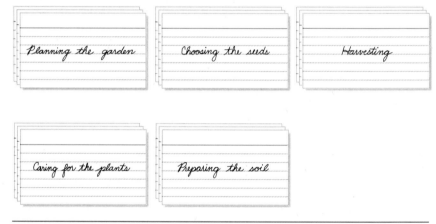

Activity A The bold word in each group below is the main topic. On your paper, write the subtopics that belong with this main topic. Ignore any subtopics that are not related to the main topic.

1) **Furniture:**   chair   table   window   sofa

2) **Books:**   magazine   dictionary almanac atlas

3) **Clothes:**   coat   hat   jewelry   shirt

4) **Sports:**   football hockey   athlete   tennis

Activity B Look over the note cards you have been making for your own report. Sort the cards by main topics. Then write your own list of main topics for your report.

Choosing an Order

Think about the main topics you have listed for your report. How will you put the information into a logical order? There are many ways to organize the information. Choose the way that seems to fit your report topic best.

Several possible arrangements are listed below. Study the list.

Chronological order:	according to time, usually from the oldest to the most recent
Order of importance:	from the most to the least important or from the least to the most important
Order of size:	from the largest to the smallest or from the smallest to the largest
Order of cost:	from the most to the least expensive or from the least to the most expensive
Spatial order:	from left to right, top to bottom, or outside to inside
Other logical groupings:	first, second, third; easiest to hardest; least to most popular; least to most practical; and so on

Reading Vocabulary

athlete (6)   practical (5)
chronologic   recent (6)
ignore (5)   relate (6)
importance (6)   sofa (5)
jewelry (5)   tennis (5)
logical (8)

■ **Presenting Activity A**

Have students use their own words to tell the difference between a main topic and a subtopic.

Activity A Answers

1) chair, table, sofa
2) dictionary, almanac, atlas
3) coat, hat, shirt 4) football, hockey, tennis

■ **Presenting Activity B**

Have students assemble the note cards they have been writing.

Activity B Answers

Answers will vary. Allow time for students to arrange and rearrange their note cards. They then write the list of main topics to be covered in their written report. A manageable number is from four to eight main topics.

LEARNING STYLES

Logical/Mathematical Ask the students to work in pairs to develop a set of symbols or icons for the first five boldfaced headings in the box on page 277. Explain that each icon should be a visual representation of its type of organization. Afterward, invite the pairs to share their five icons with the class. Decide on a set of class icons. Have someone draw these. Then post the set in the classroom to help the students remember five ways to organize information.

Reading Vocabulary
breed (5)   firefighting
electronic (5)   phrase (6)

■ **Presenting Activity C** Go over the directions with students. Tell them to use the chart on page 277 as a reference.

Activity C Answers

Answers may vary. Sample answers are given.

1) Chronologic order
2) Least to most popular
3) Least to most important
4) Least to most practical

■ **Presenting Activity D**

Have students look over the list of main topics they made in Activity B.

Activity D Answers

Answers will vary. Students should write several sentences to explain how they will order their main topics and why they think the arrangement makes sense.

GLOBAL CONNECTION

Write the continent names Africa, Asia, Australia, Europe, North America, and South America on the board. Ask students for the names of countries, cities, or other geographical regions on each continent, and add those names to the list. Have students choose one of the listed items and think about the categories of information that might be contained in a report on that place. Together, come up with a list of main topics. Discuss a likely organization of those topics.

Amanda is writing her term paper on early computers. How should she arrange her information? A logical way would be chronological order, the order in which events happened. She could start with the earliest computers and end with the invention of electronic computers.

Activity C   Read about the students' situations below. Each student must decide on an order for the main topics and subtopics in his or her report. Refer to the list of arrangements on page 277. Then write at least one way in which information could be arranged. In some cases, more than one logical order may be possible.

1) Mike's report is about growing vegetables. His main topics are planning the garden, choosing the seeds, caring for the plants, harvesting, and preparing the soil.

2) Shirley is investigating popular breeds of dogs in the United States. She has information about the five most popular breeds.

3) Laura is investigating firefighting methods. She has facts on several ways to put out a fire.

4) Derek has researched four energy sources of the future.

Activity D   Look over your list of main topics for your report. Decide on a logical arrangement for your information. Write what your arrangement is and why you think it will work.

Outlining

An outline is a kind of writer's guide. If you make an outline for your report, then you will know what to write first, next, and last. A good outline makes writing a report easier.

A topic outline lists only words and phrases. Outlines can also be written in complete sentences.

Mike has written the topic outline below. You should be able to see that Mike has chosen a chronologic order for his main topics.

- The main topics are listed after Roman numerals.

- The subtopics are indented and listed after capital letters.

- Further subtopics are indented and listed after Arabic numerals.

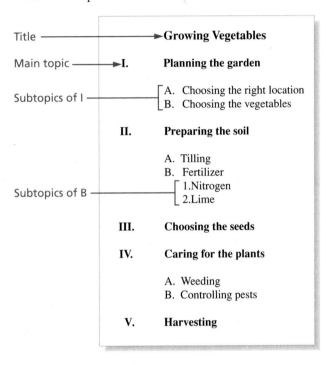

Title ——————→ **Growing Vegetables**

Main topic ——→ **I. Planning the garden**

Subtopics of I ——— A. Choosing the right location
B. Choosing the vegetables

II. Preparing the soil

A. Tilling
B. Fertilizer

Subtopics of B ——— 1. Nitrogen
2. Lime

III. Choosing the seeds

IV. Caring for the plants

A. Weeding
B. Controlling pests

V. Harvesting

Activity E On your paper, rewrite the outline above. Make each part a complete sentence.

Activity F Look at your own list of main topics for your report. Think about the order in which you plan to present them. Add subtopics to your list. Then write an outline for your report. Refer to the sample outline above as a guide.

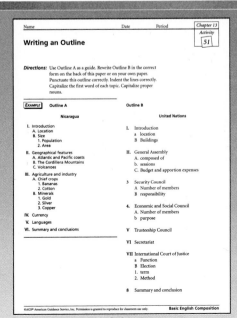

Activity 51

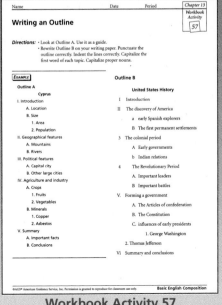

Workbook Activity 57

■ **Presenting Activity E**

Start by having students turn the first main topic and two subtopics into sentences orally.

Activity E Answers

Answers may vary. A sample sentence outline is given.

I. The first step is to plan the garden.
A. Choose the right location.
B. Choose the vegetables.
II. The next step is to prepare the soil.
A. Till the soil.
B. Fertilize the soil.
1. Use nitrogen.
2. Use lime.
III. The third step is to choose the seeds.
IV. The fourth step is to care for the plants.
A. Weed the garden.
B. Control any pests.
V. The final step is to harvest the vegetables.

■ **Presenting Activity F**

Have students refer to their note cards to decide on subtopics that belong with each main topic they listed in Activity B.

Activity F Answers

Answers will vary. Students should write a topic or sentence outline showing the main topics and subtopics they will cover in their report.

Reading Vocabulary

aside	lubrication
electrical	radiator (6)
filter (7)	system (5)

Part A Answers

Answers will vary. A sample answer is given.

Title: Olympic Games
How the games began
Summer games
Winter games
Famous Olympic athletes
The importance of the Olympics

Part B Answers

Order of entries may vary.

Basic Car Care
I. The electrical system
  A. Battery
  B. Spark plugs
II. Engine lubrication
  A. Changing engine oil
  B. Replacing the oil filter
III. The cooling system
  A. The water pump
  B. The radiator
  C. The hoses

Follow-up Activity

Show students that long encyclopedia articles are often accompanied by outlines. Explain that readers can use the outline to locate specific sections of information in the article. You can also use one or more encyclopedia outlines to play a mix-and-match game. Copy the main topics and subtopics from the encyclopedia outline, and list each on a slip of paper. Challenge students to rearrange the slips to match the original outline of main topics and subtopics.

Lesson 3   Review

Organize your notes. You will find that you are ready to begin writing your report.

- Sort your notes into groups of main topics and subtopics.
- Set aside the information that does not fit anywhere. You will not use it in your report.
- Arrange your main topics in a logical order. Refer to the list on page 277.
- Write a topic outline or a sentence outline. Refer to the example on page 279.

Part A   Read this list of main topics for a report on the Olympic Games. Decide on a logical order in which the topics could be presented. List the topics in the order in which you would present them. Be ready to tell why you think your order is a good one.

Title: Olympic Games

Summer games

Famous Olympic athletes

How the games began

Winter games

The importance of the Olympics

Part B   Read the list of topics and subtopics below. Rearrange them into a logical order. Then write a topic outline. Refer to the example on page 279 as a guide.

Title: Basic Car Care	Battery
The electrical system	Replacing the oil filter
The water pump	The cooling system
Engine lubrication	Changing engine oil
The radiator	Spark plugs
The hoses	

Workbook Activity 58

Refer to your outline as you write your report. You will find that an outline makes the writing easier. Begin the report with a topic paragraph. Think of this paragraph as an introduction to your report. A topic paragraph tells your reader what the report will be about. Remember the three main parts of a paragraph:

- A *topic sentence* states the main idea.

- A *body* lists the main topics (I, II, III, and so on in your outline).

- A *summary sentence*.

Read the sample topic paragraph below. Compare the sentences in this paragraph to Mike's outline on page 279. Notice that the main topics are included. Subtopics will be discussed in the rest of the report.

Growing Vegetables

You can successfully grow vegetables in your own back yard. Five steps are involved. Begin by carefully planning the garden. Next, prepare the soil properly. Choose the best seed. During the growing season, give the plants the necessary care. Follow the detailed directions in this report to accomplish each of these steps. Harvest time will come much sooner than you may think!

Lesson at a Glance

Chapter 13   Lesson 4

Overview This lesson offers guidance in writing a clearly organized report.

Objectives

- To use an outline as a guide to writing.
- To develop a report with a topic paragraph, a body, and a summary paragraph.

Student Pages 281–285

Reading Vocabulary

accomplish (6)   successfully
introduction (6)   summary (8)

Teaching Suggestions

- **Introducing the Lesson**
Tell students that professional writers of factual information almost always work from an outline. A publishing company usually asks to see a writer's outline before buying the book. Ask students why an outline is so important to professional writers (and to student writers, too).

- **Reviewing Skills** Have students offer suggestions for a topic sentence that could introduce a paragraph on each of these topics: Choosing a Pet, Careers in Construction, How to Take a Great Photograph.

Reading Vocabulary

advise (5)   nursery (5)
attitude (6)   parentheses
effective (7)   reputable (10)

■ **Presenting Activity A**

Have students compare Mike's topic paragraph on page 281 with his outline on page 279. Help them to see how the main topics are worked into the sentences of this topic paragraph.

Activity A Answers

Answers will vary. A sample topic paragraph is given.

Keeping in Shape

People always say they want to look good and feel good. How can they accomplish their goals? Keeping in shape means sticking to a routine. It is essential to eat the right foods. Daily exercise and proper rest are important. A person's attitude can make a big difference, too.

■ **Presenting Activity B**

Have students refer to the main topics of their outline as they develop their topic paragraph.

Activity B Answers

Answers will vary. Review students' topic paragraphs, encouraging them to come up with their own improvements.

Activity A Write a topic paragraph to introduce a report on keeping in shape. Use the outline below. Write at least one sentence about each main topic.

Keeping in Shape

  I.   Eating the right foods

  II. Exercising daily

  III. Getting proper rest

  IV. Having a good attitude

Activity B Write a topic paragraph for your own report. Write at least one sentence for each main topic from your outline. Try to make the topic of your report sound interesting to your readers.

Using Direct Quotations

Most of your report should be written in your own words. Sometimes it is effective to write the exact words of an author of one of your sources. When you were taking notes, you paraphrased most information. You used quotation marks around any words you copied. You jotted down the page where you found the quotation.

Study the example below. Notice how Mike has included a direct quotation in his paragraph. Notice the page number in parentheses. It tells where the quotation was found.

> Choosing the best seed for your garden is important. Scientists Robert Wiest and Augusta Low make this point: "Except in special cases, it pays the gardener to buy seeds from reputable nurseries and not to depend on home-grown supplies." (p. 24) They also advise gardeners to order seed well ahead of planting time.

Activity C   Read Mike's bibliography card and note card below. Then write the answers to the questions that follow.

Wiest, Robert, and Augusta Low. "Backyard Vegetables." Natural Homes Magazine 3 (January 1995) 24-28.

Preparing Soil

To have good soil you need organic matter — that's partly rotten plants. Leaves, lawn clippings, and straw will do. Gardeners should have a compost pile. "On some soils with naturally high fertility, only nitrogen or compost may be needed." (p. 25) Only add lime if tests show that it is needed.

Wiest & Low, p. 25

---

1) What was the source of Mike's information?

2) Was this information taken from a book or from a magazine?

3) Which sentence is a direct quotation? How can you tell?

4) From what page was this direct quotation copied?

Activity D   Write a paragraph about preparing soil. Paraphrase the information from the note card above. Use the direct quotation in your paragraph. Remember to indicate the source and to use quotation marks. Include the page number after the direct quotation.

Reading Vocabulary

compost	organic (10)
fertility	rotten (5)
indicate (6)	

■ Presenting Activity C

Compare the bibliography card and the note card shown. Briefly review the purpose of each.

Activity C Answers

1) The source of Mike's information was the article "Backyard Vegetables" by Robert Wiest and Augusta Low.   2) The article came from a magazine titled *Natural Homes Magazine*.
3) "On some soils with naturally high fertility, only nitrogen or compost may be needed." The quotation marks show that this sentence was copied exactly from the article.   4) The quotation was copied from page 25 of the article.

■ Presenting Activity D

Have a volunteer read aloud the information on Mike's note card. Briefly discuss the information before students proceed to write their paragraphs.

Activity D Answers

Answers will vary. A sample paragraph is given.

Gardeners should remember that good soil is really rotten! Plants need soil filled with rotting plants, also called organic matter. Gardeners can work leaves, lawn clippings, and straw into the soil, and they should keep a compost pile. Scientists Robert Wiest and Augusta Low say that some soils have "naturally high fertility" (p. 25). Fertile soils may need only nitrogen or compost. A soil test will tell whether lime is needed.

Reading Vocabulary

definite (6)   pluck (5)
limit (5)   satisfaction (6)

■ Presenting Activity E

Have students compare the summary paragraph sample shown on this page with the topic paragraph for the same report, shown on page 281. They should see that each paragraph presents the same ideas in different ways.

Activity E Answers

Answers will vary. A sample summary paragraph is given.

Fitness is not just a fad. Keeping fit makes people feel better. To become fit and stay fit, people should eat healthy foods, exercise daily, and get the proper rest. Perhaps the most important requirement for keeping in shape is having a positive attitude with plenty of enthusiasm.

LEARNING STYLES

 Visual/Spatial
Have the students illustrate the summary paragraph on page 284. First, divide the class into five groups. Assign Group 1 sentences #1 and 2 of the paragraph. Assign Group 2, sentence #3; Group 3, sentence #4; Group 4, sentence #5; Group 5, sentence #6. Ask each group to create one or more illustrations for its sentence or sentences. Post these pictures in sequence. Then ask someone to read the paragraph aloud while pointing to the appropriate picture. Discuss the logic and sequence of the paragraph's ideas.

Writing Summary Paragraphs

End your report with a summary paragraph. It repeats the main points of your report. A summary paragraph does not have to be long. It brings the report to a definite end.

Mike wrote this summary paragraph for his report. Notice how it sums up the main topics of his outline on page 279.

> Vegetables will grow even where there is limited space. If you want to see for yourself, just follow the steps that have been given in this report. Start by making a plan, preparing the soil, and choosing seeds. Caring for the plants can bring great satisfaction. Then you can have the satisfaction of plucking ripe vegetables. Finally, you will enjoy many delicious meals!

Activity E   Look back to the topic paragraph you wrote for Activity A. Think about the information that might have been included in the report "Keeping in Shape." Write a summary paragraph that could come at the end of that report.

Lesson 4 Review

Follow your outline, and you will write your report smoothly. Remember the three main parts of a report: the topic paragraph, the body, and the summary paragraph.

Part A Review your knowledge of reports. Write the letter of the correct answer for each question below.

1) When you put an author's information into your own words, what are you doing?
   a) outlining   b) paraphrasing   c) reporting

2) What do you use as a guide when you write your report?
   a) note cards   b) the title   c) an outline

3) Which part of the report is always more than one paragraph?
   a) the topic sentence   b) the body   c) the summary

4) What is another name for the topic paragraph?
   a) an introduction   b) an outline   c) a term paper

5) Why should you put quotation marks around an author's exact words?
   a) to show that you have borrowed someone else's words
   b) to show that you are paraphrasing
   c) to show a bibliography

Part B Continue writing your report. You should have a collection of note cards, an outline, a title, and a topic paragraph. Take these remaining steps:

1) Write the body of your report. Write good paragraphs about the main topics and subtopics. Remember to include facts, details, examples, illustrations, and reasons. Use direct quotations (with page numbers) to emphasize important facts.

2) Make your last paragraph a summary of important points.

3) After you write your report, proofread it carefully. Revise it and rewrite it. Correct any mistakes.

4) Write the final report. Use a word processing program if possible. If you are handwriting, use ink.

Reading Vocabulary

emphasize (7)   process (6)
handwriting

Part A Answers

1) b 2) c 3) b 4) a 5) a

Part B Answers

Answers will vary. Set a deadline that allows enough time for students to turn their outlines and note cards into a report. Each report should begin with a topic paragraph, include a body of several paragraphs, and end with a summary paragraph. Remind students to proofread using the tips on page 185 of the student book. The final version should be word-processed or neatly written in ink. Students will complete the report with a bibliography, discussed in the next lesson.

Follow-up Activity

Each student may create a five-question multiple choice quiz about the information in his or her report. Partners then exchange reports. After reading the other's report, each partner takes the quiz. By discussing quiz answers, partners can make decisions about improving their own reports—clarifying points, adding missing information, and so on.

Lesson at a Glance

Chapter 13   Lesson 5

Overview This lesson presents guidelines for writing a bibliography.

Objective

- To complete a report with a bibliography.

Student Pages 286–289

Teacher's Resource Library

   Activity 52

   Workbook Activity 59

Reading Vocabulary

data (9)   journal (5)
italics (6)

Teaching Suggestions

■ Introducing the Lesson

Show students a bibliography from a published work of nonfiction. Ask for their ideas about why bibliographies are included in such works. They may express their understanding that the author of the book is showing the thoroughness of the research, giving credit to other authors, and also helping readers who want to do more research on the subject.

■ Reviewing Skills
Write on the board the words *comma, colon, quotation marks, period, exclamation point, parentheses,* and *abbreviation.* Have volunteers come to the board to show an example of each being used in a sentence.

The last step in writing a report or term paper is completing the bibliography. You have been using index cards to record information about each source. Your report will end with an alphabetic list of the sources you used.

Study the sample bibliography below. Notice the different forms used for a book, a periodical, and an encyclopedia. Here are two points to remember:

- If you are word processing, use italics for all titles of books or magazines. Otherwise, underline the titles.

- Use quotation marks around titles of articles in magazines or encyclopedias.

Bibliography

Allen, G., and M.K. Howard. *The History of Computers.* Chicago: Acme Books Co., 1996.

Brown, J.K., ed. *The Computer Encyclopedia.* New York: Computer Publications, Inc., 1995.

"Computer." *World Encyclopedia.* Vol. 3, 1996, 119–127.

"Computers of the Nineteenth Century." *Data World* 8 (March 1997) 54–57.

Evan, Stacey. "Computers Yesterday and Today." *The Computer Journal* 2 (August 1998) 9–11.

Activity A Use the sample bibliography on page 286 to answer these questions.

1) Why is the book *The History of Computers* listed before *The Computer Encyclopedia*?

2) What information comes first in each entry?

3) Who wrote the article in *The Computer Journal*?

4) What does the abbreviation *ed.* mean?

5) Which two entries are periodicals?

6) In book entries, what punctuation mark is used after the place of publication?

7) If you were handwriting this bibliography, how would you show the title of a book or periodical?

8) What does the number 2 mean after the title *The Computer Journal*?

9) When was the book by Allen and Howard published?

10) Read carefully. What happens if the author is unknown?

Activity B Study the sample bibliography entries on page 286. Then write the following entries in alphabetic order. Put each set of facts into the correct form. Be sure that your punctuation is correct.

<u>Basic Car Care</u> by Blakeley Richard. The book was published in Seattle by Automotive Publications in 1995.

"Fix It Yourself," an article by T. Ramirez in <u>The Car Magazine</u>, Volume 7, March 1999, on pages 67–72.

"Automobiles," in <u>Universal Encyclopedia</u>, Volume 1, 1995, on pages 144–152. No author is given.

<u>The History of Automobiles</u>, K.L. Lee, editor. The book was published in Boston by Cars and Company in 1996.

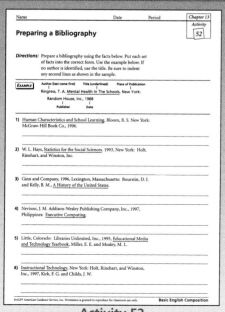

Activity 52   Workbook Activity 59

Reading Vocabulary
automotive   universal (8)
punctuation (7)

■ **Presenting Activity A** Go over the sample bibliography entries on page 286 with students. Answer their questions about any points in it.

Activity A Answers
1) The author's last name *Allen* comes before the last name *Brown* in the alphabet. **2)** The first word is the last name of an author or the first important word of the title. **3)** The article "Computers Yesterday and Today" was written by Stacey Evan. **4)** The abbreviation *ed.* stands for *editor.* **5)** The two periodical entries are "Computers of the Nineteenth Century" in *Data World* and "Computers Yesterday and Today" in *The Computer Journal.* **6)** A colon comes after the place of publication. **7)** The title of a book or periodical should be underlined. **8)** The number 2 is the volume number. **9)** The book by Allen and Howard was published in 1996. **10)** If the author is unknown, the title of the work is listed first.

■ **Presenting Activity B** Tell students to decide whether a book, an encyclopedia, or a periodical is named in each entry. They then look for that kind of entry in the sample bibliography on page 286 and use it as a model.

Activity B Answers
"Automobiles." <u>Universal Encyclopedia.</u> Vol. 1, 1995, 144–152.

Lee, K.L., ed. <u>The History of Automobiles.</u> Boston: Cars and Co., 1996.

Ramirez, T. "Fix It Yourself." <u>The Car Magazine</u> 7 (March 1999) 67–72.

Richard, Blakely. <u>Basic Car Care.</u> Seattle: Automotive Publications, 1995.

■ Presenting Activity C

Read through the four listed steps with students. Have them assemble and alphabetize their bibliography cards.

Activity C Answers

Answers will vary. Students should list each source used alphabetically by author's last name or by title if no author is given. They should italicize or underline each book or magazine title and use quotation marks around each article title.

Activity C Make a bibliography for your report. Start by getting your stack of bibliography cards. Then follow these steps.

1) Put your cards in alphabetic order according to the author's last name.

2) If there is no author, use the first important word of the title of the article or book.

3) Copy the information from each bibliography card to make a list.

4) Use the correct bibliographic form. Refer to the samples in this lesson on page 286.

Lesson 5 | Review

The last pages of your report should be your bibliography. A bibliography is an alphabetic list of all the sources you used to write your report. Make sure to record all details about authors, titles, publishers, and dates. Use the correct form for each bibliographic entry.

Part A   Read the five bibliographic entries below. Rewrite them in correct alphabetic order. Find the mistakes in each entry. Look for order, capitalization, and punctuation. Write each entry correctly.

Eating the right foods, A.L. Smith. Good Food Journal, May 1999, Volume 7, page 19.

Franklin, Sandra. Food and You. Nutrition Books, Inc., Chicago, 1997.

Gomez, C.V. The Right Kind of Exercise. NY, New York Book Co., 1998.

W.L. Fisher. Think Positive! 1998, Boston: Good Thoughts Press, Inc.

Young, J.F., ed. A Good Night to All. Carson City, NE: Carson City Press, 1996.

Part B   Proofread the bibliography you wrote for your report. Revise it if you need to. Correct any mistakes.

Part A Answers

Fisher, W.L. Think Positive! Boston: Good Thoughts Press, Inc., 1998.

Franklin, Sandra. Food and You. Chicago: Nutrition Books, Inc., 1997.

Gomez, C.V. The Right Kind of Exercise. New York: New York Book Co., 1998.

Smith, A.L. "Eating the Right Foods." Good Food Journal 7 (May 1999) 19.

Young, J.F., ed. A Good Night to All. Carson City, NE: Carson City Press, 1996.

Part B Answers

Answers will vary. Students should complete a correct final version of their bibliography.

Follow-up Activity

Students may choose any five books or magazines. They use them to write five correct bibliographic entries in an alphabetic list.

Chapter 13 Review

The Teacher's Resource Library includes two parallel forms of the Chapter 13 Mastery Test. The difficulty level of the two forms is equivalent. You may wish to use one form as a pretest and the other form as a posttest.

Final Mastery Test

The Teacher's Resource Library includes the Final Mastery Test. This test is pictured on pages 304–305 of this Teacher's Edition. The Final Mastery Test assesses the major learning objectives of this text, with emphasis on Chapters 7–13.

Reading Vocabulary

dialogue (7)	memo
directory (7)	outfielder
footnote	outstanding (6)
irregular (7)	textbook
lifetime	waltz (6)

Part A Answers

1) Yes 2) Yes 3) Yes 4) Yes
5) Yes 6) No 7) Yes 8) No
9) Yes 10) Yes

Part B Answers

Names of sources may vary.

1) waltz, dictionary 2) Myanmar, atlas 3) motorcycle, encyclopedia
4) peach, encyclopedia
5) computer, encyclopedia
6) crow, blue jay; encyclopedia
7) basketball, encyclopedia
8) mile records, almanac
9) Anderson, biographical dictionary 10) US presidents, almanac

Part C Answers

Answers will vary. A sample paraphrase is given for each sentence.

1) Roberto Clemente played outfield for the Pittsburgh Pirates. He had a lifetime batting average of .317 and was an outstanding player. 2) Nicaragua is larger than other Central American countries.

Part A   Decide which topics listed below are included in this textbook, *Basic English Composition*. Use the table of contents and the index. If the topic is included, write *Yes*. If the topic is not included, write *No*.

1) Punctuating dialogue
2) Forms of irregular verbs
3) Using a dictionary
4) Topic sentences
5) Chronologic order
6) Footnotes
7) Outlines
8) Using telephone directories
9) Writing memos
10) Writing a summary

Part B   Read each question below. For each one, name the key words you would look up to find the answer. Tell what source you would use to find the answer.

1) What is the dance called the waltz?
2) Where is the Asian country of Myanmar?
3) When were motorcycles invented?
4) Can peaches be grown in a cold climate?
5) How big was the first electronic computer?
6) Are crows and blue jays related?
7) Where did basketball begin?
8) What is the record for running the mile?
9) Who was Marian Anderson?
10) Who was the president of the United States after Abraham Lincoln?

Part C   Read these sentences of information. Paraphrase each one. Write the same information in your own words.

1) With a lifetime batting average of .317, Pittsburgh Pirates outfielder Roberto Clemente was an outstanding baseball player.
2) Nicaragua is the largest nation in Central America.

Chapter 13 Mastery Test A

(Teacher's Resource Library pages shown)

Chapter 13 Mastery Test A
Chapter 13 Mastery Test A page 1

Part A Match each step in planning a report with the correct purpose of the step. Write the letter of the purpose on the blank line.

1) _____ Prepare a bibliography
2) _____ Make an outline
3) _____ Choose a topic
4) _____ Write the report
5) _____ Find information and take notes

a) To narrow your subject to one you can handle in a report
b) To prepare a clear report on your chosen topic
c) To gather enough information to cover your subject
d) To organize the information in the report
e) To provide the source of the information in your report

Part B Write the reference that is the best place to find the information needed. Write *Almanac, Atlas, Who's Who, Periodicals, Encyclopedia, Library catalog,* or *Reader's Guide.*

1) A short description of a famous living athlete
2) Current information about safety
3) Titles of magazine articles about football
4) Maps of the United States
5) Current facts about many topics

Chapter 13 Mastery Test A, continued
Chapter 13 Mastery Test A page 2

Part C Rearrange this list of topics and subtopics into a logical order. Write a topic outline.

Title: Dental Care

Fillings, crowns, and other repairs
Flossing
Periodic x-ray examinations
Special care
Brushing
Rinsing between meals
Professional care
Daily care
Regular dental visits
Braces

Part D Alphabetize these bibliography entries. Write a number from 1 to 5 in front of each item to show the correct alphabetic order.

1) _____ Pruitt, B. E. "Drug Abuse Prevention Programs: Do They Work?" *NASSP Bulletin* (April 1993) 37–49.
2) _____ "Alcohol and Youth." *Alcohol World* 15 (1991) 1.
3) _____ Taylor, C. *The House That Crack Built.* San Francisco: Chronicle Books, 1991.
4) _____ Hyde, M. *Know About Abuse.* New York: Walker & Company, 1992.
5) _____ Collingwood, T. R., R. Reynolds, B. Jester, and D. Debord. "Enlisting Physical Education for the War on Drugs." *The Journal of Physical Education, Recreation, and Dance* 63 (February 1992) 25.

Chapter 13 Mastery Test A

3) The animal known as the big brown bat is actually only about four inches long.

4) Hurricanes are damaging storms often accompanied by rain and high tides.

5) Whatever is stored in a computer's RAM (Random Access Memory) is lost when the computer is turned off.

Part D Make a neat, final copy of your own report. Make a title page.

The History of Computers
Amanda O'Hara
June 9, 1998

Assemble the report in this order:

1. Title page

3. Bibliography

2. Report

4. Blank page at end

Your goal was to write a well-organized, fact-filled, interesting report. How well do you think you reached your goal? Write a few sentences to answer that question.

Test Taking Tip Study any examples that follow a set of directions in a test. Make sure you understand why the example is done as shown. If the example is not clear to you, read the directions again.

Writing a Report Chapter 13 **291**

(Part C Answers, continued)
3) The big brown bat is not really big. It is only four inches long.
4) Hurricanes bring rain, high tides, and damage.   **5)** RAM is a computer's Random Access Memory. When the computer is turned off, RAM is lost.

Part D Answers

Review and display students' final reports. Have a conference with each student to discuss their self-evaluations.

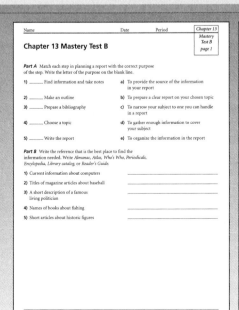

Chapter 13 Mastery Test B

Glossary

Action verb—(ak´shən vèrb) a word that expresses action in a sentence; it tells what someone or something does: *Throw* the ball. They *run* fast. Please *think* of an answer. (p. 50)

Adjective—(aj´ ik tiv) a word that describes a noun or pronoun; it tells how many, what kind, or which one (p. 47)

Adverb—(ad´ vèrb) a word that answers questions about a verb, an adjective, or another adverb; it tells *when, how, how often, where,* or *to what degree* (p. 135)

Agreement—(ə grē´ mənt) the logical match between two elements of a sentence (p. 32)

Anecdote—(an´ ik dōt) a very short story about an interesting or amusing happening (p. 194)

Antecedent—(an tə sēd´ nt) the noun to which a pronoun refers (p. 40)

Apostrophe—(ə pos´ trə fē) a punctuation mark used to replace missing letters in a contraction *(doesn't)* or to show possession *(Mary's* coat) (p. 65)

Bibliography—(bib lē og´ rə fē) a list of books and periodicals that have been used to find information (p. 272)

Body—(bod´ ē) the part of a paragraph that discusses the main idea; these sentences can include reasons, facts, examples, or illustrations (p. 169)

Business letter—(biz´ nis let´ ər) a formal message written to a person or an organization (p. 249)

Capital letter—(kap´ ə təl let´ ər) the uppercase form of a letter: *A, B, C,* and so on (p. 2)

Case—(kās) the form of a noun or pronoun that tells its relation to other words in a sentence (p. 43)

Catalog—(kat´ l og) a list of items arranged in a special way (p. 262)

Chronological order—(kron ə loj´ ə kəl ôr´ dər) arrangement according to time, usually from oldest to most recent (p. 196)

Command—(kə mand´) a sentence that tells or orders someone to do something (p. 12)

Common noun—(kom´ ən noun) the general name of a person, place, thing, or idea; it begins with a lowercase letter: *child, playground, swing, happiness* (p. 47)

Comparative form—(kəm par´ ə tiv fôrm) the form of an adjective or adverb used to compare two people, places, things, or actions; it is formed by adding *-er* to the base word or by using the word *more* or *less*: small, *smaller*; quickly, *more quickly, less quickly* (p. 138)

Compare—(kəm pâr´) to point out ways in which two or more things are alike or different (p. 211)

Comparison—(kəm pâr´ ə sən) a statement about how two or more things are alike or different (p. 211)

Compound subject—(kom´ pound sub´ jikt) two subjects joined by *and* (p. 38)

Conclusion—(kən klü´ zhən) a logical judgment based on evidence; often presented at the end of a paragraph or an essay (p. 173)

Conjunction—(ken jungk´ shən) a word used to connect words or phrases or to combine complete ideas in sentences: *and, or, but* (p. 118)

Consistent—(kən sis´ tənt) following the same rules; staying the same (p. 53)

Contraction—(kən trak´ shən) a shortened form of one or two words; an apostrophe stands for the missing letters: *they're, he'll, jumpin'* (p. 86)

Dependent clause—(di pen´ dənt klöz) a group of related words that contains a subject and a verb but that does not express a complete idea *(Before the phone rang)* (p. 156)

Dialogue—(dī´ ə lòg) the words that people or story characters say to each other (p. 17)

Direct comparison—(də rekt´ kəm par´ ə sən) an expression showing that two things have similar qualities; also called a *metaphor* (p. 212)

Direct quotation—(də rekt´ kwō tā´ shən) sentences reporting the exact words that someone said; quotation marks enclose these exact words (p. 22)

Discuss—(dis kus´) to tell about; a discussion should include the good and the bad characteristics of a topic; a discussion may include the writer's opinion about the topic (p. 225)

E

End punctuation mark—(end pungk chü ā´ shən märk) a mark that comes at the end of a sentence and tells the reader where the complete idea ends; the three end punctuation marks are: *period (.), question mark (?),* and *exclamation mark (!)* (p. 2)

Essay—(es´ ā) a short piece of writing about a single subject or topic (p. 223)

Exaggerate—(eg zaj´ ə rāt) to overstate; to say that something is greater than it is (p. 213)

Exclamation—(ek sklə mā´ shən) an expression of strong feeling (p. 12)

F

Feminine pronoun—(fem´ ə nen prō´ noun) a word that replaces a noun naming a female person; the feminine pronouns are *she, her, hers, herself* (p. 42)

Fiction—(fik´ shən) an imaginary story; writing based largely on the writer's imagination (p. 194)

Fragment—(frag´ mənt) a group of words that does not express a complete thought; a phrase or clause incorrectly treated as a sentence (p. 122)

G

Gender—(jen´ dər) the characteristic of nouns and pronouns that tells they are masculine *(man, he)*, feminine *(woman, she)*, or neuter *(puppy, it)* (p. 42)

H

Helping verb—(hel´ ping vėrb) a verb form that helps main verbs to express time: We *must* go. I *have* cooked. Laura *will* see us. The dog *has been* eating. (p. 50)

Homonyms—(hom´ ə nimz) words that sound alike but have different meanings and spellings (p. 74)

I

Identify—(ī den´ tə fī) to tell the most important characteristics of something; these characteristics make the person, place, or thing different or recognizable (p. 221)

Independent clause—(in də pen´ dənt klòz) a group of words that includes a subject and a verb; it may be written alone as a complete sentence, or it may be combined with another clause (p. 155)

Index—(in´ deks) an alphabetic list of all topics and subtopics in a book; each listing is followed by the numbers of pages on which information is found (p. 267)

Indirect comparison—(in də rekt´ kəm pâr´ ə sən) an expression using *like* or *as* to show that things are like each other in a certain way; also called a *simile* (p. 212)

Indirect quotation—(in də rekt´ kwō tā´ shən) sentences that report what someone said without using the speaker's exact words (p. 22)

Investigate—(in ves´ tə gāt) to search thoroughly; to examine (p. 264)

Irregular plural noun—(i reg´ yə lər plùr´ əl noun) a noun that forms its plural in an unusual way, not with the usual *-s* or *-es*: mouse, *mice;* foot, *feet;* man, *men* (p. 66)

Irregular verb—(i reg´ yə lər vėrb) a verb that does not form its past and past participle by adding *-ed* to the present tense form: *eat, ate, eaten* (p. 56)

K

Key words—(kē wėrdz) the words you look up to find information on a topic; they name what your question is about (p. 270)

M

Masculine pronoun—(mas´ kyə lin prō´ noun) a word that replaces a noun naming a male person; the masculine pronouns are *he, him, his, himself* (p. 42)

Memorandum—(mem ə ran´ dəm) an informal message written in special form and frequently used in the business world; often shortened to *memo* (p. 235)

a	hat	e	let	ī	ice	ò	order	ù	put	sh	she	ə	a in about
ā	age	ē	equal	o	hot	oi	oil	ü	rule	th	thin		e in taken
ä	far	ėr	term	ō	open	ou	out	ch	child	ᴛʜ	then		i in pencil
â	care	i	it	ȯ	saw	u	cup	ng	long	zh	measure		o in lemon
													u in circus

Message—(mes´ij) communication, either written or spoken (p. 232)

Metaphor—(met´ ə fôr) see *Direct comparison* (p. 212)

Modifier—(mod´ ə fī ər) a word that describes another word in a sentence (p. 132)

N

Neuter pronoun—(nü´ tər prō´ noun) a word that replaces the name of any place, thing, or idea in a sentence; neuter singular pronouns are *it*, *its*, *itself* (p. 42)

Nominative case—(nom´ ə nə tiv kās) the form of a pronoun that shows it is being used as a subject: *I* sing; *he* dances; *we* perform (p. 43)

Nonfiction—(non fik´ shən) writing that expresses facts and ideas; a true story, rather than an imaginary one (p. 194)

Noun—(noun) the name of a person, place, thing, or idea: *teacher, museum, ball, heroism* (p. 32)

Number—(num´ bər) the characteristic of a noun or pronoun that tells whether it is singular or plural (p. 43)

O

Objective case—(ab jek´ tiv kās) the form of a pronoun that shows it is being used as an object: sing with *me*; hold *him*; perform for *us* (p. 43)

Outline—(out´ līn) a list of information arranged by main topics and subtopics; an outline is a plan; an outline provides a framework for a report (p. 276)

P

Paragraph—(par´ ə graf) a group of sentences about one idea or topic; it usually has three parts: a topic sentence or introduction, a body, and a conclusion or summary (p. 164)

Paraphrase—(par´ ə frāz) to express someone else's ideas in your own words (p. 274)

Past participle—(past pär´ tə sip əl) a principal part of a verb, used to form the perfect tenses (p. 55)

Periodicals—(pir ē od´ ə kəlz) any printed materials published at regular intervals; magazines and newspapers (p. 269)

Personal letter—(pėr´ sə nəl let´ ər) an informal message written to a friend or a relative (p. 242)

Personal narrative—(pėr´ sə nəl nar´ ə tiv) a true story told from the viewpoint of the narrator (p. 194)

Persuade—(pər swād´) to write or talk in a convincing way; to give reasons and facts that convince others to act or believe in a certain way; to appeal to feelings in order to convince (p. 191)

Phrase—(frāz) a group of words that does not contain a subject or predicate, such as a prepositional phrase or a verb phrase (p. 144)

Plural—(plür´ əl) referring to more than one person, place, or thing: *houses, nations, doctors, they* (p. 32)

Point of view—(point ov vyü) an opinion; the way in which something is looked at (p. 203)

Positive form—(poz´ ə tiv fôrm) the basic form of an adjective or adverb; it makes no comparison (p. 138)

Possessive case—(pə zes´ iv kās) the form of a pronoun that shows ownership or relationship: The song is *mine*; hold *his* hand; watch *our* performance (p. 43)

Possessive noun—(pə zes´ iv noun) a noun that names the owner of something or names a relationship between people or things; a possessive noun must have an apostrophe: *Mary's* coat; the *woman's* car; the *voters'* opinions (p. 65)

Predicate—(pred´ ə kit) the part of a sentence that tells something about the subject; it always contains a verb (p. 123)

Prepositional phrase—(prep ə zish´ ə nəl frāz) a group of words made up of a preposition and its object; it may be used as either an adjective or an adverb (*to the store, by the road*) (p. 144)

Pronoun—(prō´ noun) a word used in place of a noun (p. 34)

Proofread—(prüf´ rēd) to look for mistakes in spelling, grammar, punctuation, and other things (p. 185)

Proper adjective—(prop´ ər aj´ ik tiv) a describing word formed from a proper noun: *French food* (p. 47)

Proper noun—(prop´ ər noun) the name of a particular person, place, thing, or idea; it begins with a capital letter: *Frances, Osgood Park, U.S. Senate, Stone Age* (p. 47)

Q

Question—(kwes´ chən) a sentence that asks for information (p. 12)

Quotation—(kwō tā´ shən) a passage containing someone's exact spoken or written words; the words are enclosed in quotation marks (" ") (p. 17)

R

Report—(ri pôrt´) an organized summary of information about a topic that has been researched; a report may be written or spoken (p. 260)

Request—(ri kwest´) a mild command; it politely tells someone to do something; it often includes the word *please* (p. 12)

Research—(rē´ sėrch) to look for information about a topic by reading books and periodicals, by observing events, or by questioning experts (p. 264)

Revise—(ri vīz´) to correct errors or to make changes (p. 185)

Rewrite—(rē rīt´) to write again (p. 185)

Run-on sentence—(run on sen´ təns) two or more complete ideas that are not connected correctly: *I have read that book many times I'll read it again, it is my favorite and you'll like it too.* (p. 116)

S

Sentence—(sen´ təns) a group of words containing a subject and a verb and expressing a complete idea (p. 2)

Simile—(sim´ ə lē) see *Indirect comparison* (p. 212)

Singular—(sing´ gyə lər) referring to one person, place, or thing: *house, nation, doctor, it* (p. 32)

Statement—(stāt´ mənt) a sentence that expresses a fact or gives information (p. 12)

State-of-being verb—(stāt ov bē´ ing vėrb) a word that expresses the condition of the subject; it connects the subject with a noun, pronoun, or adjective: Richard *is* my brother. The woman *looks* tired. (p. 50)

Subject—(sub´ jikt) the person, place, or thing that the sentence tells about: *Donald ate a sandwich.* (subject: *Donald*) (p. 32)

Subordinating conjunction—(sə bôrd´ n āt´ ing kən jungk´ shən) a conjunction that joins a dependent clause to an independent clause *(because, when, since)* (p. 156)

Subtopic—(sub´ top ik) a division or a part of a larger topic: *Video games* is one subtopic under the main topic *Computers* (p. 261)

Summary—(sum´ ər ē) a statement that briefly repeats main points, often as the last sentence of a paragraph or the last sentences of an essay (p. 173)

Superlative form—(sə pėr´ lə tiv fôrm) the form of an adjective or adverb used to compare more than two people, places, things, or actions; it is formed by adding *-est* to the base word or by using the word *most* or *least*: small, *smallest*; quickly, *most quickly, least quickly* (p. 138)

Synonyms—(sin´ ə nimz) words that have a similar meaning: *big* and *large; happy* and *glad* (p. 134)

T

Table of contents—(tā´ bəl ov kon´ tents) a list of the parts of a book and the page on which each part begins (p. 267)

Tense—(tens) the form of a verb that expresses time (p. 52)

Term paper—(tėrm pā´ pər) a formal report in which a writer tries to prove a thesis or an idea about a chosen topic (p. 260)

Thesaurus—(thi sôr´ əs) a reference source that lists words and their synonyms (p. 134)

Topic sentence—(top´ ik sen´ təns) a sentence that states the main idea in a paragraph; it is often the first sentence (p. 164)

Transition—(tran zish´ ən) an expression that connects ideas, sentences, or paragraphs *(however, therefore, on the other hand, in the meantime)* (p. 208)

V

Variety—(və rī´ ə tē) a number or collection of many different things (p. 205)

Verb—(vėrb) a word used to express action or state of being: *Donald ate a sandwich.* (action verb: *ate*) *Donald was hungry.* (state-of-being verb: *was*) (p. 32)

Verb phrase—(vėrb frāz) a group of words including a main verb and any helping verbs (p. 50)

a	hat	e	let	ī	ice	ȯ	order	u̇	put	sh	she		a	in about
ā	age	ē	equal	o	hot	oi	oil	ü	rule	th	thin	ə	e	in taken
ä	far	ėr	term	ō	open	ou	out	ch	child	ᴛʜ	then		i	in pencil
â	care	i	it	ȯ	saw	u	cup	ng	long	zh	measure		o	in lemon
													u	in circus

Index

Command, 12
Commas, 5
  with conjunction *and,* 152
  as incorrect end punctuation, 116–19
  in quotations, 17
Common noun
  capitalization of, 47
  defined, 47
Comparative form
  defined, 138
  irregular, 141
Compare, 211
Comparisons, 138–43
  defined, 211
  direct, 212
  indirect, 212
  making, 211–15
Complete idea, 2
Complete sentences, 122
  answering questions with, 126
  in test answers, 220
  writing, 115–29
Complimentary close, 249
Compound sentence, 118
Compound subject, 38
Computer catalog, 262, 266
  periodical records in, 269
Conclusion
  defined, 173
  in essay answer, 223
Conjunction
  and as, 151–54
  but as, 153–54
  correct usage of, 120
  defined, 118
  other than *and* and *but,* 155–56
  to show connections among ideas, 151
  subordinating, 156–58
Connections
  of ideas, 151–59
  transitions and, 208
Consistent, 53
Contractions
  defined, 86
  list of commonly used, 86–87
  possessive pronouns and, 88–89
Council/counsel, 77
Course names, 47

D

Definitions, 181
Degree, adverbs of, 135
Dependent clause, 156–58

Description
  in essay answer, 224–25
  of event in invitation, 243
Dialogue
  defined, 17
  in story, 195
  words of direct address in, 21
  writing, 17–24
Direct address, 21
Direct comparison, 212–13
Directions, 25
Direct quotation
  defined, 22
  in reports, 282–83
Discuss, 225

E

Either...or, 155
Encyclopedia, 268
End punctuation mark, 2
  choosing correct, 5–7
  for questions, 18
  with quotations, 18
  for statements, 18
Envelope
  for business letters, 254–55
  for personal letters, 244–45
Essay
  answers, 223–27
  defined, 223
Exact adjectives, 134
Exaggerate, 213–14
Exclamation, 12
Exclamation point, 2, 5
  as end punctuation, 15
  quotations and, 17
Explanations, 180–83

F

Feminine pronoun, 42
Fiction, 194
Form
  comparative, 138–41
  positive, 138–41
  superlative, 138–41
Formally/formerly, 83
Fragment, 122–27
Future perfect tense, 52
Future tense, 52

G

Gender, 42
Grammar and usage skills
  antecedents, 40–46

case, 43–44
clauses, 155–58
comparisons, 138–43, 211–15
phrases, 50–51, 144–50
plurals, 32–35, 38, 42–44, 65–69, 91–98
questions, 12, 126, 182, 189–90, 219–29
sentences, 1–9, 11–29, 31–71, 73–113, 115–29,
    131–61, 163–77, 179–99, 201–17, 219–29,
    231–39, 241–57, 259–91
singular, 32–35, 42–44, 66
subject-verb agreement, 32–39
Greeting
    business letter, 249
    personal letter, 242

H

Heading, 249
Hear/here, 75
Helping verbs
    defined, 50
    list of common, 51
    in verb phrase, 51
Homonym, 74
How-to paragraph, 184–87

I

Ideas
    complete, 2
    connecting, 118–19
    incomplete, 124–25
    relating vs. contrasting, 154
    in run-on sentence, 116
    in topic sentence, 164–66
Identify, 221
Incomplete idea, 124–25
Independent clause, 155
Index, 267
Indirect comparison, 212–13
Indirect quotation, 22
Information
    asking for, 188–90
    in business letter, 249
    finding for report, 264–75
    in magazines and newspapers, 269–70
    in memos, 235
    in messages, 232
    paragraphs giving, 180–83
    in reference books, 268
    sentences and, 25–27
Inside address, 249–50
Investigate, 264
Invitation, 243
Irregular comparative and superlative forms, 141

Irregular plural noun, 66, 95
Irregular verbs
    defined, 56
    tables of, 56, 58–63
Its/it's, 88

K

Key words, 270

L

Language names, 47
Less/least, 140–41
Letterhead, 251
Letters
    business, 249–55
    commas in, 21
    to keep in touch, 246–47
    parts of, 242, 249–50
    personal, 242–48
    thank-you, 244
    writing, 241–57
Library catalog, 262, 264
    reference books in, 268
Loose/lose, 84

M

Mailing address, 245
Main idea
    developing the, 169–72
    in paragraph title, 167
    in summary sentence, 173
    in topic sentences, 167
Main verb, 51
Masculine pronoun, 42
Memo/memorandum
    defined, 235
    messages and, 231–39
Messages
    defined, 232
    memorandums and, 231–39
    writing, 232–34
Metaphor, 212. *See also* Direct comparison
Microfiche, 262
Modified block style, 251
Modifier, 132
More/most, 139, 141–42

N

Names, plurals of, 96–97
Neither...nor, 155
Neuter pronoun, 42
Newspaper, 269

Nominative case
    defined, 43
    personal pronouns in, 44
Nonfiction, 194
Notes, taking, 271–73
Not only…but also, 155
Nouns
    common, 47
    defined, 32
    irregular plural, 66
    as objects of prepositions, 144
    plural, 32
    pronouns and, 40
    proper, 47
    singular, 32
Number
    defined, 43
    pronoun and antecedent agreement in, 43–44

O

Object of preposition, 144
Objective case
    defined, 43
    personal pronouns in, 44
Optional notations, 250
Order, report topics, 277
Outline, 276, 278–79

P

Paragraphs
    answering questions in, 182
    art of persuasion in, 191–93
    asking for information in, 188–90
    based on definitions, 181
    body of, 169
    business letter, 250
    combining, 171
    comparing in, 211–15
    conclusions of, 173–75
    defined, 164
    essay answer, 223–27
    goals of, 180
    how-to, 184–87
    improving, 201–17
    informative and explanatory, 180–83
    in letters, 242–44, 249–53
    main idea of, 169–72
    parts of, 163–77
    proofreading and revising, 185–86
    purpose of, 179–99
    sentences in, 180–99, 205–07
    summary, 173–75, 284
    telling story in, 194–97

topic, 281
    topic sentence of, 164–68, 202–04
    transitions in, 208–10
Paraphrase, 274
Parts of speech
    adjectives, 47, 132–34, 136
    adverbs, 135–37, 205–06
    conjunctions, 118, 151–58
    nouns, 32, 40, 47, 66, 144
    prepositions, 144–50, 205–06
    pronouns, 34–35, 40–46, 144
    verbs, 32–39, 50–64
Past participle, 55
Past/passed, 77
Past perfect tense, 52
Past tense, 52
Period
    at end of answer, 14
    as end punctuation, 2, 5
    at end of statement, 12, 18
Periodicals, 269–70
Personal letter, 242–48
Personal narrative, 194
Personal/personnel, 83
Personal pronouns, 44
Persuade, 191
Phrase
    adjective, 146, 148–50
    adverb, 147–50
    defined, 144
    prepositional, 144–50
    title as, 167
    verb, 50
Piece/peace, 76
Plain/plane, 78
Planning to write
    essay answers, 223–27
    letters
        business, 249–53
        personal, 242–44, 246–48
    memos and messages, 232–37
    paragraphs, 164–75, 180–97
    reports, 260–63
    sentences, 132–59
Plural nouns, 32–33
    apostrophe with, 66
    irregular, 66, 95
    of nouns ending with
        -f or *-fe,* 93
        -o, 94
        -y, 92
    plural pronouns and, 42
    proper, 96–97

Midterm Mastery Test

Midterm Test Page 1

Midterm Mastery Test

Part A Find 30 spelling, punctuation, and capitalization mistakes in these sentences. Circle the errors. Then rewrite each sentence correctly on the blank lines.

1) our familys are definately intresting.

2) they are all diffrent in some ways.

3) Amanda O'Haras family is small it only has too people.

4) Amanda and her mom go two danceing class togather.

5) The O'Hara's live in a plesant apartment.

6) Laura's father had gave Laura her own room after her older sister Francie got marryed.

7) Before Francie was married it was nessary for Laura and Francie to share a room.

8) Derek is the only "child" at home, to, his sister Tamara works for the goverment in Washington.

9) Mikes family has liveed in Springfield for a long time.

10) Mike's family had lived in Illinois ohio florida, and oregon.

Midterm Test Page 2

Midterm Mastery Test, continued

Part B Write a complete sentence for each item as directed. Punctuate each sentence correctly.

1) Write a sentence that makes a statement.

2) Write a sentence that includes a direct quotation.

3) Write a sentence that uses the conjunction *and*.

4) Write a sentence that includes a proper noun.

5) Write a sentence that joins two complete ideas using the conjunction *however*.

6) Write a sentence that includes a possessive noun.

7) Write a a sentence that is a question.

8) Write a sentence that uses a past tense verb.

9) Write a sentence that uses a prepositional phrase.

10) Write a sentence that uses the contraction *you're*.

11) Write a sentence that uses the possessive pronoun *its*.

Midterm Test Page 3

Midterm Mastery Test, continued

12) Write a sentence that uses an adverb of degree.

13) Write a sentence that makes an exclamation.

14) Write a sentence that joins two complete ideas using the conjunction *but*.

15) Write a sentence that gives a command.

Part C Choose the word in parentheses that correctly completes each sentence. Write the word on the blank line.

1) There are six _____ in Mike's family. (children, childrens)

2) Mike is the _____ child. (older, oldest)

3) The youngest boy, Tim, _____ six. (am, is, are)

4) Tim is the only child who _____ born in Springfield. (was, were)

5) Mike _____ taught his brother Tim to play tennis. (has, have)

6) Tim already plays very _____. (good, well)

7) Because Tim wants to play well, he _____ often. (practices, practiced)

8) Tim's parents _____ him a racket for his birthday. (buyed, bought)

9) _____ racket was not expensive. (Tims, Tim's)

10) Mike thinks that Tim _____ will be a champion. (probable, probably)

11) Tim _____ to enter his first tournament next summer. (plan, plans)

12) He _____ care if he wins or not. (doesn't, don't)

13) Mike _____ Tim to see himself as a winner, however. (telled, told)

14) _____ tennis, swimming, and yard work, the boys will have plenty to do. (Among, Between)

15) Thankfully, the boys _____ a lot of energy. (has, have)

Midterm Test Page 4

Midterm Mastery Test, continued

Part D Circle the correct spelling in each pair of words.

1) acheive — achieve
2) sceince — science
3) beleive — believe
4) foreign — foriegn
5) separate — seperate
6) knifes — knives
7) wifes — wives
8) deer — deers
9) nineteen — ninteen
10) shoping — shopping

Part E Find five sentences in this paragraph. Rewrite them in a list on the lines. Use correct capitalization and punctuation.

Tennis players seem to be younger every year some of the young players are beating their older opponents tim is only six but he can almost beat his brother mike tim has a mean serve and a wicked backhand hey give me a break laughs mike.

1)

2)

3)

4)

5)

Final Mastery Test

Final Mastery Test

Part A Write a complete sentence for each item as directed. Punctuate each sentence correctly.

1) Write a sentence that uses the past participle of the irregular verb *grow*.

2) Write a sentence that uses both a proper noun and a proper adjective.

3) Write a sentence that uses a prepositional phrase as an adverb.

4) Write a sentence that joins two complete ideas using the conjunction *but*.

5) Write a sentence that makes a statement.

Part B Circle the correct spelling in each pair of words.

1)	speeches	speechs	11)	leafs	leaves
2)	cheif	chief	12)	calfs	calves
3)	theifs	thieves	13)	neighbor	nieghbor
4)	weird	wierd	14)	trout	trouts
5)	potatoes	potatos	15)	writeing	writing
6)	cities	citys	16)	boating	boatting
7)	beged	begged	17)	drugist	druggist
8)	consceince	conscience	18)	starry	stary
9)	referal	referral	19)	refusal	refuseal
10)	libary	library	20)	February	Febuary

Basic English Composition

Final Mastery Test Page 1

Final Mastery Test, continued

Part C Find ten sentences in this paragraph. Rewrite them in a list on the lines. Use correct capitalization and punctuation.

The biggest challenge to decision making is knowing your real goals usually we think we understand why we want something it seems clear but it's not have you ever seen a small child scream for a toy and then throw it down when she finally gets it that's because she had a hidden goal everyone has hidden goals sometimes suppose you're buying a new CD are you buying it because you like the songs on it could you have hidden reasons for buying it if you aren't aware of your real goals it's hard to make a good decision that will meet your real needs.

1) _____
2) _____
3) _____
4) _____
5) _____
6) _____
7) _____
8) _____
9) _____
10) _____

Basic English Composition

Final Mastery Test Page 2

Final Mastery Test, continued

Part D Write a topic sentence for each of these titles.

1) My Favorite Movie

2) My Idea of a Perfect Pet

3) The Hobby I Would Like Most

4) The Month I Like Best

5) The Actor or Actress I Most Admire

Part E Write a five-sentence paragraph explaining one of these topics. Write the main idea in the topic sentence. Write three sentences that support the main idea. Write a summary or conclusion as the last sentence.

• What is good music? • What is honesty? • The value of education

Basic English Composition

Final Mastery Test Page 3

Final Mastery Test, continued

Part F Rewrite these sentences to give them variety. Begin each sentence with an adverb or a prepositional phrase.

1) I enjoyed our last vacation.

2) We drove to a campground.

3) We climbed trails.

4) We rode mountain bikes and paddled a canoe.

5) We had campfires and roasted corn.

Part G Write the answer to each question in a complete sentence. Use sentence variety.

1) What is the purpose of a topic sentence?

2) What is the difference between a short answer and an essay?

3) What are the three parts of a paragraph?

4) What does *chronologic order* mean?

5) What is a *sentence fragment*?

Basic English Composition

Final Mastery Test Page 4

Final Mastery Test

Final Mastery Test, continued

Part H Write a memo to your teacher about a question you have. Write the message in a paragraph. Use today's date.

MEMO

To: _____

From: _____

Date: _____

Subject: _____

_____

_____

_____

_____

_____

_____

Part I Write a personal letter to a friend about plans to see each other. Use today's date. Indent each new paragraph. Include the five parts of a personal letter. Sign your letter.

_____

_____

_____

_____

_____

_____

_____

_____

Basic English Composition

Final Mastery Test Page 5

Final Mastery Test, continued

Part J Write an essay in pencil explaining how to write a report. Include the five steps. Include facts about each step. Proofread your work. Erase and revise or correct your essay as needed.

_____

_____

_____

_____

_____

_____

_____

_____

_____

_____

_____

_____

_____

_____

_____

_____

_____

_____

_____

_____

_____

_____

Basic English Composition

Final Mastery Test Page 6

Activity

Activity 1–Looking for Sentences

1) In the spring we have cheerleading tryouts. They last two weeks. Twelve girls are chosen to be on the squad. **2)** Amanda received her yearbook today. She had her friends autograph it. The book was full of color pictures. **3)** The seniors will graduate at the Capital Center. This is an exciting event. Derek will miss his friends. **4)** During the summer Derek will work at a full-time job. He needs to make money for college. He hopes to work many hours. **5)** College is expensive. It is important to plan. Derek will need to choose his classes.

Activity 2–Expressing Ideas in Different Order

Some answers may vary.
1) Immediately we got into traffic. We got into traffic immediately. **2)** Usually everyone goes on vacation in the summer. In the summer everyone usually goes on vacation. **3)** I suddenly saw a huge black rain cloud. I saw a huge black rain cloud suddenly. **4)** Lately the weather has been hot and humid. The weather lately has been hot and humid. **5)** They often have a picnic to celebrate. They have a picnic to celebrate often. **6)** Finally we finished our last exam. We finished our last exam finally. **7)** They ran down the hill carefully. Carefully they ran down the hill. **8)** The sun always is shining on a gorgeous day. On a gorgeous day, the sun is always shining.

Activity 3–Capitalizing and Punctuating Sentences.

1) Getting the yearbook is exciting to Laura. **2)** What is your favorite subject? **3)** Go and answer the phone, Amanda. **4)** The graduation announcement was sent last week. **5)** Did you receive it in the mail? **6)** Here is my report card. **7)** My final grade for math was a *B*. **8)** She cannot wait for school to be out.

Activity 4–Find the Sentences

1) The first president of the United States was George Washington. **2)** He was the son of Augustine Washington and Mary Ball. **3)** His early childhood was spent on the Ferry Farm near Fredericksburg, Virginia. **4)** At the age of 16, he went to live with his half brother Lawrence, who built and named Mount Vernon. **5)** Lawrence died in 1752, and George acquired his property by inheritance. **6)** In 1759, he married Martha Dandridge Custis and managed his family estate at Mount Vernon. **7)** He was unanimously elected president by the electoral college and inaugurated on April 30, 1789, on the balcony of New York's Federal Hall. **8)** He was reelected in 1792 but refused to consider a third term and retired to Mount Vernon. **9)** He had acute laryngitis after a ride in the snow and rain around his estate and died on December 14, 1799.

Activity 5–The Purpose of a Sentence

1) d) What a beautiful day it is! **2) a)** I want a hamburger. **3) c)** Stop asking so many questions. **4) b)** When are we leaving? **5) a)** We will be ready soon. **6) c)** Please be patient. **7) a)** His parents were shocked. *or* **d)** His parents were shocked! **8) a)** I got straight *A*'s for grades. **9) c)** Go get the newspaper.

10) a) He read the sports section. **11) b)** What time are we leaving? **12) a)** The book was due yesterday. **13) a)** A friend is a special person. **14) d)** That's wonderful! **15) c)** Give me twenty dollars.

Activity 6–Find the Purpose of the Sentence

1) Statement–Playing a sport is good exercise. **2)** Question–What is your favorite sport? **3)** Question–Does it matter? **4)** Command–Go and get my dinner, please. **5)** Exclamation–That's beautiful! **6)** Statement–Skiing is an expensive sport. **7)** Question–How many miles did you run? **8)** Command–Stop immediately. *or* Exclamation–Stop immediately! **9)** Statement–A vacation should be a time to relax. **10)** Exclamation–I was shocked! *or* Statement–I was shocked.

Activity 7–Writing Dialogue

1) Laura said, "I don't have enough money." **2)** "I'll lend you some," answered Derek. **3)** "Are you sure?" asked Laura. **4)** Laura said, "I will pay you later when I get my allowance." **5)** "The movie starts at 8:00 P.M.," said Derek. **6)** "Will you be on time?" asked Laura. **7)** "Of course I will!" said Derek. **8)** Amanda asked, "Can I come?" **9)** "Sure, come along," laughed Derek. **10)** "What movie are we going to see?" asked Amanda.

Activity 8–Direct and Indirect Quotations

Answers may vary. Sample answers are given.
A. 1) Amanda said, "I enjoyed the movie." **2)** They said, "We will go to the movies together again." **3)** Laura said, "I will choose the movie next time." **4)** She asked, "Can I call for next week's shows?" **5)** Derek laughed and said, "I am not paying."

B. 1) The lady answered that she was not sure what movies would be playing next week. **2)** Laura asked her when she would know. **3)** The lady answered that they change their movies every Friday. **4)** Laura said that she would call back on Friday. **5)** Amanda said that she should have her allowance by Friday.

Activity 9–Subject and Verb Agreement

1) plans **2)** love **3)** knows **4)** makes **5)** sits **6)** likes **7)** jumps **8)** complete **9)** call **10)** wants

Activity 10–Recognizing Antecedents

1) his–Derek **2)** it–car **3)** her–Laura **4)** his–Derek **5)** his–teacher **6)** their–Laura and Amanda **7)** his–Mr. Smith **8)** I–Amanda **9)** their–boys **10)** it–house

Activity 11–Capitalization of Proper Nouns

Some answers will vary. Sample answers are given.
1) building **2)** Spanish, French **3)** city **4)** Monday, Saturday **5)** Ritz Theater, Radio City Music Hall **6)** president **7)** Ford, Porsche, Honda **8)** continent **9)** holiday **10)** the Rocky Mountains, the Alps **11)** falls *or* waterfalls **12)** *Star Wars, Apollo 13* **13)** soft drink, soda, pop **14)** William Shakespeare, Edgar Allan Poe **15)** Pacific Ocean, Atlantic Ocean

Activity 12–sing Verbs Correctly

Helping verbs are bold.

1) should help **2) has** visited **3) will** collect **4)** jogged
5) is watching **6)** stopped **7) will** receive **8)** purchased

Activity 13–Homonyms

1) to **2)** two **3)** too, to **4)** Two **5)** to, to **6)** too, to
7) two **8)** to **9)** too **10)** to, two

Activity 14–Sound-Alike Words

1) capital **2)** capital **3)** Capitol **4)** capital **5)** capitol
6) capital **7)** Capitol **8)** capital **9)** capitol **10)** capital

Activity 15–Almost Alike

1) advice **2)** advise **3)** advise **4)** advice **5)** advice
6) advice **7)** advise **8)** advice **9)** advice **10)** advise

Activity 16–Find the Misspelled Words

1) friend, runner **2)** Finally, believed, decision **3)** Stopping,
relief, stepping **4)** secretary, piece **5)** experienced, different
6) surprise **7)** forty **8)** realized, minute **9)** immediately,
recommended **10)** privileged, taking

Activity 17–No More Run-On Sentences

1) The weather was not good today. It rained very hard. The power
went off. **2)** I stayed up late last night. I wrote a letter to my sister.
She always enjoys hearing from me. **3)** The baseball game begins
at 7:30 P.M. I will leave after I get off work. I hope that we will get
there on time. **4)** My vacation to Florida was great. It was an
enjoyable and a relaxing trip. It was my first trip to Florida.
5) The test tomorrow will be difficult. It will cover everything that
we have studied for the past month. I plan to go to the library and
study for many hours tonight.

Activity 18–Separating the Ideas

Graduation

Graduation takes place after students have completed a course of
study. People can graduate from a school or college. Graduates
receive a diploma or degree during a ceremony. The ceremony
connected with graduation is called commencement.

Yearbook

A yearbook editor is a person in charge of producing a yearbook.
The position involves many responsibilities. The editor carries out
many duties to meet deadlines. Many hours are usually spent in
drawing layouts, taking pictures, and proofreading pages. One of the
most important responsibilities is to meet the deadlines. Missing
deadlines will result in a fee and a late publication.

Activity 19–Correcting Sentence Fragments

Some answers will vary. Bold words indicate corrections.

1) Sentence **2)** Fragment–The store around the corner **is closed.**
3) Fragment–**Amanda** wrote a letter yesterday. **4)** Sentence
5) Fragment–**We** answered the phone all day. **6)** Fragment–
I got a present from my sisters and brothers. **7)** Sentence
8) Fragment–**Jill worked** on the computer all day. **9)** Fragment–
Sandy went to work at eight o'clock. **10)** Sentence

Activity 20–Completing Sentences

Some answers will vary. Bold words indicate corrections.

1) Run-on–Amanda will **baby-sit. She** expects to be paid well.
2) Fragment–**She is** looking for a job. **3)** Sentence **4)** Run-on–
The sun was **shining. We** enjoyed the day. **5)** Fragment–While he
was doing his homework, **the phone rang.** **6)** Run-on–My teacher
is very proud of **me. She** hopes that I will continue my good study
habits. **7)** Sentence **8)** Fragment–On top of the table **was a
book.** **9)** Run-on–Derek will continue to live at **home. He** wants
to get an apartment soon. **10)** Fragment–Being in a good mood
is **pleasant.**

Activity 21–Comparisons

1) better **2)** fastest **3)** more satisfying **4)** least **5)** worse
6) smaller **7)** oldest **8)** slower **9)** best **10)** happier

Activity 22–Adding Adjectives and Adverbs

Answers will vary. Bold words are sample adjectives or adverbs.
1) I like **chocolate** ice cream with **strawberries** and **butterscotch**
sauce on it. **2)** Derek drives **slowly** in **bad** weather. **3)** The
red-haired girl asked Derek to go to the **early** movie on **Friday**
night. **4)** The **long-distance** runner was **hot** and **exhausted** after
a **ten-mile** run. **5)** The **English** exam lasted **two** hours and was
very difficult. **6)** In **gym** class we had to run **two** miles around the
muddy track. **7)** The **public** library has **reference** books we can
use for **research** projects. **8)** The **delicious** and **filling** dinner was
spinach lasagna. **9)** The florist made an **attractive** arrangement
for the **summer** wedding. **10)** We **always** go to the **beautiful**
beach on the **Fourth of July** weekend.

Activity 23–Prepositional Phrases

1) under the table **2)** with us **3)** at the movies **4)** by plane
5) For lunch **6)** in the front, of the class **7)** from noon, until
one o'clock **8)** on time **9)** with fresh strawberries
10) to the library

Activity 24–Combining Sentences

Answers may vary. Sample answers are given.
1) Monday, Tuesday, and Wednesday it snowed. **2)** Amanda,
Laura, and I like shopping. **3)** Derek was bored, tired, and
hungry. **4)** Laura is sixteen and can drive a car. **5)** She went
shopping and bought an expensive, attractive outfit.
6) McDonald's, Wendy's, and Hardee's are fast food restaurants.

Activity 25–Choosing a Topic Sentence

1) a **2)** b **3)** b **4)** a **5)** b **6)** a **7)** b **8)** a

Activity 26–Choosing a Title

Answers will vary. Two suggested titles are given for each paragraph.
1) Naturalization; Becoming a Citizen of the United States
2) The History of the Liberty Bell; The Philadelphia Liberty Bell
3) The American Flag; The Stars and Stripes

Activity 27–Building a Paragraph With Facts

Responses will vary. A sample paragraph is given.
Skiing is a popular sport. Learning to ski takes much time and
effort. Learning to ski well takes excellent coordination and balance.
Various slopes for different abilities are open in many states. People's

ability to ski changes as they practice. Good snow conditions will have a major effect on how people ski. Skiing takes a lot of energy and is good exercise. No wonder skiing is a popular activity!

Activity 28–Writing a Paragraph
Paragraphs will vary. They should have a topic sentence, a three- or four-sentence body, and a conclusion.

Activity 29–Asking for Information
Answers will vary. Sample questions are given.
1) a) What sizes do you have?   **b)** How much does it cost?
c) Do you guarantee it?   **2) a)** Does it have a warranty?
b) What special features does it have?   **c)** Can I bring it back if it is defective?   **3) a)** Does it have any attachments?   **b)** Does it have a warranty?   **c)** What type of film does it use?   **4) a)** How many bedrooms does it have?   **b)** For how long can it be rented?
c) What is the monthly rent?

Activity 30–Chronologic Order
A) 2   **B)** 6   **C)** 4   **D)** 1   **E)** 5   **F)** 3
Paragraphs will vary. Students must add a topic sentence and a conclusion.

Activity 31–A Short Story
Responses will vary. Events should be in chronologic order.

Activity 32–Explaining Your Ideas
Answers will vary. Sample answers are given.
1) People need to be well informed when buying life insurance.
2) People need to be well informed because many companies are changing their plans, because insurance is expensive, and because many types of insurance exist.   **3)** Understanding a policy is important.   **4)** Answers will vary.

Activity 33–Improving Topic Sentences
Answers will vary. Sample answers are given.
1) A surprise birthday party is always fun.   **2)** Homework can be helpful if you do the assignments.   **3)** Going shopping for a gift can be a very difficult task.   **4)** Valentine's Day is a time to send your sweetheart roses.   **5)** Playing a sport can be not only fun but also challenging.   **6)** Eating crabs for the first time can be an unusual experience.   **7)** A summer vacation should be enjoyable and relaxing.   **8)** Getting a letter in the mail can add a smile to my day.   **9)** Halloween is a time when children like to dress up in costumes.   **10)** Regular exercise is good for the body.

Activity 34–Transitional Words and Phrases
1) Next weekend   **2)** At the end of the day   **3)** however
4) At last   **5)** For example   **6)** Last night   **7)** As a result
8) However   **9)** Soon   **10)** Later that evening

Activity 35–Making Comparisons
1) Direct   **2)** Indirect   **3)** Direct   **4)** Indirect   **5)** Indirect
6) Direct   **7)** Indirect   **8)** Direct   **9)** Indirect   **10)** Indirect

Activity 36–Comparisons
Answers will vary. Sample answers are given.
1) The sunset over the horizon looked like crystal.   **2)** My first day at school seemed like a century.   **3)** My senior term paper was like a nightmare.   **4)** High school graduation was like a miracle come true.   **5)** The dessert was as light as a cloud.   **6)** The Porsche was as expensive as a tray full of diamonds.   **7)** Almost slipping on a banana peel was the funniest thing I ever did.   **8)** In the terrible thunderstorm, our rescue from the boat was like a dream come true.
9) Sky diving is more frightening than a roller coaster ride.
10) The glimpse of the movie star passed as quickly as the flicker of an eyelid.

Activity 37–Writing Short Answers
Some answers will vary.
1) Benjamin Franklin invented the lightning rod and experimented with electricity.   **2)** Yellowstone National Park is located in Wyoming, Idaho, and Montana.   **3)** Edgar Allan Poe was a famous writer.   **4)** The first permanent English colonial settlement in America was in Jamestown, Virginia.   **5)** The planet closest to the sun is Mercury.   **6)** The capital of the United States is Washington, D.C.   **7)** Christopher Columbus was an explorer who came to America in 1492.   **8)** Walt Disney is famous for his motion pictures and his theme parks.   **9)** The Japanese bombed Pearl Harbor on December 7, 1941.   **10)** The first president of the United States was George Washington.

Activity 38–Identifying People, Places, and Things
Some answers will vary.
1) Joseph Stalin was the general secretary of the Communist party of the former U.S.S.R. from 1922 to 1953.   **2)** Posology is the scientific study of drug dosages.   **3)** Hong Kong is a city in China on the southeast coast of the mainland.   **4)** Melton is a heavy woolen cloth with a smooth surface and a short nap.
5) A scatterbrain is a giddy or forgetful person who is incapable of concentrating on important matters or of doing serious thinking.
6) Theodore Roosevelt was the 26th president of the United States.
7) NASA stands for the National Aeronautics and Space Administration.   **8)** An observation car is a railway car with extra large windows in an upper level for viewing the scenery.
9) A trackwalker is a person whose work involves walking along and inspecting sections of railroad track.   **10)** A riot is violence and fighting in a community.

Activity 39–Completing Sentences
Answers may vary slightly.
1) New York City has the largest population.   **2)** Christopher Columbus sailed across the Atlantic Ocean to America in 1492.
3) Washington, D.C., is the capital of the United States.   **4)** The Declaration of Independence was adopted by the Continental Congress on July 4, 1776.   **5)** The oldest national park is Yellowstone.   **6)** Benjamin Franklin invented the lightning rod and bifocal eyeglasses.   **7)** The Japanese attacked and bombed Pearl Harbor, Hawaii, on December 7, 1941.   **8)** The Grand Canyon is located in Arizona.   **9)** The two tallest buildings in the United States are the World Trade Center in New York and the Sears Tower in Chicago.

Activity 40–Writing Essays
Essays will vary.

Activity 41–Messages

All messages are missing both the date and the time. Other missing information is indicated below.

1) When were they supposed to go to the movies?   **2)** Which teacher? When is she calling back?   **3)** Who left the message? When will he or she talk to Coach Jones? Why won't he or she be at practice?   **4)** What message did Derek leave?   **5)** Who left the message? When will they stop by? Which homework assignment?   **6)** Who left the message? What is the phone number? When should the call be returned?   **7)** Who left the message? What message did the boss leave?

Activity 42–Leave a Message

Messages will vary. A sample message is given.

```
To  Rick Bailey
Date [Today's date]  Time [Current time]
      WHILE YOU WERE OUT
Mrs. Bailey
of _____
Phone No. _____

| TELEPHONED        | ✓ | PLEASE CALL    |   |
| WAS IN TO SEE YOU |   | WILL CALL BACK |   |
| WANTS TO SEE YOU  |   | URGENT         |   |
| RETURNED YOUR CALL|   |                |   |

MESSAGE Your dentist appointment
is canceled. Your mother will pick
you up after school to take
you to work.
_____
_____
             Mrs. Johnson
             Message Taken by
```

Activity 43–More About Memos

Answers will vary. Students should include all necessary information in these two memos.

Activity 44–Writing Memos

MEMO

Date: September 10, 20–
To: Mrs. Smith
From: Mrs. K. Hall
Subject: John Hall's doctor's appointment

John Hall has a doctor's appointment today at 1:30 P.M. Please excuse him from school at 1:00 P.M. for this appointment.

MEMO

Date: May 5, 20–
To: Mr. White
From: Elizabeth Proctor
Subject: School spirit

The student body would like to see more school spirit and involvement. We would like to plan a special Brownsville High Sports Day. Would you help us in any way that you can?

Activity 45–Label the Parts of a Personal Letter

Labels are given top to bottom.
Date, Greeting or Salutation, Body, Closing, Signature

Activity 46–Addresses

1) Christopher Jones 1528 Pikestown Road Daytona Beach, FL 32018   **2)** Melissa Thomas Rt. 1, Box 561 Annapolis, MD 21401
3) Mr. John Kennedy 1976 East Gate Way Chula Vista, CA 92013
4) Paul Jacobs 12 Ocean Drive, Apt. 6 San Francisco, CA 94101
5) Ms. Beth Hall Rt. 5, Box 1 Columbus, OH 43085
6) Mary Moran 1375 Maryland Way Hollywood, MD 20636
7) Tom Smith 612 Tenth Avenue Salt Lake City, UT 84110

Activity 47–Writing a Personal Letter

Letters will vary. They should include a date, salutation or greeting, message (body), closing, and signature.

Activity 48–Understanding the Letter

A. 1) No **2)** Yes **3)** No **4)** Yes **5)** No **6)** No **7)** Yes
8) Yes **9)** No **10)** Yes

B. 1) a) the heading or return address **b)** the date **c)** the inside address **d)** the salutation or greeting **e)** the body
f) the closing (or complimentary close) **g)** the handwritten signature **h)** the typed name
2) Accept any three of the following answers.
Business letters: **a)** use standard size paper **b)** usually use white or off-white paper **c)** use only one side of the paper **d)** contain a return address or imprinted letterhead **e)** have a more formal closing **f)** should be typed if possible **g)** have the name of the sender typed under the handwritten signature **h)** have a colon after the salutation **i)** include an inside address

Activity 49–Choosing a Topic

1) a) Narrow **b)** Broad **2) a)** Narrow **b)** Broad
3) a) Broad **b)** Narrow **4) a)** Narrow **b)** Broad
5) a) Broad **b)** Narrow **6) a)** Broad **b)** Narrow
7) a) Narrow **b)** Broad **8) a)** Broad **b)** Narrow

Activity 50–Finding Information

1) Atlas, encyclopedia, almanac **2)** *Who Was Who*, almanac, encyclopedia **3)** Almanac **4)** Encyclopedia **5)** Almanac, encyclopedia **6)** *Who Was Who*, almanac, encyclopedia
7) Almanac, atlas, encyclopedia **8)** Almanac **9)** Encyclopedia, almanac **10)** Almanac

Activity 51–Writing an Outline

Outline B: United Nations
  I. Introduction
      A. Location
      B. Buildings
 II. General Assembly
      A. Composed of
      B. Sessions
      C. Budget and apportion expenses
III. Security Council
      A. Number of members
      B. Responsibility
 IV. Economic and Social Council
      A. Number of members
      B. Purpose
  V. Trusteeship Council
 VI. Secretariat

Activity 52–Preparing a Bibliography

1) Bloom, B.S. <u>Human Characteristics and School Learning</u>. New York: McGraw-Hill Book Co., 1996. **2)** Hays, W.L. <u>Statistics for the Social Sciences</u>. New York: Holt, Rinehart, and Winston, Inc., 1993. **3)** Bourstin, D.J. and B.M Kelly. <u>A History of the United States</u>. Lexington, Massachusetts: Ginn and Company, 1996. **4)** Nevison, J.M. <u>Executive Computing</u>. Philippines: Addison-Wesley Publishing Company, Inc., 1997. **5)** Miller, E.E. and M.L Mosley. <u>Educational Media and Technology Yearbook</u>. Little, Colorado: Libraries Unlimited, Inc., 1995. **6)** Kirk, F.G. and J.W Childs. <u>Instructional Technology</u>. New York: Holt, Rinehart, and Winston, Inc., 1997.

Workbook Activities

Workbook Activity 1–Finding Sentences

1) In the spring we planted a garden. We planted cabbages and peas first. Later we planted tomatoes. **2)** My aunt sent me a book for my birthday. I wrote a letter to thank her. She was pleased. **3)** My friends and I started a band. We practiced three times a week. Soon we sounded very good. **4)** Last night it snowed again. The streets were slippery. This morning we looked in the garage for our sleds. **5)** There was an ad in the newspaper for a file clerk. The person had to put papers in alphabetic order. I decided to apply for the job. **6)** Yesterday my sister went to the library. She wanted to find a book about guitars. Her music teacher told the class to write a report about a musical instrument. **7)** Today there was an announcement on the public address system at school. The coach is having tryouts for the basketball team. My friend and I decided to go. **8)** Every year the senior class produces a play. Usually it is a musical. We have a lot of talent at our school. **9)** What two things must a writer always do? A writer must capitalize the first word of a sentence. He or she also must put a punctuation mark at the end.

Workbook Activity 2–Expressing Ideas

Answers will vary. Sample answers are given.
1) We watch television seldom in the summer. **2)** Usually we are too busy with outdoor activities. **3)** The weather is always sunny and warm where we live. **4)** We have not had much rain lately in our town. **5)** In the background, I suddenly heard thunder rumbling. **6)** Immediately everyone was sure that we would have rain. **7)** The thunder stopped in a few minutes. **8)** We opened the door slowly and looked outside. **9)** As far as we could see at that moment, the sky was clear. **10)** I'm sure we will finally get some rain someday soon.

Workbook Activity 3–Writing in Sentences

Answers will vary. Sentences should be complete.

Workbook Activity 4–What's the Purpose?

1) Statement–. **2)** Question–? **3)** Question–? **4)** Statement–. **5)** Exclamation–! **6)** Statement–. **7)** Statement–. **8)** Question–? **9)** Statement–. **10)** Exclamation–! **11)** Command–. **12)** Statement–. **13)** Question–? **14)** Statement–. **15)** Question–? **16)** Statement–. **17)** Exclamation–! **18)** Command–. **19)** Question–? **20)** Statement–.

Workbook Activity 5–The Purpose of a Sentence

1) B–? **2)** A–. **3)** D–! **4)** A–. **5)** C–. **6)** A–. **7)** A–. **8)** A–. **9)** B–? **10)** A–. **11)** C–. **12)** A–. **13)** A–. **14)** C–. **15)** A–. **16)** A–. **17)** A–. **18)** D–! **19)** B–? **20)** C–.

Workbook Activity 6–Punctuating Dialogue

1) "Let's . . . weekend," Mike suggested. **2)** "That . . . me," Derek agreed. **3)** "I . . . equipment?" Mike asked. **4)** "Well," said Derek, "I . . . bag." **5)** "What . . . stove?" asked Mike. **6)** said, "I . . . boss." **7)** asked, "Can . . . too?" **8)** "Sure . . . go." **9)** "We . . . camp," Mike said. **10)** added, "Then . . . dinner." **11)** "At . . . bags," said Mike. "We'll . . . tent." **12)** "That . . . fun," laughed Tim. "We . . . time!" **13)** "Do . . . year?" asked Derek. **14)** "No chance," said Mike. "We . . . there." **15)** "Anyway . . . friendly," said Derek. **16)** "I . . . something," Tim said. **17)** "What . . . Tim?" **18)** "I think . . . weekend," he said. **19)** "Too bad," said Derek. "It . . . fun." **20)** "Sure, guys," said Tim, "but . . . time."

Workbook Activity 7–Who's Speaking Now?

Everyone met at Whitemarsh Park at 6:30 P.M. "Hey, Coach," called Clark. "What time does the game start?" The coach looked at the schedule. "It says here the game starts at 6:45 P.M. Take a turn at bat and then get out in the field. Be sure to warm up thoroughly." "Sure thing, Coach," Clark smiled and picked up his favorite bat. Soon the game got under way. "Batter up," the umpire yelled.

Workbook Activity 8–Direct and Indirect Quotations

Answers will vary. Sample answers are given.
A. 1) "Fred, do you want a second piece of cake?" asked Karen. **2)** "I'm trying to maintain my weight," Fred reminded her. **3)** Karen laughed and said, "You should have told me sooner." **4)** "I could have given you an apple for dessert," she said. **5)** Fred said, "I'd rather have the cake."

B. 1) Harold's father told Harold to sit down and have a good breakfast. **2)** He told Harold that breakfast is the most important meal of the day. **3)** Harold shrugged and told his dad he was in a hurry. **4)** Harold told his dad that beside that, he isn't hungry in the morning. **5)** Harold's father firmly told his son that he wouldn't take no for an answer.

Workbook Activity 9–Making Your Subject and Verb Agree

1) are **2)** gives **3)** makes **4)** has **5)** stay **6)** invites **7)** love **8)** like **9)** gets **10)** knows **11)** does **12)** is **13)** comes **14)** works

Workbook Activity 10–Using Pronouns

Pronouns are bold.
1) **They** agreed to meet for lunch. **2)** Sam planned to meet Eleanor after **her** French class. **3)** **Her** French teacher is Mrs. Bernstein. **4)** Mrs. Bernstein had given **her** class a long assignment. **5)** Eleanor didn't understand **it** completely. **6)** **She** was still talking to Mrs. Bernstein about it when Sam arrived. **7)** Sam paced back and forth because Eleanor was making **them** late for lunch. **8)** Finally **she** came out of the classroom. **9)** "I am sorry to keep you waiting," Eleanor said.

10) "OK, but let's hurry. The special today is spaghetti, and I don't want to miss **it**," said Sam.

Workbook Activity 11–Capitalization of Proper Nouns
Activity 1: Answers will vary.
Activity 2: Suggested common nouns are listed.
1) class **2)** language **3)** month **4)** dance **5)** theater
6) movie, play **7)** ocean **8)** mountains **9)** city **10)** state
11) building **12)** president **13)** continent **14)** lake
15) university **16)** actress **17)** book, movie, TV show
18) city **19)** writer, author **20)** place

Workbook Activity 12–Plurals and Possessives
A. 1) day–S Mrs. O'Hara–S letter–S mail–S **2)** letter–S duty–S
3) jury–S group–S people–P **4)** members–P evidence–S
5) guilt–S innocence–S **6)** men–P women–P
B. 1) the wolf's howl **2)** the calves' pen **3)** plural; no apostrophe **4)** the children's room **5)** the student's book
6) your two cents' worth **7)** a day's pay **8)** plural; no apostrophe **9)** the family's home **10)** the car's tire

Workbook Activity–13 Make Them Correct
Bold words indicate corrections.
1) Amanda and Laura **work** together. **2)** They work at a **restaurant. 3)** They are **working** as waitresses. **4)** "I **am** glad that we only work . . . Laura. **5)** "Do you **have** a date tonight?" asked Amanda. **6)** "Yes, I am **going** to a movie with . . . Laura. **7) "Bill's** father is lending us . . . explained. **8)** "I **am** going out with some of . . . Amanda. **9)** After Laura worked her shift, she **went** home. **10)** At home Laura **ate** dinner. **11)** She went to her room and **got** ready . . . date. **12)** Laura **bought** a new outfit for the date. **13)** When . . . she **looked** beautiful. **14)** Bill **said,** "Laura, you look great!" **15)** As they **left,** Laura's mother . . . late!"

Workbook Activity 14–Homonyms
A. 1) write **2)** right **3)** write, right **4)** right **5)** write
B. 1) which **2)** witch **3)** Which **4)** witch **5)** which

Workbook Activity 15–Confusing Words
A. 1) pare, pears **2)** pears **3)** pair **4)** pare **5)** pair
B. 1) course **2)** coarse **3)** course **4)** coarse **5)** course

Workbook Activity 16–Sound-Alike Words
A. 1) buy, by **2)** bye **3)** bye **4)** by
B. 1) isle **2)** aisle **3)** aisle **4)** I'll

Workbook Activity 17–Words That Sound Alike
1) dessert **2)** Desert **3)** desert **4)** desert **5)** dessert
6) desert **7)** dessert **8)** desert **9)** dessert **10)** desert

Workbook Activity 18–Little Words, Big Trouble
1) it's **2)** its **3)** its **4)** there **5)** They're **6)** their
7) It's **8)** their **9)** It's **10)** Their **11)** its **12)** it's

Workbook Activity 19–A Camping Trip
1) Wednesday **2)** because, weather, to **3)** their, supplies
4) clothes **5)** two **6)** to, where **7)** to, two **8)** were, morning
9) necessary, for, your **10)** "We're **11)** for, week
12) experience **13)** through **14)** see **15)** Once

Workbook Activity 20–Avoiding the Comma Fault
1) Helicopters are fun to ride in. They are also scary. **2)** On her first ride, Tina fell in love with flying. Now she wants to be a pilot. **3)** Victor thought flying was OK. Mike made plans to take a bus next time. **4)** The fastest a helicopter ever flew was over 200 miles per hour. The pilot was Byron Graham. **5)** Byron Graham isn't in the National Aviation Hall of Fame. The Hall of Fame is in Dayton, Ohio. It honors outstanding pioneers. **6)** Some of the people in the Hall of Fame are Amelia Earhart, Wiley Post, and Orville and Wilbur Wright. Also in the Hall of Fame are Charles Lindbergh and Alexander Graham Bell.

Workbook Activity 21–Separating the Ideas
The Labrador Retriever The Wilsons got a labrador retriever puppy. It was eight weeks old and weighed ten pounds. By the time it was three months old, the puppy weighed over thirty pounds. The veterinarian said the puppy might be over one hundred pounds when he was full-grown. "Wow," said Jane, "the puppy will weigh more than I do!"

Rehoboth Beach Rehoboth Beach is a little town on the Atlantic Ocean. It is in the state of Delaware. Rehoboth is a popular summer resort. People go there to swim, boat, sunbathe, and fish. There is a small boardwalk where people like to walk at night.

Workbook Activity 22–Repairing Sentence Fragments
Sentences will vary. Sample sentences are given.
1) Fragment–My new computer was not so expensive.
2) Sentence **3)** Sentence **4)** Fragment–The computer was a birthday present from my father, mother, and grandparents.
5) Fragment–Word processing is the main use I expect to have for the computer. **6)** Fragment–Word processing is also called electronic typesetting. **7)** Sentence **8)** Fragment–That is to say, the computer would balance my checkbook if I had one.
9) Sentence **10)** Fragment–I am looking forward to playing the games right after I finish my homework.

Workbook Activity 23–Writing Complete Sentences
Corrected sentences may vary. Sample sentences are given.
1) Run-on–We watch the Super Bowl. It's the best game of the year.
2) Fragment–Last year we went skiing. Next year we will go ice skating. **3)** Run-on–What's your favorite sport? Mine is hockey.
4) Fragment–There was rain, wind, lightening, and thunder for hours. **5)** Fragment–Under the chair, the dog slept.
6) Fragment–In Florida and California, they usually have sunny skies. **7)** Fragment–In April, all I think of is taxes, taxes, and more taxes! **8)** Run-on–The weather was pleasant, and we enjoyed the day. **9)** Run-on–What's BASIC? It's a computer programming language. **10)** Run-on–Do you agree that a complete sentence is best?

Workbook Activity 24–Improving Sentences
A. and **B.** Answers will vary.

Workbook Activity 25–Combining Short Sentences
Answers will vary. Suggested answers are given.
1) A dog, a cat, and a horse are animals. **2)** Last winter there was snow and sleet. **3)** Frank and his brother walked to school.
4) Rob and Lee are bakers at a bakery on Chester Avenue.
5) John filled out a long, complicated application. **6)** Twenty-year-old Amanda was interviewed for a job. **7)** The young girl

named Joan goes to school.   **8)** Rob and David are going to the concert, but Frank isn't.   **9)** Schools were closed because there had been a blizzard.   **10)** When Bill was jogging, he fell and hurt his knee and ankle.   **11)** The family went on vacation to Maine and stayed for two weeks.   **12)** Chris is studying medicine at a large college in Virginia.

Workbook Activity 26–Connecting With Semicolons

A. 1) Pick up your room; otherwise, you will be in big trouble.
2) You want to be a star; therefore, you must practice.   **3)** We exercised for an hour; then we rested.   **4)** We enjoy exercise; moreover, it makes us feel better.   **5)** Allen ate too much; consequently, he had indigestion.

B. Answers will vary. Sample answers are given.
1) I like to swim in warm weather; however, today is cold.   **2)** We worked all day; consequently, we got the job done.   **3)** Kenny would like to be an engineer; furthermore, he would also like to be an architect.   **4)** Joan wants a Gold Medal; therefore, she practices many hours a day.   **5)** Class began at 9 o'clock; accordingly, the teacher expected the students to be there on time.

Workbook Activity 27–Sentences to Improve

Sentences will vary. Sample answers are given.
A. 1) Everyone was out for the evening.   **2)** The kitten on the step looks sad.   **3)** The team for our school got three new players.
4) The winters in Maine are cold.   **5)** Marlene is hungry in the morning.

B. 1) We like the beach, so we go there every summer.   **2)** Jackie's uncle has a farm, and she goes horseback riding.   **3)** Sometimes there is nothing to do, so I can just go for a walk.   **4)** The city streets are noisy, but they are also exciting.   **5)** Dena and Karl got tickets for the concert.

Workbook Activity 28–Punctuating With Subordinating Conjunctions

A. 1) If Dana has a chance, he will go to summer camp.
2) While he is there, he will earn money as a counselor.
3) Although Dana will be busy, he will find time for recreation himself.   **4)** He plans to swim every day after he finishes his chores.   **5)** Because he likes kids and the great outdoors, Dana always enjoys camp.

B. Answers will vary.

Workbook Activity 29–Choosing a Topic Sentence

1) A   **2)** B   **3)** B   **4)** A   **5)** A   **6)** A   **7)** A   **8)** B   **9)** B
10) A

Workbook Activity 30–Does It Belong?

1) Joe had homework to do.   **2)** Reading is an enjoyable hobby.
3) The children wanted new bicycles.   **4)** Robert enjoys driving.
5) The zoo was crowded.   **6)** Everyone will enjoy the cake.
7) Education is important.   **8)** An airplane travels by air.
9) Meat provides protein.   **10)** Mexico is not involved in space exploration.

Workbook Activity 31–Building a Paragraph With Facts

Answers will vary.

Workbook Activity 32–Good Endings

1) b   **2)** b   **3)** a   **4)** a   **5)** a   **6)** b

Workbook Activity 33–Paragraph Writing Practice

Sample responses are given. Several acceptable arrangements can be used.

A. A Fire Protection Engineer
Most people have never heard of a fire protection engineer. Communities hire fire protection engineers to decide where fire hydrants should be placed. Builders consult these engineers to be sure the building follows the fire safety codes. After a fire, these engineers investigate to find out the cause. A fire protection engineer does an important job in a community.

B. Being Letter Perfect
Your writing says something about you. Every paper that you write in school says something more than words. Are you neat or sloppy? Are you careful or careless? Do you think before you speak or write? A reader can tell many things about a writer.

Workbook Activity 34–Writing a Paragraph

Answers will vary. Paragraphs should have a topic sentence, three or four sentences about the subject, and a conclusion.

Workbook Activity 35–Asking for Information

Answers will vary. Acceptable responses are given.
A. 1) How much is the rent?   **2)** Are utilities included?
3) Does the apartment complex have a pool?

B. 1) What kind of warranty does the car have?   **2)** What is the total cost of the car?   **3)** What is the EPA rating on the car?

C. 1) What special features does the telephone have?   **2)** What colors does it come in?   **3)** How much does it cost?

D. 1) Has the puppy had its shots?   **2)** How old is the puppy?
3) Could I return the puppy if it is not healthy?

Workbook Activity 36–Chronologic Order

I. A) 4   **B)** 3   **C)** 2   **D)** 5   **E)** 6   **F)** 1
II. A) 2   **B)** 3   **C)** 4   **D)** 1   **E)** 5

Workbook Activity 37–Paragraph Purpose

1) A   **2)** D   **3)** C   **4)** B

Workbook Activity 38–Rewriting Topic Sentences

Answers will vary. Sample sentences are given.
1) Playing baseball well requires concentration and practice.
2) Good novels often explain people's behavior.   **3)** Many attics contain old and interesting items.   **4)** Gourmet foods often need unusual spices.   **5)** Good-paying jobs demand people with special skills.   **6)** Every swimmer should know certain safety rules.
7) Watching a sunset can be a moving experience.   **8)** Insect behavior can often be compared to human behavior.   **9)** Television can influence the attitudes of children.   **10)** Charles is the most forgetful person I know.   **11)** Tennis and baseball have several common elements.   **12)** The twins Jill and Jean are different in many respects.   **13)** Old newspapers can be put to many practical uses.   **14)** The behavior of curious kittens is often amusing.

Workbook Activity 39–Transitional Words and Phrases

1) ALSO   **2)** AS A RESULT   **3)** AT LAST   **4)** AT THE END
5) BEFORE   **6)** FINALLY   **7)** FIRST   **8)** FOR EXAMPLE
9) FURTHERMORE   **10)** HOWEVER   **11)** IN CONCLUSION
12) IN THE MEANTIME   **13)** LATER   **14)** MEANWHILE

15) NEXT **16)** NOW **17)** SOON **18)** THEN
19) THEREFORE **20)** TOMORROW

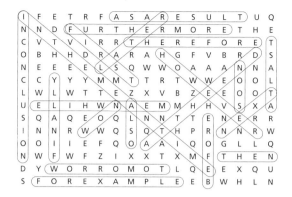

Workbook Activity 40–Using Transitional Words

Transitional words may vary. Sample answers are given.

Anthony walked onto the tennis court. Now, he was ready to serve. He tossed the ball into the air and then hit it hard. At last, he really wanted to win the match.

Computers do many things to help us. For example, they keep banking records. Also, they can do difficult problems in math. Furthermore, they can even change big city traffic lights.

Suzanne watched the waves coming in. Then, she looked around for her parents. At last, she saw them. Finally, she decided to hold their hands. The ocean looked too rough today.

Pete studied the pitcher carefully. Now, it was his turn to bat. A solid hit would bring in the winning run. First, he stepped up to the plate. Then his eyes followed the ball right until it met his bat. Immediately, he knew he helped win the game.

Workbook Activity 41–Making Comparisons

A. 1) Indirect **2)** Indirect **3)** Direct **4)** Indirect
5) Indirect **6)** Direct

B. Other answers will vary.

Workbook Activity 42–Improving a Paragraph

Answers will vary. A suggested paragraph is given.
Reference sources are books and files that enable us to find information of all kinds. Most are available at your local library. However, they cannot be taken home. A library catalog lists all the books in a library. If you know the title or author of a book, you can easily look it up in the library catalog. The dictionary, atlas, and encyclopedia are other reference sources. *Who's Who in America* is a less familiar one. It contains information about well-known people. A thesaurus gives synonyms and antonyms. *The Reader's Guide* lists articles from major magazines. An almanac contains facts, statistics, and records from current and past years. All of these reference sources can help you with your schoolwork.

Workbook Activity 43–Proofreading Practice
Why I Quit Bowling

For many years, I enjoyed bowling. Two years ago I quit my team, and this is the reason why. The name of my team was the Starframers. A starframe in bowling means that everyone got a spare or a strike in that frame. We were great. Everyone's averages kept improving. Naturally, we were in first place all year. Finally, it was the last night of the season. My team went into the final position round three games ahead of the second place team. Confidence was our middle name that night! We only had to win one game to take home the first place trophy! All I can say is that I am looking right now at a second place trophy.

Workbook Activity 44–Identifying People, Places, and Things

1) Neapolitan ice cream is brick ice cream in layers of different colors and flavors. **2)** Naugahyde is a trademark for an imitation leather used in upholstery. **3)** A haberdasher is a dealer in men's clothing and accessories. **4)** Winston Churchill was the prime minister of England from 1940 to 1945 and from 1951 to 1955. **5)** Carson City is the capital of Nevada. **6)** Casablanca is a seaport in Morocco, a country in Northern Africa. It is also the name of a famous movie starring Humphrey Bogart and Ingrid Bergman. **7)** A bighorn is a type of wild sheep that is usually grayish brown in color and that has large curving horns. It is also called the Rocky Mountain sheep because it lives in the mountainous areas of western North America. **8)** Thanksgiving is a holiday in the United States that falls on the fourth Thursday in November. **9)** A rya rug is a decorated, handwoven, thick area rug made in Scandinavia. **10)** A trinket is a small ornament, a piece of jewelry, or a toy. **11)** A trilogy is a series of three dramas, literary works, or sometimes musical compositions that are closely related and that develop a single theme. **12)** NATO stands for the North Atlantic Treaty Organization.

Workbook Activity 45–Become an Essayist

Answers will vary. Students are to include all three parts of a paragraph and proofread their essay.

Workbook Activity 46–Developing a Brief Essay From Facts

Answers will vary. Sample responses are given.
A. No longer in existence today, the mammoth was a large elephant-like creature. It was about nine feet tall and had long, curved tusks. Scientists today believe the mammoth also had hairy skin.

B. Antarctica is the continent located around and near the South Pole. Since it is extremely cold for most of the year, very little life inhabits its 5,000,000 square miles.

C. At 36,000,000 miles away, moonless Mercury is the closest planet to the sun. Although its year is shorter than ours (Mercury takes only 88 days to orbit the sun), its day is much longer. How long? A whopping 58 earth days equals one day on Mercury.

Workbook Activity 47–Leave a Message

```
To  Audrey
Date [Today's date]  Time [Current time]
WHILE YOU WERE OUT
Ms. Dana Kurtz
of  4320 Foxhill Drive
Phone No.  555-1298
┌──────────────────┬──┬──────────────┬──┐
│ TELEPHONED       │ ✓│ PLEASE CALL  │ ✓│
├──────────────────┼──┼──────────────┼──┤
│ WAS IN TO SEE YOU│  │ WILL CALL BACK│ │
├──────────────────┼──┼──────────────┤  │
│ WANTS TO SEE YOU │  │ URGENT       │ ✓│
│ RETURNED YOUR CALL│ │              │  │
└──────────────────┴──┴──────────────┴──┘
MESSAGE  Call Ms. Kurtz about
an emergency TV repair today.
_____
_____
_____
_____
_____
                            Pete
```

Workbook Activity 48–More About Memos
Answers will vary.

Workbook Activity 49–Writing Memos
Memos will vary. Two sample memos are given below.

MEMO

DATE: Oct. 4, 20–
TO: Mrs. Wilson
FROM: Mrs. D. Neal
SUBJECT: Frankie Neal's absence last Friday

Please excuse Frankie's absence last Friday. He had the flu.

MEMO

DATE: April 19, 20–
TO: Mr. Howard
FROM: Rae Caldwell, Secretary of the Seventh Grade Girls
SUBJECT: Tennis team

The seventh grade girls would like to start a tennis team. We need your help with the arrangements.
Thank you very much.

Workbook Activity 50–Preparing a Memo
Memos will vary. A sample memo is given below.

MEMO

DATE: March 5, 20–
TO: All Students and Faculty Members
FROM: Bob Durkin, Talent Committee
SUBJECT: Talent Show Auditions

Beginning March 6 and for the next two days, Central High School will be holding auditions for its annual Student-Faculty Talent Show. If you can sing, dance, play a musical instrument, do stand-up comedy, read poetry with real feeling, or in any other way can keep an audience entertained for several minutes, then you are the kind of person we need. Come to the school auditorium at three o'clock and take that first small step to the stars. Show our talent committee what you can do. Our talent committee is ready to select. We look forward to seeing your act. For further information, contact Mary Madden, Fred Pollock, Sylvia Carino, or me in homeroom 315. You can also call 991-1256 after 7:00 P.M. Good luck!

Workbook Activity 51–Addressing an Envelope
Note: An apartment number can be placed on the same line with the street address, or it can be placed on a separate line.
1) Tony Pierce 17 Dartmouth Court Trenton, NJ 08601
2) Janet Lahney 92 Westland Drive, Apt. 13 College Park, MD 20740 **3)** Valerie Armstrong 67 Tulip Drive Lansdowne, PA 19050 **4)** Mary Jo Golato 4210 Saratoga Avenue San Jose, CA 95129 **5)** Taffy Clayton 517 Louisville Lane Cumberland, MD 21502 **6)** Jill Edmonds 43 Main St., Apt. 101 Poughkeepsie, NY 12603

Workbook Activity 52–Label the Parts of a Letter
Labels are given in order from top to bottom of letter.
Return Address, Addressee, Inside Address, Greeting, Body, Closing, Signature, Name

Workbook Activity 53–Edit Your Letters
Corrections are indicated in bold.
3412 **W**ilson **A**venue
Anderson**, IN 46011**
August 12, 20-
Mr. Harold **S**weet
1111 Albany **Blvd.**
Anderson, IN 46011
Dear **Mr. Sweet:**
I am writing in response to your advertisement in the *Anderson Daily Blade.* I am interested in the **management** trainee position that you described. I am enclosing my résumé **for your** information. I am available to begin work immediately.
I will call you for an interview on Wednesday morning.
Very sincerely yours**,**
Richard Kochert

Workbook Activity 54–Understanding the Letter
1) a) personal **b)** business **2)** business **3)** personal
4) a) heading **b)** date **c)** inside address **d)** salutation
e) body **f)** closing   **g)** signature **h)** typed name **5)** Yes
6) Probably not, but it could be if it were typed.   **7)** greeting
8) body **9)** comma **10)** colon **11)** business letter
12) comma **13)** today's date (in form of: June 1, 2001)
14) Dr. Mary Madden 41 Rutland Road Lyndhurst, NJ 07032

Workbook Activity 55–Library Catalog Entries
1) art–subject **2)** Buck, Pearl–author **3)** *Gone With the Wind*–title 4) *Hamlet*–title **5)** Hinton, S. E.–author
6) history–subject **7)** Oates, Joyce Carol–author **8)** Olympics, history–subject **9)** *The Outsiders*–title **10)** psychology–subject
11) *The Red Pony*–title **12)** Russia–subject **13)** Shakespeare, William–author **14)** Steinbeck, John–author **15)** *The Writer's Handbook*–title

Workbook Activity 56–Report Acrostic
1) Reference **2)** Atlas **3)** *Who's Who* **4)** Periodical
5) *Readers' Guide* **6)** Term **7)** Index **8)** Chronologic
9) Bibliography **10)** Mistake

Acrostic Puzzle Solution: The key to a successful report is planning.

Workbook Activity 57–Writing an Outline
United States History

I. Introduction
II. The discovery of America
   A. Early Spanish explorers
   B. The first permanent settlements
III. The Colonial Period
   A. Early governments
   B. Indian relations
IV. The Revolutionary Period
   A. Important leaders
   B. Important battles
V. Forming a government
   A. The Articles of Confederation
   B. The Constitution
   C. Influences of early presidents
     1. George Washington
     2. Thomas Jefferson
VI. Summary and conclusions

Workbook Activity 58–Organizing Topics for an Outline
Sample responses are given.
Sports Around the World

I. Outdoor Sports
   A. Baseball
   B. Soccer
   C. Tennis
   D. Football
II. Indoor Sports
   A. Volleyball
   B. Ice Hockey
   C. Basketball

A Typical Daily Menu

I. Breakfast
   A. Eggs and Bacon
   B. Cereal and Milk
   C. Fruit Juice
   D. Toast
II. Lunch
   A. Soup
   B. Sandwich
   C. Milk
III. Dinner
   A. Salad
   B. Entree (Main Dish)
   C. Vegetable
   D. Beverage
   E. Dessert

Workbook Activity 59–Preparing a Bibliography
Answers are listed in alphabetical order.
"Audio." *Television Encyclopedia*, Vol. 11, 1994, 231–235. Bannigan, Michael. *Using a Video Camera*. Washington, DC: Wilson Books, Inc., 1995. Gamble, Vic. *Operating a Television Station*. Boston: Video Productions Publications, 1996. Legarette, Collette. *The History of Television*. Seattle: BCTV Publishing Company, 1995. Stein, Ellen. "Writing a Television Play." *Video Producer's Magazine* 3 (November 1997) 56–76.

Writing Tip Sheets
The Writing Tip Sheets are meant to be quick references for students as they write papers. The sheets can be used both while students study *Basic English Composition* and when they write for other classes. The sheets can help students to proof and double-check their work. Make copies of the sheets available to students as often as needed.

Community Connection
Completed activities will vary for each student. Community Connection activities are real-life activities completed outside of the classroom by the students. These activities give students practical learning and practice of the skills taught in *Basic English Composition*. Check completed activities to see that students have followed directions, completed each step, filled in all charts and blanks, provided reasonable answers to questions, written legibly, and used proper grammar and punctuation.

Tests

Chapter 1 Mastery Test A
Part A: 1) In the fall Derek likes to go to the school basketball games. **2)** He decided to call Amanda and see if she wanted to go. **3)** What time does the basketball game start? **4)** Amanda finished her work and got ready for the game. **5)** She could not wait for the game to begin. **6)** Derek met Amanda in front of her house. **7)** They walked several blocks to the school. **8)** Unfortunately, it started to rain. **9)** Luckily, they were almost at the school. **10)** Which players will be starting the game today?

Part B: 1) In area, Canada is the second largest country in the world. It stretches 3,223 miles from east to west. The United States is on its southern border. **2)** Many stories are told about who designed the United States flag. No one knows for sure who really did. Some people think that Betsy Ross made the first flag. However, there is no historical proof that she did. **3)** Have you ever heard of the Pulitzer Prizes? They have been given since 1917. They are given to writers for outstanding work. Receiving a Pulitzer Prize is a great honor. **4)** Do you know anyone who lives in Mobile, Alabama? More than 200,000 people live in this city. It is the second largest city in Alabama. The largest city is Birmingham. **5)** Almanacs are books of facts. Do you want to know how many calories are in a banana? Do you need to know what the capital of Lesotho is? You can find the answers to these questions in an almanac.

Chapter 1 Mastery Test B
Part A: 1) Derek and Amanda saw Mike in the stands at the basketball game. **2)** Amanda always asks Derek questions during the game. **3)** Which team will get this tip-off? **4)** Which player is the best free thrower? **5)** Sometimes the school pep group sells snacks at halftime. **6)** Oh boy, they have hot dogs today. **7)** Do they have any mustard? **8)** Yes, and they have ketchup, too. **9)** Derek wants two hot dogs and a cold drink. **10)** Amanda just wants a cold drink.

Part B: 1) The average person watches television almost 30 hours each week. Do you think that men or women watch the most TV? The answer is women. They watch about five hours more each week than men do. **2)** Do you know what snowflakes are made of? Snowflakes are clumps of ice crystals. They form around bits of dust when the temperature is very cold. Ice crystals bump into each other and form snowflakes. **3)** The skeleton is the body's framework. It is made up of large and small bones. Do you know how many bones are in the human body? There are 206 bones that provide the framework for your body. **4)** Did you ever watch Lassie? Did you wish you had a collie of your own? The collie is a very smart dog. It is capable of showing a great deal of affection. You could not find a better friend and protector. **5)** Erosion wears down hills and forms valleys and canyons. Did you ever see water running down a hill after it rains? Running water, ice, wind, ocean waves, and gravity are all part of the erosion process.

Chapter 2 Mastery Test A

Part A: 1) Exclamation–! **2)** Statement–. **3)** Command/ Request–. **4)** Question–? **5)** Question–? **6)** Command/ Request–. **7)** Statement–. **8)** Exclamation–! **9)** Command/ Request–. **10)** Statement–.

Part B: 1) Indirect **2)** Direct **3)** Direct **4)** Indirect **5)** Direct **6)** Direct **7)** Indirect **8)** Direct **9)** Indirect **10)** Direct

Part C: 1) "Practice starts at eleven o'clock," said Derek. **2)** "You better not be late, Mike," he warned. **3)** "I know the coach likes to start practice on time," said Mike. **4)** "I hope the coach lets me play goalie today," said Derek. **5)** "Goalie is my favorite position," he added. **6)** "Derek, why do you like playing goalie so much?" asked Mike. **7)** Derek answered, "You don't wear yourself out running up and down the field." **8)** "Besides, the crowd goes wild every time you catch the ball," said Derek. **9)** "You always were a show-off, Derek," laughed Mike. **10)** "Just call me a crowd pleaser, Mike," replied Derek.

Chapter 2 Mastery Test B

Part A: 1) Exclamation–! **2)** Statement–. **3)** Command/ Request–. **4)** Question–? **5)** Statement–. **6)** Question–? **7)** Exclamation–! **8)** Statement–. **9)** Command/Request–. **10)** Command/Request–.

Part B: 1) Direct **2)** Direct **3)** Indirect **4)** Direct **5)** Direct **6)** Indirect **7)** Direct **8)** Direct **9)** Indirect **10)** Indirect

Part C: 1) "Laura, what time does our horseback riding lesson start?" asked Amanda. **2)** "Our lesson starts at five o'clock," answered Laura. **3)** "You better not fall off your horse again, Laura," Amanda warned. **4)** "Last time I thought I broke my leg," said Laura. **5)** "I hope we get to go trail riding today," said Amanda. **6)** "I like riding in the ring," returned Laura. **7)** "Why do you like riding in the ring so much, Laura?" asked Amanda. **8)** Laura answered, "I like it because the horse can't run away with me as easily." **9)** "Besides, having the instructor in the ring makes me feel safe," Laura added. **10)** "Laura, you always were a little too careful," laughed Amanda.

Chapter 3 Mastery Test A

Part A: 1) Derek, Laura, and Amanda all take Spanish. **2)** They all have dreams of going to Spain and Portugal. **3)** After doing her homework, Amanda sometimes calls Derek. **4)** They talk about living in the West and being in the Olympics. **5)** Derek asked Amanda what she thinks about watching a video on Friday. **6)** Amanda says, "Laura and Mike want to join us." **7)** Derek suggested they rent *Apollo 13* or *The Secret of Roan Inish*. **8)** Amanda heard her mother calling and said, "I have to hang up." **9)** She asked Derek to call their friends about Friday. **10)** Derek said he would call them on Tuesday.

Part B: 1) has/had **2)** had **3)** am **4)** begun **5)** caught **6)** fed **7)** grown **8)** ridden **9)** swung **10)** tore

Part C: 1) Ms. Jones's car has two flat tires. **2)** They are casting for three actors' parts in the play. **3)** What are people's ideas about women's basketball? **4)** This child's toy was different from other children's toys. **5)** The geese's flight patterns were interesting to study.

Chapter 3 Mastery Test B

Part A: 1) Mike does not take Spanish, but Derek, Laura, and Amanda do. **2)** Mike takes French, and he wants to ski in the French Alps. **3)** After studying his atlas, Mike wants to go to French Guiana. **4)** The four friends talk of traveling to the South someday. **5)** They like movies about the South like *Mississippi Burning* and *Fried Green Tomatoes*. **6)** Laura said to Amanda and Derek, "Mike and I want to see a movie." **7)** "Do you want to join us at a movie Saturday?" Laura asked. **8)** "I want to see a movie. Amanda, do you want to go?" Derek replied. **9)** Amanda said, "We can treat ourselves to Chinese food at the Tea House afterward." **10)** Amanda said that she herself will reserve a table for them.

Part B: 1) had **2)** has/had **3)** are **4)** blew **5)** driven **6)** forgot **7)** hidden **8)** lain **9)** stole **10)** wept

Part C: 1) Mr. Williams's boat has two sails. **2)** The boys ran for fifty cents a mile in the benefit races. **3)** Children's and men's clothes are on the store's second floor. **4)** The mice's nest and the wolves' den are warm places in winter. **5)** The number of geese is not threatened because of hunters.

Chapter 4 Mastery Test A

Part A: 1) lose **2)** already **3)** quite **4)** formally **5)** break **6)** accept **7)** counsel **8)** advice **9)** too **10)** than

Part B: 1) won't **2)** You've **3)** hasn't **4)** Let's **5)** can't

Part C: 1) you're **2)** its **3)** Who's **4)** theirs **5)** They're

Part D: 1) buses **2)** trays **3)** bodies **4)** elves **5)** teeth **6)** copies **7)** chimneys **8)** sheriffs **9)** burros **10)** moose

Part E: 1) friend **2)** receipt **3)** seize **4)** ancient **5)** lumped **6)** slipped **7)** beginner **8)** pooled **9)** safety **10)** changing

Part F: 1) We lived through the biggest blizzard that lasted three days. **2)** When the snow finally stopped we could barely get out our door. **3)** At first I thought the business of staying home from school was great. **4)** Then Mom had me cleaning my room and picking up my clothes. **5)** Next Dad gave me the privilege of shoveling snow–definitely not fun!

Chapter 4 Mastery Test B

Part A: 1) capital **2)** effect **3)** waist **4)** chose **5)** Plains **6)** past **7)** principal **8)** waste **9)** personnel **10)** choose

Part B: 1) aren't **2)** We've **3)** couldn't **4)** There's **5)** didn't

Part C: 1) Whose **2)** you're **3)** It's **4)** There's **5)** their

Part D: 1) foxes **2)** bays **3)** ladies **4)** selves **5)** feet **6)** rubies **7)** turkeys **8)** giraffes **9)** pintos **10)** sheep

Part E: 1) relief **2)** sleigh **3)** weight **4)** science **5)** pumped **6)** tripped **7)** permitted **8)** cooled **9)** wasteful **10)** nosing

Part F: 1) We are getting knowledge of writing in this class. **2)** It is helping us with our grammar and ability to describe things beautifully with words. **3)** After forty weeks we will realize which words are spelled right. **4)** We go to the library and thoroughly study topics that we choose.   **5)** We will surprise ourselves by how much we benefit from this experience.

Chapter 5 Mastery Test A

Part A: 1) Sentence   **2)** Fragment   **3)** Fragment   **4)** Sentence   **5)** Run-on   **6)** Fragment   **7)** Run-on   **8)** Run-on   **9)** Fragment   **10)** Run-on   **11)** Fragment   **12)** Run-on   **13)** Fragment   **14)** Sentence   **15)** Run-on   **16)** Sentence   **17)** Sentence   **18)** Fragment   **19)** Sentence   **20)** Run-on

Part B: Sentences will vary. Sample sentences are given.
1) She likes to drive with her mother in the car.   **2)** We go to the beach when summer comes.   **3)** Do you want to go to a play or to dinner and a movie?   **4)** On a cold and rainy night, we like to cook chili.   **5)** The hotel has vacant rooms for more than 50 people.

Part C: Sentences will vary. Sample sentences are given.
1) Ross went to the apartment, and then he went to work.
2) Milk and yogurt are sources of protein.   **3)** My computer doesn't have enough memory. I need a new computer.   **4)** Pat exercises daily. She starts her routine with a fast walk.   **5)** Bruce has fifty CDs, and he just added ten more to his collection.

Chapter 5 Mastery Test B

Part A: 1) Sentence   **2)** Run-on   **3)** Run-on   **4)** Fragment   **5)** Sentence   **6)** Fragment   **7)** Fragment   **8)** Run-on   **9)** Fragment   **10)** Sentence   **11)** Fragment   **12)** Run-on   **13)** Fragment   **14)** Sentence   **15)** Run-on   **16)** Fragment   **17)** Run-on   **18)** Sentence   **19)** Sentence   **20)** Run-on

Part B: Sentences will vary. Sample sentences are given.
1) If things were different, we would have fewer problems.
2) I need to get mittens or find my lost gloves.   **3)** We haven't heard from Tom after the other night.   **4)** When the sun came up, the day grew warm.   **5)** Since everyone went home early, we watched a video.

Part C: Sentences will vary. Sample sentences are given.
1) Because the weather was dry, the lawn needed to be watered often.   **2)** Lan brought a birthday present and birthday treats.
3) It rained on three Saturdays in June.   **4)** Juan bought a computer, and then he bought software.   **5)** The book was so exciting that she didn't put it down until three in the morning.

Chapter 6 Mastery Test A

Part A: Sentences will vary. Sample sentences with adjectives are given.
1) Don is a loyal friend.   **2)** My older sister is moving to Iowa.
3) This delicious dessert will be great for dinner.   **4)** The frightened kitten ran away and hid.   **5)** Sharon did an excellent job on her homework.

Part B: Sentences will vary. Sample sentences with adverbs are given.
1) That train is moving extremely slowly.   **2)** Buy me that book today.   **3)** Judy is amazingly bright.   **4)** Stan went to the beach last week.   **5)** Usually dinner is served at six o'clock.

Part C: Sentences will vary. Sample sentences with prepositional phrases are given.
1) Did you lose a ring in the locker room?   **2)** The man from the power company was here.   **3)** In two months, the construction crew built a house.   **4)** That family across the street likes their new home.   **5)** We read a story in the newspaper.

Part D: Sentences will vary. Sample combined sentences using a conjunction are given.
1) Eggplant, spinach, and squash are vegetables.   **2)** Today there was lightning and thunder.   **3)** You may have eaten beets, but have you ever eaten beet greens?   **4)** I missed the bus because I was late.
5) Neither Tony nor Paula had been to Alaska.

Part E: Sentences will vary. Sentences in different word order are given.
1) He often likes to relax by reading a good book.   **2)** Probably Cecilia will come late to the party.   **3)** I like to hike in the mountains in the summer.   **4)** Bart realized quickly that his shoe was untied.   **5)** The thunderstorm and high winds suddenly developed.

Chapter 6 Mastery Test B

Part A: Sentences will vary. Sample sentences with adjectives are given.
1) Mr. Smith is a superb math teacher.   **2)** Silvia's favorite brother went to college in Idaho.   **3)** The vegetable salad will be ideal to serve guests.   **4)** The playful monkey climbed all over its cage.
5) Louis got an award for his outstanding work on the project.

Part B: Sentences will vary. Sample sentences with adverbs are given.
1) Those planes are landing rapidly on all the runways.
2) Bring the cake over here tomorrow.   **3)** Jon is exceptionally clever.   **4)** Aunt Sarah volunteers at the thrift shop monthly.
5) The trash is picked up weekly.

Part C: Sentences will vary. Sample sentences with prepositional phrases are given.
1) There is a lot of food in the kitchen.   **2)** Did Grandfather go to the lake?   **3)** In the spring a large variety of flowers is blooming.
4) Nora reads the cartoons in the Sunday paper first.   **5)** Neal was seventeen years old in May.

Part D: Sentences will vary. Sample combined sentences using a conjunction are given.
1) Yesterday was sunny, warm, and beautiful.   **2)** Friends and relatives were at the party.   **3)** You may have corn dogs for lunch, but you may prefer a salad.   **4)** Lucy wanted to eat homegrown vegetables, so she planted a large garden.   **5)** Neither Alan nor Sue likes eggs.

Part E: Sentences will vary. Sentences in different word order are given.
1) On Saturday afternoon we sometimes go to a movie.   **2)** Every day, Norma comes in early.   **3)** We drive to see the colorful leaves in the fall.   **4)** Rapidly Chuck finished his homework assignment.
5) They paddled the canoe lazily down the creek.

Chapter 7 Mastery Test A

Part A: Topic sentences will vary. They should be complete sentences. Sample sentences are given.
1) My favorite book is *Walden Pond* by Henry David Thoreau.
2) The perfect vacation is spent hiking in the mountains.
3) Being a naval officer is the ideal job I would most like to have.
4) The Fourth of July is the best holiday of the year.   **5)** The person I most admire in all the world is my mother.   **6)** Bobby McFerrin, my favorite musician, is a remarkable talent.

Part B: Supporting sentences will vary. They should be complete sentences that begin with a capital letter and use proper grammar and end punctuation. They should all support the topic sentence.

Part C: 1) A   **2)** B   **3)** A   **4)** B   **5)** A   **6)** A

Chapter 7 Mastery Test B

Part A: Topic sentences will vary. They should be complete sentences. Sample sentences are given.

1) Basketball is the sport I most enjoy watching and playing.
2) Of all the 50 states, the state I most want to visit is North Carolina.   **3)** The country I want to see more than any other is Scotland.   **4)** Because I delight in reading and writing, my best class in school is English.   **5)** The teacher I most admire is the one who inspires students.   **6)** Among my many collections are teddy bears, hats, and butterflies.

Part B: Supporting sentences will vary. They should be complete sentences that begin with a capital letter and use proper grammar and end punctuation. They should all support the topic sentence.

Part C: 1) A **2)** B **3)** B **4)** A **5)** A **6)** A

Chapter 8 Mastery Test A

Part A: Paragraphs will vary. The paragraph should achieve the purpose of informing about or explaining one of the assigned topics. The paragraph should have a topic sentence, three supporting sentences, and a final sentence as a summary or conclusion. Sentences should be complete and have correct punctuation and grammar.

Part B: Paragraphs will vary. The paragraph should achieve the purpose of telling how to do something. The paragraph should have a topic sentence, three sentences explaining how to do the task, and a final summary sentence. Sentences should be complete and have correct punctuation and grammar.

Part C: Paragraphs will vary. The paragraph should achieve the purpose of requesting information about one of the assigned topics. The paragraph should have a topic sentence, three sentences explaining what is wanted, and a final sentence that is a conclusion. Sentences should be complete and have correct punctuation and grammar.

Part D: Paragraphs will vary. The paragraph should achieve the purpose of persuading someone to do something. The paragraph should have a topic sentence that states the main idea, three facts or reasons for why it should be done, and a final sentence to sum up the student's case. Sentences should be complete and have correct punctuation and grammar.

Part E: Paragraphs will vary. The paragraph should achieve the purpose of telling a personal story about a memorable weekend. The paragraph should have a topic sentence and four sentences in chronological order. Sentences should be complete and have correct punctuation and grammar.

Chapter 8 Mastery Test B

Part A: Paragraphs will vary. The paragraph should achieve the purpose of informing about or explaining one of the assigned topics. The paragraph should have a topic sentence, three supporting sentences, and a final sentence as a summary or conclusion. Sentences should be complete and have correct punctuation and grammar.

Part B: Paragraphs will vary. The paragraph should achieve the purpose of telling a friend how to do something. The paragraph should have a topic sentence, three sentences explaining how to do the task, and a final summary sentence. Sentences should be complete and have correct punctuation and grammar.

Part C: Paragraphs will vary. The paragraph should achieve the purpose of requesting information about one of the assigned topics.

The paragraph should have a topic sentence, three sentences explaining what is wanted, and a final sentence that is a conclusion. Sentences should be complete and have correct punctuation and grammar.

Part D: Paragraphs will vary. The paragraph should achieve the purpose of convincing someone about something. The paragraph should have a topic sentence that states the main idea, three facts or reasons for why its a good idea, and a final sentence to sum up the student's case. Sentences should be complete and have correct punctuation and grammar.

Part E: Paragraphs will vary. The paragraph should achieve the purpose of telling a personal story about a memorable childhood event. The paragraph should have a topic sentence and four sentences in chronological order. Sentences should be complete and have correct punctuation and grammar.

Chapter 9 Mastery Test A

Part A: Sentences will vary. Sample sentences are given.
1) A camping trip I took at age seven was an itchy experience.
2) Becoming a millionaire would make life fascinating.
3) My goal is to move to the country some day.   **4)** Collections of special treasures require lots of space.   **5)** Working at an ice-skating rink has some fun advantages.

Part B: Sentences will vary. Sample sentences are given. Sentences should start with an adverb or a prepositional phrase.
1) Between you and me, I enjoyed our visit last week.
2) Immediately, I found your family to be very likable.   **3)** Before too long, I hope that we can get together again.   **4)** Later this year, I'd like to come back.   **5)** During the spring, I'll call you to plan another visit.

Part C: Paragraphs will vary. A sample paragraph is given. The paragraph should include five transitional words or phrases.

Ruth once visited the Statue of Liberty in New York. She was fifteen **then. At first,** she climbed and climbed. **Finally,** she reached the top. **At last,** she was able to see the view of the city and the harbor. It was spectacular! She always remembered that trip **later.**

Part D: Comparisons will vary. Sample comparisons are given.
1) A thing of beauty is a joy forever.   **2)** The tornado sounded like a rumbling train.   **3)** The moon looked as white as snow.
4) Jody is as happy as a lark.   **5)** The morning hours are like precious gold.

Chapter Mastery Test B

Part A: Sentences will vary. Sample sentences are given.
1) I lost a wonderful treasure when my friend Susan moved away.
2) Being an airline pilot would be a life of adventure and excitement.   **3)** Traveling to Africa is my goal after college.
4) Being an explorer has some drawbacks.   **5)** Yard work is prosperous but hard work.

Part B: Sentences will vary. Sample sentences are given. Sentences should start with an adverb or a prepositional phrase.
1) To our delight, we flew on an airplane last month.   **2)** High above the clouds, we flew to Oregon.   **3)** Twice we went to the coast and had fun.   **4)** After only five days there, we regretted that we had to go home so soon.   **5)** On our next trip, we want to go to the mountains.

Part C: Paragraphs will vary. A sample paragraph is given. The paragraph should include five transitional words or phrases.

Hernando and his friends went on a trip to the mountains. **Surprisingly,** he loved hiking. **However,** the trails were rugged. The mountain views made it all worthwhile. **Later,** Hernando saw a steep waterfall. **Then** he saw a million stars. **At last,** they had a campfire and roasted marshmallows–Hernando's favorite treat.

Part D: Comparisons will vary. Sample comparisons are given. **1)** A ride on a merry-go-round is a trip to heaven. **2)** She ran up the hill like a streak of lightning. **3)** The clouds are like a big fluffy pillow. **4)** We all feel as full as stuffed toads. **5)** When the hail hit the roof, it sounded like a trip hammer.

Chapter 10 Mastery Test A

Part A: Sentences will vary. Samples of complete sentences are given. **1)** The St. Lawrence River is Canada's largest river. **2)** Niagara Falls is in the state of New York. **3)** California is the site of the Mojave Desert. **4)** Jane Addams won the Nobel Peace Prize. **5)** The animal that can run at speeds over 60 miles per hour is the cheetah. **6)** GOP is the abbreviation for Grand Old Party. **7)** Every four years, presidential elections are held in the United States. **8)** A one-eyed mythological giant is called a cyclops. **9)** The Blue Ridge Parkway is the longest national park in the United States. **10)** The Caspian Sea is the world's largest lake.

Part B: Essays will vary. A sample paragraph is given. Paragraphs should begin with a topic sentence and have four additional complete sentences.

Jupiter is the largest planet in the solar system in which Earth is located. The diameter of Jupiter is 88,000 miles. Planet Jupiter is eleven times bigger than planet Earth. Jupiter has at least sixteen moons, while Earth has only one. To travel once around the sun, Jupiter takes the equivalent of almost twelve Earth years.

Part C: Paragraphs will vary. They should have five complete sentences focused on one of the assigned topics. Correct grammar and punctuation should be used.

Chapter 10 Mastery Test B

Part A: Sentences will vary. Samples of complete sentences are given. **1)** The largest South American country is Brazil. **2)** The rulers of ancient Egypt were called pharaohs. **3)** In 1803 the United States gained possession of the Louisiana Purchase. **4)** The general defeated at the Battle of Little Big Horn was General Custer. **5)** The first chief justice of the U.S. Supreme Court was John Jay. **6)** The protest against the British tea tax was known as the Boston Tea Party. **7)** Acapulco is famous for beautiful beaches. **8)** Wearing moccasins that were dyed black is how a group of Native Americans got the name Blackfoot Indians. **9)** A vitamin deficiency causes beriberi. **10)** The Bering Strait is usually frozen between October and June.

Part B: Essays will vary. A sample paragraph is given. Paragraphs should begin with a topic sentence and have four additional complete sentences.

The planet Pluto is the ninth planet out from the sun in the solar system. Pluto's diameter is about 2,000 miles. Charon is the only known moon that orbits Pluto. The atmosphere that envelops Pluto is thought to be thin methane. The planet was unknown until 1930, when Clyde Tombaugh discovered it.

Part C: Paragraphs will vary. They should have five complete sentences focused on one of the assigned topics. Correct grammar and punctuation should be used.

Chapter 11 Mastery Test A

Part A: 1) The date **2)** The time of the message **3)** The name of the message recipient **4)** The information needed by the message recipient **5)** The name of the message taker

Part B: Messages will vary. A sample message is given.

[Today's date]

[Time]

[Friend's name], please meet me tonight for dinner at the Delicious Diner on First Street. Be there at 7:00 P.M. Get a table if you get there first.

[Student's name]

Part C: Memos will vary. A sample memo is given.

MEMO

To: Eileen

From: Howie

Date: [Today's date]

Subject: Safety Committee Meeting

There will be a Safety Committee meeting tomorrow at 10:00 A.M. in Room 8. Please attend, and bring a copy of your financial report with you.

Chapter 11 Mastery Test B

Part A: 1) The date **2)** Who the memo is to **3)** Who the memo is from **4)** The subject of the memo **5)** The information being transmitted

Part B: Messages will vary. A sample message is given.

[Today's date]

[Time]

Nicki, your friend Bud called to cancel your date this Friday night.

[Student's name]

Part C: Memos will vary. A sample memo is given.

MEMO

To: Taylor

From: Louise

Date: [Today's date]

Subject: Training Session

There will be a training session that you must attend this Saturday at 9:00 A.M. It will be held in the restaurant's main dining room. Please be sure to wear your uniform.

Chapter 12 Mastery Test A

Part A: 1) Date **2)** Salutation **3)** Body **4)** Closing **5)** Signature

Part B: Return addresses will vary. The student's full name, street address, city, state, and ZIP code should be included. The postal abbreviation for your state's name should be used. The rest of the mailing address should read:

234 York Road
Winchester, NE 68000-1234

Part C: Letters will vary. A sample letter is given. Letters should include all five parts of a personal letter. Paragraphs should be indented. A comma should follow the greeting. Sentences should be complete and have correct punctuation.

[Today's date]

Dear Aunt Judy,

I have three days off from the fifteenth to the eighteenth of next month. I'd like to come and visit you in Winchester. It's been a long time since I've seen you and Tassie, Barny, and Towser, too.

I've been studying hard in school. My grades show how well I'm doing. English and math are my favorites. I still manage to work part time at the drug store. The extra money helps my college fund.

Please let me know how the fifteenth to the eighteenth will work for you. I'd love to see you.

Lovingly,
[Signature]

Chapter 12 Mastery Test B

Part A: 1) Heading **2)** Inside address **3)** Salutation **4)** Body **5)** Typed name

Part B: Return addresses will vary. The student's street address should be on one line and city, state, and ZIP code on the other. The postal abbreviation for your state's name should be used. The rest of the mailing address should read:

1200 Writer's Drive
Suite 12
Loving, TX 76000-1234

Part C: Letters will vary. A sample letter is given except for the heading. The heading should be the student's complete name and address. Letters should include all eight parts of a business letter. Paragraphs should be indented. A semicolon should follow the greeting. Sentences should be complete and have correct punctuation.

[Current date]

Editor
Today's Issues
1200 Writer's Drive
Suite 12
Loving, TX 76000-1234

Dear Editor:

On April 3, [year], I sent you a copy of a story I wrote for possible publication. The story is entitled "Life in the Age of Technology."

I have not heard from you. As you can understand, I am anxious to know your response. In case you did not receive the story, a copy is enclosed.

Please write me at the address on this letter to notify me whether you are considering my story for publication.

Thank you for your consideration.

Sincerely,
[Signature]
[Typed/printed name]
Enclosure

Chapter 13 Mastery Test A

Part A: 1) e **2)** d **3)** a **4)** b **5)** c

Part B: 1) *Who's Who* **2)** Periodicals **3)** *Reader's Guide* **4)** Atlas **5)** Almanac

Part C:
Dental Care
 I. Daily care
  A. Brushing
  B. Flossing
  C. Rinsing between meals
 II. Professional care
  A. Regular dental visits
  B. Periodic x-ray examinations

III. Special care
  A. Fillings, crowns, and other repairs
  B. Braces

Part D: 1) 4 **2)** 1 **3)** 5 **4)** 3 **5)** 2

Chapter 13 Mastery Test B

Part A: 1) d **2)** e **3)** a **4)** c **5)** b

Part B: 1) Periodicals **2)** *Reader's Guide* **3)** *Who's Who* **4)** Library catalog **5)** Encyclopedia

Part C:
Yard Care
 I. Spring cleanup
  A. Raking after snow melt
  B. Early weed control
 II. Summer maintenance
  A. Regular mowing
  B. Adjusting mower height for grass growth
  C. Watering in dry periods
 III. Fall cleanup
  A. Raking leaves
  B. Covering beds for protection

Part D: 1) 5 **2)** 4 **3)** 1 **4)** 3 **5)** 2

Midterm Mastery Test

Part A: 1) Our families are **definitely interesting. 2) They** are all **different** in some ways. **3)** Amanda **O'Hara's** family is small**. It** only has **two** people. **4)** Amanda and her mom go **to dancing** class **together. 5)** The **O'Haras** live in a **pleasant** apartment. **6)** Laura's father had **given** Laura her own room after her older sister Francie got **married. 7)** Before Francie was married**,** it was **necessary** for Laura and Francie to share a room. **8)** Derek is the only "child" at home**, too. His** sister Tamara works for the **government** in Washington. **9) Mike's** family has **lived** in Springfield for a long time. **10)** Mike's family had lived in Illinois, **Ohio, Florida,** and **Oregon.**

Part B: Sentences will vary. Sample sentences are given. Each sentence should do what the directions indicate.
1) Mike is sitting between Derek and Laura. **2)** John asked, "Are we going to lunch at 12:30?" **3)** Apples and bananas are my favorite fruits. **4)** The fiftieth state is Hawaii. **5)** We went to the store; however, it was closed. **6)** Mike asked to borrow Derek's bike. **7)** When are we going to start the game? **8)** She knocked on the door. **9)** The house at the end of the street is for sale. **10)** If you follow my directions, you're going to find the house. **11)** The cat puts its paw on my arm when it wants to eat. **12)** The weather is very warm today. **13)** It's so cold in here! **14)** Tom likes to see plays, but Mary prefers to go to concerts. **15)** Answer the telephone.

Part C: 1) children **2)** oldest **3)** is **4)** was **5)** has **6)** well **7)** practices **8)** bought **9)** Tim's **10)** probably **11)** plans **12)** doesn't **13)** told **14)** Among **15)** have

Part D: 1) achieve **2)** science **3)** believe **4)** foreign **5)** separate **6)** knives **7)** wives **8)** deer **9)** nineteen **10)** shopping

Part E: 1) Tennis players seem to be younger every year. **2)** Some of the young players are beating their older opponents. **3)** Tim is only six, but he can almost beat his brother Mike. **4)** Tim has a mean serve and a wicked backhand. **5)** "Hey, give me a break," laughs Mike.

Final Mastery Test

Part A: Sentences will vary. Sample sentences are given. Sentences should be complete, start with a capital letter, and end with the correct punctuation mark.
1) Tran has grown to like his new dog.   **2)** The American capital is Washington, D.C.   **3)** We went to the store.   **4)** We went to the mall early, but the doors were locked.   **5)** The flowers are blooming late this spring.

Part B: 1) speeches   **2)** chief   **3)** thieves   **4)** weird
5) potatoes   **6)** cities   **7)** begged   **8)** conscience   **9)** referral
10) library   **11)** leaves   **12)** calves   **13)** neighbor   **14)** trout
15) writing   **16)** boating   **17)** druggist   **18)** starry
19) refusal   **20)** February

Part C: 1) The biggest challenge to decision making is knowing your real goals.   **2)** Usually we think we understand why we want something.   **3)** It seems clear, but it's not.   **4)** Have you ever seen a small child scream for a toy and then throw it down when she finally gets it?   **5)** That's because she had a hidden goal.
6) Everyone has hidden goals sometimes.   **7)** Suppose you're buying a new CD.   **8)** Are you buying it because you like the songs on it?   **9)** Could you have hidden reasons for buying it?   **10)** If you aren't aware of your real goals, it's hard to make a good decision that will meet your real needs.

Part D: Topic sentences will vary. They should be complete sentences. Sample sentences are given.
1) The movie I'd see any time, any place, and for any price is *Sense and Sensibility.*   **2)** Affectionate, loyal, and tidy, a cat is my idea of the perfect pet.   **3)** If I had lots of money and time, photography is the hobby I would most like to pursue.   **4)** Bursting with spring, May is the most glorious of all the months.   **5)** Because of his commitment to the environment, Robert Redford is the actor I most admire.

Part E: Paragraphs will vary. The paragraph should achieve the purpose of informing about or explaining one of the assigned topics. The paragraph should have a topic sentence, three supporting sentences, and a final sentence as a summary or conclusion. Sentences should be complete and have correct punctuation and grammar.

Part F: Sentences will vary. Sample sentences are given. Sentences should start with an adverb or a prepositional phrase.
1) Happily, I enjoyed our last vacation.   **2)** On a sunny day, we drove to a campground.   **3)** In the mornings, we climbed trails.
4) In the afternoons, we rode mountain bikes and paddled a canoe.
5) Contentedly in the evenings, we had campfires and roasted corn.

Part G: Sentences will vary. Sample sentences are given.
1) The purpose of a topic sentence is to express the main idea of a paragraph.   **2)** A short answer includes only one or two sentences, but an essay is one or more paragraphs long.   **3)** The three parts of a paragraph are the topic sentence, the body, and the summary or conclusion.   **4)** Chronologic order is an arrangement according to time.   **5)** A sentence fragment is a phrase or clause that is incorrectly treated as a sentence.

Part H: Memos will vary. Sentences should be complete and have correct punctuation, grammar, and spelling. Today's date should be used.

Part I: Personal letters will vary. Sentences should be complete and have correct punctuation, grammar, and spelling. Paragraphs should begin on a new line and be indented. Today's date should be used. Letters should be signed.

Part J: Essays will vary. They should begin with an introduction that will attract the reader's attention and state the main idea of the essay. The body of the essay should include each of the five steps of report writing listed in proper order: (1) choosing a topic, (2) finding information and taking notes, (3) organizing information and making an outline, (4) writing, proofreading, revising and rewriting the report, and (5) preparing a bibliography. Each paragraph should start on a new line and have a topic sentence and two or more sentences giving facts or details about each step. The essay should end with a conclusion or summary. Grammar, punctuation, and spelling should all be correct. Good sentence variety and transitions should be used.

Attention Teachers! As publishers of *Basic English Composition*, we would like your help in making this textbook more valuable to you. Please take a few minutes to fill out this survey. Your feedback will help us to better serve you and your students.

1) What is your position and major area of responsibility? _____
   _____
   _____

2) Briefly describe your setting:
   ____ regular education ____ special education ____ adult basic education
   ____ community college ____ university ____ other _____

3) The enrollment in your classroom includes students with the following (check all that apply):
   ____ at-risk for failure ____ low reading ability ____ behavior problems
   ____ learning disabilities ____ ESL ____ other _____

4) Grade level of your students: _____

5) Racial/ethnic groups represented in your classes (check all that apply):
   ____ African-American ____ Asian ____ Caucasian ____ Hispanic
   ____ Native American ____ Other

6) School Location:
   ____ urban ____ suburban ____ rural ____ other _____

7) What reaction did your students have to the materials? (Include comments about the cover design, lesson format, illustrations, etc.)
   _____
   _____
   _____

8) What features in the student text helped your students the most?
   _____
   _____
   _____

OVER ➤

9) What features in the student text helped your students the least? Please include suggestions for changing these to make the text more relevant.

_____

_____

_____

10) How did you use the Teacher's Edition and support materials, and what features did you find to be the most helpful?

_____

_____

_____

11) What activity from the program did your students benefit from the most? Please briefly explain.

_____

_____

_____

12) Optional: Share an activity that you used to teach the materials in your classroom that enhanced the learning and motivation of your students.

_____

_____

_____

Several activities will be selected to be included in future editions. Please include your name, address, and phone number so we may contact you for permission and possible payment to use the material. Thank you!

▼ fold in thirds and tape shut at the top ▼

Name: _____

School: _____

Address: _____

City/State/ZIP: _____

Phone: _____